The Right Not to Use the Internet

This pioneering collection addresses the prospective fundamental/human right not to use the Internet and the challenges that the non-use of the Internet poses for democracy.

As the Internet has increasingly ceased to be a mere option and rather turned into a *de facto* obligation for anyone who exercises their rights or fulfils duties, these developments bring about profound ramifications for the very existence and the functioning of democracy, and therefore merit a critical reflection. With contributors from academia and legal practice from all over Europe, this edited volume offers timely critical analysis of the right not to use of the Internet, at times supplemented with policy advice and postulates for law reform.

This book is of key interest to scholars and students of – predominantly – law, political science and philosophy as well as to policymakers, judges and non-governmental organisations at national, supranational and international levels.

Dariusz Kloza is a postdoctoral researcher at the Faculty of Law of UCLouvain Saint-Louis Bruxelles, Belgium.

Elżbieta Kużelewska is Associate Professor at the Faculty of Law of the University Bialystok, Poland.

Eva Lievens is Associate Professor of Law and Technology at the Faculty of Law and Criminology of Ghent University, Belgium.

Valerie Verdoodt is a postdoctoral researcher at the Faculty of Law and Criminology of Ghent University, Belgium.

Current Debates in European Integration

This peer-reviewed Series focuses on the contemporary challenges to democracy *sensu largo*, the rule of law (*Rechtsstaat*) and the respect for fundamental (human) rights, which are – these challenges – related to the European integration project. Each volume in the Series offers a timely critical analysis of a single pressing challenge, possibly supplemented with policy advice, thus making it useful for fellow academics and policymakers. The Series analyses these challenges from a multidisciplinary perspective, yet law and political science dominate.

Series editors: *Elżbieta Kużelewska of the University of Białystok, Poland, and Dariusz Kloza of UCLouvain Saint-Louis Bruxelles, Belgium.*

Geopolitical and Humanitarian Aspects of the Belarus-EU Border Conflict
Edited by Elżbieta Kużelewska, Agnieszka Kasińska-Metryka, Karolina Pałka-Suchojad and Agnieszka Piekutowska

The Right Not to Use the Internet
Concept, Contexts, Consequences
Edited by Dariusz Kloza, Elżbieta Kużelewska, Eva Lievens and Valerie Verdoodt

The Right Not to Use the Internet

Concept, Contexts, Consequences

Edited by Dariusz Kloza, Elżbieta Kużelewska, Eva Lievens and Valerie Verdoodt

Routledge
Taylor & Francis Group
LONDON AND NEW YORK

First published 2025
by Routledge
4 Park Square, Milton Park, Abingdon, Oxon OX14 4RN

and by Routledge
605 Third Avenue, New York, NY 10158

Routledge is an imprint of the Taylor & Francis Group, an informa business

The book is financially supported by the Polish Ministry of Science under the Regional Initiative of Excellence (RID) programme.

Regionalna Inicjatywa Doskonałości

Ministry of Science and Higher Education
Republic of Poland

British Library Cataloguing in Publication Data
A catalogue record for this book is available from the British Library

Library of Congress Cataloging in Publication Data
Names: Kloza, Dariusz, editor. | Kużelewska, Elżbieta, editor. |
Lievens, Eva, 1979– editor. | Verdoodt, Valerie, editor.
Title: The right not to use the Internet : concept, contexts, consequences /
edited by Dariusz Kloza, Elżbieta Kużelewska, Eva Lievens, and Valerie Verdoodt.
Description: Abingdon, Oxon [UK] ; New York, NY : Routledge, 2025. |
Series: Current debates in European integration |
Includes bibliographical references and index.
Identifiers: LCCN 2024054176 (print) | LCCN 2024054177 (ebook) |
ISBN 9781032866314 (hardback) | ISBN 9781032866321 (paperback) |
ISBN 9781003528401 (ebook)
Subjects: LCSH: Internet–Access control–Law and legislation. | Internet governance–Law and legislation. | Internet–Law and legislation. | Right to Internet access.
Classification: LCC K4345 .R54 2025 (print) | LCC K4345 (ebook) |
DDC 343.09/944–dc23/eng/20241118
LC record available at https://lccn.loc.gov/2024054176
LC ebook record available at https://lccn.loc.gov/2024054177

ISBN: 978-1-032-86631-4 (hbk)
ISBN: 978-1-032-86632-1 (pbk)
ISBN: 978-1-003-52840-1 (ebk)

DOI: 10.4324/9781003528401

Typeset in Times New Roman
by Newgen Publishing UK

Contents

Notes on contributors

Sarah Anrijs (PhD) is a postdoctoral researcher at imec-mict, Ghent University. She combines post-positivist and critical-constructivist perspectives to study digital literacy and digital exclusion in relation to the digitisation of public and civic services. Sarah is currently engaged in both academic and policy- and practice-oriented research on these topics.

Sabrina Aouici (PhD in sociology) is a researcher at the French National Pension Fund. Her research on transitions to retirement considers the family, social and professional trajectories. She also works on the effect of solidarity on residential mobility patterns in retirement, on the risks of exclusion and the (social and digital) isolation of elderly people.

Barbora Badurova (PhD) is a researcher focusing on philosophy, ethics and education, who has been involved in several interdisciplinary international projects focused on selected aspects of the digital world such as Erasmus + KA2 PLATO´S EU (Philosophical Learning Applied to Online Surroundings) and COST Global Digital Human Rights Network.

David de Segovia Vicente is a doctoral researcher at imec-mict, Ghent University (Belgium) where he investigates how smartphones and emotions interact in everyday life from a media-psychological perspective. His most recent publication explores the relation between mindless scrolling and guilt, which can be found in the Journal of Computer-Mediated Communication.

Elise Degrave (PhD) is Professor at the Law Faculty of the Université de Namur and Academic Director of the E-government research group at the Namur Digital Institute. She is the author of numerous publications in the field of digital public law, especially human rights and ICT.

Władysław Jóźwicki (PhD) is Assistant Professor at Constitutional Law Chair of Adam Mickiewicz University in Poznań (AMU). PhD in Law (2018, AMU),

MA in Law (2011, AMU), MA in Political Sciences (2009, University of Warsaw) and BA in Political and International Studies with Joint Degree (2006, Middlesex University – London). Main fields of research: relations between EU MSs constitutional courts and the CJEU; conflicts between EU and domestic law, especially in human rights matters; constitutional identity; EU and the ECHR; international human rights protection; international courts; and principle of proportionality.

Jonathan Keller is a senior consultant in Techlaw and Policy at the Sublimis Institute and a doctor in public law specialising in IT issues and conflicts with fundamental rights. His work focuses on the crossroad between organic public law with economic concerns.

Dariusz Kloza is a postdoctoral researcher (*chargé de recherche auprès du Fonds de la Recherche Scientifique – FNRS*) at the Faculty of Law of UCLouvain Saint-Louis Bruxelles, Belgium, focusing on privacy and personal data protection law. Previously, he was at Ghent University, Belgium (2021–2024), where he worked on Internet governance and co-edited this volume.

Elżbieta Kużelewska is Associate Professor at the Faculty of Law, University of Bialystok, Poland, where she is Vice-Dean for Science (2019–2028) and Chair of the Comparative Constitutional Law Department. Her expertise concentrates on constitutional law, direct democracy and human rights.

Pauline Lagasse joined the Belgian Council of State in 2016 after eight years as a lawyer specialising in public and administrative law, to become an auditor in the Legislation Section. For several years, Pauline has been an assistant in administrative law at the UCLouvain (Saint Louis-Bruxelles).

Eva Lievens is Associate Professor at the Faculty of Law and Criminology of Ghent University, where she leads the research group Law & Technology. She researches the legal impact of technology design and deployment, human and children's rights in the digital environment, and alternative regulatory instruments to regulate tech phenomena.

Oskar MacGregor is Senior Lecturer in Informatics at the University of Skövde in Sweden. He has an extensive background in philosophy (in particular applied ethics) and cognitive neuroscience (in particular electrophysiology). His current research interests include neuroprivacy, AI ethics, human rights and research methods more broadly.

Kamil Mamak is a philosopher (MA, PhD) and a legal scholar (MA, PhD). He is a postdoctoral researcher at the University of Helsinki and Assistant Professor at Jagiellonian University. He has authored 5 book monographs and more than 50 articles and chapters. In 2024, he won the ERC Starting Grant.

Marijn Martens (PhD, Ghent University) is a postdoctoral researcher at imec-mict, Ghent University (Belgium). He employs a critical and interpretative mixed method research design focussing on digital disconnection, digital well-being and the evaluation of algorithmic decision-making systems from the perspective of laypeople. He coordinates the Disconnect-2-Reconnect research project.

Leonor Moral Soriano is Professor of Public Law at the University of Granada. Her current areas of interest are the use of AI in legal reasoning and the right of education. She is a guarantor of the Centre of Excellence 'Digital Society' at the Law Faculty of Granada University where she focuses on the governance of AI.

Michał Ożóg is Assistant Professor at the Department of Constitutional Law at the University of Bialystok and author of more than 50 scientific publications, including articles, glosses, expert opinions, reports and reviews. His research work deals with constitutional and religious law issues in an interdisciplinary approach.

Paolo Passaglia (PhD in Constitutional Justice at the University of Pisa and in Law at the University of Aix-Marseille III – 2001) is Full Professor of Comparative Law, at the University of Pisa. His current research activities are mostly related to comparative law and new technologies, with special attention to new forms of social exclusion and to online disinformation.

Radosław Puchta is Assistant Professor at the Department of Constitutional Law at the University of Bialystok, specialising in the issues related to the constitutional justice and fundamental rights. His current research activities are concentrated on new challenges for the constitutionalism, such as climate change and digitalisation.

Julien Rossi is Associate Professor at Université Paris 8, and researcher at the Centre d'études sur les médias, les technologies et l'internationalisation (CÉMTI). He is also co-chair of the Working Group on Internet Governance and Regulation of the CNRS' Research Network on Internet, AI and Society. His work focuses on data protection and Internet governance.

Mart Susi is Professor of Human Rights Law at Tallinn University. Recently, he has established several global research groups focusing on digital and new human rights. His scholarly innovations include the Internet balancing formula and the non-coherence theory of digital human rights.

Łukasz Szoszkiewicz (PhD) is Assistant Professor at Constitutional Law Chair of Adam Mickiewicz University in Poznań (AMU). PhD in Law (2021, AMU), MA in Law (2015, AMU). Main fields of research: international human rights law, particularly in the context of new technologies such as artificial intelligence and neurotechnology; child rights; and natural language processing of legal texts.

Georgios Terzis is Professor in Communications and Ethics at the Brussels School of Governance, Vrije Universiteit Brussel. Throughout his academic career his research focused on media and security, research and media ethics, media governance, disinformation and media literacy, science diplomacy and the right not to access the Internet and for an analogue life.

Sara Van Bruyssel is a doctoral researcher in communication sciences at Ghent University. Through a feminist lens, Sara works on understanding the role of digital dis/connective work in maintaining a sense of digital well-being in everyday life. Her most recent publication can be found in New Media and Society.

Sébastien Van Drooghenbroeck is Prorector 'Equity, Diversity and Inclusion' at the UCLouvain, and Full Professor at this University. He is also guest professor at the Université Paris Panthéon Assas, Assessor in the Belgian Council of State, and national expert for the European network of legal experts in gender equality and non-discrimination.

Mariek M. P. Vanden Abeele (PhD, KULeuven) is Associate Professor in Digital Culture at imec-mict, Ghent University (Belgium). Mariek combines media psychological and media sociological perspectives to understand the role that digital media use plays in everyday life and society. She received a 2020 European Research Council Starting Grant for her work on digital well-being.

Valerie Verdoodt is a postdoctoral researcher at the Faculty of Law and Criminology of Ghent University, where she is a member of the research group Law and Technology. Her research focuses on the legal and fundamental rights questions originating from the development of new media and technology, in particular (but not exclusively) regarding the protection and participation of children online.

Series editors' preface

In 2021, when one of us proposed to invoke human rights to protect the non-use of the Internet, or at least a degree thereof,[1] such a proposition was probably received as a bit mischievous. Yet, just a few years later, as society has become more and more dependent on the Internet, already a considerable body of earnest scholarship,[2] political debate, legislative effort and jurisprudence has addressed the right not to use the Internet, however conceptualised and termed. This multidisciplinary edited volume fits squarely in these debates as it offers a pioneering, timely and rich analysis of this right. The present book might equally be a voice in a much-needed debate on the boundaries of (new, emerging) technologies – such as artificial intelligence – in society and individual lives. We are hence pleased to include it in our book series.

During the gestation of this book, also acting as its co-editors, we have enjoyed many thought-provoking discussions with many authors and we have reflected on their chapters. Although diverse opinions emerged in this book, we now perceive the non-use of the Internet as a human right in the making, to be accommodated with other rights, interests, needs, desires, etc., possibly with the help of the principle of proportionality.[3] It is conventional wisdom that once a need for a new human right is established, it requires careful crafting.[4] Thus, we believe that legislators, policymakers, magistrates and judges – at national, supranational and international levels – will find this book useful in better understanding the subject matter and informing their policies and decisions in this context. Given its significant influence on the regulation of technology worldwide, Europe could promote its values, and shape policies and practices also in this area.[5] Exportable examples thus far include the employee's right to disconnect after working hours, granted in some Member States of the European Union,[6] or a constitutional *droit à l'intégrité numérique* in the Swiss canton of Geneva.[7] Similarly, we wish for this book to inspire fellow researchers, journalists, civil society organisations, etc. in their investigations, commentaries or advice.

We furthermore expect that the right not to use the Internet – or, perhaps, the right not to use a technology – will soon cause even more interest, both in academic and professional circles. Hence, we invite prospective authors and/or editors to submit their proposals for subsequent volumes in our book series on 'Current Debates in European Integration'.

Elżbieta Kużelewska
Dariusz Kloza[8]
Białystok – Brussels, January 2025

Notes

1 Dariusz Kloza, 'It's All About Choice: The Right Not to Use the Internet' (2021) Völkerrechtsblog https://voelkerrechtsblog.org/its-all-about-choice.

2 Possibly informed by disconnection studies and movements such as digital detox or deep work. Cf., e.g., Mariek M. P. Vanden Abeele and others, 'Why, How, When, and for Whom Does Digital Disconnection Work? A Process-Based Framework of Digital Disconnection' (2024) 34 Communication Theory 3; Dariusz Kloza, 'A Behavioural Alternative to the Protection of Privacy' in Dan Jerker B. Svantesson and Dariusz Kloza (eds.), Trans-Atlantic Data Privacy Relations as a Challenge for Democracy (Intersentia 2017) https://doi.org/10.5281/zenodo.5121331; Joao Batalheiro Ferreira, 'Exhausted and Not Doing Enough? The Productivity Paradox of Contemporary Academia' (2022) 8 She Ji 181 http://dx.doi.org/10.1016/j.sheji.2022.05.001.

3 Jacco Bomhoff, 'Proportionality' in Jan M. Smits and others (eds.), Elgar Encyclopedia of Comparative Law (Edward Elgar 2023) www.elgaronline.com/view/book/9781839105609/b-9781839105609.proportionality.xml

4 Andreas von Arnauld, Kerstin von der Decken and Mart Susi (eds.), The Cambridge Handbook of New Human Rights (Cambridge University Press 2020).

5 Anu Bradford, The Brussels Effect: How the European Union Rules the World (Oxford University Press 2020); Lee A. Bygrave, 'The "Strasbourg Effect" on Data Protection in Light of the "Brussels Effect": Logic, Mechanics and Prospects' (2021) 40 Computer Law & Security Review 105460.

6 E.g., Belgium – cf. Articles 29–33, Loi du 3 octobre 2022 portant des dispositions diverses relatives au travail / Wet van 3 oktober 2022 houdende diverse arbeidsbepalingen.

7 Article 21A, Constitution de la République et canton de Genève.

8 This preface contains solely my personal views and not those of any organisation I may be affiliated with.

Abbreviations

3Ps	provision, participation and protection
ADHD	attention-deficit hyperactivity disorder
ADM	automated decision-making
AI	artificial intelligence
ARCOM	*Autorité de régulation de la communication audiovisuelle et numérique* (Regulatory Authority for Audiovisual and Digital Communication)
AWS	Amazon Web Services
BVerfG	German Constitutional Court
CCP	Code of Civil Procedure of 17 November 1964
CCPA	California Consumer Privacy Act
CESCR	Committee on Economic, Social and Cultural Rights
CJEU	Court of Justice of the European Union
CNAV	*Caisse nationale d'assurance vieillesse* (French National Pension Fund)
CNIL	*Commission nationale de l'informatique et des libertés* (French Data Protection Authority)
CREDOC	*Centre de Recherche pour l'Étude et l'Observation des Conditions de Vie* (Centre for the Study and Observation of Living Conditions)
CROUS	*Centres Régionaux des Œuvres Universitaires et Scolaires*
DARPA	Defense Advanced Research Projects Agency
DESI	Digital Economy and Society Index
DRM	Digital Right Management
ECHR	European Convention on Human Rights
ECtHR	European Court of Human Rights
EDPB	European Data Protection Board
EGDI	E-Governance Development Index
eHealth	electronic health
eID	electronic identification
ESC	economic, social and cultural rights
ETSI	European Telecommunications Standards Institute
EU	European Union

EULA	End-User Licence Agreement
e-waste	electronic waste
FTC	Federal Trade Commission
GDPR	General Data Protection Regulation
HITLFE	human-in-the-loop-for-exceptions
HRC	Human Rights Committee
IACtHR	Inter-American Court of Human Rights
ICF	International Classification of Functioning, Disability and Health
ICTs	Information and Communication Technologies
IGF	Internet Governance Forum
IHRL	International Human Rights Law
INSEE	*Institut National de la Statistique et des Études Économiques* (French National Statistics Office)
IP	Intellectual Property
IP	Internet Protocol
IS	Information Society
IT	information technology
ITU	International Telecommunication Union
LIME	Local Interpretable Model-Agnostic Explanations
LMS	learning management system
MMORPG	massively multiplayer online role-playing game
NGO	non-governmental organisation
OECD	Organisation for Economic Co-operation and Development
ONEM	National Employment Office
PPPs	public-private partnerships
SDGs	Sustainable Development Goals
SLCE	Legislation Section of the Belgian Council of State
SNCF	*Société Nationale des Chemins de Fer* (French National Railway Company)
TFEU	Treaty on the Functioning of the European Union
UD	Universal Design
UDHR	Universal Declaration of Human Rights
UPR	Universal Periodic Review
UN	United Nations
UNCRC	United Nations Committee on the Rights of the Child
UNESCO	United Nations Educational, Scientific and Cultural Organization
UNIA	Centre for Equal Opportunities and Opposition to Racism
USA	United States of America
VR	virtual reality
WHO	World Health Organization
WSIS	World Summit on the Information Society
WTO	World Trade Organization
XAI	Explainable AI
Y2K	year 2000 problem

Introduction[1]

Dariusz Kloza, Elżbieta Kużelewska, Eva Lievens and Valerie Verdoodt

Can people be forced to use the Internet to exercise their rights or fulfil their duties? This burning question emerges in the aftermath of the recent public health crisis where the reliance on the Internet and other (new or emerging) technologies has soared, often nudged or (*de facto*) coerced by both state and private actors. To address this intriguing development, some commentators have recently invoked fundamental/human rights[2] as an appropriate means either to protect and promote the individual *choice* not to use such technologies or to acknowledge the individual *inability* to use them; the latter due to unaffordability or unavailability of technology, or the lack of necessary skills.[3] Proponents often assert that human rights law not only offers the highest level of protection by reflecting the most important values in society but also continually evolves to address new challenges and cater to the evolving needs and wishes of individuals and communities.

The modern plea to protect non-use starkly contrasts with more than decade-old calls to safeguard the use of technologies such as the Internet under the banner of human rights; these calls have already been discussed extensively and a few of them have even made it to the legal realm.[4] At the same time, this plea starkly contrasts with the fierce efforts to close the so-called digital divide;[5] furthermore, non-use often comes at a price and runs against the efficiency or convenience of the functioning of a state or an organisation (e.g., a need to offer some analogue alternatives to digital services).

However, the proposition to safeguard the non-use of such technologies through human rights has not yet been conceptualised nor comprehensively analysed. It brings to the fore profound consequences for democracy, the protection and promotion of human rights and the rule of law (*Rechtsstaat*), and thus merits academic attention. In this pioneering edited volume, we explore protecting the non-use of a single technology – the Internet – through human rights. We aim to contribute to closing the research gap while offering insights for policymaking and – possibly – law reform.

To achieve our goal, this book is organised into 15 chapters, divided into two parts. Part I explores the conceptual aspects of the prospective human right not to use the Internet. More specifically, it looks at the rationale, role and functioning of such a right, including an ethical perspective. The prospect of legal

DOI: 10.4324/9781003528401-1

recognition – whether as a new, standalone right or one derived from existing rights (e.g., through the doctrine of human rights as 'living instruments')[6] – necessitates a debate on the very understandings, the extent of protection thus far stemming from human rights legal instruments and jurisprudence of senior courts as well as its coherence with existing rights.

Part II analyses the (legal) consequences of the human rights protection of the non-use of the Internet, frequently from a national perspective, in various contexts, such as legal practice, criminal justice, public administration, healthcare, education and entertainment. It also considers the implications for various vulnerable groups, such as children and the elderly.

The authors featured in this volume originate largely from academia, spanning various levels of seniority, and from legal practice. While we aimed to embrace diverse perspectives, the book predominantly showcases viewpoints from law, political science and philosophy. As such, it primarily targets fellow researchers as well as policymakers, judges and non-governmental organisations at national, supranational and international levels. Although our focus primarily centres on Europe, due to its advanced system of protection of human rights, we aim for the analysis and findings to hold universal relevance.

This book received funding under the Weave programme from the National Science Centre, Poland (NCN) in the OPUS LAP 26 call (agreement No. UMO-2023/51/I/HS5/01417) and from the Fonds Wetenschappelijk Onderzoek Vlaanderen – Research Foundation Flanders, Belgium (FWO) (agreement No. G000325N). It has been published in open access with the financial support of the Polish Minister of Science under the Regional Initiative of Excellence programme.

Notes

1 This introduction contains solely my personal views and not those of any organisation I may be affiliated with (DK).

2 Although this distinction is not watertight and these terms are frequently used interchangeably, 'fundamental rights' typically form a part of national constitutional law and 'human rights' – a part of international law.

3 Cf., e.g., Bart Custers, "New Digital Rights: Imagining Additional Fundamental Rights for the Digital Era," *Computer Law and Security Review* 44 (2022): 105636, https://doi.org/10.1016/j.clsr.2021.105636; Dariusz Kloza, "The Right Not to Use the Internet," *Computer Law & Security Review* 52 (2024): 105907, https://doi.org/10.1016/j.clsr.2023.105907; Dariusz Kloza and Julien Rossi, 'Du Droit d'accéder à Internet à La Liberté de – Ne Pas – l'utiliser?' (2024) 68 La revue européenne des médias et du numérique (La Rem) 17.

4 Cf. e.g., Paul De Hert and Dariusz Kloza, "Internet (Access) as a New Fundamental Right. Inflating the Current Rights Framework?," *European Journal of Law and Technology* 3, no. 3 (2012), https://ejlt.org/index.php/ejlt/article/view/123; Başak Çalı, "The Case for the Right to Meaningful Access to the Internet as a Human Right in International Law," in *The Cambridge Handbook of New Human Rights*, ed. Andreas von Arnauld, Kerstin von der Decken, and Mart Susi (Cambridge: Cambridge University Press, 2020), 276–284, https://doi.org/10.1017/9781108676106.022; Lina Jasmontaite and Paul De Hert,

"Access to the Internet in the EU: A Policy Priority, a Fundamental, a Human Right or a Concern for EGovernment?," in *Research Handbook on Human Rights and Digital Technology: Global Politics, Law and International Relations*, ed. Ben Wagner, Matthias C. Kettemann, and Kilian Vieth (Cheltenham: Edward Elgar, 2019), 157–179, https://doi.org/10.4337/9781785367724.00017; Oreste Pollicino, "The Right to Internet Access," in *The Cambridge Handbook of New Human Rights*, ed. Andreas von Arnauld, Kerstin von der Decken, and Mart Susi (Cambridge: Cambridge University Press, 2020), 263–275, https://doi.org/10.1017/9781108676106.021.

5 Jan van Dijk, *The Digital Divide* (Cambridge: Polity Press, 2020).

6 Cf. e.g., Eva Brems and Janneke Gerards, eds., *Shaping Rights in the ECHR* (Cambridge: Cambridge University Press, 2014), https://doi.org/10.1017/CBO9781107337923.

Part I

The concept and its consequences

1 Ethical meditations for a human right to an analogue life[1]

Georgios Terzis

1.1 Introduction

This chapter examines the intricate ethical dimensions surrounding the right to be excluded from the Information Society (IS) and maintain the choice for an analogue life in the context of the rapidly evolving information age. The IS, characterised by extensive digital connectivity and technological advancements, presents both advantages and challenges. As detailed in the foundational, as well as more recent literature review, the IS represents a web of inequality, shaped by interwoven social, economic, cultural and geographical factors that creates an inequitable access to technology broadly termed as the 'digital divide' (Van Dijk, 2006). Literature also suggests that individual hesitancy towards technology, whether due to fear, scepticism or a lack of perceived benefit, needs addressing (Ragnedda and Muschert, 2013).

While IS offers improved communication, access to knowledge and economic opportunities, it also raises concerns related to privacy, data protection, social equity or individual autonomy, among others. The latter has led to a number of recent 'opposition movements' in several countries. There is intensifying opposition to, for example, the *Bruxelles numérique* ordinance in 2024 that aims to digitise all administrative services. Opponents, including NGOs, social workers, unions and jurists, argued that the ordinance will exacerbate inequalities and discrimination in a city where nearly half of the inhabitants struggle with digital technology (Laloux, 2023).

A noticeable trend also shows that individuals are increasingly seeking analogue experiences, such as attending unplugged retreats or spending time offline to focus on personal relationships, favouring traditional mediums like books, vinyl records and handwritten materials over digital alternatives. This preference underscores, for example, the European Economic and Social Committee's (EESC, 2019) stance that the digital transition should incorporate analogue elements to be broadly accepted, cautioning against an over-reliance on digital replacements.

Examining this ethical conundrum, the chapter navigates through philosophical foundations, the issues of inclusivity to the IS and social consequences of the digital divide *vis-a-vis* those of individual autonomy and privacy considerations, and the balance between individual rights and societal interests (Aissaoui, 2021).

DOI: 10.4324/9781003528401-3

While recognising the potential productivity and other benefits and cost savings associated with digitalisation, the chapter contends that safeguarding individual freedom, even at a fractional cost of financial and social capital, is paramount in a democratic society.

The concluding remarks underscore the complex and multifaceted nature of the right to be excluded from the IS and to an analogue life. It calls for inclusive policymaking within ethical frameworks that strike a delicate balance between individual preferences and societal interests in an evolving digital landscape and eventually for the establishment of a *human right to analogue life* similar to the one recently enacted in the Constitution of Geneva – a *droit à l'intégrité numérique* (cf. its Article 21A). This invocation of a right to be excluded from the IS and an analogue life does not represent a Luddite retreat from technology, but rather a selective engagement on one's own terms, resonating with the Cynic tradition of autonomy and asceticism. In this light, the right to exclusion becomes an essential counterbalance to the IS's overreach, providing a necessary space for individuality, creativity and critical thought.

1.2 Information Society inclusion

1.2.1 Introduction

As the inclusion in the IS is an ideal, the concept of 'digital divide' denotes the disparity among individuals, households, businesses or geographic regions at varying socio-economic strata concerning their access to information and communication technologies (ICTs) and their utilisation of the Internet for diverse activities. Policymakers, academics and civil society organisations have long argued that addressing the digital divide is vital for promoting – *inter alia* – economic development, enhancing educational opportunities, fostering social inclusion, improving healthcare access, stimulating innovation and competitiveness and strengthening democratic participation.

In their analyses of the digital divide, Vassilakopoulou and Hustad (2023) conduct a systematic review of recent literature examining the factors influencing the digital divide and identifying emerging areas of division. They categorise factors affecting the digital divide into sociodemographic, socioeconomic, personal elements, social support, type of technology, digital training, infrastructure and large-scale events like COVID-19. The review suggests potential new levels of the digital divide, including algorithmic awareness also related to digital vulnerability, dataveillance and data inequalities (Dymacz, 2023). Elsewhere, literature argues that a significant number of people are unable to read and write, and so the focus should be promoting basic literacy before turning our attentions to digital literacy, thus calling for a more holistic approach. Monahan (2001) and Hamelink (2015), among others, argue that the issue can be more accurately and holistically described as an 'analogue divide' or 'development divide' that the digital divide operates within and thus would never narrow if we do not address it also more holistically in this context. Finally, other authors call for nuanced research that goes beyond established determinants to explore variations within demographic groups and the impact of attitudes, beliefs and the quality of social support related to the IS (Vartanova, 2017) and question the fundamental premises to be or not to be included in the IS, as the next two sections will illustrate.

1.2.2 To be …?

1.2.2.1 Why *digital inclusion can be beneficial*

Academic and policy literature provides a variety of arguments *why* digital inclusion is critical. First, it argues that economic development and innovation are fostered by the IS by expanding access to information, resources and markets as it enables individuals to participate in the digital economy, enhances productivity, entrepreneurship and creates employment.

Second, ICTs provide critical tools for social inclusion and equality, offering opportunities for individuals to improve their quality of life by providing access to social networks (Warschauer, 2004). Third, digital inclusion ensures that individuals can be active participants in the political decision-making processes as information and communication tools allow them to voice their opinions, mobilise for social causes and hold governments accountable (Shirky, 2011).

Fourth, education and lifelong learning through digital technologies provide opportunities for personalised learning, access to knowledge and digital literacy skills (Selwyn, 2010), while cultural diversity and creativity are enhanced through digital platforms that enable cultural expression and exchange through sharing heritage and engaging in creative collaborations (Jenkins, 2006). As a consequence, policymakers and academics have argued that individuals would gain a broader perspective on global issues, promoting peace and mutual understanding by participating in the global information network (Hamelink, 2015).

1.2.2.2 Where *digital inclusion can be beneficial*

In order to achieve the above, IS inclusion should be used across all sectors *where* ICTs are employed and should be focused on areas where the risk of exclusion is highest. The literature suggests the following areas and conditions for the application of IS inclusion. First, education is a key area where IS inclusion is important from primary schools to higher education to allow all learners access to educational content and participate in digital learning (Warschauer, 2004; Education International, 2021).

Second, in the area of healthcare, there is a need for telemedicine and e-health services to be inclusive to provide access to health services to patients from diverse backgrounds, including the elderly and rural populations (Eysenbach, 2001). Third, the public services area involves creating inclusive e-government initiatives to allow all individuals to access official services and engage in the democratic process (West, 2004). Fourth, at the labour market, there is a need for digital inclusion so that everyone, especially those from low-income or rural areas, can access job opportunities, training and professional development, while rural and remote areas need particular attention as these areas often have limited ICT infrastructure. The aim should be to reduce the urban-rural digital divide (Salemink et al., 2017). Finally, financial services inclusion is crucial for accessing digital financial services, including online banking and financial information (Manyika et al., 2016).

1.2.2.3 Who *can benefit from digital inclusion?*

The literature also provides a wide range of arguments of *who* should be the relevant and 'legitimate' stakeholders that could play a critical role in ensuring that the benefits of the IS are accessible to all. First, governments who are primarily responsible for creating policies and regulatory frameworks that promote IS inclusion by developing and implementing national strategies, investing in infrastructure and creating policies for digital literacy programmes (Van Dijk and Hacker, 2003). Second, international organisations like the United Nations (UN) and the International Telecommunication Union (ITU), as well as supranational organisations such as the European Union (EU) that play a crucial role in setting global agendas, fostering cooperation and providing guidance. They also have the capacity to track progress and encourage nations to invest in IS initiatives (Mansell and When, 1998).

Third, private sector companies are also crucial for driving innovation and providing the necessary technology and services for IS inclusion. They can also engage in public-private partnerships (PPPs) to develop affordable and accessible solutions for underserved populations such as the low-cost Aakash Tablets in India (Cullen, 2003; Sarvi et al., 2015). Fourth, civil society organisations, such as NGOs, advocacy groups and trade unions, can promote IS inclusion by raising awareness, providing training and ensuring that marginalised voices are heard, while local communities and grassroots initiatives are vital for understanding local needs and can be effective in tailoring inclusion efforts to specific contexts so that they are sensitive to local cultural and socioeconomic needs (Gurstein, 2003). Finally, fifth, educational institutions are also important players and can contribute to IS inclusion by offering digital literacy and skills training (Selwyn, 2004).

1.2.2.4 What *digital inclusion can be beneficial*

The academic literature around IS inclusion pertains to various dimensions of *what* individuals and groups can access, use and benefit from ICTs. First, digital access inclusion refers to ensuring that individuals have access to the physical infrastructure necessary to connect to the digital world, like the Internet, computers and mobile devices as well as content (Van Dijk, 2006), while digital skills inclusion focuses on equipping individuals with digital literacy and training to enable them to engage with digital content and tools including artificial intelligence (AI) (Hargittai, 2002; Goralski, 2020).

Socioeconomic inclusion acknowledges the need to address IS inclusion disparities related to income, education and socioeconomic status (Norris, 2001), and sociocultural and linguistic inclusion involves ensuring that the IS is inclusive of different sociocultural backgrounds and linguistic groups and promotes the preservation and representation of cultural diversity in the digital space (Graham, 2011; Warschauer, 2004). Jenkins (2006) also highlights the need for a participatory culture in the context of new media, where users are not only consumers but also content creators who contribute to and shape the development of IS. Moreover, inclusion of persons with disabilities involves designing technology and content that is accessible by following universal design (UD) principles and so inclusive to one of the groups most at risk of exclusion (Goggin and Newell, 2003).

1.2.2.5 When *digital inclusion can be beneficial*

The literature supports also several key arguments for the optimal timing and context for deploying IS inclusion strategies. IS inclusion strategies are most effectively employed *when* they are integrated proactively into the planning and implementation stages of technology development and policymaking. First, incorporating inclusion early in technological development reduces the risk of creating new forms of exclusion and helps design technologies that are accessible and usable for a wider range of populations (Schradie, 2011; Ragnedda and Muschert, 2013). Second, prioritising inclusion during the launch of digital education and health initiatives and e-government services ensures that citizens from all backgrounds have equal opportunities to benefit from e-learning and e-health technologies (Warschauer and Matuchniak, 2010; Azaare et al., 2024; Hollands, 2008; Kleine, 2010).

1.2.2.6 How *digital inclusion can be beneficial*

Finally, based on the literature, the following strategies are key to *how* to successfully implement IS inclusion. First, infrastructure development ensures that there is robust but also widespread ICT infrastructure (Servon, 2002) in order to serve the principle of universal access. Second, inclusive policymaking is vital so that the views of all stakeholders, including those from marginalised communities, are incorporated (Munyoka, 2022). Third, UD principles need to be applied to ensure accessibility for users of all abilities (Scherer, 2005). Fourth, affordability issues like subsidies, financing plans or free access points in community centres can help bridge inclusivity gaps (Chinn and Fairlie, 2007). Fifth, monitoring and evaluation on an ongoing basis are important to ensure that inclusion strategies are meeting their intended goals and necessary adjustments could be made (Selwyn, 2004). Sixth, PPPs between governments, private companies, non-profits and community organisations can leverage resources and expertise for IS inclusion efforts (Marx, 2019).

1.2.3 … or not to be?

1.2.3.1 Why *digital inclusion can be detrimental*

The literature review also offers many counterarguments to the promotion of inclusion in the IS that centre on concerns about potential negative impacts, misaligned priorities and the complexities of implementing inclusion effectively. First, the assumption that access to the IS automatically leads to growth and innovation may overlook other needs such as a skilled workforce and institutional capacity. Moreover, labour market digitisation could potentially lead to job displacement, as automation and AI become more prevalent and this could disproportionately affect low-skilled workers who are not equipped for the digital economy (Autor, 2015), and financial services in the digital space risks leaving behind those who are technologically illiterate, as well as raise concerns about increased financial fraud targeting vulnerable populations (O'Neil, 2016; Anakpo et al., 2023).

Additionally, political empowerment and participation to digital platforms may not ensure meaningful participation in the decision-making processes as there could be systemic barriers to participation such as lack of information and/or social capital that technology alone cannot remove. Moreover, the digital space can sometimes give an illusion of participation without leading to actual influence or change (Roth, 2020; Van Dijk, 2006). Critics also argue that increased digital interaction with the government could lead to the misuse of personal data and privacy infringement (Lyon, 2003).

Furthermore, critics argue that education and lifelong learning through digital tools is not a panacea for educational disparities as technology could exacerbate existing inequalities by privileging those who have access to digital devices and high-speed Internet over those who do not (Selwyn, 2016) or presented as a cheap alternative to well-qualified and well-paid teachers (Education International, 2021). Technology could also be a distraction and may not always lead to better educational outcomes (Education International, 2009).

At the same time, while ICTs have the potential to reduce social inequalities, they can also perpetuate and even deepen them. Unequal early adoption to technology, along with a lack of relevant skills, can leave marginalised groups further behind, creating a new form of digital underclass (Unwin, 2017). Similarly, telemedicine might exacerbate health disparities due to unequal access to technology. Vulnerable populations, such as the elderly or those with lower tech literacy, may face difficulties navigating e-health systems (Lupton, 2021).

Moreover, while the intent is to bridge the urban-rural divide, overemphasis on ICT infrastructure may neglect more pressing needs like basic amenities and services. Ragnedda and Muschert (2013) raise concerns about creating new forms of stratification through unequal implementation of IS inclusion since technology access in urban areas in most cases improves faster than in rural areas, increasing the urban-rural divide.

Likewise, cultural diversity and creativity may actually be homogenised through technology as dominant languages and narratives overshadow the diversity of local and indigenous content, while the commercialisation of digital spaces can lead to the commodification of culture and creativity, potentially stifling genuine and original cultural expression (Couldry and Mejias, 2019a).

Finally, critics have argued that increased connectivity does not necessarily lead to understanding or peace (Milan and Treré, 2019). Global networks could also facilitate the spread of misinformation; enable cyber warfare and become tools for political manipulation rather than mutual understanding (Hamelink, 2015).

1.2.3.2 Who *can be detrimental for digital inclusion*

In academic and policy discourse, critics also point out several potential pitfalls associated with the involvement of the 'legitimate' stakeholders and their agendas. Governments for example are often presented as primary change agents for IS inclusion, but Couldry and Mejias (2019b) caution that official policies may lag behind technological change and government interests may also not always align with the ideals of digital inclusion, as policies could favour national security or economic interests of specific groups over equitable access.

International organisations have also been criticised by Milan and Treré (2019) for advocating a homogenised approach to inclusion at variance to the needs of different nations, as well as potentially being swayed by agendas of more powerful nations and the corporate world. Furthermore, private sector involvement could lead to the commodification of public goods, where inclusion efforts are directed more by profit motives than by the public interest (Fuchs, 2009). At the same time, civil society groups and local communities might lack the necessary resources and political clout to sustain and scale their efforts in initiatives, which may take place over long periods of time (Hintz et al., 2019). Finally, an emphasis on technical skills may detract from holistic educational goals like critical thinking and interpersonal development (Education International, 2021).

1.2.3.3 What *digital inclusion can be detrimental*

The literature also highlights the several counter arguments or critiques as to what kind of IS inclusion should be pursued. Selwyn (2006) for example argues that access does not automatically lead to digital literacy or meaningful use, and may not justify the cost when compared to other pressing social needs, while Hargittai and Hsieh (2013) contend that even with training, some individuals may not see the Internet as relevant to their lives or they might abstain from the IS due to the perception of harmful content or side effects on their thinking processes and social and emotional skills.

Furthermore, socioeconomic inclusion efforts might lead to superficial engagement that does not address underlying economic inequalities and with the introduction of AI most recent debates have shifted to the disproportionate negative impact on disadvantaged socio-economic groups and developing countries (van Dijk, 2005; Korinek and Stiglitz, 2021; Mhlanga, 2021; Wakunuma et al., 2020; Lutz, 2019).

Additionally, overemphasising linguistic diversity inclusion can create fragmentation and inefficiencies in communication and information exchange, according to Crawford (2000). He questions whether the effort to support all languages and dialects is sustainable. Emphasising local content can also unintentionally limit exposure to global perspectives and potentially reinforce local prejudices or misinformation.

At the same time, UD for the purposes of inclusion may lead to a 'lowest common denominator' approach to the development of technology and constrain innovation (Goggin and Newell, 2007). Finally, participatory inclusion concerns posit that participatory design might slow down the development process and lead to a compromise on the quality or functionality of technology. As Feenberg (1999) argues, not all user input may be equally beneficial or practical to implement.

1.2.3.4 When *digital inclusion can be detrimental*

The optimal timing debate on IS inclusion also has its counterarguments. Some scholars argue that pushing for IS inclusion before a population is ready can lead to premature technology adoption and underutilisation or rejection of technology. Second, Morozov (2013) criticises what he perceives as an overly idealistic view of digital technology's role in society, where the current focus limits the development of more appropriate bottom-up technologies. Critics also point out that in some instances the cost of implementing inclusion outweighs the benefits, especially where technology becomes obsolete quickly or fails to deliver the expected social improvements (Benkler, 2006). Finally, rushing to implement inclusion can lead to overlooking data privacy and security concerns, especially if inclusion is prioritised over the development of robust cybersecurity measures (Zuboff, 2019).

1.2.3.5 Where *digital inclusion can be detrimental*

Counterarguments arise also from challenges associated with the practicalities of implementation, unintended consequences and differing perspectives on responsibility. First, infrastructural development by itself, according to Diga (2007), does not bridge the digital divide due to persistent socioeconomic inequalities. Moreover, as stated already above, simply building infrastructure does not ensure meaningful usage (Helsper and Reisdorf, 2017). Second, the complexity of inclusive policymaking means that involving many legitimate stakeholders, though ideal, makes the process more complex and slower, potentially leading to conflicts between different interest groups. Braman (2006) for example argues that the complexity of policymaking in the IS often leads to exclusion rather than inclusion. At the same time, critics of UD also argue that it is not always feasible or cost-effective to design products to meet all user needs. Some features that make a product accessible for one group may hinder another. Goggin and Newell (2003) note that UD can sometimes lead to 'one-size-fits-none' solutions.

1.2.3.6 How *digital inclusion can be detrimental*

An insightful report by the World Economic Forum (WEF, 2023) sets out six categories of online harms: threats to personal and community safety encompassing issues such as child exploitation and extremist content; health and well-being where content promotes suicide or disordered eating; hate and discrimination, including algorithmic discrimination; violation of dignity through, for example, online bullying and sexual extortion; privacy, highlighting concerns such as doxing and image-based abuse; and deception and manipulation covering disinformation and scams. Other harms relate to the side effects on human capabilities with studies indicating a correlation between extensive social media use and a reduction in attention spans and maintaining focus on tasks or activities for prolonged periods (Wang et al., 2020).

Finally, PPP can be powerful but they may lead to an over-reliance on the private sector, with public interests taking a backseat to corporate profits. Already in 1998, Schiller raised the issue of the potential loss of public control over critical infrastructure and services, while Sørensen and Torfing (2009) discuss how such collaborations can be fraught with governance challenges. At the same time, Bauer and Latzer (2016) discuss how market-driven approaches to affordability may neglect the needs of the least advantaged and also argue that on the other hand focusing on affordability may compromise quality or rely on outdated technology. Finally, effective monitoring and evaluation are important to assess progress but it can be resource-intensive and may not accurately reflect the impact on the ground due to the complexity of measuring social change (Heeks, 2010).

1.2.4 Discussion

As we have seen in this section, the literature highlights the multifaceted benefits of digital inclusion, ranging from fostering economic growth to enhancing social equality and empowering global connectivity (Hamelink, 2015). However, it also confronts the idealistic advocacy of naïve Internet utopians of digital inclusion policies with a realistic critique of its potential to inadvertently widening existing gaps and introduce new forms of inequalities and abuse of human rights. The discourse around IS inclusion reflects a balancing act between leveraging the connective power of technology and mitigating its divisive and harmful effects. It calls for a nuanced, evidence-based approach to policymaking that aligns with local needs and global development goals, as well as human rights. The following section attempts to offer a framework for such an approach through the application of different ethics lenses offered by the six foundational ethical theories of utilitarian, contractualist, deontological, virtue, discourse and care ethics.

1.3 Meditations of IS inclusion *via* different ethical lenses

1.3.1 Introduction

A small number of researchers to this day have discussed the ethical dimensions of the above debate and reference to those seems to be silenced the past 20 years. In 2003, Tavani examined the ethical implications of the digital divide and considered whether access to ICT should be considered a right, given its increasingly crucial role in enabling participation in the economy, education, health services and politics. Also in 2003 Hacker and Mason examined the ethical oversights in digital divide research, suggesting that a lack of ethical consideration influences data collection and interpretation, thus affecting policy decisions. Van der Velden's (2005) analysis also reveals the deep ethical and political implications embedded in ICT choices, arguing for a nuanced understanding of digital inclusion that recognises the diverse ways knowledge is produced, owned and shared. All the aforementioned authors acknowledge shortcomings in the debate on inclusivity and the digital divide, a trend that persists to the present.

This chapter will attempt to fill the gap in this discussion by examining the inclusivity to IS through various ethical frameworks and highlight a number of underlining issues and policy assumptions while proposing that virtue, discourse and care ethical approaches are missing from the debate despite the fact that they might be providing a more appropriate framework to approach them.

1.3.2 Utilitarian ethics

First, *utilitarian ethics*, which prioritises the greatest happiness for the greatest number of people, often underpins arguments for the widespread inclusion of individuals in the IS. This perspective suggests that the benefits accrued from digital platforms justify efforts to integrate as many people as possible. The approach has its critics. One argument centres around presuming that inclusion inherently leads to happiness or is uniformly desired. As we have seen in the previous section, scholarship acknowledges that the IS presents challenges ranging from privacy concerns to information overload, which may not contribute to everyone's well-being (Zuboff, 2019). Sen (1997) highlights that utilitarian approaches often fail to consider the heterogeneity of happiness itself, which is subjective and can manifest differently across cultures and individuals. The implication that productivity inherently leads to pleasure is also contested; as Marx (1844/2009) pointed out, in the realm of labour and production, alienation can occur when individuals do not find intrinsic value in their work, despite its productivity. Newport (2021) further argues that digital tools, while designed to increase productivity, instead create interruptions and fragmented attention spans and so undermine our ability to perform deep, focused work and significantly decrease our substantive productivity and satisfaction.

In addition, individuals or groups may wish to opt out of certain digital engagements for reasons, including cultural preservation, psychological well-being or the desire for autonomy (Lanier, 2018). Alas, within the utilitarian framework, the minority who resist inclusion can be overlooked or their well-being sacrificed for the larger benefit, despite the fact that theorists contend that the mere aggregation of happiness does not justify harm to a few (Sandel, 2009). The adverse effects on these minorities have significant ethical costs that must be factored into any comprehensive utilitarian calculus. The balance between collective benefit and individual harm becomes a critical point of contention. Recent discourses in digital ethics propose that autonomy and respect for individual choice are paramount, even if this results in fewer people being part of the IS (Vallor, 2016). This view suggests that individuals should have the right to determine the extent of their engagement with IS, challenging the assumption that inclusion is universally beneficial. Thus, while the utilitarian argument for IS inclusion appears compelling, it must be reconciled with the principle of respect for individual autonomy and the recognition that happiness is subjective and cannot be assumed to arise uniformly from IS participation. The ethical imperative to mitigate the negative impacts on minorities who opt-out or are less engaged with the IS becomes a counterbalancing force against the utilitarian drive for maximal inclusion.

Finally, utilitarian approaches often drive policymaking towards IS inclusion, with an emphasis on immediate benefits like increased access to information, improved connectivity and economic growth. However, there is a growing academic discourse questioning the scope of utilitarian foresight, particularly in relation to the long-term implications of technological advancements on happiness, including the impacts of AI. Recent literature emphasises that while utilitarianism considers the outcomes of actions, it may not adequately address the long-term consequences that span generations. Bostrom (2014) argues for the importance of incorporating an 'existential risk' assessment when evaluating the implications of rapidly advancing technologies, like AI, which might have irreversible effects on humanity's future (Floridi and Cowls, 2019). The principles of 'techno-utilitarianism', which merge technological progress with utilitarian ethics, must therefore be critically examined. As technology increasingly shapes the structure of societies, the ethical models that support inclusion must evolve to consider not only the sum of immediate benefits but also the potential impacts on social structures, human welfare and environmental sustainability in the long term.

1.3.3 Contractualist ethics

Second, *contractualist ethical* approaches justifying IS inclusion often hinge on the assumption that life before or outside the digital realm is poorer, and that the IS enhances the quality of life. This argument posits that the collective welfare of individuals is improved through a contract of IS inclusion. Critics have challenged the premises of this view. They argue that the notion of a low quality of life in the 'state of nature' outside the digital realm overlooks the value of non-digital cultures and experiences. Indeed, Escobar (2018) stresses the richness and diversity of life that thrives outside the bounds of digitisation, where community, traditional knowledge and connection to nature play central roles in well-being. These critics suggest that digitisation erodes cultural diversity and is responsible for the loss of vital skills and knowledge that are not dependent on, or even compatible with, the digital world.

Furthermore, the contractualist premise that an IS inclusion social contract is indispensable for human survival is contested. Nussbaum (2011) offers a capability approach as an alternative ethical framework, arguing that human development should focus on expanding people's capabilities and choices rather than coercively integrating them into a digital society. From this perspective, the value of IS inclusion should be measured not by its ubiquity but by its ability to enhance individuals' freedom to lead lives of value (Lanier, 2018).

Moreover, the contractualist framework, particularly as it pertains to Hobbes's philosophy (1651/1968) and much more to more modern contractualists such as Rawls (1971), posits that the legitimacy of societal arrangements, such as the inclusion in the IS, hinges on the voluntary consent of individuals. Hobbes's central claim was that ethical and political systems gain their authority from a social contract, a mutual agreement among individuals. Thus, this notion of consent should underlie contemporary debates about the ethical inclusion in the IS. Recent literature on digital ethics argues that if such consent is not given, the right to opt out of the IS and maintaining analogue options must be upheld (Friedman and Nissenbaum, 1996). This perspective is significant in the digital age, where participation in the IS is often assumed to be mandatory or, at least, the default position (Cohen, 2019). It argues that, just as citizens have the right to resist the sovereign when the social contract is breached, individuals should be able to resist participation in the IS, if it conflicts with their personal values or if it poses risks to their privacy and autonomy.

Furthermore, the notion of consent in the IS is complex and often obscured by the opaque terms and conditions presented by digital platforms, which few read and even fewer understand. This problematises the very notion of consent within the IS, as it challenges whether users can truly give informed consent (O'Neil, 2016).

1.3.4 Deontological ethics

Third, interpreting IS inclusion through the *deontological ethics* lens raises questions about the universality and morality of mandating such inclusion. Kant's imperative calls for actions to be made into universal law, applicable to all. If policymakers, academics and civil society advocates applied this imperative to IS inclusion, it would imply a moral obligation for universal participation in digital life, without exceptions. The perspective is, however, subject to scrutiny in academic discourse (Ess, 2013). Critics argue that a Kantian approach would fail to address the nuanced and contextual nature of ethical decision-making in the digital age. Mandating IS inclusion universally also ignores the autonomy of individuals who choose to limit their digital footprint, which conflicts with Kant's emphasis on autonomy and rational agency. Recent advancements in AI and big data analytics have also intensified debates about privacy and autonomy within the IS.

Thus, while the categorical imperative provides a robust framework for ethical action, its application to IS inclusion necessitates a delicate balance. It must acknowledge the moral weight of potential harms and the importance of respecting individual autonomy, as well as the diversity of cultural norms and values. Metz (2013) suggests that a modified Kantian framework, one that considers relational factors and the social implications of technology, may be more suitable for ethical decision-making in the context of the IS.

In conclusion, while a Kantian imperative towards universal IS inclusion may strive towards a world where digital access and literacy are as fundamental as any other right, it must also accommodate the realities of the complex digital landscape. As human dignity becomes more and more exposed to risks online and we can easily be '*mere means*' of someone else online, people would like to opt out to avoid such risks. It is not merely then the inclusion itself but the quality and terms of this inclusion that must be universally ethical, especially in the context of a fast moving AI landscape. It requires a more pluralistic and context-sensitive approach aligning with the core principles of respect for persons, justice as well as promoting human flourishing that necessitates that right to be excluded from the IS and an analogue life, that discourse, virtue and care ethics provide as we will see in the sections hereunder.

1.3.5 Discourse ethics

Fourth, in the context of *Habermasian discourse ethics*, the validity of moral claims depends on the consensus reached through rational discourse, without coercion and manipulation (Habermas, 1984/2015). When applied to IS inclusion, this framework presents significant challenges, particularly concerning fora like the Internet Governance Forum (IGF), whose mandate necessitates engaging with marginalised voices (Couldry and Mejias, 2019b). For the IGF and others aiming to be inclusive, Habermasian principles require that it must engage all stakeholders, even for those who opt to remain outside the digital fold (Fisher, 2010). This should encompass then a recognition of the rights of individuals to resist incorporation into the IS. The irony lies in the fact that individuals who do not wish to be part of the IS must participate in the IGF or other similar platforms to facilitate their exclusion. Furthermore, identifying these individuals is challenging unless they self-identify, as their preference for remaining offline and lack of a digital footprint makes them difficult to trace *via* digital means.

In practice, achieving a free discourse without coercion and manipulation is a formidable task, especially in the face of commercial interests and global inequalities that can permeate deliberative spaces on IS. Power dynamics present obstacles to achieving this ideal as those already in power often dominate conversations, and less powerful voices are at risk of being overshadowed or outright ignored, leading to a form of coercion or manipulation by omission (Hintz et al., 2019). Carefully scrutinised, the IGF procedures and those of other fora do not ensure that all participants engage on equal footing. Literature suggests that the mechanisms of discourse themselves may be subject to inequalities and biases that can marginalise certain groups, for instance because of power inequalities of financial or social capital, as well as the language that often reflects a particular cultural and technical vernacular that may be less accessible, and so effectively exclude non-experts or those from different cultural backgrounds from meaningful participation (Milan and Treré, 2019).

The question then becomes whether the IGF, or any other fora advocating for IS inclusion, can implement procedures that counteract these power dynamics and create an environment where genuine consensus building is possible. To align with Habermasian ethics then, there is a need for continuous reform of governance structures of fora to ensure they are inclusive in theory and equitable in practice. It involves actively seeking out and facilitating the participation of those who may be opposed to IS inclusion, ensuring their perspectives are given weight and consideration in the shaping of the digital world and their right to be excluded from the IS and an analogue life.

1.3.6 Virtue ethics

Fifth, the *virtue ethics* perspective discussion, with its emphasis on character and the well-lived life, centres around the concept of human flourishing or eudaimonia, and the importance of moderating between the extremes of deficiency and excess. Within this ethical lens, the deficiency would be digital exclusion with limited or no access at all, while the excess would involve compulsory inclusion in the IS, where individuals are forced into a digital sphere. Virtue ethicists suggest that virtues are about finding a balance between deficiency and excess. The virtuous path involves seeking a midpoint that thoughtfully recognises the complexity of the human-technology relationship. It calls for a compassionate, reflective approach that upholds the dignity and agency of all individuals to embrace or opt out of the digital world. Applying this to IS inclusion, the virtuous action offers individuals the right to participate in the digital realm while simultaneously upholding their right to opt out, a position that acknowledges autonomy and respects individual decisions (Swanton, 2003).

In considering the right to be excluded and an analogue life, the virtue ethics framework offers arguments for advocates of a society that cultivates *digital wisdom* – a virtue involving a judicious use of technology, an elevated media literacy and netiquette, which does not only explain the Internet but also reflects on digital citizenship that recognises when it serves human flourishing and when it detracts from it. Digital wisdom would entail creating spaces that allow for meaningful choice and consent, ensuring that technology serves to enhance, rather than dictate, the course of one's life (Vallor, 2016).

1.3.7 Care ethics

Finally, the *care ethics* approach underscores the interdependence of human beings and the centrality of caring relationships. Rooted in the idea that moral value stems from practices, relationships and responsibilities of care (Gilligan, 1982), care ethics insists that digital inclusion policies be contextually grounded, responsive to individuals' specific circumstances and reflective of embedded relations of care and responsibility (Held, 2005). The central tenets of care ethics, empathy and compassion, should guide actions and lean towards fair treatment rather than mere calculations of utility (Slote, 2007).

This ethical lens highlights the necessity of guarding against the risks of mandatory digital inclusion, which may lead to undermining well-being and cultural integrity. The care ethics framework advocates a move away from one-dimensional ethical frameworks for digital inclusion, towards policies rooted in empathy, attentive to the diversity of human relationships and committed to fostering human flourishing (Held, 2005). This leads to adaptable and tailored policies that recognise different levels and forms of engagement with technology (Noddings, 1984) and allow opting out (Tronto, 1993).

A care ethics approach also calls for a holistic consideration of human needs, incorporating support for education, fair wages and environmental protection alongside the development of digital infrastructure.

1.4 Conclusion

Hamelink already in 2005 explored the complexities and shortcomings of digital inclusion at the World Summit on the Information Society's (WSIS) Declaration of Principles. Critiquing these references with regard to the lack of context and lack of concrete implementation plans, Hamelink pointed out that digital divide and inclusion references in the WSIS declaration were made in a socio-political void that lacked historical context and concrete resource allocations.

Extending even further on the above arguments, in *Human Rights in the IS*, Sartor (2010) warns of several risks associated with digital advancements. They include Orwell's nightmare of increased surveillance; Kafka's concerns of control and judgement; Huxley's dread of using technologies to discriminate and exclude and Bradbury's fears of ignorance and indifference. With these dystopian scenarios he underscores the need for a balanced approach that safeguards human rights. Exploring the legal and moral dimensions of specific rights like privacy, freedom of expression and access to information he underscores the importance of adapting human rights to the realities of the IS.

More recently, Kloza (2024) in *The Right Not to Use the Internet* examines the increasingly *de facto* obligation to use the Internet in contemporary society and questions whether such an obligation aligns with democratic ideals. Outlining the evolution of Internet use from a choice towards a near-mandatory way to exercise rights and fulfilling duties, Kloza suggests that the current trajectory towards the obligatory Internet use should be reassessed to ensure that it remains optional and justified only in cases of absolute necessity. He questions whether existing human rights law could protect individuals from this implicit obligation and proposes the possibility of framing protection from mandatory use either as a new standalone right or through the reinterpretation of existing rights to ensure more comprehensive protection for individuals.

Kloza's (2017) further argument for a behavioural alternative to privacy protection stems from the observation that existing legal, organisational and technological measures often fall short in effectively safeguarding privacy. He states the mechanisms to protect privacy must adjust to the evolving societies and technologies and behavioural alternatives are an essential complement to traditional protections. This approach involves adjusting own behaviour to protect privacy, even if it comes at a cost. Along the same lines, Wyatt (1999) also argued that these voluntary, informed and conscious choices to reject the Internet, are often overlooked in the debate centred on barriers to access and way of promoting technology adoption. She urged incorporating the perspectives of those who reject the Internet in shaping societal and technological landscapes.

Moreover, building upon Fortner's (1995) taxonomy of factors for the exclusion from the IS, it is possible to view this ascetic exclusion as part of a digital resistance movement that advocates for the right to disconnect in tech-free analogue-life spaces to preserve mental health and well-being (Turkle, 2016). The right to be excluded and for an analogue life can also be viewed within a pleonastic framework of the modern paradox of choice, where an abundance of digital options leads to the cannibalisation of our free time and previous cultural practices by new digital products (Wajcman, 2015).

Furthermore, the right to exclude oneself from the IS and have an analogue life is also related to the right to silence, to privacy and to a life less exposed to the often pervasive data collection mechanisms of our time (Zuboff, 2019). Inclusion without the real possibility of exclusion may result in a form of digital totalitarianism, where the individual's freedom is subsumed by the wider societal digital embrace.

This discussion opens the floor for further debate on the safeguarding lives outside the digital world with the introduction of the right for an analogue life similar to the one recently enacted in the Constitution of Geneva for *l'intégrité numérique* (cf. its Article 21A). In a world where digital footprints are often perceived as synonymous with existence, the right to an analogue life of choosing to remain 'offline' is, for many, a statement of autonomy and self-determination and a necessary counterpart to digital inclusion efforts.

1.5 Epilogue

In our information age, the right to be excluded and have an analogue life manifests as the prerogative to remain autonomous and detached from the pervasive digital networks and the ever-present gaze of data surveillance. This contemporary form of self-imposed exile is not driven by the disdain for technology *per se*, but rather by a conscious choice to preserve one's mental space and personal data from the omnipotent reach of corporations and officialdom, positioning privacy and autonomy as modern equivalents of the ancient philosophical pursuit of eudaimonia.

The right to be excluded from the IS and to an analogue life parallels the ancient Cynics' desire for self-sufficiency and independence from the conventional expectations of civic life. The Cynics, with Diogenes of Sinope as a prototypical figure, excluded themselves from the political life of the polis. Their philosophy, grounded in the pursuit of virtue through asceticism and the rejection of conventional desires, advocated a life lived in accordance with nature rather than societal norms.

Similarly, the assertion of the right to be excluded from the IS today and have an analogue life is a direct challenge to the structures of digital power and the commodification and commercialisation of personal information. It embodies a modern-day Diogenes' barrel, a symbolic retreat from the complexities and intrusions of digital life. Diogenes' assertion of his autonomy from the power structures and societal expectations is encapsulated through his infamous encounter with Alexander the Great, when he asked Alexander to move out of the way as he was blocking him sunlight. Individuals today assert their autonomy from the modern day 'Alexandrian' digital powers by demanding that tech giants and their surveillance apparatuses not encroach on their personal space with data collection and targeted advertisements.

This stance negates not only the desire for the supposed benefits of omnipresent connectivity but also questions the very nature of desire as shaped by the IS (Sloterdijk, 1983). It is an ethical conscious stand against the algorithmic determinism that directs human wants and needs, an affirmation of the power of individuals to define their desires independently of the IS's imperatives. It is a recognition of empowerment and self-determination and the ability to choose one's level of engagement within the contemporary digital world. It is a reimagining of Cynics withdrawal from the polis and Diogenes' barrel, one that values the unfettered 'sunlight' of personal freedom over the allure of constant digital connectivity.

Acknowledgements

This chapter benefited from the comments of my colleagues Alfonso Garcia Figueroa, Nadia Tjahja and Stephanie Arnold.

Note

1 ChatGPT4 was used for the editing of this chapter.

Bibliography

Aissaoui, N. (2021). *The digital divide: A literature review and some directions for future research in light of COVID-19*. Global Knowledge, Memory and Communication, February 2021.

Anakpo, G., Xhate, Z., and Mishi, S. (2023). The policies, practices, and challenges of digital financial inclusion for sustainable development: The case of the developing economy. *FinTech*, 2(2), 327–343.

Autor, D. (2015). Why are there still so many jobs? The history and future of workplace automation. *Journal of Economic Perspectives*, 29(3), 3–30.

Azaare, J., Dagadu, J. C., and Otoo, S. N.-A. (2024). Evaluating e-government development among African Union member states: An analysis of the impact of e-government on public administration and governance in Ghana. *Sustainability*, 16(3), 1333.

Bauer, J. M., and Latzer, M. (2016). *Handbook on the economics of the internet*. Edward Elgar.

Benkler, Y. (2006). *The wealth of networks: How social production transforms markets and freedom*. Yale University Press.

Bostrom, N. (2014). *Superintelligence: Paths, dangers, strategies*. Oxford University Press.

Braman, S. (2006). *Change of state: Information, policy, and power*. MIT Press.

Brynjolfsson, E., and McAfee, A. (2014). *The second machine age: Work, progress, and prosperity in a time of brilliant technologies*. W.W. Norton and Company.

Cardona, M., Kretschmer, T., and Strobel, T. (2013). ICT and productivity: Conclusions from the empirical literature. *Information Economics and Policy*, 25(3), 109–125.

Castells, M. (1996). *The rise of the network society*. Blackwell Publishers.

Castells, M. (2008). The new public sphere: Global civil society, communication networks, and global governance. *The Annals of the American Academy of Political and Social Science*, 616(1), 78–93.

Chinn, M. D., and Fairlie, R. W. (2007). The determinants of the global digital divide: A cross-country analysis of computer and internet penetration. *Oxford Economic Papers*, 59(1), 16–44.

Cohen, J. (2019). *Between truth and power: The legal constructions of informational capitalism*. Oxford University Press.

Constitution de la République et canton de Genève. (2012, octobre 14). https://silgeneve.ch/legis/program/books/rsg/pdf/rsg_a2_00.pdf

Couldry, N., and Mejias, U. A. (2019a). Data colonialism: Rethinking big data's relation to the contemporary subject. *Television & New Media*, *20*(4), 336–349. https://doi.org/10.1177/1527476418796632

Couldry, N., and Mejias, U. A. (2019b). Making data colonialism liveable: how might data's social order be regulated? *Internet Policy Review*, *8*(2). https://doi.org/10.14763/2019.2.1411

Crawford, J. (2000). *At war with diversity: US language policy in an age of anxiety*. Multilingual Matters. www.dawsonera.com/depp/reader/protected/external/AbstractView/S9781853596766

Cullen, R. (2003). The digital divide: A global and national call to action. *The Electronic Library*, 21(3), 247–257.

Diga, K. (2007). Mobile cell phones and poverty reduction: Technology spending patterns and poverty level change among households in Uganda. *Information Technologies and International Development*, 4(3), 17–23.

Dymacz, A. (2023). Digital vulnerability of the AI-assisted consumers, Maastricht University Blog, www.maastrichtuniversity.nl/blog/2023/02/digital-vulnerability-ai-assisted-consumers.

Education International. (2009). Bridging the digital divide. www.ei-ie.org/en/item/20644:bridging-the-digital-divide.

Education International. (2021). *Poor families and digital technologies: The nuances of digital appropriation*. www.ei-ie.org/en/item/25177:poor-families-and-digital-technologies-the-nuances-of-digital-appropriation.

Escobar, A. (2017). *Designs for the Pluriverse: Radical Interdependence, Autonomy, and the Making of Worlds*. Duke University Press. www.jstor.org/stable/j.ctv11smgs6

Ess, C. (2013). *Digital media ethics*. Polity.

European Economic and Social Committee (EESC). (2019). Opinion of the European Economic and Social Committee on 'The digital revolution in view of citizens' needs and rights' (own-initiative opinion). *Official Journal of the European Union*, C 190/17. https://eur-lex.europa.eu/legal-content/EN/TXT/PDF/?uri=CELEX:52018IE4168andrid=1

Eysenbach, G. (2001). What is e-health? *Journal of Medical Internet Research*, 3(2), e20.

Feenberg, A. (1999). *Questioning technology*. Routledge.

Fisher, E. (2010). *Media and new capitalism in the digital age: The spirit of networks*. Palgrave Macmillan.

Floridi, L., and Cowls, J. (2019). A unified framework of five principles for AI in society. *Harvard Data Science Review*, *1*(1). https://doi.org/10.1162/99608f92.8cd550d1

Fortner, R. S. (1995). Excommunication in the information society. *Critical Studies in Media Communication*, *12*(2), 133–154.

Friedman, B., and Nissenbaum, H. (1996, April). User autonomy: who should control what and when? In *Conference Companion on Human Factors in Computing Systems* (p. 433).

Fuchs, C. (2009). Information and communication technologies and society: A contribution to the critique of the political economy of the internet. *European Journal of Communication*, 24(1), 69–87.

Gilligan, C. (1982). *In a different voice: Psychological theory and women's development.* Harvard University Press.

Goggin, G., and Newell, C. (2003). *Digital disability: The social construction of disability in new media.* Rowman and Littlefield.

Goggin, G., and Newell, C. (2007). The business of digital disability. *The Information Society*, 23(3), 159–168. https://doi.org/10.1080/01972240701323572

Goralski, M. (2020). Artificial intelligence and sustainable development. *International Journal of Management Education*, *18*(1), 100330.

Goralski, M. A., and Tan, T. K. (2020). Artificial intelligence and sustainable development. *International Journal of Management Education*, 18(1), 100330.

Graham, M. (2011). Time machines and virtual portals: The spatialities of the digital divide. *Progress in Development Studies*, 11(3), 211–227.

Gurstein, M. (2003). Effective use: A community informatics strategy beyond the digital divide. *First Monday*, 8(12). doi: 10.5210/fm.v0i0.1798

Habermas, J. (1984/2015). *The theory of communicative action: Reason and the rationalization of society* (Vol. 1). Polity.

Hamelink, C. (2015). *Global communication.* Sage

Hargittai, E. (2002). Second-level digital divide: Differences in people's online skills. *First Monday*, 7(4). doi: 10.5210/fm.v7i4.942

Hargittai, E., and Hsieh, Y. P. (2013). Digital inequality. In W. H. Dutton (Ed.), *The Oxford handbook of Internet studies* (pp.129–150). Oxford University Press.

Heeks, R. (2010). Do information and communication technologies (ICTs) contribute to development? *Journal of International Development*, 22(5), 625–640.

Held, V. (2005). *The ethics of care: Personal, political, and global.* Oxford University Press.

Helsper, E. J., and Reisdorf, B. C. (2017). The emergence of a "digital underclass" in Great Britain and Sweden: Changing reasons for digital exclusion. *New Media and Society*, 19(8), 1253–1270.

Hintz, A., Dencik, L., and Wahl-Jørgensen, K. (2019). *Digital citizenship in a datafied society.* Polity Press.

Hobbes, T. (1651). *Leviathan.* Penguin Books.

Hollands, R. G. (2008). Will the real smart city please stand up? *City*, 12(3), 303–320.

Jenkins, H. (2006). *Convergence culture: Where old and new media collide.* New York University Press.

Johnson, D. G. (2001). *Computer ethics* (3rd ed.). Prentice Hall.

Kleine, D. (2010). ICT4WHAT?—Using the choice framework to operationalise the capability approach to development. *Journal of International Development*, 22(5), 674–692.

Kloza, D. (2017). A behavioural alternative to the protection of privacy. In Svantesson, D. and Kloza, D. (Eds.), *Trans-Atlantic data privacy relations as a challenge for democracy* (pp. 451–505). Intersentia.

Kloza, D. (2024). The right not to use the internet. *Computer Law & Security Review, 52*, https://doi.org/10.1016/j.clsr.2023.105907.

Korinek, A., and Stiglitz, J. E. (2021). *Artificial intelligence, globalization, and strategies for economic development (Working Paper No. 28453).* National Bureau of Economic Research.

Laloux, P. (2023, Octobre 11). *Union sacrée contre le « numérique par défaut »* (p. 11). *Le Soir.*

Lanier, J. (2018). *Ten arguments for deleting your social media accounts right now*. Henry Holt.

Lupton, D. (2021). Young people's use of digital health technologies in the global North: Narrative review. *Journal of medical Internet research*, *23*(1), e18286. https://doi.org/10.2196/18286

Lutz, C. (2019). Digital inequalities in the age of artificial intelligence and big data. *Human Behavior and Emerging Technologies*, 1(2), 141–148.

Lyon, D. (2003). *Surveillance as social sorting: Privacy, risk, and digital discrimination*. Psychology Press.

Mansell, R., and Wehn, U. (Eds.). (1998). *Knowledge societies: Information technology for sustainable development*. Oxford University Press on behalf of the United Nations.

Manyika, J., Lund, S., Singer, M., White, O., and Berry, C. (2016). *Digital finance for all: Powering inclusive growth in emerging economies*. McKinsey Global Institute.

Margetts, H., and Dunleavy, P. (2013). The second wave of digital-era governance: A quasi-paradigm for government on the Web. *Philosophical Transactions of the Royal Society A: Mathematical, Physical and Engineering Sciences*, 371(1987), 1–17.

Marx, A. (2019). Public-private partnerships for sustainable development: Exploring their design and its impact on effectiveness. *Sustainability*, 11(4), 1087.

Marx, K., and Engels, F. (2009). *The economic and philosophic manuscripts of 1844 and the Communist manifesto*. Rowman & Littlefield.

Metz, T. (2013). *Meaning in life*. Oxford University Press.

Mhlanga, D. (2021). Artificial Intelligence in Industry 4.0, and its impact on poverty, innovation, infrastructure development, and the Sustainable Development Goals: Lessons from emerging economies. *Sustainability*, 13(11), 5788.

Milan, S., and Treré, E. (2019). Big data from the South(s): Beyond data universalism. *Television & New Media*, *20*(4), 319–335. https://doi.org/10.1177/1527476419837739

Monahan, T. (2001). The analog divide: Technology practices in public education. *Computers and Society*, 31(3), 22–31.

Morozov, E. (2013). *To save everything, click here: The folly of technological solutionism*. Public Affairs.

Munyoka, W. (2022). Inclusive digital innovation in South Africa: Perspectives from disadvantaged and marginalized communities. *Sustainability*, 14(9), 5372.

Newport, C. (2021). *A world without email: Reimagining work in an age of communication overload*. Portfolio.

Noddings, N. (1984). *Caring: A feminine approach to ethics and moral education*. University of California Press.

Norris, P. (2001). *Digital divide: Civic engagement, information poverty, and the internet worldwide*. Cambridge University Press.

Nussbaum, M. (2011). *Creating capabilities: The human development approach*. Harvard University Press.

O'Neil, C. (2016). *Weapons of math destruction: How big data increases inequality and threatens democracy*. Crown Publishing.

Postigo, H. (2016). The socio-technical architecture of digital labor: Converting play into YouTube money. *New Media and Society*, 18(2), 332–349.

Ragnedda, M., and Muschert, G. W. (2013). *The digital divide: The internet and social inequality in international perspective*. Routledge.

Rawls, J. (1971). *A theory of justice*. Oxford University Press.

Rothe, F.-F. (2020). Rethinking positive and negative impacts of 'ICT for development' through the holistic lens of the sustainable development goals. *Information Technology for Development*, 26(4), 653–669.

Rothe, F.-F., Van Audenhove, L., and Loisen, J. (2022). ICT for development and the novel principles of the Sustainable Development Goals. *Third World Quarterly*, 43(6), 1495–1514.

Roth-Ebner, C. (2022). Work in transition: Digital media and its transformative potential for work. In Karmasin, M., Diehl, S., and Koinig, I. (Eds), *Media and change management*. Springer. https://doi.org/10.1007/978-3-030-86680-8_7

Salemink, K., Strijker, D., and Bosworth, G. (2017). Rural development in the digital age: A systematic literature review on unequal ICT availability, adoption, and use in rural areas. *Journal of Rural Studies*, 54, 360–371.

Sandel, M. J. (2009). *Justice: What's the right thing to do?* Farrar, Straus and Giroux.

Sartor, G. (2010). Human rights in the information society. *SSRN Electronic Journal*, https://doi.org/10.2139/ssrn.1707724. https://ssrn.com/abstract=1707724

Sarvi, J., Blaji, V., Pillay, H. (2015). *Public-private partnerships in ICT for education*. Asian Development Bank Briefs, No. 49. October.

Scherer, M. J. (2005). *Living in the state of stuck: How assistive technology impacts the lives of people with disabilities*. Brookline Books.

Schiller, D. (1988). How to think about information. In *The political economy of information* (pp. 27–43). University of Wisconsin Press.

Schradie, J. (2011). The digital production gap: The digital divide and Web 2.0 collide. *Poetics*, 39(2), 145–168.

Selwyn, N. (2004). Reconsidering political and popular understandings of the digital divide. *New Media and Society*, 6(3), 341–362.

Selwyn, N. (2006). Digital division or digital decision? A study of non-users and low-users of computers. *Poetics*, 34. 273–292. 10.1016/j.poetic.2006.05.003.

Selwyn, N. (2010). Looking beyond learning: Notes towards the critical study of educational technology. *Journal of Computer Assisted Learning*, 26(1), 65–73.

Selwyn, N. (2016). Minding our language: Why education and technology is full of bullshit … and what might be done about it. *Learning, Media and Technology*, 41(3), 437–443.

Sen, A. (1997). Welfare economics, utilitarianism, and equity. In *On economic inequality*. Clarendon Press.

Servon, L. J. (2002). *Bridging the digital divide: Technology, community, and public policy*. Blackwell Publishing.

Shirky, C. (2011). The political power of social media: Technology, the public sphere, and political change. *Foreign Affairs*, 90(1), 28–41.

Slote, M. (2007). *The ethics of care and empathy*. Routledge.

Sloterdijk, P. (1983). *Kritik der zynischen Vernunft [Critique of cynical reason]*. Suhrkamp Verlag.

Sørensen, E., and Torfing, J. (2009). Making governance networks effective and democratic through metagovernance. *Public Administration*, 87(2), 234–258.

Swanton, C. (2003). *Virtue ethics: A pluralistic view*. Clarendon Press.

Tavani, H. T. (2003). Ethical reflections on the digital divide. *Journal of Information, Communication and Ethics in Society*, 1(2), 99–108.

Tronto, J. C. (1993). *Moral boundaries: A political argument for an ethic of care*. Routledge.

Turkle, S. (2016). *Reclaiming conversation: The power of talk in a digital age*. Penguin.

United Nations. (2020). *Report of the secretary-general: Roadmap for digital cooperation*. United Nations.

Unwin, T. (2017). *Reclaiming information and communication technologies for development*. Oxford University Press.

Vallor, S. (2016). *Technology and the virtues: A philosophical guide to a future worth wanting*. Oxford University Press.

Van der Velden, M. (2005). The ethics of digital inclusion: Reflections on FLOSS and diversity. Presented at the Norwegian Network on ICT and Development conference, Oslo, October 20–21.

Van Deursen, A. J., and Van Dijk, J. A. (2014). The digital divide shifts to differences in usage. *New Media and Society*, 16(3), 507–526.

Van Dijk, J. A. G. M. (2005). *The deepening divide: Inequality in the information society*. SAGE. https://doi.org/10.4135/9781452229812

Van Dijk, J. A. G. M. (2006). Digital divide research, achievements and shortcomings. *Poetics*, 34(4–5), 221–235.

Van Dijk, J. A. G. M., and Hacker, K. (2003). The digital divide as a complex and dynamic phenomenon. *Information Society*, 19(4), 315–326.

Vartanova, E. L. (Ed.). (2017). *World of media – Journal of Russian Media and Journalism Studies*. National Association of Mass Media Researchers, Faculty of Journalism, Lomonosov Moscow State University.

Vassilakopoulou, P., and Hustad, E. (2023). Bridging digital divides: A literature review and research agenda for information systems research. *Information Systems Frontiers: A Journal of Research and Innovation*, 25(3), 955–969. https://doi.org/10.1007/s10796-020-10096-3

Vu, K. M. (2011). ICT as a source of economic growth in the information age: Empirical evidence from the 1996–2005 period. *Telecommunications Policy*, 35(4), 357–372.

Wajcman, J. (2015). *Pressed for time: The acceleration of life in digital capitalism*. University of Chicago Press.

Wakunuma, K., Jiya, T., and Aliyu, S. (2020). Socio-ethical implications of using AI in accelerating SDG3 in Least Developed Countries. *Journal of Responsible Technology*, 4, 100006.

Wang, Z., Tchernev, J. M., and Solloway, T. (2020). A dynamic longitudinal examination of social media use, needs, and gratifications among college students. *Computers in Human Behavior*, 28(5), 1829–1839.

Warschauer, M. (2003). Demystifying the digital divide. *Scientific American*, 289(2), 42–47.

Warschauer, M. (2004). *Technology and social inclusion: Rethinking the digital divide*. MIT Press.

Warschauer, M., and Matuchniak, T. (2010). New technology and digital worlds: Analyzing evidence of equity in access, use, and outcomes. *Review of Research in Education*, 34(1), 179–225.

West, D. M. (2004). E-government and the transformation of service delivery and citizen attitudes. *Public Administration Review*, 64(1), 15–27.

World Economic Forum. (2023). *Typology of Online Harms*. World Economic Forum.

Wyatt, S. (1999). *They came, they surfed, they went back to the beach: Why some people stop using the internet*. Society for Social Studies of Science Conference.

Zuboff, S. (2019). *The age of surveillance capitalism: The fight for a human future at the new frontier of power*. Public Affairs.

2 An attempt to conceptualise the right to access the Internet and its impact on the right not to use it

Paolo Passaglia

2.1 Introduction

Ever since the Internet has become an essential means for people to communicate and the basis for the technological development of society, scholars have been called upon to define it (Abbate, 1999). The task is still not yet fully accomplished, as different definitions still coexist, especially if one focuses on difficulties deriving from the distinction between technical and legal definitions. Indeed, "[t]he forces and directions of the Internet are so new, so protean, and so far reaching" (U.S. Supreme Court, *Packingham v. North Carolina*, 582 U.S. 98 (2017), at 105), that lawyers could hardly identify the key elements of any comprehensive definition. As a result, attention has been increasingly focused on a specific aspect, namely access to the Internet (Best, 2004, 23–31; Cruft, 2021). A rather odd shift occurred: to define an instrument (i.e., the Internet), rather than searching for its main features and peculiarities, the focus has become the act of using it, just as if the way in which an instrument is used could establish the inherent nature of the instrument itself.

From a theoretical point of view, this shift seems more than questionable, at least because it has left undefined something (the Internet) that produced unprecedented societal and even anthropological changes (Castells, 2010). Actually, the purpose became the premise and the definition of the Internet left room for the analysis of how this legally U.V.O. (Unidentified Virtual Object) could be used and could concretely reshape individuals' lives.

The purpose of this chapter is not to criticise the approach adopted in defining the Internet. The above-mentioned shift, however, is remarkably interesting for this chapter, because it has oriented the way in which the use of the Internet has been conceived.

It is no coincidence that the issue of non-use of the Internet has hardly ever been addressed (with notable exceptions, such as Kloza, 2021, 2024). Or, rather, it has been effectively considered, but mainly as an expression of shortcomings in the possibility of accessing the Internet. As a result, to provide a conceptualisation of the non-use of the Internet, the inevitable starting point of the analysis is the legal definition of the access. In other words, to ascertain whether there is a right not to (access and) use the Internet, one must, first of all, establish what kind

DOI: 10.4324/9781003528401-4

of conceptualisation is provided for the access. In particular, the first issue to deal with is which kind of right might be proper to define the access to the Internet as such and in relation to the activities that individuals carry out online. Logically speaking, the existence of a hypothetical right not to use the Internet should thus be considered a sort of secondary issue. As time passes, this logical secondary issue tends to become a major issue from a legal perspective that is likely to increase its impact as technologies develop.

2.2 The various possible definitions of the right to access the Internet …

As comparative law research shows, access to the Internet has been progressively identified as a right of the individual, thus currently the definition as a right is largely established (even though critical voices can also be heard in this regard: e.g., Tomalty, 2017, 8–11).

In this regard, some constitutions (such as the Portuguese, the Greek, the Ecuadorian, the Bolivian and the Mexican) are (more or less) explicit in considering the use of and/or the access to new technologies and connections as a right. But much more conclusive is the high number of judgments delivered by supreme and constitutional courts around the world (some examples will be provided in the following), which emphasise the importance of access to the Internet and the need for this access to be granted the status of an "individual right". The same approach is shared by some U.N. bodies (see, for instance, the 2011 *Report of the Special Rapporteur on the promotion and protection of the right to freedom of opinion and expression, Frank La Rue* and the 2016 resolution of the Human Rights Council on *The promotion, protection and enjoyment of human rights on the Internet*), which have sometimes qualified access to the Internet as a real "human right" (Çalı, 2020, 276–284; Kaur, 2021, 767–806; Banihashemi, 2023).

Notwithstanding a consensus concerning the qualification of access to the Internet as a right, uncertain remains the nature of the right: the issue is often avoided, but when it is addressed, the proposed solutions are considerably diverse. The point is not to recognise the right as "human" or "fundamental" (on this alternative: Jasmontaite & De Hert, 2019, 157–179; Pollicino, 2020, 263–275), because its concrete impact depends, primarily, on the type of protection that the access is given. What really matters is thus whether access to the Internet should be considered as a freedom, or whether it should be ranked among the social rights, or whether other definitions could be suggested (De Hert & Kloza, 2012; Passaglia, 2024, 155–168). In the following paragraphs, the different possible definitions will be considered, to establish the impact of each one on the non-use of the Internet.

2.3 … and their relevance for the identification of a possible right not to use the Internet

The title of the chapter clearly expresses the initial assumption of the research, i.e., the idea that the definition that is given of the right to access the Internet has a significant, if not essential, impact, first, on whether a right not to use the Internet can be identified and, second, where appropriate, on the kind of right to deal with.

This statement may seem a little weird, or even paradoxical, but it is far from being so: to understand what it means (from a legal point of view) not to use something, one must first have a clear perception of the thing that is not used: thus, it is essential to clearly distinguish, from a legal point of view, between the thing (i.e., the Internet) and the human conduct (namely, the action of using or not using the Internet).

To say it in more concrete words, and adopting a more legally oriented approach, waiving a freedom cannot produce the same effects as waiving a social right. Indeed, the consequences of non-use may be different, and, even more so, the assumptions underlying non-use may change and find different justifications and reasons.

It is bearing this idea in mind that I have outlined an overview of the different definitions of access to the Internet. The elements that this overview provides should be particularly useful for trying to answer the research question, namely what means, from a legal point of view, the non-use of the Internet (and therefore, also the refusal to use it).

2.3.1 Not using the Internet as an expression of a right not to exercise a freedom

A comparative law analysis on the access to the Internet could never neglect the U.S. Supreme Court case law. The Court's first ruling on Internet law, in 1997, has exerted a deep influence on many jurisdictions, thus spreading the idea that access to the Internet is a freedom (*Reno v. American Civil Liberties Union*, 521 U.S. 844 (1997): Jacques, 1997, 1945–1992; Djavaherian, 1998, 371–388). Indeed, according to the Court, the Internet is "a unique and wholly new medium of worldwide human communication", to which "[i]ndividuals can obtain access […] from many different sources" (*id.*, at 850); "[a]nyone with access to the Internet may take advantage of a wide variety of communication and information retrieval methods" (*id.*, at 851).

Access to the Internet as an expression of an act of freedom (to use a medium of communication) was confirmed by the U.S. Supreme Court in a more recent ruling declaring the unconstitutionality of the general ban for sex offenders to access social media (*Packingham v. North Carolina*, 582 U.S. 98 (2017): M. Burnette-McGrath 2019). The legal reasoning was strongly oriented, in fact, by the finding that "[a] fundamental principle of the First Amendment is that all persons have access to places where they can speak and listen, and then, after reflection, speak and listen once more" (*id.*, at 104).

The link established by the U.S. Supreme Court between access to the Internet and the exercise of a freedom can be detected in many rulings delivered by constitutional and supreme courts. A notable example is provided by Judgment No. 2009-580 DC of 10 June 2009 (the so-called *Hadopi I Judgment*: Passaglia, 2016, 141–143) delivered by the French Constitutional Council. The key principle of the judgment reads as follows: "[i]n the current state of the means of communication and given the generalised development of public online communication services and the importance of the latter for participation in democracy and the expression of ideas and opinions", the right to free communication of ideas and opinions "implies the freedom to access such services" (para. 12).

According to their definition, all the freedoms are recognised to allow individuals to express themselves in the forms and by the means they deem proper, with the limits and conditions that are established by the law. Their protection is the result of the absence of limitations deriving from government intervention: indeed, their full exercise depends on the omission of interventions by others (government officials, in particular).

While the basis and origin of the recognition of freedoms are related to the purpose of enabling individuals to exercise a freedom, it has become increasingly evident over time that protection cannot be limited to the "positive side" of the coin, since it must also extend to the "negative side". A few examples may help to make the concept clearer.

The case law of many constitutional and supreme courts expressly defines the freedom of expression as a vital condition for the establishment, consolidation and preservation of democracy in contemporary societies: thanks to debates and comparison between personal opinions develops the marketplace of ideas that allows (at least in theory) the identification of the best possible solutions to the problems and challenges that societies must face. The freedom to express one's thoughts, however, cannot become an obligation to do so. Indeed, on a certain topic, a person may feel that he or she has nothing to say or may not want to say anything at all. Freedom of expression must therefore also protect these cases, i.e., those in which a person does not express him/herself, regardless of the reason for his/her choice (Seidman, 2007). An aphorism (probably wrongly) attributed to Plato could not be clearer in defending those who wish to remain silent: "Wise men speak because they have something to say; fools speak because they have to say something".

This conclusion concerning the freedom of expression can be applied to many other freedoms that form part of the essential core of the protection of human beings within a legal system. Freedom of worship, for example, also implies the freedom to have no faith and no worship: indeed, atheism and agnosticism are protected precisely as a mode of expression of the individual in a free society. Freedom of assembly and freedom of association are other examples (among many others) that can be mentioned.

In the end, the "negative side" of the coin of freedoms is an essential part of every freedom, a component that cannot be neglected and that, therefore, must be regulated and protected, in principle, in the same way as the "active" forms of exercising freedoms. From this point of view, in particular, the same limits must be recognised for the two sides of the coin: if freedom of expression is not absolute, but is subject to conditions and limits, even silence cannot always be invoked, because there are cases in which the legal system imposes on the individual to express him/herself (e.g., this is what happens to the witness in a trial), just as it is possible to impose on the individual to associate and be part of a community (one could mention the compulsory military service, in countries where it still exists). Another example, which the COVID-19 pandemic has made very topical, is that of the right to health, from the viewpoint of the freedom to accept to be cured: this freedom has its downside in the freedom to refuse care and, in general, health treatments; but this freedom has limits, which in the case of refusing health treatments are expressed in many forms, including that of compulsory vaccination, if provided for.

These remarks concerning the right not to exercise a freedom have obvious consequences on the non-use of the Internet, once the access to it is conceived as a freedom. If access to the Internet is a right that the individual must be able to exercise as an expression of his or her freedom, then its protection cannot be limited only to the positive decision to access, since the decision not to access must also be protected. In other words, the individual who has the possibility of using the Internet cannot be forced to use it, because that would be an unlawful restriction of his freedom.

A further point deserves some attention. In the case of access to the Internet, the protection of the refusal to use it is strengthened by a consequence of the access that is often overlooked, or at least not sufficiently highlighted. Accessing the Internet, for the average user (i.e., the one who does not have computer skills so developed to use special hardware and software) inevitably means "leaving traces": any access to the Internet, in fact, implies the production of connection data that, in a more or less direct way, can be retrieved by service providers or by the government requesting them from service providers (Martin & Fargo, 2015, 311–376; Moyakine, 2016). Anonymity on the Internet is never absolute, not to say that it is a mere illusion unless the user falls within that small circle of people capable of truly guaranteeing it to themselves.

If this assumption is true, the non-use of the Internet cannot be protected merely as an expression of the "negative side" of a freedom: it is also an expression of an active exercise by the individual of the protection of his personal data. Indeed, whether he or she is aware of it or not, the individual who does not access the Internet is an individual who, for that simple fact, limits the possibility of others having access to his or her data. Data that are obviously of significant importance because they allow access to a great deal of information about the individual: in this regard, the case law of the French Constitutional Council (as well as that of many other courts) is noteworthy. Indeed, the Council pointed out the need to limit the collection of connection data to what is strictly necessary, since "[c]onnection data include in particular data relating to the identification of individuals, their location and their telephone and digital contacts, as well as the online public communication services they consult", thus, "[g]iven their nature, their diversity and the processing to which they may be subjected, connection data provide numerous and precise details about the individuals in question and, where applicable, about third parties, which are particularly invasive of their privacy" (Judgment No. 2022-1000 QPC, of 17 June 2022, para. 11).

Joining the "negative side" of the freedom to the protection to the personal data issue, the right not to use the Internet results considerably strengthened. This does not mean, however, that it is an absolute right: like any other freedom, the "negative side" of the right to access the Internet can be restricted. That happens if special conditions arise that make access to the Internet the only way to perform certain activities. The situation that arose with the pandemic is, in this respect, a very pertinent example: in a state of generalised emergency, the right not to use the Internet was severely restricted, because access to the Internet was, on the one hand, the only way to exercise a relevant number of rights (right to health, right to education, freedom of assembly, etc.) and, on the other, the only way to ensure the provision of certain public services and an appearance of normalcy in social life (Archer & Wildman, 2021, 29–33; Pollicino, 2022, 125–138). But it was, indeed, a state of emergency, in which there was room to apply exceptions to ordinary rules. And among the latter, there must be counted the one that protects the right not to use the Internet.

2.3.2 Not using the Internet as a shortcoming of (the implementation of) a social right

The right to access the Internet has been conceived primarily as a freedom. However, the conditions to exercise this freedom are not always easy to meet; as a result, difficulties in ensuring equal network conditions become a major issue. In particular, these difficulties have clearly demonstrated the inadequacy of the definition of access as simple freedom.

The freedom to access the Internet may, in fact, prove to be only theoretical. This is what happens when certain conditions make it impossible for an individual to exercise the right of access. Thus, the right can be theoretically asserted and can also be deemed essential to the full development of the human being, but this same right can suffer a lack of implementation.

The statements that can be read in some judgments or international documents are very explicit in recognising the importance of being able to access the Internet to be fully part of contemporary society. In this respect, the quotation of the above-mentioned resolution adopted by the Human Rights Council of the United Nations on 18 July 2016, concerning *The promotion, protection, and enjoyment of human rights on the Internet* is highly revealing: "The global and open nature of the Internet as a driving force in accelerating progress towards development in its various forms, including in achieving the Sustainable Development Goals" (Para. 5: Reglitz, 2020, 314–331).

Precisely because of the importance of the Internet in contemporary societies, defining access to it as a (mere) freedom can be inadequate since it does not help to ensure the full availability of the Internet for all individuals. This leads to advocating for the recognition of a social right: if there are situations in which access to the Internet is prevented, the government's duty is to find solutions (or at least try to find them) so that the obstacles to access are removed.

Two rulings can be mentioned as examples of the commitment that is required of governments to close gaps and inequalities in access to the Internet.

The first is the Italian Constitutional Court Judgment No. 307 of 21 October 2004, concerning some provisions that "foster[ed] the dissemination of a culture of information technology", with financial aid aimed at the purchase of personal computers enabled to connect to the Internet. To confirm the consistency of the provisions with the Constitution, the Court pointed out that the legislature "pursue[d] an objective of general interest, such as the development of culture, in particular through the use of computers" (*Conclusions on points of law*, Para. 3.1). This crucial commitment assigned to government to fight against the digital divide relating to one's knowledge of information technology was the expression of the struggle against inequality that characterises (or should characterise) the Italian model of Welfare State from its very origins, and that requires public authorities "to remove those obstacles of an economic and social nature which in fact limit the freedom and equality of citizens [and] impede the full development of the human person" (Article 3, Para. 2, of the 1947 Constitution: Peruginelli, 2022, 274–282).

The second ruling was delivered by the Constitutional Chamber of the Supreme Court of Justice of Costa Rica (Judgment No. 12790 of 30 July 2010), that recognised the government's failure to promptly implement the obligation to make the telecommunications market competitive. Since "technologies have impacted how human beings communicate, facilitating the connection between people and institutions worldwide and eliminating the barriers of space and time", in the current state "of the information or knowledge society, the public authorities must promote and guarantee universal access to these new technologies for the benefit of the public" (Para. V).

These two rulings refer to different obstacles that hinder access to the Internet. Indeed, many obstacles contribute to create digital divide between individuals (Peacock, 2019; van Dijk, 2020) so that even the plural form, "digital divides", is increasingly used (Hynes, 2021, 103–120; Vassilakopoulou & Hustad, 2023, 955–969). The list of these obstacles includes, at the very least: economic gaps, resulting from unequal individuals' financial conditions; cultural gaps, which are the result of different computer skills; physiological gaps, linked to possible physical or psychological handicaps of Internet users; and geographical gaps, resulting from disparities in Internet coverage between different territories. All these gaps must be considered potential challenges. And the definition of access to the Internet as a social right serves precisely to force governments to address these challenges, to overcome a situation in which freedom of access is concretely available for one part of the population, but only theoretically for the other.

From this viewpoint, the non-use of the Internet acquires a completely different meaning from the one I described regarding the definition of access to the Internet as a freedom.

Looking at the "negative side" of freedom, the non-use means that the individual refuses access to the Internet. His/her refusal is voluntary and is the result of a more or less conscious and meditated choice between the possibility of taking advantage of the contents of the Net and the possibility of living his/her life without them.

On the contrary, when access to the Internet is conceived as a social right, then the non-use of the Internet is not of the result of a refusal, but it is, primarily, the outcome of the impossibility of access. The obvious consequence of this difference is the shift in the meaning of non-use from a legal perspective. At first glance, one could even consider useless to continue talking about a "right" not to use the Internet. Adopting this point of view, the focus could rather be on the inadequacy of the government's action: indeed, the non-use of the Internet is mainly the result of the omissions and inadequacies of the government's policies, which have been unable to overcome the multiple digital divide grounds that affect societies.

Actually, the alternative between freedom and social right should not lead to the assumption that when access to the Internet is defined as a social right, the non-use of the Internet cannot be defined itself as a right. Such a conclusion would be erroneous for several reasons.

From a general perspective, the protection granted by the existence of a social right does not exclude the existence, at the same time and on the same matter, of a freedom. In other words, if access to the Internet is a social right, this does not mean that its exercise cannot be an expression of a freedom.

The government must do its utmost to make a right exercisable, but even assuming that the government's policy has fully achieved all its objectives, a further issue needs to be addressed, namely, to determine how the (social) right to access the Internet is exercised. In this respect, it must be pointed out that ensuring that the conditions for exercising a right are in place does not necessarily imply that the right must be exercised. Among the more "typical" social rights, there are examples of compulsory exercise (e.g., education for minors) as well as examples of exercise left to individual choice (e.g., the right to health, which is a social right, since the government must ensure the possibility of treatment, but which, as mentioned previously, is exercised, in general, on the basis of the individual's self-determination).

In light of this alternative, it must be established whether access to the Internet is a social right of the first or second kind. On this subject, also considering what I exposed concerning data protection (see above, Section 2.3.1), it seems more logical to opt for the free exercise approach. In support of this position, one can first point out that when needed, the legal system can impose access to the Internet, so it would make no sense to impose a generalised obligation, beyond what is necessary. After all, in a liberal democracy, limits to individual self-determination should be exceptional, especially in a case such as the one at stake, in which the limits necessarily also impact the right to personal data protection. However, there is also another argument, perhaps even more significant, that leads one to exclude the existence of an access obligation. It is a factual argument: no matter how effective policies to combat the digital divide are, inequalities will inevitably remain between individuals in accessing the Internet, not to mention outright exclusions, affecting categories of particularly weak individuals, for economic or cultural reasons, disability, or geographical area of residence. As a result, imposing an obligation to access the Internet would mean ignoring the shortcomings of the government's policies and, at the same time, pretending that they have achieved results that have not been achieved, or that have been achieved only in part.

It is essential to always keep in mind the risk of exclusions that an access obligation may produce. To demonstrate this assumption, reference may be made to Judgment No. 106/2004 of 16 June 2004 delivered by the Belgian Court of Arbitration, that directly addressed the issue, even if not in relation to a social right. The challenged law replaced official paper publication of legislation with online publication, thus making the Internet almost the only means to gain knowledge of the legislation. The Court declared the new regulation unconstitutional, drawing attention to the fact that the challenged provisions made "a significant number of people" (those who were unable to access the Internet) "deprived of effective access to official texts". Therefore, the lawmaker had to pass some provisions aimed at allowing anyone to know legislation without been required to necessarily access the Internet (the new regulation that Belgian Parliament passed was considered adequate to avoid unconstitutionality on the ground of discrimination in Judgment No. 10/2007 of 17 January 2007).

The publication of legislation and its knowledge by citizens is an essential element of the legal system so by no means it can be subject to the application of exceptional rules. As a result, it is simply impossible to establish an obligation to access the Internet in this field. But once the obligation is excluded, the way is open to individual's self-determination and thus to recognise the freedom to refuse access to the Internet.

These findings seem obvious if the failure to overcome digital divide has created a situation in which access to the Internet is prevented: for those who suffer the digital divide, non-use is nothing more than inevitable. Less obvious, but maybe more interesting from a legal point of view, is what happens when access to the Internet is not fully prevented but it is difficult to implement, because of digital divide (and shortcomings in the government's action). Leaving aside the issues related to inequalities between Internet users, the key element to consider is the degree of difficulty in accessing the Internet, and in particular whether or not the difficulty can concretely affect the choice to access. In other words, if access to the Internet is difficult, but not impossible, it is likely to have to balance the individual's self-determination against other competing interests; and this balancing can lead, in certain cases, to giving prevalence to the latter by founding an obligation to access (e.g., to fulfil a duty during pandemics).

In order to determine the outcome of the balance, however, one must always take into account how difficult access to the Internet is. The possibility of access that is recognised in theory may be of minimal relevance in practice if the individual must overcome too heavy an impediment to concretely use the Net. In such a case, an access obligation would create the conditions for social exclusion to the detriment of some categories of vulnerable subjects. In other words, the social exclusion would hit subjects who have difficulties in accessing the Internet, because of their economic situation, their illiteracy, their location, etc. If access to the Internet were required to exercise some rights, these vulnerable people would be excluded precisely because of their vulnerability. In fact, there is no room for them to choose whether to use or not use the Internet: rather, the recognition of the right not to use the Internet becomes a pivotal right, since it is an essential protection for the individual and his social life.

2.3.3 The right not to use the Internet as a tool to exercise one's rights

Access to the Internet is not always considered an autonomous right. This is the assumption of those who consider the Internet to be nothing more than an instrument (Cerf, 2012). By accessing the Internet, one can conduct many activities and, among them, also exercise a large number of rights (as well as fulfil duties). The Internet is therefore an "enabler of rights", because the real right would not be the right to access the Internet, but rather all those rights that are exercised through access. From a legal point of view, the Internet would be no different from any other medium of communication: the relevant right is not to switch the television on or to find and buy the newspaper; what matters is rather to express one's opinion or to be informed, through television or the newspaper. The same applies to the Internet.

It follows that access to the Internet is a component of the right that it allows to implement, and therefore its protection is the result of the rights that the Internet enables to exercise. In other words, access to the Internet can be protected only if, and to the extent that, it actually enables a certain right (an echo of this approach can be found in the judgment delivered by the Indian Supreme Court in the case *Anuradha Bhasin v. Union of India*, W.P.(C) No. 001031 / 2019, 10 January 2020, notwithstanding its apparent critique of the "enabler of rights" definition: Pajagopal, 2020).

This definition implies significant changes, not only in the legal status of access to the Internet but also, consequently, in the meaning of the non-access.

Theoretically, excluding a real right to access could ease the issues concerning its "negative side": if there is no right related to the action, it makes no sense to search for a right related to the omission. This deduction turns out to be too simple to be correct.

Firstly, one needs to clarify whether the Internet is an instrument for exercising rights that is truly equivalent to others. In the affirmative, it is possible to state that the individual has a real choice among the tools, thus, from a legal viewpoint, access to the Internet or refusal to access it are only the result of personal self-determination. For instance, this is the case of the choice of the means through which communicate with a friend: one can freely choose between a telephone call or a VOIP service. If no equivalence can be determined (and it is, of course, what happens most of the times), the choice is only theoretical; thus access to the Internet is actually the only tool that allows the exercise of the rights, or at least a certain type of exercise or, perhaps, a complete exercise of the rights.

Facing this alternative, it is fair to state that even excluding that access to the Internet is an autonomous right, one still must assume that the individual, in many cases, has no real choice between the Internet and any other means to exercise a right, since the Internet is much more comprehensive and effective than any other. The issue of the right not to use the Internet is thus far from being irrelevant, although it needs to be considered from a different perspective than in the previous paragraphs: since the right is no longer to access the Internet, the focus of the analysis becomes the type of rights that are exercised thanks to the access.

Against this backdrop, freedom and social rights must be clearly distinguished.

Concerning social rights, the core of the issue is quite simple. The exercise of a social right implies government action, and this action is specifically addressed to those who could not exercise the right without the support of public authorities, because of economic, social, health, age or other reasons. As a result, if, to benefit from government action, one must have access to the Internet, then it is highly likely that a deadlock takes place: those who need support cannot get it because they cannot use the instrument (i.e., the Internet) through which they obtain it. In other words, as long as a digital divide exists, certain categories of individuals are excluded from using the Internet. There is a very high risk that these categories of individuals coincide, at least in part, with those who are entitled to receive the government's support (e.g., many elderly people do not have access to the Internet, thus if a social right were available only through online booking, then a case of patent exclusion would occur: European Union Agency for Fundamental Rights, 2023).

To avoid such a paradox, the availability of the instruments that allow the exercise of a social right must have an essential part in the definition of the services that the government must offer. Indeed, defining these services means defining the social right itself. Therefore, since the Internet is the "enabler", the instrument of the social right, the latter necessarily encompasses access to the Internet. In short, even though it is not an autonomous right, access to the Internet must be considered as if it were a social right whenever access is the way through which a social right is exercised. Consequently, to assert a right not to use the Internet, one can refer to the considerations made previously (Section 2.3.2).

When access to the Internet is aimed at exercising a freedom, further difficulties appear, because one needs to distinguish depending on the individual's choices. Of course, no problem exists if a person decides not to exercise a certain freedom. On the contrary, if he/she decides to exercise it, then he/she must be enabled to do so, otherwise, it is not a freedom at stake but rather a luxury. From this point of view, access to the Internet, as a means of exercising freedom, must be guaranteed, just like social rights. That is to say that the non-use of the Internet should never be the result of the impossibility of using it: even regarding the exercise of rights of freedom, one must be able to refuse access to the Internet and not be forced to waive it. If this were the case, a major problem would arise, at the very least, because of a possible infringement of equality.

This reference to equality introduces a further issue to be addressed. Since the digital divide could be fully removed only in a perfect world, the recognition of a right not to use the Internet in relation to the possible exercise of social rights was the means to prevent vulnerable categories of people from suffering further discrimination. When it comes to the exercise of freedoms, the issue becomes considerably more complex. For two reasons.

First, being able to access the Internet undoubtedly enables one to exercise many freedoms more effectively than with other means. In this respect, establishing the right not to use the Internet would not avoid discrimination, but would rather give the individual nothing more than the right to … accept being subject to discrimination.

Second, the right not to use the Internet is not deprived of relevance, but its scope is extremely limited. Indeed, as a rule, it is hard to imagine freedoms that necessarily require access to the Internet: the latter can be useful, but not indispensable. In this respect, the right not to use the Internet cannot function as a protection against a *de facto* obligation, likewise for the case of social rights. There is room, however, for some exceptions. When they occur, the right not to use the Internet turns out to be a relevant form of protection.

The most important exception is related to the freedom of having recourse to judicial guarantees. As became usual during the COVID-19 pandemic, massive use of digital technology can have a deep impact on the conduct of judicial proceedings. Even in normal situations, videoconferencing is quite frequently used. Nevertheless, these possibilities offered by the Internet can have negative repercussions, for example, on a defendant who feels uncomfortable in front of a video-camera. Consequently, asserting a right not to use the Internet can have the effect of protecting fundamental rights, which may be restricted only under exceptional conditions (such as a pandemic) or only after a balance carried out between individual self-determination and equally important needs (e.g., public safety that requires the accused prisoner not be let out of prison).

At first, among the exceptions, one might be tempted to also include freedom of expression, which can be exercised on the Internet in a much more extensive form than in any other medium of communication. Actually, as important as the Internet is for freedom of expression, this freedom can be fully exercised offline: with much greater obstacles, much longer time and a much more laborious research, what is found on the Internet should also be found offline, what can be communicated on the Internet can be communicated offline. Moreover, the difference between freedom of expression online and offline does not consist only of the advantages of the former over the latter. Indeed, the Internet also has its dark side, which cannot be overlooked precisely concerning freedom of expression.

2.4 The dark side of the Internet and the right not to use it: Final remarks

The huge amount of information that characterises the Internet does not necessarily mean that the individual can improve her/his knowledge (Passaglia, 2022). This is, of course, a driving factor for putting Internet policies at the top of the government's agenda. Oddly enough, such an important factor is generally not called into question, probably because of the original definition of the Internet as an area of freedom, a "new home of Mind" (Barlow, 1996), in which individuals are free to express themselves as they wish.

The issue is, therefore, whether this definition is still valid. To say it in a few words, if the idea of freedom remains the milestone of our conception of the Internet, irrespective of its governance, its main actors (the so-called "gatekeepers"), and the use and abuse of algorithms and artificial intelligence raise the question whether social, spiritual and intellectual growth on the Internet can still be considered genuinely "free". Chamber echoes, filter bubbles, rankings and other tools heavily influence the communication and knowledge transfer of individuals, and somehow determine their social digital life.

These considerations cannot lead to the stigmatisation of the Internet and the denial of its potential in terms of freedom of expression and its impact on personal and collective self-development. However, the time is ripe for a deep reconsideration of the original conception of the Internet.

And, thanks to such a different approach, greater attention should be paid to the right not to use the Internet.

The aim of this chapter was precisely to suggest possible points of view from which to analyse this right. The analysis that was carried out showed that this is a complex right since it has many possible concrete repercussions.

Indeed, taking into consideration the different legal conceptualisations of access to the Internet, one can define the lack of access as the result of a refusal, a waiver, or the effect of an inability for an individual to access the Net. Therefore, in some cases, the Internet is not used because of a (free) choice, while in other cases there are external factors that prevent use. On the one hand, the importance and diffusion of the Internet in contemporary societies require that barriers that do not allow an individual to use the Internet be overcome; on the other hand, the principles of any liberal democracy require that individual self-determination be protected. The right not to use the Internet aims to implement both requirements: this remark *per se* makes it surprising that it is still a very neglected and, often, even denied right.

On the contrary, it is an increasingly essential right. Actually, it is necessary that, in parallel with the development of technology and the Net, a legal framework be developed in which individuals are protected when they are users of new technologies. At the same time, it is no less necessary to focus on the need to constantly ensure the possibility of avoiding the use of technologies available on the Net. Only in this way can the proper development of the Internet in society be guaranteed, because only in this way can one think of building a society where the Internet can be developed without individuals becoming dependent on it.

Bibliography

Abbate, J. (1999). *Inventing the Internet*. MIT Press.

Archer, A., & Wildman, N. (2021). Internet access as an essential social good. In E. Aarts, H. Fleuren, M. Sitskoorn, & T. Wilthagen (Eds.), *The new common* (pp. 29–33). Springer.

Banihashemi, P. (2023). International law and the right to global internet access: Exploring internet access as a human right through the lens of Iran's Women-Life-Freedom Movement. *Chicago Journal of International Law*, *24*(1), 31–49.

Barlow, J. P. (1996). *A declaration of the independence of cyberspace*. Electronic Frontier Foundation.

Best, M. L. (2004). Can the Internet be a human right? *Human Rights & Human Welfare*, *4*(1), 23–31.

Burnette-McGrath, M. (2019). Packingham v. North Carolina. *Ohio Northern University Law Review*, *44*(1).

Çalı, B. (2020). The case for the right to meaningful access to the internet as a human right in international law. In A. von Arnauld, K. von der Decken, & M. Susi (Eds.), *The Cambridge handbook of new human rights* (pp. 276–284). Cambridge University Press.

Castells, M. (2010). *The rise of the network society*. Wiley.

Cerf, V. G. (2012). *Internet access is not a human right*. The New York Times.

Cruft, R. (2021). Is there a right to internet access? In C. Véliz (Ed.), *The Oxford handbook of digital ethics* (pp. C4.S1–C4.N27). Oxford University Press.

De Hert, P., & Kloza, D. (2012). Internet (access) as a new fundamental right. Inflating the current rights framework? *European Journal of Law and Technology*, *3*(3), https://ejlt.org/index.php/ejlt/article/view/123/268.

Djavaherian, D. K. (1998). Reno v. ACLU. *Berkeley Technology Law Journal*, *13*(1), 371–388.

European Union Agency for Fundamental Rights. (2023). *Fundamental rights of older persons. Ensuring access to public services in digital societies*. Report. Publications Office of the European Union.

Hynes, M. (2021). Digital divides. In The *social, cultural and environmental costs of hyper-connectivity: Sleeping through the revolution* (pp. 103–120). Emerald Publishing Limited.

Jacques, S. C. (1997). Reno v. ACLU: Insulating the internet, the first amendment, and the marketplace of ideas. *American University Law Review*, *46*(6), 1945–1992.

Jasmontaite, L., & De Hert, P. (2019). Access to the internet in the EU: A policy priority, a fundamental, a human right or a concern for eGovernment? In *Research handbook on human rights and digital technology: Global politics, law and international relations* (pp. 157–179). Elgar Publishing.

Kaur, H. (2021). Protecting internet access: A human rights treaty approach. *Brooklyn Journal of International Law*, *46*(2), 767–806.

Kloza, D. (2021). *It's all about choice: The right not to use the internet*. Völkerrechtsblog.

Kloza, D. (2024). The right not to use the internet. *Computer Law & Security Review*, *52*, https://doi.org/10.1016/j.clsr.2023.105907.

Martin, J. A., & Fargo, A. L. (2015). Anonymity as a legal right: Where and why it matters. *North Carolina Journal of Law & Technology*, *16*, 311–376.

Moyakine, E. (2016). Online anonymity in the modern digital age: Quest for a legal right. *Journal of Information Rights Policy and Practice*, *1*(1), https://jirpp.winchesteruniversitypress.org/articles/10.21039/irpandp.v1i1.21.

Pajagopal, K. (2020). SC has no views on if 'access to Internet' is a fundamental right. *The Hindu*.

Passaglia, P. (2016). Protection of fundamental rights and the internet: A comparison between Italian and French systems of constitutional adjudication. In O. Pollicino & G. Romeo (Eds.), *The Internet and Constitutional Law. The protection of fundamental rights and constitutional adjudication in Europe* (pp. 118–165). Routledge.

Passaglia, P. (2022). *Behind the curtain: Questioning the right to access the internet, in search of definitions (and conditions)*. Völkerrechtsblog.

Passaglia, P. (2024). Access to the internet, a right (still) in search of definition. In G. Tieghi (Ed.), *Comparative law and global English for legal studies. A law-linguistic journey* (pp. 155–168). Jovene.

Peacock, A (2019). *Human rights and the digital divide*. Routledge.

Peruginelli, G. (2022). Internet access as a fundamental right: An overview of the Italian debate. *The International Information & Library Review*, *54*(3), 274–282.

Pollicino, O. (2020). The right to internet access. In A. von Arnauld, K. von der Decken, & M. Susi (Eds.), *The Cambridge handbook of new human rights* (pp. 263–275). Cambridge University Press.

Pollicino, O. (2022). The right to internet access. A comparative constitutional legal framework. In *The Cambridge handbook of information technology, life sciences and human rights* (pp. 125–138). Cambridge University Press.

Reglitz, M. (2020). The human right to free internet access. *Journal of Applied Philosophy*, *37*(2), 314–331.

Seidman, L.M. (2007). *Silence and freedom*. Stanford University Press.

Tomalty, J. (2017). Is there a human right to internet access? *Philosophy Now*, *118*, 8–11.

van Dijk, J. (2020). *The digital divide*. Polity Press.

Vassilakopoulou, P., & Hustad, E. (2023). Bridging digital divides: A literature review and research agenda for information systems research. *Information Systems Frontiers*, *25*, 955–969.

3 Framing the right not to use the Internet

Mart Susi

3.1 Introduction

Analogy with astronomy produces, for illustrative purposes, an image capturing key features of a new human right formation. A viewer from the space observatory and a sleepless poet both know that more stars mean more light at night. An idealistic onlooker from the ivory tower supposes that every new human right expands the existential[1] normative horizon.[2] I have used the expression "existential normative horizon" to point at the dilemma whether the human rights horizon has limits or whether human rights can, *sense stricto*, grow endlessly. Such endlessness, as I will show in the following, turns into uselessness at some point.

Yet both in astronomy and human rights architecture appears a limit against the claim of "more is better". Like Olbers' paradox[3] in astronomy questions the infinity of the external universe and claims boundaries to the number of stars in connection with our observational capability, so does the human rights inflation[4] phenomenon reject the ubiquity of human rights. It points to the necessity of establishing epistemic and ontological criteria for validating a new human right claim. A metaphysical argument, from a commoner's perspective, which has to be endorsed here, draws on John Milton's statement from *Areopagitica* that a positive feature of something is only recognizable because the opposite to the positivity exists in parallel.[5] Ergo, stars exist only because there are objects which do not meet the criteria of temperature, colour, luminosity, mass and size; and human rights exist only because there are other rights which do not meet the criteria of universality and priority over other rights.[6]

The epistemic commonality between astronomy and human rights science concerns knowledge development about the "new kid in the block". Astronomers' enthusiasm when detecting the appearance of a new object which may or may not develop into a separate star is comparable to that of human rights scholars' when a claim of a new human right is raised. Yet detecting a new object in the space through the Hubble Space Telescope, or advancing an argument that some entitlement merits the label of a human right is just the first step along the road before confirmations. In human rights discourse this road is labelled as the period of contestations which may lead to the recognition of a new human right, or to its rejection, or to perpetuating the process of validation against doubts.[7] There can be

DOI: 10.4324/9781003528401-5

formation failures in both fields. The claim of a new human right may never gain sufficient critical mass of recognition and thereby may not extend the human rights regime;[8] and in space brown dwarfs may lack the mass needed to jumpstart the nuclear fusion necessary for star formation.[9]

The ontological commonality is related to the characteristics of the newborns. There are difficulties to observe these characteristics in the first glance. The interstellar medium obscures the clear image of the new object in space, because the process of a new star formation is usually connected to molecular clouds and dust.[10] The same can be observed for a new human right claim emergence, especially in relation to the digital sphere. Elsewhere I have shown that the online domain can alter the meaning of well-established human rights to a wider or narrower extent, impacting core concepts such as transparency, legal certainty and foreseeability.[11] Benedek has advanced the argument that the danger of fragmentation of international regulation may evolve in the digital sphere due to competing regulations each claiming to apply globally.[12] Several countries and regions have adopted "digital constitutions",[13] which, without having the space here to enter into their detailed review, indicates the need to address human rights transposition away from their traditional offline setting in specific normative instruments. Pointing to the view that technicism of the digital domain leads to "digital constitutionalism"[14] suffices to complete the argument that the digital domain can be compared to a cloud or dust surrounding the formation of a new star. The challenge is to look beyond such cloud for comprehending the features of possible new digital-domain specific rights.

The period of contestations in human rights development creates uncertainties. For instance, how an existing "traditional" human right may become a "parent" right when new rights are formed.[15] This chapter now will look inside the digital discursive dust with an attempt to establish the contours of the claim that a new human right may be justifiable – the right not to use the Internet.

3.2 The analysis – framing and questions

The analytical part will start by formulating the claim of the new human right under review.

It will then proceed to review this claim under different theoretical frameworks concerning human rights development. Ontological questions will thereafter be raised: first, whether the right not to use the Internet has the potential to develop into a self-standing new human right or whether it is more suitable to speak of an extension of an existing human right; second, what can be said to constitute its "parent" rights; and third, whether there are other claims of new human rights which may be closely connected to this right.

3.2.1 The claim

3.2.1.1 About recognition

The right not to use the Internet is not recognized as a general entitlement in international or national legal instruments. Yet there are moves from the phase of an idea to acceptance in specific circumstances – for instance Belgium and France have adopted laws to allow employees from the public sector to "disconnect" after working hours and not communicate with employers, except in extraordinary circumstances.[16] Although within the three phases of recognition articulated by von der Decken and Koch – the "idea", the "emergence" and "full recognition" – it is not always possible to determine in which phase a new human right is situated at any given point in time,[17] at the time of writing this chapter, the claim of this new right has clearly not passed beyond the state of an idea. This is because of the absence of normative activity by legislatures, non-inclusion of such right into any policy agendas, or activism by courts to suggest that such right "might exist". Calls for applying "evolutionary treaty interpretation" regarding the entitlement not to use the Internet are scarce.[18]

3.2.1.2 The idea

The so-called norm entrepreneurship triggering the articulation of a new human right idea is usually based on the assumption that the current body of international human rights law has limitations in protecting some important human interests.[19] Von Arnaud and Theilen have adduced appellative and contesting functionality arguments in relation to the emergence of the idea of a new human right, and they claim essentially the same.[20] The appellative function draws attention to a certain situation which is deemed sufficiently unjust so as to qualify as a human rights issue,[21] and the contesting function refers to the usage of the phrase "a human right to …" to remedy a situation which is considered undesirable by those who propose the right.[22] The claim of the right not to use the Internet has not moved beyond these functional stages, for instance into the jurisgenerative stage, where the initial content meaning imagined by civil society activists and scholars would become constrained by state institutions and courts.[23] It is too early to speak of an explicit rhetorical paradigm shift, which may never happen. A restless reader might at this point abandon reading and conclude that return to this topic becomes relevant once there are signs of a discursive struggle, having the capacity to initiate normative paradigm shift.[24] Yet as will be shown soon in this chapter, the rhetoric about a closely related right – the right to a decision by a human – can expand to affect justifiability of rights protecting similar interests. This also alerts the reader to the possibility of accelerated maturation of the idea not to use Internet, should the right to a decision by a human move fast forward along the phases of recognition. We can introduce here the clustering hypothesis in human rights development. It says that new human rights claims originating from the same parent rights and protecting closely related interests can be justified or rejected through similar arguments, and consequently should pass through the recognition phases with relative proximity in time. This hypothesis is not confirmed and will be addressed below further.

A question about the degree of flexibility has to be raised concerning the idea of a new human right. We can call this the problem of initial justification. That is, how to decide about the sufficiency of reasons which allow to speak of a new human right instead of a collection of emotions and sporadic observations that "something is structurally wrong"? Return to analogy with astronomy is about the cloud of dust which blocks a view to inside in order to determine whether elements of a new star are there. Any position abandoning the requirement of at least some reasons would lead to arbitrariness and weakening of human rights architecture, because the label of a human right could be extended too easily and early. In summer 2024, the right not to use the Internet has not moved beyond the phase of an idea, and related rhetoric does not exhibit all functional elements associated with the development of a new human right. Is it therefore justified at all to speak of such a new right, or is it still an intellectual venture? The problem of initial justification disappears after discourse emerges about the content, related obligations and position of the new human right in the existing legal system.[25] We need to view therefore the status of contextual discourse around the proposed new right not to use the Internet.

3.2.1.3 The rationale

The rationale of the proposed new right not to use the Internet rests on reversal of the right to use the Internet into an obligation to use the Internet. Such reversal can be considered a phenomenon of the non-coherence between the digital and non-digital domains.[26] Recent claims to recognize free Internet access as a self-standing human right are built upon the recognition that people need this right to live their daily lives. Merten Reglitz assertion that "The internet has unique and fundamental value for the realization of many of our socio-economic human rights ..." is an example.[27] Nicholas Nugent's Viewpoint Access Theory builds five Internet rights on the assumption of inseparability of the digital domain from our existence.[28] Dariusz Kloza has shown the implicit obligation to use the Internet because it contributes to the efficiency or convenience of the functioning of the state or an organization and decreases costs of traditional person-to-person communication models, which are replaced by digital ones.[29] Many examples could be given and anecdotal, yet truthful stories told – which will not be done here, of how people not having access to the Internet or not wishing to use it have complications to interact with the public power. Take for instance Estonia's e-governance system,[30] where someone wishing to communicate with a taxation official in person or make an appointment with a doctor by phone call faces considerable hardship in terms of time and effort. The spread of the obligation to use the Internet in public and private communication is a reason enough to raise the question whether a specific right countering such obligation can be justified. Kloza has put forward concrete arguments to support such right – first, the matter of personal choice; second, the matter of affordability – some people simply are unable to acquire the equipment; and third, the absence of required skills.[31]

3.2.1.4 Formulations

Building upon the reflections given, the following is an attempt to offer some alternatives for formulating the right not to use the Internet. The first alternative is:

> Everyone has the right not to use the internet. Governments must secure through laws and appropriate means to everyone equal and efficient access to public services and essential services from private entities through the communication channels of their choice.

The second alternative is:

> Everyone is guaranteed access to public services and essential services from private entities through the communication channels of their choice. There is no obligation to use the Internet for accessing these services.

The third alternative would simply and explicitly add a specific factor into the catalogue of features which can constitute discrimination – that is, people should not be discriminated on the basis of their choice to use or not to use the Internet.

The answer to the initial justification problem – formulated at the start of this section – cannot be sufficiently discussed here. I will confine myself to the assertion that the initial justification of a new human right should build upon one or several of the core fundamental values, such as dignity, equality, non-discrimination and personal choice. Both alternatives proposed are direct guarantees of personal choice, equality and non-discrimination.

3.2.2 Theoretical frameworks

Among the frameworks conceptualizing human rights development the question about sufficiency of moral standards and value judgments occupies a central position. That is, whether the existence of a new human right can be justified merely on the basis of qualitative indicators, although requiring high degree of judicial and political consensus, or whether metrical indicators can be applied separately instead, or as a supplement to qualitative indicators. The choice of conceptual framework has far-reaching consequences for human rights architecture, the feature of human rights universality, and primarily for the phenomenon of human rights inflation. This chapter is interested only in the last aspect – whether the exclusion of quantitative criteria from human rights development conceptualization and reliance only on morality and values may give a different response to the question if, in principle, human rights can expand endlessly.

3.2.2.1 The quality control approach

Phil Alston represents the approach relying on qualitative indicators only. His *appellation contrôlée* test is about the matter when a new human right has matured to the degree that is can be recognized as a self-standing right by an international institution.[32] Others have expressed similar ideas conditioning the recognition of a human right to values and consensus only. For instance, James Nickel links the justification of a new human right to its dealing with some very important good and its response to a common and serious threat to that good, as well as it being feasible in most countries of the world.[33] Brems conditions the establishment of a new human right to the threshold criterion (a human right should protect interests that are of great importance) and universality criterion (a new human right should be universally valid).[34]

The pursuit of this practice-dependent approach to new human rights development, which Alston and others represent, does not exclude the possibility that the universe of human rights is endlessly growing. It is dependent on what states can agree on and what is considered to be socially important at a given time. This approach underlying the rights inflation proposition is utilitarian and, surprisingly, can in principle be mirrored in the opposite process as well – the deflation of human rights, or the shrinking of the number of human rights, should the global community become tired of the human rights language.

Although Alston has the aspiration of putting forward a universally applicable mechanism of rights' development quality control, the essential element of what constitutes quality is actually missing. The only element close to the idea of quality is that a new right needs to reflect of a fundamentally important social value. Other elements are related to political consensus building and rights enforcement practicalities. Yet the notion of a fundamentally important social value is construed in isolation from specifying standards. It therefore is open to excesses from relativism or geopolitical agendas from states claiming hegemony. It is here where metrics should assume a restrictive function.

Because a very concrete and individual idea can also meet the standard of an important social value, Alston's new human rights quality control method turns into something completely different – it enables unlimited expansion of new human rights. Alston's filter would not block entry of very specific digital rights into the status of a fundamental rights, provided that countries agree to this. Its logical consequence if applied to online rights, is that most rights in digital constitutions, provided they are repetitive, can be justified as fundamental rights. The meaning and value of fundamental rights would then wither through a process called by others as rights inflation. This is sufficient to say that additional components need to be added to Alston's list, so that it can be turned into an approach where qualitative standards and non-relative and non-political characteristics prevent the inflation.

With respect to the right not to use the Internet, the Alston approach shows the following image. This potential right is about enhancing choice how to be engaged with public power and access vital services from the private or public/private sectors (such as education or finance) – therefore it reflects a fundamentally important social value of personal freedom. Considering that this right is a derivate of the right to privacy, it is relevant throughout different value systems, although such relevance stays at a high general level. This right can be considered an interpretation of the UN Charter Article 12 obligation to protect privacy. Although at present value systems around the world are more and more polarized – a statement which does not need confirmations – recognizing the right not to use the Internet might not reach the depth of political differences. Thus is can be considered that establishment of a considerable degree of international consensus cannot be excluded, especially since the digital domain poses similar threats to states across the globe. Since we apply the Alston approach at the phase of a new human right idea, the aspect of existing states' practice enforcing the right does not apply. Yet provided that such right would become recognized by states from different political families, courts' practice shall definitely follow to meet this criterion. The final criterion of sufficient preciseness to give rise to identifiable right and corresponding obligations is met through the definitions proposed in the previous section. States and private entities have the obligation to enable to communicate with rights' holders both *via* Internet and non-Internet based channels. This preliminary sketch allows to suggest that under the qualitative criteria approach, of which Alston's quality control proposal is an example, the right not to use the Internet can be justified as a new human right. It is conditional upon the assumptions of consensus building and fitting into different value systems.

3.2.2.2 The decrease in universality and abstractness thesis

The approach to replace or supplement the values-based-only criteria with metrics-based criteria is represented by the decrease in universality and abstractness thesis, which I have articulated and explained elsewhere.[35] I have claimed in the context of the thesis that

> There are two distinct categories of new human rights claims. First, there are new human rights clams connected with the incapability of the discursive practice of established rights to provide sufficient protection to certain groups.[36]
>
> Second, there are new human rights claims which are meant to enhance some specific aspect of an established human right.[37]
>
> … the process of new human rights development has two directions: either towards the decrease of universality, as is the case with the rights for specific groups, or towards the decrease in abstractness, as is the case with rights derived from or being implied by established rights.[38]

For illustrative purposes Figure 3.1 can be presented.

With the increase of the aspect of individuality, at some point the element of universality connected by definition with a human right is lost. Likewise, with the increase of concreteness, at some point the new human rights claim loses the aspect of abstractness associated by definition with any human right. The decrease of abstractness and universality do not necessarily go hand in hand. A human right can retain a strong abstract character and at the same time decrease in universality. And conversely, a human right can retain a high degree of universality and at the same time decrease in abstractness. The box labelling a right as a "human right" is a matter of choices, but in principle the thesis excludes the possibility of endless growth of human rights. This is because the levels of abstractness and universality of any human right claim cannot by definition fall below certain degree.

This thesis when applied to the right not to use the Internet has to be viewed on both axes – universality and abstractness. The statistical information available shows that as of April 2024 there were 5.44 billion Internet users worldwide,

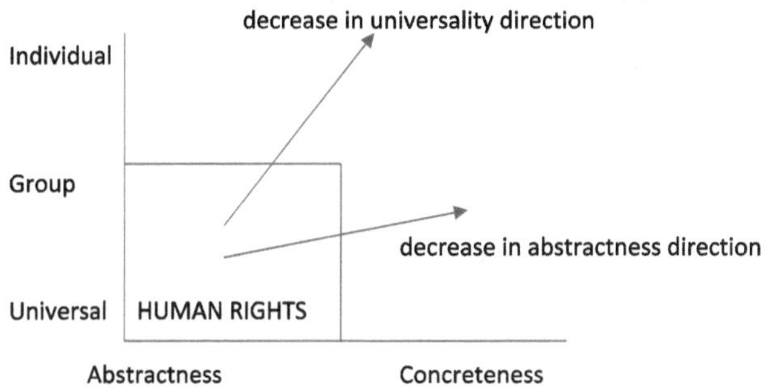

Figure 3.1 Visual depiction of the decrease in universality and abstractness thesis.

amounting to around 67.1 percent of the global population.[39] The United Nations led EGDI (E-Governance Development Index)[40] most recent report of 2022 shows 60 countries having EGDI values between 0.75 and 1.00; and 73 countries having the values between 0.5 and 0.75.[41] The maximum figure 1.00 shows that a resident of the particular country can accomplish all official affairs *via* websites only, if he or she so chooses. These statistical figures show that Internet usage for communication with the public power stands far beyond a group interest and meets the criterion of universality for the purpose of our analysis.

Next we have to see where the criterion of abstractness positions the idea of the right not to use the Internet in the visual description figure. Although there is no generally shared definition about abstractness in human rights discourse, the view of close connection to core human rights principles has to be endorsed here. Alexy has defined this as the *simpliciter* argument[42] of clear referral to fundamental values, Sano points to the level of generality, which is higher for abstract principles and more concrete for obligations.[43] We observe several layers between the entitlement not to use the Internet and fundamental values. Because this entitlement is not related to the usage of Internet *per se*, but in relation to its concrete functionality as the enabler to manage one's official business with the state and/or obtain essential services from the private sector. If this entitlement was labelled as an overall right not to use the Internet in any communication with anyone, its justifiability as a human right would move significantly towards higher degree of abstractness. But this scenario would be the intrusion of public power into private sphere, where any online company would be compelled by law to offer their services offline as well, and as such it is unrealistic even in theory. Therefore the right not to use the Internet as a human right idea can be still limited to cases related to managing its public affairs or accessing vital services. More aspects about ontology of the entitlement not to use the Internet will be looked at in the next section, which can open a more nuanced image. Yet the first glance about its abstractness leads either towards the rejection of the right not to use the Internet as a human right or positions it at the margin of the human rights box in the graphical description due to high degree of concreteness.

3.2.3 The ontology of the idea of a human right not to use the Internet

One of the main conclusions from the collective intellectual work of more than 40 scholars working on the Cambridge Handbook on New Human Rights[44] reflect the ontology of new human rights. It was formulated as follows:

> All the new human rights … can be traced to some uncontested, globally accepted and long-standing human right norm or multiple norms in conjunction, which can thus be considered an overarching conceptual framework for the emergence of any new human rights claim.[45]

The book confirmed the correctness of the derivation approach[46] – through analysis of various emerging new human rights. Derivation means that most new rights are derived from already existing ones with adding new elements. At one point separation of a new human rights from the "parent" right may be justified. In order to derive a new human right, it must be shown through discourse that the new right is "implied" or "inherent" in one or several already existing human rights.

Since discourse about the right not to use the Internet is scarce and the proposition stays at the phase of an initial idea, the question about connection to existing rights will be guided by intuitionistic logic. A careful reader notices the word "initial" before the word "idea", which is a call to further differentiate the first phase of idea in new human right development. I will limit this novel point here with the suggestion that the justification of the initial idea of a new human right can be sufficiently accomplished by intuition, but for moving beyond the phase of idea discursive arguments need to appear. The intuition says that the right not to use the Internet has ontological connection to the right to privacy, the right to good administration and the right to a decision by a human.

3.2.3.1 Connection to the right to privacy

The formulation of the right to privacy in the contemporary era is widely credited to Warren and Brandeis' formulation from 1890 as an interest "to be let alone".[47] Yet privacy in the digital domain differs to a considerable degree from privacy in the non-digital domain. For instance, Richards has declared privacy online "dead" or "dying".[48] Facebook's Zuckerberg says that "privacy is no longer a social norm".[49] Thomas has asserted that today nobody appears "to have any very clear idea what privacy is".[50] The doctrine of privacy fatalism is advanced by some to characterize the distortion of the traditional meaning of privacy online.[51] The possibilities to intrude privacy by media are considered more readily available and with broader impact, in comparison when Warren and Brandeis critiqued "the press" which was "overstepping in every direction" beyond common decency and engaging in "vicious" and "unseemly" gossip.[52] It is suggested that the Internet has given birth to modern privacy rights, as proposed by some scholars focusing on new technology and associated data practices and threats and challenges to privacy, particularly the development of new computing and data-based technologies.[53] The result of this process is that defining and conceptualizing privacy has become an increasingly complex and complicated task, as noted by Lin.[54] Penney asserts that difficulties associated with defining privacy online may have the "chilling effect" of deterring people from exercising their rights and freedoms on the Internet. These views do not mount to denying that privacy exists in the online domain, but contestation to the "traditional" offline meaning of privacy is prevalent.

The right not to use the Internet means, given the change of privacy meaning upon transposition from offline to online and explainable by the non-coherence theory, the entitlement to be let alone by the Internet. The single point of interest is whether such general formulation entails any need for the separation of the entitlement to be let alone by the Internet from the overall entitlement to be let alone. At such general level this need does not exist. It may appear through concretization and ontological comparison with other rights.

3.2.3.2 Connection to the right to good administration

Such right is protected under the EU Charter of Fundamental Rights[55] Article 41 and includes three entitlements: the right to be heard before an individual measure, the right to have access to his or her file and the obligation of administration to give reasons. Several countries have included comparable entitlements into national legal systems.[56] The right to good administration has generic roots in the physical domain and has the focus anchoring several human rights principles such as *accountability, responsiveness and openness*[57] into how the state should conduct its affairs with rights holders.

The elements of accountability, responsiveness and openness can be merged under the umbrella principle of transparency. But the features of transparency in the digital and non-digital domains are non-coherent. There seems a desire to move from quantity-based meaning of transparency towards a feature entailing certain qualitative elements enabling to explain decisions. For instance, European Commission expert group of artificial intelligence has published a set of standards for transparency, which should enable the identification of the reasons why an AI-decision was erroneous which, in turn, could help prevent future mistakes.[58] As a next step, the EU Artificial Intelligence Act enlarges the meaning of online transparency regarding artificial intelligence decisions to reveal input and output elements.[59] There are attempts to implicitly accept that the meaning of transparency online has changed and put this into normative shape, which would now be the explicit acceptance of the variance in the meaning. For instance, UNESCO has endorsed an assertion that "a third way is increasingly being proposed: to focus more on issues of process, rather than content, and especially to focus on greater transparency of the processes used by the platform companies".[60] All this has led me elsewhere to assert[61] that upon transposition into the digital domain core principles of human rights architecture – as we know them – change. Transparency turns into non-transparency, legal certainty into uncertainty and foreseeability into non-foreseeability. Since the right to good administrative is a highly specific human right – doubts can be expressed whether it fits into the box of Figure 3.1 – containing epistemic features, and since the non-coherence theory shows that these features undergo considerable change upon transposition into the digital domain, it can be asserted that the right to good administration no longer is an offline-domain centred right and its substance can be evoked both offline and online. The right not to use the Internet says that administration has to be provided also offline, and the right to good administration refers to the characteristics of this administration. The right not to use the Internet is a gatekeeper from moving all administration into the digital domain.

3.2.3.3 Connection to the right to a decision by a human

The General Data Protection Regulation (GDPR) contains in Article 22(1) this right: "The data subject shall have the right not to be subject to a decision based solely on automated processing, including profiling, which produces legal effects concerning him or her or similarly significantly affects him or her". Shany's analysis[62] of the present discourse shows that "the right to a human decision maker appears to be well on its way to becoming recognized as a universal human right, recognized under IHRL".[63] His listing of claims justifying the recognition of the right to a decision by a human as a human right include concerns about arbitrariness and abuse of power of automated decisions, their lack of accountability and democratic legitimacy, the inability of data subjects to participate in decision-making, fears of algorithmic discrimination and unfairness, and finally the incompatibility of algorithmic decisions with human dignity where the absence of empathy is substituted by "data shadows".[64]

Despite what one would expect prior to contemplation, the right not to use the Internet and the right to a decision by a human share a very limited common area in content. They are both related to the digital space, but this similarity is at a very high level. Concretization shows separate areas of focus. The right not to use the Internet is concerned with privacy and not having to rely on certain communication model for obtaining public and private services. The quality of these services remains outside of this new right's scope. The right to a decision by a human is concerned with the opposite – the quality of public and private services is of central importance and whether the service is provided through Internet or not remains outside of its scope.

3.3 Concluding remarks

This chapter has applied two theoretical frameworks to consider whether the right not to use the Internet can be justified as a new human right. The approach relying on qualitative indicators only, represented by Alston's quality control idea, shows the potential to give an affirmative response. The decrease in universality and abstractness thesis leads to a contrary response. Although the universality of such new right has to be accepted, it remains highly concrete and therefore doubts prevail about its justifiability as a human right.

The right not to use the Internet is about the entitlement not to be forced to use the Internet for conducting one's official affairs with the state, nor for obtaining vital services from private companies. It is an aspect of the right to privacy and there are not enough reasons to speak of its extension into a new self-standing right. There is some functional connection to the right to good administration, because the latter can be better enforced outside of the digital domain. There may be some who choose to evoke the right not to use the Internet in order to benefit from the right to good administration, but there also may be some who do not care about the quality of administration.

The right not to use the Internet is no guarantee for the right to a decision by a human. Therefore, the clustering hypothesis formulated in this chapter could not be confirmed, because these two rights are not originating from the same parent right and are not protecting closely related interests. To recapitulate, the parent right of the right not to use the Internet is the right to privacy, and the parent right of the right to a decision by a human is the right to good administration. Yet it is important to develop the idea of the right not to use the Internet further and try to push it from the phase of an idea into the phase of emergence through scholarly discourse and advocacy. This right should be viewed as a shield against the increasing pressures to conduct all business with the governments *via* the digital domain. The final speculation of this chapter asserts that the more the obligation to use the Internet strengthens, the more justifiable becomes the right not to use the Internet. Such general speculation has to suffice as the end of this chapter. The topic of interconnectedness of various entitlements and their possible positive or negative correlations will be explored elsewhere in the future.

Notes

1 Existentialist justification of human rights concerns the introduction of the ideal aspect into the human rights architecture. Alexy claims that without such justification we could still not be certain whether human rights exist, and as such completes the catalogue of human rights justifications – see Alexy, R. (2011). The Existence of Human Rights. *Law of Ukraine: Legal Journal, 11–12*, 102–111, p. 110.

2 La Torre defines the existential normative situation as an idealistic orientation instrument of what ought to be done – see La Torre, M. (2018). Human Rights: Existential, Not Metaphysical. *Ratio Juris*, *31*(2), 188. I have used the expression "existential normative horizon" to point at the dilemma whether the human rights horizon has limits or whether human rights can, *sense stricto*, grow endlessly. Such endlessness, as I will show below, turns into uselessness at some point.

3 The Olbers' paradox addresses the conflict between the assumption of endless number of stars and the darkness of sky – because if the universe consists of infinite number of stars, the sky at night should be wholly covered by starlight – see Wesson, P. (1991). Olbers' Paradox and the Spectral Intensity of the Extragalactic Background Light. *The Astrophysical Journal*, *367*, 399–406.

4 There is a wide ongoing discussion about the phenomenon of human rights inflation. For instance, Baxi terms inflationary process as human rights overproduction – see Baxi, U. (2001). Too Many, or Too Few, Human Rights? *Human Rights Law Review*, *1*, 1–10.

There is a shared perception that "human rights inflation" has become a spectre that has haunted the debate for quite some time now – see Nickel, W. (2007). *Making Sense of Human Rights*. Malden: Blackwell, p. 96; Letsas, G. (2007) *A Theory of Interpretation of the European Convention on Human Rights*. Oxford: Oxford University Press, p. 129; Ignatieff, M. (2001). *Human Rights as Politics and Idolatry*. Princeton: Princeton University Press, p. 90. Adorno objects to the tendency of labelling everything "socially desirable" as a human right – see Adorno, R. (2020). The Relevance of Human Rights for Dealing with the Challenges Posed by Genetics, in: von Arnaud, A., von der Decken, K., and Susi, M. (eds.), *Cambridge Handbook on New Human Rights of the 21st Century: Rhetoric, Recognition and Novelty*. Cambridge: Cambridge University Press, pp. 335–349, at 336.

5 Milton claimed almost 400 years ago: "It was from out the rind of one apple tasted, that the knowledge of good and evil as two twins cleaving together leapt forth into the World" – see Milton, J. (1664). *Areopagitica, A Speech of Mr. John Milton for the Liberty of Unlicenc'd Printing to the Parliament of England*, 1st ed., London. Retrieved 19 July 2024 *via* Google Books.

6 More does not need to be said about this point here, one can also consider the seminal work – Dworkin, R. (1985). Rights as Trumps, in: J. Waldron (ed.), *Theories of Rights*. Oxford: Oxford University Press, pp. 153–167.

7 For framing the discussion of new human rights emergence process, see: von Arnaud, A., von der Decken, K., and Susi M (eds.). (2020). *Cambridge Handbook on New Human Rights of the 21st Century: Rhetoric, Recognition and Novelty*. Cambridge: Cambridge University Press.

8 For discussion about the process of recognition of new human rights see the theory of "differentiated traditionalism", which cautions against abrupt recognition of claims of new human rights in customary public law – see von der Decken, K. and Koch, N. (2020). Recognition of New Human Rights. Phases, Techniques and the Approach of "Differentiated Traditionalism", in: Arnaud, A., von der Decken K., and Susi M. (eds.), *Cambridge Handbook on New Human Rights of the 21st Century: Rhetoric, Recognition and Novelty*. Cambridge: Cambridge University Press, pp. 7–20.

9 See Taylor Tillman, N. (2024). *Brown Dwarfs: Failed Stars Resembling Planets*. www.space.com/23798-brown-dwarfs.html. Accessed on 21 July 2024.

10 See for reference: Herbst, E. (1995). Chemistry in The Interstellar Medium. *Annual Review of Physical Chemistry*, *46*, 27–54.

11 Susi, M. (2024). *Non-coherence Theory of Digital Human Rights*. Cambridge: Cambridge University Press.

12 Benedek, W. (2023). Digital human rights and artificial intelligence. *Pravni Zapisi*, XIV(2), 227–237.

13 See for instance the Italian Declaration of Internet Rights – for discussion see: Rodotá, S. Towards a Declaration of Internet Rights, date unknown, www.camera.it/application/xmanager/projects/leg17/attachments/upload_file/upload_files/000/000/194/Internet_Libe_inglese.pdf. Accessed 17 July 2024; or the Spanish Charter of Digital Rights – The original text in Spanish is accessible, for example, *via* the following website: Cities Coalition for Digital Rights, "Spain presents its Charter of Digital Rights", date unknown, https://citiesfordigitalrights.org/spain-presents-its-charter-digital-rights. Accessed 17 July 2024.

14 Pollicino, O. and De Gregorio, G. (2022). Constitutional Law in the Algorithmic Society, in: Micklitz, H., Pollicino, O. Reichman, A., Simoncini, A., Sartor, G. and De Gregorio G. (eds.), *Constitutional Challenges in the Algorithmic Society*. Cambridge: Cambridge University Press, p. 5.

15 For instance how the right to privacy can be viewed as one of the "parents" of the right to gender identity – see Lau, H. (2020). Right to Gender Identity, Arnaud, A., von der Decken K., and Susi M. (eds.), *Cambridge Handbook on New Human Rights of the 21st Century: Rhetoric, Recognition and Novelty*. Cambridge: Cambridge University Press, pp. 191–214.

16 Since there may be developments regarding this entitlement, it is advisable for the reader to look for updates from the website of the World Economic Forum at: www.weforum.org/agenda/2023/02/belgium-right-to-disconnect-from-work/.

17 von der Decken, K. and Koch, N. (2020). Recognition of New Human Rights. Phases, Techniques and the Approach of "Differentiated Traditionalism", in: Arnaud, A., von der Decken K., and Susi M. (eds.), *Cambridge Handbook on New Human Rights of the 21st Century: Rhetoric, Recognition and Novelty*. Cambridge: Cambridge University Press, p. 8.

18 For context see: Thienel, T. (2014). The "Living Instrument" Approach in the ECHR and Elsewhere: Some Remarks on the Evolutive Interpretation of International Treaties, in: Delbrück, J. et al. (eds.), *Aus Kiel in die Welt: Kiel's Contribution to International Law.* Berlin: Duncker & Humboldt, p. 165.

19 Finnemore, M. and Sikkink, K. (1998). International Norm Dynamics and Political Change. *International Organization*, *52*, 894–905.

20 von Arnaud, A. and Theilen, J. T. (2020). Rhetoric of Rights. A Topical Perspective on the Functions of Claiming a "Human Right to …", in: von Arnaud, A., von der Decken K., and Susi, M. (eds.), *Cambridge Handbook on New Human Rights of the 21st Century: Rhetoric, Recognition and Novelty*. Cambridge: Cambridge University Press, pp. 34–49.

21 von Arnaud, A. and Theilen, J. T. (2020). Rhetoric of Rights. A Topical Perspective on the Functions of Claiming a "Human Right to …", in: von Arnaud, A., von der Decken K., and Susi, M. (eds.), *Cambridge Handbook on New Human Rights of the 21st Century: Rhetoric, Recognition and Novelty*. Cambridge: Cambridge University Press, p. 39.

22 von Arnaud, A. and Theilen, J. T. (2020). Rhetoric of Rights. A Topical Perspective on the Functions of Claiming a "Human Right to …", in: von Arnaud, A., von der Decken K., and Susi, M. (eds.), *Cambridge Handbook on New Human Rights of the 21st Century: Rhetoric, Recognition and Novelty*. Cambridge: Cambridge University Press, p. 41.

23 See about the normative constraints imposed during the legislative process, possibly impacting the core of the initial idea: Cover, R. M. (1983). The Supreme Court 1982 Term. Foreword: Nomos and Narrative. *Harvard Law Review*, *97*(4), 4–68.

24 The example usually given to illustrate the context of such discursive struggle leading to normative changes is related to the fight for women's rights, so I will use the same reference here for context: Kapur, R. (2006). Revisioning the Role of Law in Women's Human Rights Struggles, in: Meckled-García, S. and Çalı, B. (eds.), *The Legalization of Human Rights: Multidisciplinary Perspectives on Human Rights and Human Rights Law.* London and New York: Routledge, p. 105.

25 See for context discussion about activities and questions raised, signalling that justification of a new human right has started: what will be the content of the newly proposed human rights, what obligations it ensues and for whom, how may the new human rights be properly fitted into the existing legal system – Nickel, J. (1987). *Making Sense of Human Rights: Philosophical Reflections on the Universal Declaration of Human Rights.* Berkeley: University of California Press, pp. 27–35.

26 See Susi, M. (2024). *Non-coherence Theory of Digital Human Rights*. Cambridge: Cambridge University Press. Reversal of some human rights feature to the opposite can occur upon transposition from non-digital domain to the digital domain. For instance, involuntary entry into privacy claim in the non-digital domain turns into voluntary entry into privacy claim in the digital domain. This is because we do not choose to enter the physical world but do so for the non-physical world.
27 Reglitz, M. (2024). *The Human Right to Free Internet Access*. Cambridge: Cambridge University Press. In his comment to the book Reglitz lists such activities as submission of job applications, sending medical information to professionals, management of finances and business, making social security claims and submission of educational assessments.
28 Nugent, N. J. (2023). The Five Internet Rights. *Washington Law Review*, *98*, 527.
29 Kloza, D. (2023). The Right Not to Use the Internet. *Computer Law & Security Review*, *52*, 3. https://doi.org/10.1016/j.clsr.2023.105907.
30 To access most recent "success stories" of digitalization of Estonia's public services, it is best to enter the respective website at: https://e-estonia.com/estonia-a-european-and-global-leader-in-the-digitalisation-of-public-services/.
31 Kloza, D. (2023). The Right Not to Use the Internet. *Computer Law & Security Review*, *52*, pp. 2–3. https://doi.org/10.1016/j.clsr.2023.105907
32 Alston, P. (1984). Conjuring Up New Human Rights: A Proposal for Quality Control. *American Journal of International Law*, *78*, 607–621. According to his criteria a new human right is ready to be recognized by an international organ if the following conditions apply: the right reflects a fundamentally important social value, is relevant throughout the world in different value systems, it is an interpretation of UN Charter obligation, it introduces a new aspect into the existing body of international human rights law, there is already a high degree of international consensus about the claim, states have already a practice enforcing the right, and it is sufficiently precise to give raise to identifiable rights and corresponding obligations.
33 Nickel, J. (2014). Human Rights, in E. N. Zalta (ed.), *Stanford Encyclopedia of Philosophy*. Available at https://plato.stanford.edu/entries/rights-human/.
34 Brems, E. (2020). Birthing New Human Rights: Reflections around a Hypothetical Human Right of Access to Gestational Surrogacy, in: von Arnaud, A., von der Decken K., and Susi M. (eds.), *Cambridge Handbook on New Human Rights of the 21st Century: Rhetoric, Recognition and Novelty*. Cambridge: Cambridge University Press, pp. 326–334.
35 Susi, M. (2020). Novelty in New Human Rights: The Decrease in Universality and Abstractness Thesis, in: von Arnaud, A., von der Decken, K., and Susi, M. (eds.), *Cambridge Handbook on New Human Rights of the 21st Century: Rhetoric, Recognition and Novelty*. Cambridge: Cambridge University Press, pp. 21–33.
36 Susi, M. (2020). Novelty in New Human Rights: The Decrease in Universality and Abstractness Thesis, in: von Arnaud, A., von der Decken, K., and Susi, M. (eds.), *Cambridge Handbook on New Human Rights of the 21st Century: Rhetoric, Recognition and Novelty*. Cambridge: Cambridge University Press, p. 26.
37 Susi, M. (2020). Novelty in New Human Rights: The Decrease in Universality and Abstractness Thesis, in: von Arnaud, A., von der Decken, K., and Susi, M. (eds.), *Cambridge Handbook on New Human Rights of the 21st Century: Rhetoric, Recognition and Novelty*. Cambridge: Cambridge University Press, p. 27.
38 Susi, M. (2020). Novelty in New Human Rights: The Decrease in Universality and Abstractness Thesis, in: von Arnaud, A., von der Decken, K., and Susi, M. (eds.),

Cambridge Handbook on New Human Rights of the 21st Century: Rhetoric, Recognition and Novelty. Cambridge: Cambridge University Press, p. 28.

39 See the website of digital statistics, which is regularly updated: www.statista.com/statistics/617136/digital-population-worldwide/. Accessed on 28 July 2024.

40 For further insights into the methodology and results, one can visit the site of the Index at: www.statista.com/topics/2420/e-government/#topicOverview. Accessed on 28 July 2024.

41 Reports are available through the previously referenced source.

42 Alexy, R. (2011). The Existence of Human Rights. *Law of Ukraine: Legal Journal*, 12.

43 Sano, H. O. (2013). Human Rights and Development: Human Rights Principles and Their Indicators. *Nordic Journal of Human Rights*, 31(3), 399.

44 von Arnaud, A., von der Decken, K., and Susi M (eds.). (2020). *Cambridge Handbook on New Human Rights of the 21st Century: Rhetoric, Recognition and Novelty*. Cambridge: Cambridge University Press.

45 Susi, M. (2020). Novelty in New Human Rights: The Decrease in Universality and Abstractness Thesis, in: von Arnaud, A., von der Decken, K., and Susi, M. (eds.), *Cambridge Handbook on New Human Rights of the 21st Century: Rhetoric, Recognition and Novelty*. Cambridge: Cambridge University Press, p. 25.

46 For discussion see von Arnaud, A., von der Decken, K., and Susi M (eds.). (2020). *Cambridge Handbook on New Human Rights of the 21st Century: Rhetoric, Recognition and Novelty*. Cambridge: Cambridge University Press.

47 Warren, S. D. and Brandeis, L. D. (1890). The Right to Privacy. *Harvard Law Review*, *4*(5), 193.

48 Richards, N. (2015). Four Myths of Privacy, in: Sarat, A. (ed.), *A World Without Privacy: What the Law Can and Should Do*. Cambridge: Cambridge University Press, pp. I–II.

49 Johnson, B. (2010). Privacy No Longer a Social Norm, Says Facebook Founder. *The Guardian*, 11 January 2010, www.theguardian.com/technology/2010/jan/11/facebook-privacy. Accessed 27 July 2024.

50 Thomas, J. J. (1984). The Right to Privacy, in: Schloeman, F. D. (ed.), *Philosophical Dimensions of Privacy: An Anthology*. Cambridge: Cambridge University Press, pp. 272–289.

51 Mims, C. (2018). Privacy Is Dead. Here's What Comes Next. *Wall Street Journal*, 6 May 2018, www.wsj.com/articles/privacy-is-dead-heres-what-comes-next-1525608001. Accessed 19 July 2024; and Tan, A. (2018). Privacy Is Dead. *The Business Times*, 9 June 2018. Accessed 19 July 2024; and Bonnell, K. (2018). Privacy Is Dead and We All Helped Kill It. *Ottawa Citizen*, 2 April 2018. Accessed 19 July 2024; and Kerry, C. F. (2018). Why Protecting Privacy Is a Losing Game Today and How to Change the Game. *Brookings*, 12 July 2018, www.brookings.edu/research/why-protecting-privacy-is-a-losing-game-today-and-how-to-change-the-game/. Accessed 19 July 2024.

52 See also Glancy, D. J. (1971). The Invention of the Right to Privacy. *Arizona Law Review*, 21(1), pp. 1–39.

53 Rosenberg, M. J. (1995). *The Death of Privacy*. Random House; and Regan, P. M. (1995). *Legislative Privacy: Technology, Social Values, and Public Policy*. Chapel Hill and London: University of North Carolina Press; and Froomkin, M. (2000). The Death of Privacy? *Stanford Law Review*, *52*, 1461; and Garfinkel, S. (2000) *Database Nation: The Death of Privacy in the 21st Century*. O'Reilly Media.

54 Lin, E. (2002) Prioritizing Privacy: A Constitutional Response to the Internet. *Berkeley Technology Law Journal*, *17*, 1088.

55 Charter of Fundamental Rights of the European Union, OJ C 202, 7.6.2016, pp. 389–405.
56 For comprehensive comparative review of the right to good administration see: Corder, H. (2020). A Right to Administrative Justice: "New" or Just Repacking the Old?, in: von Arnaud, A., von der Decken K., and Susi M. (eds.), *Cambridge Handbook on New Human Rights of the 21st Century: Rhetoric, Recognition and Novelty*. Cambridge: Cambridge University Press, pp. 493–506.
57 Corder, H. (2020). A Right to Administrative Justice: "New" or Just Repacking the Old?, in: von Arnaud, A., von der Decken K., and Susi M. (eds.), *Cambridge Handbook on New Human Rights of the 21st Century: Rhetoric, Recognition and Novelty*. Cambridge: Cambridge University Press, pp. 493–506.
58 European Commission High-Level Expert Group on AI, "Ethics Guidelines for Trustworthy AI", 8 April 2019, p. 18. https://digital-strategy.ec.europa.eu/en/library/ethics-guidelines-trustworthy-aip.
59 Regulation (EU) 2024/1689 of the European Parliament and of the Council of 13 June 2024 laying down harmonized rules on artificial intelligence and amending Regulations (EC) No 300/2008, (EU) No 167/2013, (EU) No 168/2013, (EU) 2018/858, (EU) 2018/1139 and (EU) 2019/2144 and Directives 2014/90/EU, (EU) 2016/797 and (EU) 2020/1828 (Artificial Intelligence Act), OJ L, 2024/1689, 12.7.2024, Article 13.
60 Puddephatt, A. (2021). Letting the sun shine in: transparency and accountability in the digital age. UNESCO document CI-2021/WTR/5 (2021), p. 7.
61 Susi, M. (2024). *Non-coherence Theory of Digital Human Rights*. Cambridge: Cambridge University Press.
62 Shany, Y. (2023). From Digital Rights to International Human Rights: The Emerging Right to a Human Decision Maker, *AI Ethics at Oxford Blog* (11th December 2023). Available at www.oxford-aiethics.ox.ac.uk/blog/digital-rights-international-human-rights-emerging-right-human-decision-maker.
63 Shany, Y. (2023). From Digital Rights to International Human Rights: The Emerging Right to a Human Decision Maker, *AI Ethics at Oxford Blog* (11th December 2023). Available at www.oxford-aiethics.ox.ac.uk/blog/digital-rights-international-human-rights-emerging-right-human-decision-maker
64 Shany, Y. (2023). From Digital Rights to International Human Rights: The Emerging Right to a Human Decision Maker, *AI Ethics at Oxford Blog* (11th December 2023). Available at www.oxford-aiethics.ox.ac.uk/blog/digital-rights-international-human-rights-emerging-right-human-decision-maker

Bibliography

Alexy, R. (2011). The Existence of Human Rights. *Law of Ukraine: Legal Journal*, 4, 21–31.
Alston, P. (1984). Conjuring Up New Human Rights: A Proposal for Quality Control. *American Journal of International Law*, 78, 607–621.
Baxi, U. (2001). Too Many, or Too Few, Human Rights? *Human Rights Law Review*, *1*, 1–10.
Benedek, W. (2023). Digital Human Rights and Artificial Intelligence. *Pravni Zapisi*, XIV (2), 227–237.
Bonnell, K. (2018). Privacy is Dead and We All Helped Kill It. *Ottawa Citizen*, 2 April 2024. https://ottawacitizen.com/news/local-news/bonnell-privacy-is-dead-and-we-all-helped-kill-it. Accessed 19 July 2024.
Brems, E. (2020). Birthing New Human Rights: Reflections around a Hypothetical Human Right of Access to Gestational Surrogacy, in: von Arnaud, A., von der Decken K.,

Susi M. (eds.), *Cambridge Handbook on New Human Rights of the 21st Century: Rhetoric, Recognition and Novelty*. Cambridge: Cambridge University Press, pp. 326–334.

Charter of Fundamental Rights of the European Union, OJ C 202, 7.6.2016, pp. 389–405.

Corder, H. (2020). A Right to Administrative Justice: "New" or Just Repacking the Old?, in: von Arnaud, A., von der Decken K., Susi M. (eds.), *Cambridge Handbook on New Human Rights of the 21st Century: Rhetoric, Recognition and Novelty*. Cambridge: Cambridge University Press, pp. 493–506.

Cover, R. M. (1983). The Supreme Court 1982 Term. Foreword: Nomos and Narrative. Harvard Law Review, 97(4), 4–68.

Dworkin, R. (1985). Rights as Trumps, in: J. Waldron (ed.), *Theories of Rights*. Oxford: Oxford University Press, pp. 153–167.

European Commission High-Level Expert Group on AI. (2019). Ethics Guidelines for Trustworthy AI, 8 April 2019, https://digital-strategy.ec.europa.eu/en/library/ethics-guidelines-trustworthy-ai.

Finnemore, M. and Sikkink, K. (1998). International Norm Dynamics and Political Change. *International Organization*, 52, 894–905.

Froomkin, M. (2000). The Death of Privacy? *Stanford Law Review*, 52, 1461–1543.

Garfinkel, S. (2000). *Database Nation: The Death of Privacy in the 21st Century*. O'Reilly Media.

Glancy, D. J. (1971). The Invention of the Right to Privacy. *Arizona Law Review*, 21(1), 1–39.

Herbst, E. (1995). Chemistry in the Interstellar Medium. *Annual Review of Physical Chemistry*, *46*, 27–54.

Ignatieff, M. (2001). *Human Rights as Politics and Idolatry*. Princeton: Princeton University Press.

Johnson, B. (2010). Privacy No Longer a Social Norm, Says Facebook Founder. *The Guardian*, 11 January 2010, www.theguardian.com/technology/2010/jan/11/facebook-privacy. Accessed 27 July 2024.

Kapur, R. (2006). Revisioning the Role of Law in Women's Human Rights Struggles, in: Meckled-García, S. and Çalı, B. (eds.), *The Legalization of Human Rights: Multidisciplinary Perspectives on Human Rights and Human Rights Law*. London and New York: Routledge.

Kerry, C.F. (2018). *Why Protecting Privacy Is a Losing Game Today and How to Change the Game*. Brookings, 12 July 2018, www.brookings.edu/research/why-protecting-privacy-is-a-losing-game-today-and-how-to-change-the-game/. Accessed 19 July 2024.

Kloza, D. (2023). The Right Not to Use the Internet. *Computer Law & Security Review*, *52*, 3. https://doi.org/10.1016/j.clsr.2023.105907.

La Torre, M. (2018). Human Rights: Existential, Not Metaphysical. *Ratio Juris*, 31(2), 183–195.

Lau, H. (2020). Right to Gender Identity, in: Arnaud, A., von der Decken K., and Susi M. (eds.), *Cambridge Handbook on New Human Rights of the 21st Century: Rhetoric, Recognition and Novelty*. Cambridge: Cambridge University Press, pp 191–214.

Letsas, G. (2007). *A Theory of Interpretation of the European Convention on Human Rights*. Oxford: Oxford University Press.

Lin, E. (2002). Prioritizing Privacy: A Constitutional Response to the Internet. *Berkeley Technology Law Journal*, 17, 1085–1154.

Milton, J. (1664). *Areopagitica, A Speech of Mr. John Milton for the Liberty of Unlicenc'd Printing to the Parliament of England*, 1st ed., London. Retrieved 19 July 2024 *via* Google Books.

Mims, C. (2018). Privacy Is Dead. Here's What Comes Next. *Wall Street Journal*, 6 May 2018, www.wsj.com/articles/privacy-is-dead-heres-what-comes-next-1525608001. Accessed 19 July 2024.

Nickel, J. (1987). *Making Sense of Human Rights: Philosophical Reflections on the Universal Declaration of Human Rights*. Berkeley: University of California Press, pp. 27–35.

Nickel, J. (2014). Human Rights, in E. N. Zalta (ed.), *Stanford Encyclopedia of Philosophy*. Available at https://plato.stanford.edu/entries/rights-human/.

Nickel, W. (2007). *Making Sense of Human Rights*. Malden: Blackwell.

Nugent, N. J. (2023). The Five Internet Rights. *Washington Law Review*, 98, 527–624.

Pollicino, O. and De Gregorio, G. (2022). Constitutional Law in the Algorithmic Society, in: Micklitz, H., Pollicino, O. Reichman, A., Simoncini, A., Sartor, G. and De Gregorio G. (eds.), *Constitutional Challenges in the Algorithmic Society*. Cambridge: Cambridge University Press.

Puddephatt, A. (2021). *Letting the Sun Shine in: Transparency and Accountability in the Digital Age*. UNESCO document CI-2021/WTR/5 (2021).

Regan, P. M. (1995). *Legislative Privacy: Technology, Social Values, and Public Policy*. Chapel Hill and London: University of North Carolina Press.

Reglitz, M. (2024). *The Human Right to Free Internet Access*. Cambridge: Cambridge University Press.

Richards, N. (2015). Four Myths of Privacy, in: Sarat, A. (ed.), *A World Without Privacy: What the Law Can and Should Do*. Cambridge: Cambridge University Press.

Rosenberg, M. J. (1995). *The Death of Privacy*. New York: Random House.

Sano, H. O. (2013). Human Rights and Development: Human Rights Principles and Their Indicators. *Nordic Journal of Human Rights*, 31(3), 381–401.

Shany, Y. (2023). From Digital Rights to International Human Rights: The Emerging Right to a Human Decision Maker. *AI Ethics at Oxford Blog* (11th December 2023). Available at www.oxford-aiethics.ox.ac.uk/blog/digital-rights-international-human-rights-emerging-right-human-decision-maker.

Susi, M. (2020). Novelty in New Human Rights: the Decrease in Universality and Abstractness Thesis, in: von Arnaud, A., von der Decken, K., and Susi, M. (eds.), *Cambridge Handbook on New Human Rights of the 21st Century: Rhetoric, Recognition and Novelty*. Cambridge: Cambridge University Press, pp. 21–33.

Susi, M. (2024). *Non-coherence Theory of Digital Human Rights*. Cambridge: Cambridge University Press.

Tan, A. (2018). Privacy Is Dead. *The Business Times*, 9 June 2018. www.businesstimes.com.sg/opinion-features/columns/privacy-dead. Accessed 19 July 2024.

Taylor Tillman, N. (2024). *Brown Dwarfs: Failed Stars Resembling Planets*. www.space.com/23798-brown-dwarfs.html. Accessed on 21 July 2024.

Thienel, T. (2014). The "Living Instrument" Approach in the ECHR and Elsewhere: Some Remarks on the Evolutive Interpretation of International Treaties, in: Delbrück, J., et al. (eds.), *Aus Kiel in die Welt: Kiel's Contribution to International Law*. Berlin: Duncker & Humboldt.

Thomas, J. J. (1984). The Right to Privacy, in: Schloeman, F. D. (ed.), *Philosophical Dimensions of Privacy: An Anthology*. Cambridge: Cambridge University Press, pp. 272–289.

von Arnaud, A. and Theilen, J. T. (2020). Rhetoric of Rights. A Topical Perspective on the Functions of Claiming a "Human Right to …", in: von Arnaud, A., von der Decken K., and Susi M. (eds.), *Cambridge Handbook on New Human Rights of the 21st Century: Rhetoric, Recognition and Novelty*. Cambridge: Cambridge University Press, pp. 34–49.

von Arnaud, A., von der Decken, K., and Susi, M. (eds.). (2020). *Cambridge Handbook on New Human Rights of the 21st Century: Rhetoric, Recognition and Novelty*. Cambridge: Cambridge University Press.

von der Decken, K. and Koch, N. (2020). Recognition of New Human Rights. Phases, Techniques and the Approach of "Differentiated Traditionalism", in: Arnaud, A., von der Decken K., and Susi M. (eds.), *Cambridge Handbook on New Human Rights of the 21st Century: Rhetoric, Recognition and Novelty*. Cambridge: Cambridge University Press, pp. 7–20.

Warren, S. D. and Brandeis, L. D. (1890). The Right to Privacy. *Harvard Law Review*, 4(5), 193–220.

Website of the World Economic Forum at: www.weforum.org/agenda/2023/02/belgium-right-to-disconnect-from-work/

Wesson, P. (1991). Olbers' Paradox and the Spectral Intensity of the Extragalactic Background Light. *The Astrophysical Journal*, *367*, 399–406.

4 Human rights and the digital divide

Recent developments in the case law of the Belgian Council of State[1]

Pauline Lagasse and
Sébastien Van Drooghenbroeck

4.1 Introduction

In April 2024, Prof. Elise Degrave suggested in newspaper *Le Soir* (Degrave, 2024) that a new fundamental right should be enshrined in the Belgian Constitution: the right not to use the Internet (see also, Degrave, 2023: 212–244; Kloza, 2024).

In Belgium, constitutional amendment itself presupposes a preliminary step: the Constitution must be first declared open to revision on the point in question, either to incorporate the proposed new provision or to amend an existing provision (Belgian Constitution, art. 195).[2]

In view of the data currently available, this preliminary hurdle could be considered to have been passed. The declaration of revision of the Constitution, published in the Belgian Official Journal on 27 May 2024, indeed allows for the insertion, in Article 23 of the Constitution, of a right to a universal communication service, the negative aspect of which could, among other things, include the right not to use the Internet (*Moniteur belge*, 2024). All that remains is to find the necessary governmental majority to proceed – after the constitution of the Federal Government – with the actual revision.

There are undoubtedly very good reasons for producing such a constitutional effort. If the right not to use the Internet implies, among other things (Kloza, 2024), the need to provide an alternative to "all-digital" for the victims of the "digital divide", then, according to the latest figures available (King Baudouin Foundation, 2022; UNIA, 2023), there is a real urgency to do so in Belgium. According to figures from the King Baudouin Foundation (King Baudouin Foundation, 2024), in 2023, 40% of people aged 16 to 74 are in a situation of digital vulnerability (compared to 46% in 2021): 5% do not use the Internet and 35% have low digital skills. Despite this positive development, the proportion of Belgians with weak digital skills remains higher than the European average and, more importantly, higher than that of our neighbouring countries. Furthermore, in terms of digital vulnerability, the gap between low- and high-income individuals widens by 3 percentage points.

The aim of this chapter is to show that, while awaiting the desired constitutional revision, the Belgian legal system has already, on more "classical" legal bases, produced some interesting solutions to the problem at hand. The principle

DOI: 10.4324/9781003528401-6

of equality and non-discrimination were important levers in this respect (Section 4.2). More recently, the constitutional provision dedicated to the inclusion of people with disabilities also offered a welcome boost (Section 4.3). However, the ideal of "concrete and effective rights", to use the famous words of the European Court of Human Rights (ECHR, *Airey*, 1979), cannot be satisfied with these early achievements, and will require more than the pure and simple inclusion in the Constitution of a new provision that would merely codify this *constitutional acquis*: this is what will be outlined in Section 4.4.

This contribution is essentially based on an observation of the advisory practice of the Legislation Section of the Belgian Council of State (*Conseil d'Etat*),[3] to whose office the two authors contribute as, respectively, auditor and assessor.

4.2 Digitalisation, equality and non-discrimination: the aftermath of the "Moniteur belge" judgment

"Indirect" discrimination occurs when an apparently neutral practice is likely to cause particular harm to a category of people because of their age, disability, sex or particular socio-economic situation.[4]

Clearly, the increasing digitisation of the provision of goods and services – both private and public – will come into tension with this aspect of the ban on discrimination (Langlois & Van Drooghenbroeck, 2023). Statistically, elderly people, those with disabilities, or in situations of socio-economic hardship are indeed overrepresented in the category of victims of the digital divide. Access to these goods and services for these categories of people will become increasingly difficult, if not impossible.

Although this precise concept of "indirect discrimination" was not used at the time, this tension first came to light in the ruling handed down by the Belgian Constitutional Court on the changeover from the paper version to the electronic version of the Belgian official journal (*Moniteur belge*, *Belgisch Staatsblad, Belgisches Staatsblatt*).

At the end of 2002, a legislative reform abolished the paper version of the *Moniteur* and replaced it with an electronic version,[5] which was considerably less expensive. Only three paper copies remained, deposited with the Royal Library, the Ministry of Justice and the Directorate of the *Moniteur*, respectively. The resulting reform was challenged before the Constitutional Court on the grounds that, in breach of Articles 10 and 11 of the Constitution (i.e., principles of equality and non-discrimination), it resulted in a *de facto* disadvantage for certain categories of people, i.e., the victims of the "digital divide". The Court, in judgment no. 106/2004 of 16 June 2004 (Constitutional Court, 2004), accepted this argument:

> B.14. The contested provisions do not in themselves create any difference in treatment, since all persons to whom legislative and administrative acts apply can acquaint themselves with them in the same way. But the criticism levelled against those provisions is precisely that they fail to take account of the fact that not everyone has equal access to computer technology. The principle of equality

> and non-discrimination may be breached when the legislature treats people in essentially different situations in the same way.

The aim pursued by the legislator was certainly legitimate. However, it was still necessary to ensure compliance with the proportionality requirement. To this end, judgment no. 106/2004 had listed the accompanying measures that had been put in place (retention of three paper copies, right to demand a particular document in print, …) or vaguely envisaged (promise of computer equipment for municipalities), but found that they were not sufficiently effective, *hic et nunc*. The Court therefore concluded that:

> B.21. The paper edition of the *Moniteur belge* no doubt did not ensure that everyone was aware of the texts that were binding on them. For some people, making the texts available on a website will even make them more accessible and less expensive.
>
> But the fact remains that, as a result of the measures taken, a large number of people will be deprived of effective access to official texts, in particular due to the absence of accompanying measures that would give them the opportunity to consult these texts, whereas previously they were able to consult the content of the *Moniteur belge* without having to have any special equipment and without having any qualifications other than knowing how to read.
>
> B.22. In the absence of sufficient measures to ensure equal access to official texts, the contested measure has disproportionate effects to the detriment of certain categories of persons.
>
> It is therefore incompatible with Articles 10 and 11 of the Constitution.

Aware of the difficulties likely to arise in terms of legal certainty as a result of the annulment it had pronounced, the Constitutional Court nevertheless maintained the effects of the annulled provisions until a year after, i.e., 31 July 2005.

The legislator therefore had to adapt the system. This was done with an Act of 20 July 2005. Unlike its predecessor, this reform introduced accompanying measures, in particular the introduction of a free telephone helpdesk at the *Moniteur*'s head office. The reform was again challenged before the Constitutional Court which, taking into account the aforementioned accompanying measures, no longer considered that Articles 10 and 11 of the Constitution had been violated (Constitutional Court, 2007).

This line of reasoning has been emulated in a number of ways in the advisory practice of the Legislation Section of the Belgian Council of State.[6] We will mention here the most significant and recent examples: older others have already been analysed in a previous publication (Langlois & Van Drooghenbroeck, 2023).

A first series of recent advisory opinions was issued in the field of education.

First of all, mention should be made of advisory opinion no. 73.507/2 issued on 5 June 2023 (Council of State, 2023b) on a draft decree of the French-speaking Community[7] relating, in substance, to the digitisation of the pupil's support file

(*Dossier d'accompagnement de l'élève*; DACCE).[8] The explanatory memorandum to the draft stated that

> digitalising the procedure will make it possible (…) to simplify the work of schools and the Administration by facilitating the transmission of documents between the various parties, and to secure these exchanges. This project also seeks to prevent the effects of a possible digital divide. To this end, alternatives are systematically envisaged for parents who do not have access to IT tools (consultation within the school or CPMS [*Centres Psycho-Médico-Sociaux/ Psycho-Medico-Social Centers*], provision of a paper copy, sending copies of decisions by post, etc.).

However, the Council of State considered that

> Although *many* provisions do indeed provide for an alternative to the service of documents on interested parties by digital means, it has been noted that this alternative is not *systematically* provided for (emphasis added).

The French-speaking Community was therefore invited to complete its draft on this point.

Still on the subject of digitalisation in schools, advisory opinion no. 71731/2 of 1 August 2022 (Council of State, 2022) stated the following in relation to the guarantee of equality specifically set out in Article 24(4) Constitution:

> The Legislation Section notes that the draft regulation examined and its appendix 1 establish a set of rights for parents or students of legal age which can only be exercised electronically and to an electronic address.
>
> Such a system, which is aimed at the general population and not at recipients who can reasonably be assumed to have an e-mail address and to be familiar with exercising their rights 'online', therefore assumes that 'parents' or students of legal age have a computer and the basic knowledge that will enable them to effectively exercise the rights that the system under review is designed to grant them.
>
> Although the digital divide is constantly shrinking, it still affects a significant percentage of the population living in the French-speaking Community.
>
> In the view of the Legislation Section, it would therefore be contrary to Article 24(4) of the Constitution not to provide for the right of parents who are victims of the digital divide to be given a computer session at the school or CPMS centre [*Centres Psycho-Médico-Sociaux/Psycho-Medico-Social Centers*] and to obtain specific assistance in carrying out all the procedures that the draft text provides must be carried out electronically.

The advisory opinion adds: "It would even be preferable for the parents concerned to consider written procedures". The "paper" procedure or, at the very least, "specific assistance" is also the alternative recommended by the Legislation

Section in the name of the principle of equality in its advisory opinion of 6 November 2023 on the registration of cats in an electronic database (Council of State, 2023e). The draft decree examined in this opinion established an official database for the registration of cats, allowing the identification of the responsible party when an abandoned or lost cat is found, monitoring compliance with the obligation for cat identification and sterilisation, monitoring compliance with the conditions for the approval of shelters and breeders, and monitoring the trade and movement of cats. In this context, an obligation for the electronic registration and updating of data was specifically imposed on individuals, cat owners or custodians, who regularly manage or directly supervise the animal. According to the Council of State:

> (s)uch a system, which targets the general population (…), therefore assumes that 'individuals, cat owners or custodians who regularly manage or directly supervise the animal' have access to a computer and possess basic knowledge that will allow them to meet the obligations imposed by the examined system. However, the digital divide continues to affect a non-negligible percentage of the population living in the Walloon Region.

The digitisation of justice is also a recurring point of attention in the practice of the Council of State (see Council of State, 2015). In an opinion no. 72.861/1-2 (Council of State, 2023a), the Legislation Section stated the following about the organisation of hearings by videoconference:

> the draft legislation introduces a difference in treatment between litigants depending on whether or not they have access to an internet network, a connection of sufficient technical quality to this network and the computer equipment to enable effective and efficient use of videoconferencing in accordance with the 'practical arrangements' to be specified later by the King.
>
> In these conditions, some litigants could find themselves in situations where they are unable to appear by videoconference or are obliged to do so under unacceptable technical conditions.
>
> It is the duty of the author of the draft legislation to take into account, by means of accompanying measures, the situation of litigants who currently do not have access to the Internet or who do not have technical equipment of sufficient quality to be able to appear by videoconference, otherwise there will be disproportionate effects to the detriment of certain categories of people.

It is certainly remarkable that, in a subsequent advisory opinion, the Council of State emphasised that these considerations relating to the digital divide and the need to take accompanying measures, can be applied even when the litigant is not a natural person but a legal entity. Indeed, according to advisory opinion no. 74.291/1-2-3 (Council of State, 2023a) people who are digitally disadvantaged "may be the organs of legal entities, particularly when these are small or even one-person entities".

Additionally, in the case law of both the Constitutional Court and the Council of State, the accompanying measures required under the prohibition of indirect discrimination must remain "reasonable and proportionate". This requirement needs a contextual assessment.[9] One key to analysis may lie in whether we are dealing with the public or private sector: it is indeed reasonable to expect more from a public actor than from a private one (Langlois & Van Drooghenbroeck, 2023). However, this first "organic" criterion still needs to be refined in the light of the possibly essential nature of the service provided by the private actor, which may justify a heavier "burden". This seems to be the conclusion of an advisory opinion issued by the Legislation Section on 23 June 2023 (Council of State, 2023c). The main purpose of the proposed draft law was to require financial institutions to guarantee "sufficient access, throughout the country, to basic non-digital financial payment services (…)". In the idea of the MPs who drafted the bill, this accessibility should entail "collectively guaranteeing that ATMs, self-banking machines and systems for printing bank statements are spread throughout the country at a minimum level". According to the Council of State, such an obligation does restrict the freedom of enterprise of the establishments concerned. However, this restriction was admissible in the view of the Council. Firstly, it pursues a legitimate aim of "consumer protection" and "combating the digital divide in the banking sector". With regard to proportionality, the advisory opinion states that "even if it does not fall within the scope of the public service, the profession of banker is nevertheless exercised in a context of general interest". The Legislation Section therefore concludes that

> (t)aking into account the 'digital divide' within society and the fact that not everyone has equal access to information technology, the obligations imposed on credit institutions by the proposal under consideration can be analysed as support measures for the digitally disadvantaged.

According to the Council, however, it is important that when defining the concrete measures for implementing the law, the King should "ensure that these accompanying measures are reasonable, by balancing the interests involved".[10]

4.3 The right to inclusion for people with disability as a boost

Article 22*ter*, inserted into the Belgian Constitution in March 2021 (see Hachez, 2022), states that

> Every person with a disability has the right to full inclusion in society, including the right to reasonable accommodation.
>
> The law, federate law or rule referred to in Article 134 guarantees the protection of this right.

The preparatory work for this provision is not very precise on what it requires, and the issue of the digital divide is not mentioned (see Hachez, 2022). It is clear, however, that it can usefully be mobilised to "reinforce" the conclusions that can already be drawn from the implementation of the "general" principle of equality and non-discrimination. Article 22*ter* in fact highlights the particular need for protection of people with disabilities, and explicitly states the need to adopt reasonable accommodation measures for their benefit.

On 17 August 2023, the Legislation Section issued an advisory opinion on this subject that is of the utmost importance for the issues we are dealing with here (Council of State, 2023d). In essence, the proposed legislation aimed to further the digital transition in the functioning of public services in Brussels, and, among other things, to systematise the digitisation of online administrative procedures and communications with public authorities. The Council of State considered that in combination with Articles 10, 11 and 23[11] of the Constitution, and Articles 9, 19 and 27 of the United Nations Convention on the Rights of Persons with Disabilities, Article 22*ter* of the Constitution requires that a "non-digital alternative" to the electronic administrative procedure be provided. This alternative, in the terms of the advisory opinion, must have certain precise characteristics in order to secure its real effectiveness. Firstly, it is, in the words of Article 22*ter*, subject to a principle of legality: "the essential elements of the right to digital support and to continued interaction with an official of the public authority, such as cost, minimum quality requirements and minimum requirements in terms of timetables and proximity", must be specified in the legislative text itself. Furthermore, the alternative must be effective. In this respect, the Legislation Section does not take it for granted that, as a non-digital alternative, and in addition to organising contact by post, the public authority may choose at its discretion to organise "either a physical reception or a telephone service". According to the Council of State, "Telephone reception by definition requires access to a telephone". Consequently, it is up to the legislator to demonstrate that the open option does in fact make it possible to guarantee the desired inclusiveness and accessibility.

4.4 A new constitutional provision. And what next?

The foregoing developments show that, on the basis of existing constitutional law, a right not to use the Internet is already firmly established. At least in part: Articles 10, 11 and 22*ter* of the Constitution in any case guarantee for the people who are digitally vulnerable, in particular because of a disability, the right to obtain the necessary accompanying measures in the event of a switch to digital access to certain services.

This is not to say that the insertion of a new, autonomous provision dedicated to the right not to use the Internet would be superfluous and deprived of any legal relevancy. A constitutional "insistence" can, beyond its purely symbolic dimension, affirm the Constituent's attachment to the protection of certain values and interests, and give them more "weight"[12] in the balance when they are opposed to other rights – for example, freedom to conduct a business. Constitutionalisation may also provide an opportunity to enshrine the other side of the right not to use the Internet – i.e., the right to access the Internet – which, in its social dimension, is also essential to effectively combating the negative effect of the digital divide.

Finally, the insertion of a new constitutional provision would be an opportunity to enrich the right not to use the Internet. It could no longer relate solely to the issue of accompanying measures for victims of the digital divide, but could be extended to new dimensions, such as the right to disconnect. The "right to disconnect" was introduced into Belgian labour law (private sector) by a law of 3 October 2022. Essentially, it is the right for workers not to be connected to professional digital tools (mobile phones, smartphones, PCs, email, etc.) outside of their working hours. Constitutionalising this right to disconnect would likely give it more substance and ensure a common baseline of guarantees for all Belgian workers – whether they belong to the private or public sector (federal, community, regional, provincial, municipal).

What is important, however, is to realise that, even with the insertion of a new constitutional provision dedicated to it, the guarantee of the right not to use the Internet, particularly in its dimension of protecting the victims of the digital divide, cannot be concrete and effective without any supplementary legislative implementation.

In this respect, the existence of appropriate and robust anti-discrimination legislation seems essential, in particular to ensure the enforceability of the right to accompanying measures in the "horizontal" relationships that develop between the victims of the digital divide on the one hand and private suppliers of goods and services on the other. In a previous contribution (Langlois & Van Drooghenbroeck, 2023), we attempted to show that Belgian anti-discrimination legislation, both federal and federated, offers a relatively effective – but still virtual at this stage[13] – tool for combating the discriminatory consequences of the digital divide thanks to its broad scope *ratione materiae* and *ratione personae*. A recent reform of this legislation has further enhanced this potential, in two respects. Firstly, the legislation now includes a ban on discrimination on the basis of "social condition", which includes a major vector of digital vulnerability.[14] Secondly, the amended legislation now explicitly authorises the competent judge to issue "positive injunctions".[15] These are better adapted and more refined tools than outright bans for preserving the "best" of digitisation while correcting its undesired discriminatory effects through targeted accompanying measures.

4.5 Conclusions

One final comment remains to be made. The assistance of the law and the Constitution is essential to guarantee a "non-digital" alternative or accompanying measures for those who, for reasons such as age or disability, are unable to handle all the consequences of the increasing digitalisation of the supply of goods and services and contacts with the authorities. However, the purpose of the right not to use the Internet should not be to create, and even to legitimise, a structural situation of dualisation or digital segregation, condemning for all eternity the victims of the digital divide to the use of alternatives and to begging for assistance. Still striving for effectiveness, positive measures must be associated with the new constitutional right, not only to effectively *counter the negative consequences* of the digital divide, but also to *reduce the divide* itself. Those who "unwillingly" benefit from the *right not to use the Internet* must also be able to benefit from the *right to use the Internet*. Victims of the digital divide must ultimately have the right to ask for positive measures which will assist in overcoming this divide.

This is where the difficulty arises. It is illusory to think that global and structural solutions to a problem as complex and "multi-polar" in terms of origins, as that of reducing the digital divide, can be obtained solely on the basis of anti-discrimination law, even if it is revitalised. This is particularly the case in the Belgian federal design. The fight against discrimination is in fact a competence shared between the Federal State, the Communities and the Regions: in principle, it is up to these authorities, and them alone, to put in place anti-discrimination measures in their areas of competence, and only in those areas. Each entity acts for itself, exclusively.

However, none of the legislators (federal or federated) responsible for combating discrimination has, on its own, all the competences needed to build a coherent and comprehensive solution to the problem of the digital divide in the areas for which it is responsible. As evidence of this, we refer to the advisory opinion no. 34.380/VR issued on 21 November 2002 by the Legislation Section of the Council of State (Council of State, 2002). In essence, the draft legislation under review was designed to grant, *via La Poste* (Belgian postal service), a subsidy to certain groups of disadvantaged people in order to provide them with access, on favourable conditions, to an Internet connection and, where appropriate, a computer interface. It aims at promoting access to communication, to resources promoted in particular with a view to e-government, and to the employment market in the context of teleworking. In this case, however, the Council of State concluded that the federal authority did not have all the necessary competence to grant such a subsidy.

In federal Belgium, reducing the digital divide (in the same way as the fight against climate change (El Berhoumi & Nennen, 2018), the fight against poverty, or the fight against the pandemic (El Berhoumi, Losseau & Van Drooghenbroeck, 2021)) is the responsibility of no one in particular, and of everyone in general: only a cooperation agreement, rather than unilateral initiatives in a scattered order, will make it possible to tackle this issue in any meaningful way.

Notes

1 The authors speak strictly in their personal capacity. Unless specified otherwise, all translations from French are made by the authors. All decisions of the Belgian *Conseil d'Etat* are available on their official website at www.raadvst-consetat.be.

2 See Article 195 of the Belgian Constitution:

> The federal legislative power has the right to declare that there are reasons to revise such constitutional provision as it determines.
>
> Following such a declaration, the two Houses are automatically dissolved.
>
> Two new Houses are then convened, in accordance with Article 46.
>
> These Houses make decisions, in common accord with the King, on the points submitted for revision.

> In this case, the Houses can only debate provided that at least two thirds of the members who make up each House are present; and no change is adopted unless it is supported by at least two thirds of the votes cast.
>
> (translation available on www.dekamer.be)

3 The Belgian Council of State, like many of its European counterparts, has two functions (article 160 of the Constitution): a jurisdictional function, performed by the Administrative Litigation Section, and an advisory function, performed by the Legislation Section. This latter function consists of issuing advisory opinions to the authority on draft legislation submitted to it by the latter: proposals or drafts of laws, decrees or orders; draft decrees of federal, community or regional executives of a regulatory nature (i.e., general and abstract).

4 This definition is reconstructed on the basis of those provided by the European directives adopted on the basis of Article 19 TFEU. See for example art. 2 (2) b of the Council Directive 2000/78/EC of 27 November 2000 establishing a general framework for equal treatment in employment and occupation:

> indirect discrimination shall be taken to occur where an apparently neutral provision, criterion or practice would put persons having a particular religion or belief, a particular disability, a particular age, or a particular sexual orientation at a particular disadvantage compared with other persons.

5 Previously, any citizen could subscribe to the *Moniteur belge* for a fee. They could also consult it at a subscribed public library. As part of the 2002 reform, only three paper copies are maintained. The first copy is deposited with the Royal Library of Belgium; a second copy is kept with the Minister of Justice; and the last copy remains with the Directorate of the *Moniteur belge*, where it is available for consultation by any interested party.

6 See also, still on the subject of the publication of normative texts, Council of State, Advisory opinion no 69.024/2-3, 19 March 2021 and Council of State, Advisory opinion no 75.§11/4, 15 April 2024.

7 Under Belgian federalism, the Communities are responsible for education (article 127 of the Constitution).

8 A fully digital file is created for each pupil. It includes information about the pupil's school career – including changes of school – and the support measures that have been put in place for them. It can be accessed by members of the educational teams responsible for the pupil, as well as the pupil's parents.

9 It should be noted that, in some cases, the Legislation Section recognises the limits of its *ex ante* control in deciding whether the accompanying measures already envisaged by the draft legislation will be sufficient, in terms of effectiveness, to adequately compensate for the disadvantages created to the detriment of the victims of the electronic divide. See Council of State, Advisory opinion no 76.470/1, 11 June 2024; Advisory opinion no 76.427/1, 6 June 2024.

10 Council of State, Advisory opinion no 76.470/1, 11 June 2024; Advisory opinion no 76.427/1, 6 June 2024.

11 Article 23 of the Constitution recognises that everyone the right to lead a life in keeping with human dignity. Paragraph 3, 2°, 3° and 5° of the said provision precises that this right includes in particular: the right to social security; the right to healthcare and to social, medical and legal aid; the right to adequate housing; and the right to cultural and social development. According to the Council of State, "(a)ll of these rights, especially for a public that is more vulnerable because of disability, age, gender, wealth or social

origin, are often based on access to administrative procedures or communication with public authorities" (Council of State, Advisory opinion no 74001/2, 17 August 2023).

12 See, by analogy, Constitutional Court, no 159/2004, 20 October 2004, B.5.6, where the Constitutional Court deduced from Articles 10(3) and 11*bis* of the Constitution that the Constitution "attaches particular importance to equality between men and women" (own translation).

13 To our knowledge, there has not yet been any specific judicial application of this legislation in the fight against the negative effects of the digital divide. However, mention should be made of a legal procedure introduced by UNIA (Belgian Equality Body) and a consumer rights organisation (Test-Achats) against *Société Nationale des Chemins de Fer Belge* (SNCB). The aim of this procedure is to have the fact that certain products or advantageous fares can only be acquired or obtained *via* the SNCB's digital application (and not *via* ticket offices and digital terminals), which necessarily requires the possession of a smartphone, declared as discriminatory. See UNIA, "Testsachats et Unia s'opposent aux tarifs discriminatoires de la SNCB", 16 July 2024, available on www.unia.be.

14 See Article 4(4) of the Federal law of 10 May 2007 "pertaining to fight certain forms of discrimination" by the Federal Act of 28 June 2023 (OJ (*Moniteur belge*), 20 July 2023. See also Article 4, 12° of the Joint Decree and Ordinance of the Brussels-Capital Region, the Joint Community Commission and the French Community Commission of 4 April 2024 establishing the Brussels Code on Equality, Non-Discrimination and the Promotion of Diversity (*Moniteur belge,* 16 April 2024). In its *Opinion on the impact of the digitalisation of services (public or private)* (February 2023), Unia also recommended that "illiteracy" be explicitly included in the list of criteria protected by law. This suggestion has not been followed yet.

15 The possibility of "positive injunction" has been introduced in the Federal law of 10 May 2007 "pertaining to fight certain forms of discrimination" by the Federal Act of 28 June 2023 (*OJ (Moniteur belge*), 20 July 2023), following a recommendation of the Final Report of the Expert Commission for the Assessment of the 2007 Anti-Discrimination Federal Acts (see https://equal.belgium.be/sites/default/files/Commission%20e%CC%81val%20lois%20antidiscrimination_Rapport_Synthe%CC%80se.pdf, pp. 134–136). The possibility to issue "positive injunction" has also been introduced in the anti-discrimination law of some federated entities. See for example article 20, § 2/1 of the Decree of 6 November 2008 on the fight against certain forms of discrimination (Walloon Region), as modified by a decree of the Walloon Region of 13 July 2023 (*Moniteur belge,* 14 September 2023); article 41, § 1, of the Joint Decree and Ordinance of the Brussels-Capital Region, the Joint Community Commission and the French Community Commission of 4 April 2024 establishing the Brussels Code on Equality, Non-Discrimination and the Promotion of Diversity (*Moniteur belge,* 16 April 2024).

Bibliography

Books, Journals, Reports

Degrave, E., "Elise Degrave: 'Inscrivons dans la Constitution le droit de ne pas utiliser internet'", *Le Soir,* 21 April 2024.

Degrave, E., "Justice sociale et services publics numériques: pour un droit fondamental d'utiliser – ou non – internet", *Revue belge de droit constitutionnel*, 2023, 212 –244.

El Berhoumi, M., Losseau, L., and Van Drooghenbroeck, S., "Le fédéralisme belge ne connaît pas la crise: la gestion de la pandémie du Covid-19 à l'épreuve de la répartition des compétences", in Frédéric Bouhon, Emmanuel Slautsky and Stéphanie Wattier (eds), *Droit public et Covid-19* (Bruxelles: Larcier, 2021), 183–241.

El Berhoumi, M., and Nennen, C, "La changement climatique à l'épreuve du fédéralisme", *Amén.*, 2018/4, 62.

Hachez, I., "La consécration constitutionnelle du droit à l'inclusion des personnes en situation de handicap (article 22*ter*). De la duplication du cadre juridique au dessin de politiques publiques", *Journal des Tribunaux*, 2022, 17–24.

King Baudouin Foundation, *Baromètre de l'inclusion numérique* 2022, https://kbs-frb.be/fr/barometre-inclusion-numerique-2022.

King Baudouin Foundation, press release of 14 June 2024, « Quatre belges sur 10 toujours à risque d'exclusion numérique », available on https://kbs-frb.be/fr/quatre-belges-sur-dix-toujours-risque-dexclusion-numerique.

Kloza, D., "The right not to use the internet", *Computer Law & Security Review*, 52 (2024), 105907.

Langlois, C., and Van Drooghenbroeck, S., "Digitalisation et discrimination: enjeux d'une rencontre, agenda d'une réforme", in Julie Ringelheim, et al. (eds), *Een hernieuwde impuls voor de strijd tegen discriminatie/Redynamiser la lutte contre la discrimination* (Brussel: Intersentia, 2023), 48–55.

UNIA, *Avis relatif à l'impact de la digitalisation des services (publics ou privés)*, 3 February 2023, www.unia.be.

Case Law

BELGIAN CONSTITUTIONAL COURT

Const. Court, Judgement no. 106/2004, 16 June 2004.
Const. Court, Judgement no. 10/2007, 17 January 2007.

COUNCIL OF STATE

Council of State, Advisory opinion no 34.380/VR, 21 November 2002.
Council of State, Advisory opinion no 58.416/2-3, 11 December 2015.
Council of State, Advisory opinion no 71731/2, 1 August 2022.
Council of State, Advisory opinion no 72891/1-2, 24 March 2023 (a).
Council of State, Advisory opinion no. 73.507/2, 5 June 2023 (b).
Council of State, Advisory opinion no 73695/2, 23 June 2023 (c).
Council of State, Advisory opinion no 74001/2, 17 August 2023 (d).
Council of State, Advisory opinion no 74.634/4, 6 November 2023 (e).

EUROPEAN COURT OF HUMAN RIGHTS

ECHR, app. No. 6289/73, *Airey v. Ireland,* 9 October 1979, § 24.

Legislation

Declaration of revision of the Constitution, *Moniteur belge,* 27 May 2024.

5 Is there a right to be offline "for no reason" in France?[1]

Julien Rossi

5.1 Introduction: using the Internet is no longer a free choice in France

Registering for school. Applying for university. Driving home. Watching television. Paying taxes. Making a medical appointment. Buying a train ticket. Retiring. Some of these tasks are casual, everyday occurrences. Others are life-defining. They all have one thing in common: it is becoming more and more difficult to be able to do them without being online. Think of all the administrative procedures that have turned online-only. Or all of the everyday items that are now connected by default. Whereas we used to oppose the "online life" with "real life", both realms become increasingly intertwined. Given the context of surveillance capitalism (Zuboff, 2018) that we live in, it may give rise to a sense of unease. As the Web has become apparently overwhelmed by "toxic" content (Chavalarias, 2022) and social media are victim of what Cory Doctorow has so poetically dubbed a process of "enshittification" (Doctorow, 2022), the initial enthusiasm for the promised wonders of "Cyberspace" has waned. Félix Tréguer (2019) concludes his book on the "fallen Utopia" of the Internet by a surprising question: should we destroy computers? The question is provocative in nature. It hints back at much older – and now almost-forgotten – debates on whether or not computers could be anything else than massive infrastructures of social control, that date back to the 1980s, and which, at the time, contributed significantly to the push for the advent of data protection (Miller, 1971; Vitalis, 1988). Thus framed, the right to live out of the watchful eye of smart devices, tracker-infused web browsers and operating systems that bully users into activating telemetry and being always authenticated, appears to be heavily intertwined with the right to privacy, which is a "right to be let alone" (Warren & Brandeis, 1890).

In France, according to a survey published in 2023 conducted by the Centre for the Study and Observation of Living Conditions (*Centre de Recherche pour l'Étude et l'Observation des Conditions de Vie* – CREDOC), in 2022, about 8% of French residents still do not use the Internet at all. This amounted to almost 5.5 million people based on population statistics published by the French public statistics office INSEE (*Institut National de la Statistique et des Études Économiques*). This did not concern only the elderly. Even if only 1% of people aged between 18 and 24 declare they do not use the Internet at all, that would still realistically concern

DOI: 10.4324/9781003528401-7

thousands of young individuals across the country. Yet there is a growing sense of pressure that one *has* to be online. In 2016, only 28% of respondents said they could not imagine spending more than a day without using the Internet. This rose to 58% in 2022 (CREDOC 2023, 20). This growing dependence (or at least sense of dependence) is influenced by public authorities as their services go online. In 2022, according to the same survey, 22% of the population identified the obligation to use e-administration procedures as one of the reason why they could no longer imagine living without the Internet, 6% more than in 2016 (CREDOC 2023, 21).

As the French state appears to not only encourage the use of online technology, but also force people to be online, it begs the question of whether there is still some room left for those who – by choice or otherwise – wish to live their life offline. In 2023, Genevan citizens voted to recognise the right to an offline life to become a part of their constitution (Zaïbi, 2023), on the grounds that this was necessary to the protect the dignity of the human being and their "digital integrity".[2] What is the situation in France?

A lot is to be said about the study of the harms caused by forcing people into living their lives online (Aouici & Peyrache, 2021; Brotcorne et al., 2019; Deville, 2018). It is also important to have a discussion on the whether it is really *desirable* to allow individuals to object to using online tools, even when they can. These matters are discussed elsewhere in this book. Here, our focus is going to be on one specific question: can public authorities force someone to use the Internet in France? To answer it, we will need to look into two separate questions: can I opt out of the use of *non-compliant* information technology (IT) services? And could I refuse to use *perfectly compliant* technology just because I do not want to use it, without providing any justification? We shall examine this question from the perspective of existing applicable law, taking into account both European and national normative acts and jurisprudence. Given that – unlike in the constitutional amendment recently adopted in Geneva – there is no provision in French law explicitly providing for a right to be offline, we will closely examine two related rights to see whether it can be derived from them: the right to non-discrimination, and the right to privacy. As we shall see, in France, there is only a right to an offline alternative under certain circumstances. A negative consequence that arises from this restriction is that in practice, it places the burden to prove their need for such an alternative on people who require it.

5.2 The right to non-discrimination and the right to be offline

The obligation to use computers creates new forms of inequalities. In an incident which made the headlines in France in 2019, an elderly and visually impaired priest was fined 100€ for boarding the train without a ticket (France Bleu Besançon, 2019). He had not been able to buy a ticket from a ticket office, because they were closed. Due to his handicap, he was not able to buy his ticket using the dedicated app, and SNCF (*Société Nationale des Chemins de Fer*), the state-owned railway company, had recently decided to stop selling tickets onboard. When the priest told the conductor he wanted to buy a ticket, the latter told him he had no choice but to fine him. The shift to online-only public services also puts many people – especially, but not only, the elderly – at high risk of renouncing their rights or having to rely on the assistance of relatives. According to a study conducted by Aouici and Peyrache (2021) based on internal data from the French public retirement fund (*Caisse nationale d'assurance vieillesse*), in 2020, up to 74% of retired people in France were unable to use the Internet to complete online procedures.

Article 14 of the European Convention on Human Rights (ECHR) prohibits discriminations in the enjoyment of fundamental rights. Disability is one of the grounds under which this article prohibits discrimination.[3] In order to ensure that disabled persons are not barred from accessing online public services, the European Union's (EU) Web Accessibility Directive[4] provides that "websites, independently of the device used for access thereto, and mobile applications of public sector bodies meet the accessibility requirements" (art. 1(2) of the said directive). It does so by imposing accessibility guidelines standardised by the European Telecommunications Standards Institute (ETSI).[5] Such an obligation has existed in France for public service bodies ever since a 2005 law on equality of rights,[6] which is supposed to impose the implementation of certain accessibility standards for e-administration services, as well as only communication services provided by companies with an annual turnover higher than 250 million euros.[7] Yet French online public services are still notoriously inaccessible. For example, when in 2022, the French government launched *Mon Espace Santé* (My Health Space), a new online application giving access to one's health data in a centralised manner and sharing it with health professionals, it did not comply with legally mandated accessibility guidelines. As of the 10 April 2024, at the time of writing, this crucial service was still "partially non-compliant" with accessibility guidelines according to its own official website.[8] Even though the government recently adopted a legislative order (*ordonnance*) giving the Regulatory Authority for Audiovisual and Digital Communication (ARCOM), France's soon-to-be Digital Services Coordinator under the Digital Services Act, the power of imposing a fine up to 50,000€ to public bodies that do not implement digital accessibility standards, change is not going to be instantaneous and the current situation is that of online public services that are largely non-compliant with the law. Under these circumstances, can people who cannot use inaccessible online public services access offline alternatives?

In 2022 and 2024, the French State Council (*Conseil d'État*), which is the highest court for of the administrative order, ruled on two cases which involved the absence of an offline alternative to online public administration procedures.

The first case concerned a decree and two orders adopted by the French government in 2021,[9] challenged by several non-governmental organisations (NGOs), which imposed the use of an online-only procedure to foreign applicants to residence permits. In a decision issued on the 3 July 2022,[10] the judges of the State Council found that the government had, in principle, a right to impose the use of an online tool for administrative procedures, without involving the Parliament in such a decision. They stated that no national or supranational norm, not even article 14 of the ECHR, forbid the executive from imposing the use of online administration.[11] However, this can *only* be allowed "under the condition that public service users are allowed normal access and able to exercise their rights".[12] The administration must therefore provide "support for people who do not possess the necessary digital equipment or experience difficulties in their use or in the accomplishment of administrative procedures",[13] as well as an alternative solution "for cases where certain users would find it impossible to use the online procedure despite this support, due to reasons arising from the design of the tool or its functioning".[14] In the case at hand, the government's decision to force applicants for residency permits was deemed illegal because the impugned decree and executive orders provided neither support nor alternative solutions for people who, due to their individual circumstances and the design of the digital tool, were unable to complete the online procedure.[15]

Given that in April 2024, almost two years after this ruling, the website where foreigners can apply for residence permit in France was still only about 60% compliant with accessibility standards, we may safely conclude that the state has to provide online alternatives at least to people who are unable to use the service because of this non-compliance.[16] On the 9th of April 2024, even the French State Council's website stated that it was only partially compliant with accessibility guidelines.[17]

In January 2024, the same State Council issued a decision on a similar case. Article 1045-1 of the Code of Civil Procedure,[18] created by article 2 of a 2022 Decree,[19] mandated the provision of a valid e-mail address to complete the procedure one must follow to be naturalised as a French citizen. Here the court ruled that:

> [...] by forcing applicants to a nationality certificate to provide an e-mail address for the reception of information and documents sent by the court services [...] without providing, as a substitution, the possibility, for the applicant who proves that he is not capable to access an electronic mail service [...], to indicate a postal address, the impugned decree creates an obstacle to the normal access of users to public services and infringes on the effective exercise of the rights of the concerned people.[20]

It must be noted here that this decree had been adopted two weeks after the previously discussed 2022 *Conseil d'État* ruling. This means that either the government failed to understand its implications, or decided to ignore them and continue to push its agenda of switching everything to online administration. However, although *de facto*, the French administration appears (thus far) to ignore the decisions of the State Council, *de jure*, based on general principles of non-discrimination and the right to equal access public services, there is a right to an offline substitute when, on a case-by-case basis, individuals can prove that they cannot complete an online procedure. This may be either because, despite the assistance provided by the state, they are unable to do so, or because the online procedure is designed in a way that cannot take into account the particular situation of an individual user. This means that, in practice, law-abiding public service providers, can never, in France, close down all their brick-and-mortar counters, as they must keep them operational to handle all the cases where, due to the reasons stated previously, they *must* provide an offline alternative. This may remain the case even once all services become compliant with legal accessibility requirements, given that even then, there may be no full-proof guarantee that *all* the needs of every single user can be met using a digital procedure. There is, however, no *general* right to an offline alternative based on non-discrimination law in France, because one can only request it when able to prove it is impossible to complete an online procedure due to specific individual circumstances. It is therefore worth examining whether right to privacy and the right to the protection of personal data may be better-suited to offer such a general right to be offline, especially due to the pervasiveness of surveillance technology embedded in most online services, and also due to the relation of these rights to broader considerations on human dignity and autonomy.

5.3 The right to object to illegal personal data processing operations

Under the French fundamental law, as interpreted by the Constitutional Council, the right to privacy is derived from article 2 of the 1789 Declaration of the Rights of Man and of the Citizen,[21] which itself is appended to the Constitution of the Fifth Republic. It is also protected under article 8 of the ECHR, to which, given it is an international treaty ratified by France and based on article 55 of the Constitution, all national legislation must comply. This also covers the right to the protection of personal data, which also enjoys autonomous protection under article 8 of the EU's Charter of fundamental rights, which is legally binding in France whenever applying EU law. The practical provisions are laid down in the EU's General Data Protection Regulation (GDPR)[22] and in the regularly updated 1978 French Informatics and Freedom Act,[23] completed by provisions laid down in the Criminal Code.[24]

Let us first examine whether there is a right to object to being online when it involves being subjected to unlawful personal data protection operations, and then what happens in an ideal and somewhat utopian scenario where the IT environment is fully compliant with privacy and data protection law.

As reminded by Karaboga et al.:

> in a world of automated data processing, being offline is the most genuine form of the right to respect of private life with regard to data protection [...]. So to speak, it is the 'default setting'. Any changes to the 'default' need justification.
> (Karaboga, 2018, p. 43)

Indeed, two of the key principles of data protection, as provided in article 5 of the GDPR and in other international instruments, such as the Convention 108 of the Council of Europe, are data minimisation and purpose limitation, which, in a nutshell, can be summarised as a mandate to respect the principle of proportionality (De Marco, 2018). Following this principle, a data controller must always prefer the least-invasive solution, or at least provide it as an alternative to a more data-hungry offer which can be proposed to a data subject. In cases where a given processing operation, like a new online public procedure, may, if incorrectly implemented, present a high risk for the rights and freedoms of natural persons, then there is an obligation to conduct a data protection impact assessment. Given the nature and the scope of online public services, they almost always do. In 2022, the *Commission nationale de l'informatique et des libertés* (CNIL), France's data protection authority, found the impact assessment of a government application allowing French retirement beneficiaries living abroad to prove their continued existence to be lacking, and pointed out that the Ministry of Health should provide information to its users telling them that using this application is just an option, and that there are offline alternatives that they can use. This, however, was motivated at least as much by the right to non-discrimination (on the basis of age and/or health) as by the rights to privacy and data protection.[25]

Generally speaking, whenever the processing of personal data is not lawful, data subjects enjoy a right to object by demanding the erasure of the said data (under article 17 (1) (d) of the GDPR). It may however be difficult to exercise it in practice. For example, cafeterias run by student welfare offices called *Centres régionaux des œuvres universitaires et scolaires* (CROUS), which are state-controlled public service providers, often forbid their users to pay using cash, thus forcing them to choose between using payment cards – which create new data flows towards payment institutions or banks that are not strictly necessary – or a digital application called Izly, operated by S-Money, a subsidiary of Natixis, which is a major private banking institution. This prevents cafeteria users from choosing not to generate data on their purchase. Not only is refusing cash forbidden unless a specific exception applies, such as payments above 1,000€,[26] but in 2017, journalists also found out that the mobile application that can be used to manage Izly accounts was snooping illegally on the location of its users for advertising purposes (Untersinger, 2017). More recently, the introduction of a new digital identity scheme called FranceConnect+ forced individuals wanting to access certain online procedures, such as those related to their continued education funds (*compte personnel de formation*), to use an application developed by the postal service which only worked on Android and iOS devices. This is viewed by the administration as a security feature.[27] This forced people to accept the use of such an application, either on their own devices or on a device held by a postal office worker, even despite the fact that both operating systems have been criticised for their improper compliance with data protection law.[28] Google has even been fined twice already by the CNIL for the illegal data protection practices of their operating system, including a 50 million euro fine for illegal ad targeting on Android.[29] Even assuming that Google's and Apple's services are now fully compliant – and they might or might not be, this chapter is not making any claims on this topic – the point is that forcing people into using certain applications to access essential public services effectively renders them unable to object to their use should they at some point be noncompliant. Given the history of Big Tech providers, it would not be a huge stretch of the imagination that, at some point, they might. Furthermore, by forcing people into using services that process personal data in order to be able to access certain public services, the state effectively becomes a joint controller, in this case, with not only *La Poste* (which provides the only e-ID scheme currently recognised under FranceConnect+) but also Google and Apple.[30] This may have consequences for the state as it would share the responsibility of non-compliance with them.

Of course, just because a procedure or a service is offered online does not mean that it collects more data than necessary, or more data than an offline alternative. Data collected offline can be processed manually, or entered into a database. Contrary to popular belief, not *all* websites collect data on their users. From a technical standpoint, the only personal data necessary to establish a connection and give a user access to content is an IP address, but it needs not be stored for longer than the said connection, and in many cases, the vast majority of website operators will never be able to identify a user from just that piece of information. However, mobile applications and services often rely on an underlying technical architecture that is not necessarily compliant with all other data protection requirements.

Let's imagine, for example, that a publicly owned train operator – like, in France, the SNCF – forces some of its users living near small remote stations without physical offices, to use its website or mobile application to buy tickets. And let's imagine a not-so-far-fetched scenario in which they contain trackers and rely on an underlying infrastructure that is not fully compliant with data protection law. Given that under article L1111-1 of the Transportation Code:

> the organisation of transportation on the whole territory must satisfy the needs of users and make effective everyone's right to move around freely and to choose one's means of transportation, including for those whose mobility is reduced or who suffer from a handicap.[31]

it follows that, in this scenario, the public transport provider forces people who want to access a public service to be subjected to a violation of their rights. If this transporter is a private person (e.g., a competitor to the SNCF), then, still, refusing to sell a consumer a good or a service for an illegitimate reason (like the refusal to use non-compliant software) is forbidden according to the Consumer Protection Code.[32] In this scenario, one should, *de jure*, be able to object to the processing of their personal data in an illegal manner and be offered a compliant alternative, which would most likely have to be offline. In practice, however, public transport users do not have a real choice.

To date, French courts have not dealt with the issue, but it does appear quite clearly that there is indeed a *de jure* right to object to the use of online tools imposed by public authorities whenever they are unable to prove compliance with all applicable data protection rules. In practice, however, the burden of proof lies heavily on the data subjects' shoulders, who need to litigate to demand an offline alternative and would be asked to argue why they have genuine cause to believe the service they are asked to use is non-compliant. A more useful way to object to being bullied into using online services that violate data protection laws would be to have a general right to be offline.

5.4 Privacy, dignity and the right to offline alternatives

The right to privacy been criticised by some as designating a bunch of unrelated rights that were already protected before its recognition, such as the right to private property, the right to be protected against slander, and other personal rights (Thomson, 1975). Although it does indeed cover a very diverse range of situations – i.e., not only data privacy but also reproductive rights, and the right to a family life – these are all grounded in the need to protect human autonomy (Westin, 1967), making it a coherent category of fundamental rights, as recognised by the countries (including France) that have ratified the ECHR. Under the terms of article 8 of this convention, the right to privacy may only be restricted when "necessary in a democratic society". Despite the French government's tendency to believe that it can disregard the European Court of Human Rights' (ECtHR) rulings, French courts also apply the convention and are able to resist such wild fantasies (Van Drooghenbroeck, 2024). Given that the right to privacy "can embrace multiple aspects of the person's physical and social identity"[33] and includes the right to personal development as well as to develop contacts with other human beings, it could be interpreted as covering a right to offline life. It can indeed be framed as a desire for personal autonomy – especially in the context of surveillance capitalism (Zuboff, 2018). Whether it is indeed covered by the convention is still an open question, as neither the ECtHR nor any French court has, to date, ruled on this issue. It is still worth exploring this possibility by following reasoning applied to previous cases on the right to privacy.

The French Constitutional Council found as early as 2009 that the freedom of expression protected under article 11 of the Declaration of the Rights of Man and of the Citizen encompasses the right to access the Internet, which can only be restricted by an independent judge.[34] The ECtHR came to similar conclusions a few years later, based on article 10 of the Convention.[35] Sometimes, the exercise of a right is not an option. This is the case with schooling, which is both a right under article 13 of the Preamble of the 1946 Constitution, and an obligation imposed on children. Other times, there is also a right not to exercise the said right. The ECtHR has, for example, ruled that trade union membership could not be compulsory, given that article 11 of the ECHR also encompasses a "negative right of association".[36] Can there be a "negative right to freedom of expression exercised by accessing the Internet" justified under article 8 of the ECHR? And if so, would it be a general right going beyond a right to an offline alternative in certain specific situations?

Very often, the court in Strasbourg has ruled in favour of protecting the right of individuals to make their own choices with regard to their private life. For example, on the right to choose one's appearance, this court has ruled that Lithuania could not ban prisoners from growing beards.[37] It

> consider[ed] that the applicant's decision on whether or not to grow a beard was related to the expression of his personality and individual identity, protected by Article 8 of the Convention, and that the Government has failed to demonstrate

> the existence of a pressing social need to justify an absolute prohibition on him growing a beard while he was in prison.[38]

Furthermore, in *SAS v. France*, it ruled that

> criminalisation of the wearing of a full-face veil is a measure which is disproportionate to the aim of protecting the idea of "living together" – an aim which cannot readily be reconciled with the Convention's restrictive catalogue of grounds for interference with basic human rights.[39]

But there have also been times when the ECtHR found that the state had a right to limit the right to privacy. In *Gough v. the United Kingdom*, the Court decided that the state could force someone to wear clothes in public (even if in principle one should be free to choose one's appearance),[40] and in *Stevens v. United Kingdom*, it stated that one does not have a right to refuse wearing a school uniform where it is legally mandated.[41] Even state surveillance[42] or the surveillance of employees[43] can at times be necessary and proportionate. An infringement must also reach a certain degree of seriousness before it is deemed a violation of Convention. In *Diana Vučina v. Croatia*, for example, the Court found that:

> although [it] accept[ed] that the erroneous placement of the name of the Mayor's wife next to her photograph might have caused some distress to the applicant, the level of seriousness associated with that erroneous labelling of her photograph and the inconvenience that she suffered do not give rise to an issue – neither in the context of the protection of her image nor her honour and reputation [...] – under Article 8 of the Convention.[44]

Assuming that a state which is party to the ECHR (such as France) imposes the use of the Internet (i.a. to complete administrative procedures) in a way that is indeed prescribed by law and pursues a legitimate public interest (e.g., in pursuit of the "economic wellbeing of the country" assuming it can indeed be proven to effectively reduce the costs of public administration), then in order to establish that forcing one to the use the Internet is a breach of article 8, we need to prove that:

1. forcing one to use the Internet is indeed a limitation of one's right to privacy,
2. even if it is prescribed by law, it is either not necessary or not proportionate or both.

On the first point, it should be noted once again that the right to privacy is very broad. It includes even the right to apply for adoption,[45] reproductive rights – including the right not to have children[46] but only going as far as to cover abortion for health reasons,[47] or sexual orientation and sexual life.[48] All share the purpose of safeguarding human dignity and autonomy, which are necessary conditions for the development of one's welfare (Moore, 2003; Westin, 1967; Whitman, 2004). Although there has not yet been any case, to date and to my knowledge, on the right to be offline, one case on the right to beg can offer – in my opinion – a blueprint to examine the extent to which article 8 ECHR could be extended to protect offline life.

In *Lacatus v. Switzerland*[49] the Court ruled that the applicant, who was illiterate and came from a very poor background, could not be deprived from her right to beg people in the street for help, as that would seriously compromise her means of survival, and therefore her dignity.[50] It also declared that, given the circumstances of the applicant, depriving her of the possibility to ask for assistance would infringe on her right to personal development, which is also covered by article 8 ECHR.[51] Being barred from access to essential public services would also prevent someone from essential conditions for personal development and it would also similarly go against principles of human dignity. This case is relevant for the subject matter of this book, because following this reasoning, it is easy to make the point that forcing one to use the Internet violates the right to privacy, given that refusing means being deprived from services that are essential for one's dignity, personal development and, at times, survival (in cases where one is deprived from social security, education or other essential public services if refusing the use of the Internet). The first condition we set out is therefore fulfilled.

With regard to the second condition, it should however be noted that in the Lacatus decision, the ECtHR emphasised the particular situation of the applicant. It did not rule that there is a general right to beg in public spaces. There is only protection for people who have no other means of surviving and keeping some level of personal dignity and accomplishment. Only in such cases would the Strasbourg court be likely to judge that forcing somebody to use the Internet to access certain essential services violates the right to privacy in a disproportionate manner. Applying this reasoning to previously discussed examples related to the right to be offline, we could predict that the Court would find that the fine imposed on the blind priest who was unable to buy a ticket online and was not offered any alternative would constitute a violation of articles 8 and 14 ECHR. If the French State Council had not ruled that foreigners wishing to apply in France should be offered an offline alternative if they find it impossible to complete the online procedure, there would probably also have been an infringement, most likely – again – of both provisions at the same time. Therefore, based on current ECtHR case law, I would argue that any argument against the obligation to use online public services based on the right to privacy is bound to bring the same results as the arguments made on the basis of non-discrimination law in front of the French State Council in the two cases that were discussed earlier. The outcome would differ only if an applicant is able to prove that the online service at hand does not comply with data protection law, based on the fact that prescribing the use of something that is illegal cannot be "prescribed by law". But the burden of proof and, more dauntingly, the burden to initiate litigation, would, in practice, still lies squarely on the applicant's shoulders.

5.5 Conclusion: there is (thus far) no autonomous right to an offline life in France

The practical difficulty encountered by people who cannot use the Internet to use online public services to access offline alternatives, or who do not wish to use a piece of software they suspect violates their right to the protection of their personal data, pleads in favour of the recognition of a general right to an offline life, at the very least for reasons of technical practicality. However, there is no general right to an offline life in France, even in vertical relations between individuals and public services or authorities. Based on the rights to non-discrimination, data protection and privacy – encompassing the right to human dignity – there is, however, a right to an offline alternative under specific circumstances. When somebody is able to use an online public service, that person can only refuse if he or she is able to argue that the said service is illegal, for instance by alleging that it violates the GDPR. Violations of data protection law are indeed commonplace, but despite the fact the burden of proving compliance lies *de jure* on data controllers, in practice, applicants challenging the measure imposing the use of an online service would need to at least provide reasonable grounds to suspect a serious infringement for any judge to take the case seriously. Furthermore, people who use public services usually need them rather quickly. One cannot afford to wait the time it takes to bring a case to the ECtHR to be able to apply for university, ask for a driver's license or to receive one's retirement pension. Emergency procedures do exist, but they put an even greater burden on applicants to prove the urgency of their case. French courts are not easily receptive to the urgency of emergency measures to prevent violations of the right to the protection of personal data. This was illustrated in 2024, as the French State Council refused to grant an emergency ruling to stop the French government's plan to host health data on infrastructure provided by Microsoft, despite arguments highlighting the high risk that it would violate the GDPR and the very sensitive nature of the data.[52] It is possible, however, that the situation may evolve. The French State Council does already acknowledge that it is the state's duty to continue operating offline alternatives to online services for when they are required by individuals due to special circumstances. It also recently called in one of its non-binding reports for the recognition of a right for public service users to revert to a non-digital alternative to digital public services, and for the systematic existence of such offline alternatives (*Conseil d'État*, 2023, 4).

In this chapter, we only discussed whether the state could impose the use of an online service to individuals. Yet discussions on the "right to disconnect" from the workplace, recently enshrined in the French Labour Code,[53] or calls from the Austrian federal chancellor for a right to pay in cash (Hülsemann, 2023), show that the right to live offline would only be complete if there was also a positive obligation on the state to protect individuals from private persons wishing to force them online. Would this be desirable? Should an individual be free to live removed from the collective socio-technical fabric of the society where he or she lives? What would be the impacts on society? Are computers inherently tools of surveillance and control that one should be able to opt out from, or should the right to be offline remain a right to opt out only as long as it is the only way to protect oneself from intrusive technology? As discussed in this book's introduction, reflection on this topic is still relatively new, and there are no definitive answers to these questions. Although the outcome of these emerging debates cannot be predicted, we can expect further developments on this topic, both from a legal and a political perspective.

Notes

1 This chapter is derived from a working paper (Rossi, 2023) summarising exploratory research results and reflections which were presented at the *Álom és Valóság* conference at the University of Szeged on September 29, 2023. It was then presented at a workshop organised in Paris, on the 22nd of November 2023, by the Working Group on Internet Governance and Regulation of the Research Network on Internet, AI and Society of the CNRS (GDR 2091), at Université Paris 8, which in turn led to the publication of a paper written together with Dariusz Kloza (Kloza & Rossi, 2024). I would like to extend my heartfelt thanks to all the organisers and participants of these events for their invaluable input which has significantly enriched the findings presented in this chapter.

2 See: Loi constitutionnelle modifiant la constitution de la République et canton de Genève pour une protection forte de l'individu dans l'espace numérique du 22 septembre 2022.

3 See i.a. ECtHR 30 April 2009, *Glor v. Switzerland*, 13444/04, §80.

4 Directive 2016/2102/EU of the European Parliament and of the Council of 26 October 2016 on the accessibility of the websites and mobile applications of public sector bodies.

5 ETSI standard EN 301 549.

6 See article 47 of the loi n° 2005-102 du 11 février 2005 pour l'égalité des droits et des chances, la participation et la citoyenneté des personnes handicapées.

7 See article 2 of Decree nr. 2019-768.

8 See: http://web.archive.org/web/20240330212023/https://www.monespacesante.fr/accessibilite (at the time of writing, the latest archive of this webpage available on the WayBack Machine had been made on the 30th of March, 2024).

9 Décret nr. 2021-313 of 24 March 2021, Arrêté du 27 avril 2021 pris en application de l'article R. 431-2 du code de l'entrée et du séjour des étrangers et du droit d'asile relatif aux titres de séjour dont la demande s'effectue au moyen d'un téléservice, and Arrêté du 19 mai 2021 modifiant l'arrêté du 27 avril 2021 pris en application de l'article R. 431-2 du code de l'entrée et du séjour des étrangers et du droit d'asile relatif aux titres de séjour dont la demande s'effectue au moyen d'un téléservice.

10 *Conseil d'État*, 3 June 2022, decision nr. 452798, Conseil national des barreaux et autres.

11 See §8 of the decision.

12 Translated from French. Original text: "à la condition de permettre l'accès normal des usagers au service public et de garantir aux personnes concernées l'exercice effectif de leurs droits" (§9 of the decision).

13 §10 of the abovementioned decision. Translated from French. Original text: "un accompagnement les personnes qui ne disposent pas d'un accès aux outils numériques ou qui rencontrent des difficultés soit dans leur utilisation, soit dans l'accomplissement des démarches administratives".

14 §10 of the abovementioned decision. Translated from French. Original text: "[…] pour le cas où certains demandeurs se heurteraient, malgré cet accompagnement, à

l'impossibilité de recourir au téléservice pour des raisons tenant à la conception de cet outil ou à son mode de fonctionnement".

15 See §11 and 12 of the ruling.

16 On the 10th of April, 2024, the web portal where foreigners could apply for residence permits stated the following:

> The Foreigners in France portal is partly compliant with the General Framework for the Improvement of Accessibility (RGAA), version 4.0, due to the following non-compliance findings and derogations.
>
> Test Results
>
> The compliance audit realised by the CGI company reveals that 60.60% of items in the RGAA version 4.0 are correctly implemented.
>
> Translated by the author from French. Original quote:
>
> État de conformité
>
> Le portail Étrangers en France est en conformité partielle avec le référentiel général d'améloration de l'accessibilité (RGAA), version 4.0 en raison des non-conformités et dérogations énumérées ci-dessous.
>
> Résultats des tests
>
> L'audit de conformité réalisé par la société CGI révèle que 60,60% des critères du RGAA version 4.0 sont respectés.
>
> Quoted from: https://administration-etrangers-en-france.interieur.gouv.fr/particuliers/#/declaration-conformite-rgaa, on 10 April 2024. Page saved on the Internet Archive's WayBack Machine on the 12th of April: https://web.archive.org/web/20240412150514/https://administration-etrangers-en-france.interieur.gouv.fr/particuliers/#/declaration-conformite-rgaa

17 *Conseil d'État*, Déclaration d'accessibilité de Ariane Web, https://www.conseil-etat.fr/pages/declaration-d-accessibilite-de-ariane-web (accessed on the 9th of April 2024).

18 Code de la procédure civile.

19 Décret n° 2022-899 du 17 juin 2022 relatif au certificat de nationalité française.

20 *Conseil d'État*, 17 January 2024, GISTI et al., nr. 466052, §5.
Translated from French. Original text:

> [...] en exigeant d'un demandeur de certificat de nationalité qu'il indique une adresse électronique pour la réception des informations et documents qui lui seront communiqués par le greffe [...], sans prévoir, à titre de solution de substitution, la possibilité, pour le demandeur qui établit qu'il n'est pas en mesure d'accéder à une messagerie électronique [...], d'indiquer une adresse postale, le décret attaqué fait obstacle à l'accès normal des usagers au service public et porte atteinte à l'exercice effectif de leurs droits par les personnes concernées.

21 See: Cons. const., 23 July 1999, nr. 99-416 DC.

22 Regulation 2016/679/EU of the European Parliament and the Council of 27 April 2016 on the protection of natural persons with regard to the processing of personal data and on the free movement of such data, and repealing Directive 95/46/EC (General Data Protection Regulation).

23 Loi n° 78-17 du 6 janvier 1978 relative à l'informatique, aux fichiers et aux libertés.

24 See articles 226-1 to 226-7, 226-16 to 226-24, R623-4, R625-9 and R625-10 to R625-13 of the Criminal Code.

25 Délibération n° 2022-068 du 9 juin 2022 portant avis sur un projet de décret autorisant la création d'un traitement automatisé de données à caractère personnel pour le contrôle de l'existence des bénéficiaires d'une pension de vieillesse résidant à l'étranger.

26 See article R642-3 of the Code pénal, and article D112-3 of the Code monétaire et financier.

27 See the answer provided by *Mon Compte Formation* on user feedback published on a government website called Services Publics+: www.plus.transformation.gouv.fr/experiences/4468647_impossible-dacceder-au-cpf-sans-smartphone-ou-attendre-4-semaines (last accessed on the 10th of April, 2024).

28 See Leith (2021) for a recent example of a study showing privacy concerns with data management practices by both mobile operating systems. NGOs such as the Electronic Frontier Foundation have also criticised both operating systems, despite recognising some effort made to limit the invasiveness of their user tracking policies (Cyphers 2022). Making a list of press articles which – whether deservedly or not – criticise Google and Apple for the perceived lack of privacy on their mobile operating systems would be the topic of a separate article and would require additional research. However, the point here is not to assess the real compliance of these operating systems, but to stress the fact that users may be forced to use software they perceive as non-compliant if they wish to access certain essential public services.

29 CNIL, Délibération SAN-2019-001 du 21 janvier 2019, and *Conseil d'État* 19 juin 2020, Google contre CNIL, nr. 430810.

30 The ECJ has ruled in favour of an extensive understanding of joint controllership. Anyone taking part in setting the means and ends of a personal data processing operation is a joint controller. Liability under the GDPR is shared by all joint controllers, who have to sign an agreement mapping out their respective duties with regard to the processing operations and data subject rights. See: ECJ 5 June 2018 Unabhängiges Landeszentrum für Datenschutz Schleswig-Holstein contre Wirtschaftsakademie Schleswig-Holstein GmbH, C-210/16; ECJ 29 July 2019 Fashion ID GmbH & Co.KG contre Verbraucherzentrale NRW eV, C-40/17.

31 Translated from French. Original text:

> L'organisation des mobilités sur l'ensemble du territoire doit satisfaire les besoins des usagers et rendre effectifs le droit qu'a toute personne, y compris celle dont la mobilité est réduite ou souffrant d'un handicap, de se déplacer et la liberté d'en choisir les moyens […].

32 See art. L121-11 of the Code de la consommation.

33 ECtHR 4 December 2008, *S. and Marper v. the United Kingdom*, 30562/04 and 30566/04, §66.

34 Conseil constitutionnel, 10 June 2009, decision 2009-580 DC, "Hadopi".

35 ECtHR 18 December 2012, *Ahmet Yıldırım v. Turkey*, 3111/10; see also ECtHR 17 January 2017, *Jankovskis v. Lithuania*, 21575/08.

36 ECtHR 30 June 1993, *Sigurður A. Sigurjónsson v. Iceland*, 16130/90, §35.

37 ECtHR 14 June 2016, *Biržietis v. Lithuania*, 49304/09, §§ 54 and 57-58.

38 §58 of the above case.

39 ECtHR 1st July 2014, *SAS v. France*, 43835/11, §25.

40 ECtHR 12 June 2018, *Gough v. United Kingdom*, 2153/13.

41 ECtHR 3 March 1986, *Stevens v. United Kingdom*, 11674/85.

42 See i.e., ECtHR 2 September 2009, *Uzun v. Germany*, 35623/05.

43 ECtHR 22 February 2018, Libert contre France, 588/13.
44 ECtHR 24 September 2009, *Diana Vučina v. Croatia*, 58955/13, §50.
45 ECtHR 17 January 2021., H. and others versus Russia, nr. 6033/13, 8927/13, 10549/13, 12275/13, 23890/13, 26309/13, 27161/13, 29197/13, 32224/13, 32331/13, 32351/13, 32368/13, 37173/13, 38490/13, 42340/13 and 42403/13.
46 ECtHR 10 April 2007, *Evans v. United Kingdom*, 6339/05.
47 ECtHR 20 March 2007, *Tysiąc v. Poland*, 5410/03, §107; ECtHR 16 December 2010, *A B C v. Ireland*, 25579/05 §214.
48 ECtHR 22 October 1981, *Dudgeon v. UK*, 7525/76.
49 ECtHR 19 January 2021, *Lacatus v. Switzerland*, 14065/15.
50 ECtHR, Lacatus case, §56.
51 ECtHR, Lacatus case, §55.
52 *Conseil d'État*, référé, 22 March 2024, *Clever Cloud v. CNIL*, nr. 492369.
53 Article L2242-17 7° of the Labour Code (Code du travail).

Bibliography

Aouici, S., & Peyrache, M. (2021). Le soutien d'un tiers pour limiter le non-recours face à l'e-administration: Enjeux et limites. *Retraite et société*, *87*(3), 191–202. https://doi.org/10.3917/rs1.087.0191

Brotcorne, P., Bonnetier, C., & Vendramin, P. (2019). Une numérisation des services d'intérêt général qui peine à inclure et à émanciper tous les usagers. *Terminal. Technologie de l'information, culture & société*, 125–126. https://doi.org/10.4000/terminal.4809

Chavalarias, D. (2022). *Toxic Data*. Flammarion.

Conseil d'État. (2023). 12 propositions pour réussir le dernier km de l'action publique. *Étude annuelle* 2023. www.conseil-etat.fr/Media/actualites/documents/2023/septembre-2023/dossier-de-presse-etude-sur-le-dernier-kilometre-de-l-action-publique

CREDOC. (2023). *Baromètre du numérique. Édition 2022*. www.credoc.fr/publications/barometre-du-numerique-edition-2023-rapport

Cyphers, B. (2022). *How to Disable ad ID Tracking on iOS and Android, and Why You Should Do It Now*. Electronic Frontier Foundation. www.eff.org/deeplinks/2022/05/how-disable-ad-id-tracking-ios-and-android-and-why-you-should-do-it-now

De Marco, E. (2018). *Comparative Study Between Directive 95/46/EC & the GDPR Including Their Relations to Fundamental Rights*. Inthemis. www.inthemis.fr/ressources/INFORM_D2.10_Comparative_analysis_GDPR_Dir9546EC.pdf

Deville, C. (2018). Les chemins du droit. Ethnographie des parcours d'accès au RSA en milieu rural. *Gouvernement et action publique*, *7*(3), 83–112. https://doi.org/10.3917/gap.183.0083

Doctorow, C. (2022, August 17). *Pluralistic: How Monopoly Enshittified Amazon/28 Nov 2022 – Pluralistic: Daily Links from Cory Doctorow*. https://pluralistic.net/2022/11/28/enshittification/

France Bleu Besançon. (2019, June 27). *Jura: Un prêtre malvoyant ne peut pas acheter son billet de train sur une borne, il écope d'une amende de 100 euros*. Franceinfo. www.francetvinfo.fr/economie/transports/sncf/jura-un-pretre-malvoyant-ne-peut-pas-acheter-son-billet-de-train-sur-une-borne-il-ecope-d-une-amende-de-100-euros_3510465.html

Hülsemann, L. (2023, August 4). *Austrian Chancellor: Right to Use Cash Should Be in Constitution*. POLITICO. www.politico.eu/article/austria-chancellor-karl-nehammer-cash-use-constitution/

Karaboga, M. (2018). The emergence and analysis of European data protection regulation. In *Managing Democracy in the Digital Age,* Springer, pp. 29–52.

Kloza, D., & Rossi, J. (2024). Du droit d'accéder à Internet à la liberté de—Ne pas—L'utiliser? *La Revue Européenne Des Médias et Du Numérique*, *68*, 17–20.

Leith, D. J. (2021). Mobile Handset Privacy: Measuring the Data iOS and Android Send to Apple and Google. In *17th EAI International Conference, SecureComm 2021 Proceedings, Part II*, Springer, pp. 231–251.

Miller, A. R. (1971). *The Assault on Privacy: Computers, Data Banks, and Dossiers.* University of Michigan Press.

Moore, A. D. (2003). Privacy: Its Meaning and Value. *American Philosophical Quarterly*, *40*(3), 215–227.

Rossi, J. (2023, October 3). A Few Thoughts on the Right to be Offline. *Personal blog.* www.julienrossi.com/blog/2023/10/03/a-few-thoughts-on-the-right-to-be-offline/

Thomson, J. J. (1975). The Right to Privacy. *Philosophy and Public Affairs*, *4*(4), 295–314.

Tréguer, F. (2019). *L'utopie déchue: Une contre-histoire d'Internet, XVe-XXIe siècle.* Fayard.

Untersinger, M. (2017, October 20). Izly, l'appli du Cnous qui géolocalise des étudiants et renseigne des sociétés publicitaires. *Le Monde.* www.lemonde.fr/pixels/article/2017/10/20/izly-l-appli-du-cnous-qui-geolocalise-des-etudiants-et-renseigne-des-societes-publicitaires_5203902_4408996.html

Van Drooghenbroeck, S. (2024). La France défie la CEDH. *Esprit*, *Janvier-Février* (1–2), 25–28. https://doi.org/10.3917/espri.2401.0025

Vitalis, A. (1988). *Informatique, pouvoir et libertés* (2e éd.). Economica. http://gallica.bnf.fr/ark:/12148/bpt6k3334793f

Warren, S. D., & Brandeis, L. D. (1890). The Right to Privacy. *Harvard Law Review*, *4*(5), 193–220. https://doi.org/10.2307/1321160

Westin, A. F. (1967). *Privacy and Freedom.* Atheneum.

Whitman, J. (2004). The Two Western Cultures of Privacy: Dignity Versus Liberty. *Yale Law Journal*, *113*(6), 1151–1221.

Zaïbi, S. (2023, June 18). Genève veillera à l'intégrité numérique de ses citoyens. *Le Temps.* www.letemps.ch/suisse/geneve/geneve-veillera-a-l-integrite-numerique-de-ses-citoyens

Zuboff, S. (2018). *The Age of Surveillance Capitalism: The Fight for a Human Future at the New Frontier of Power* (1st ed.). PublicAffairs.

6 The right not to use the Internet

Toward a negative digital freedom in Polish law

Michał Ożóg and Radosław Puchta

6.1 Introduction

In an information society, access to a computer and the Internet seems to be taken for granted. Unfortunately, despite attempts to counteract it, the phenomenon of digital exclusion is still present in the Polish society (Kowalik, 2009, p. 73–27; Batorski, 2009, p. 223–249). The reasons for this phenomenon are multiple and could be the subject of a separate study. One way to remedy this situation is to recommend expanding the catalog of human rights by adding a new category: the right to the Internet. Without a doubt, every person should be able to use it. Countering digital exclusion is the task of public authorities and is aimed to provide equal development opportunities. Without questioning the importance of the problem and the role of law in this regard, it is also important to recognize the danger of idealizing the right to access the Internet, as it can turn into an actual coercion to use a computer and the Internet when someone does not wish to do so. It seems that the key value in a democratic society should be the protection of the freedom of choice – the ability to make a free choice when deciding on an issue within one's decision-making autonomy. However, the digital revolution that is currently underway may very soon lead to an increasing restriction of choice in this sphere, which should be counteracted by democratic societies.

With the above in mind, it is worth undertaking a scientific analysis of the legal basis of the right not to use the Internet in Polish law. The current legislation will be the starting point for formulating *de lege ferenda* recommendations. An attempt should be made to determine to what extent the current legislation allows, based on its normative content, to construct the right not to use the Internet, and what is the extent of the appropriate legislative changes.

In its essence, the right not to use the Internet means that an individual can decide not to use the Internet and any of the services offered online. Every person should remain free from any coercion when it comes to using the Internet. This includes freedom from any sanctions for refusing to use the Internet in a given area of social relations, as well as from the threat of depriving access to certain services in the event of lack of consent to carry out certain activities using Internet access. The essence of this right should be inviolable and protected in accordance with the

DOI: 10.4324/9781003528401-8

standards applicable to restrictions on human rights set forth in Article 31(3) of the Constitution of the Republic of Poland of 2 April 1997 (hereinafter: Constitution).

Most importantly, everyone should be given the freedom to choose whether he or she wants to receive certain services in the analogue form that involves direct contact with a human being, or by using applications operating on the Internet. This above requirement applies to both horizontal (individual–individual) and vertical (individual–public authority) relations. In both categories of legal relations, it is necessary to adopt appropriate legislation to protect everyone from forced use of the Internet in the absence of the will to do so. An analysis of the content of the right not to use the Internet requires separate research on the above categories of social relations due to their different characteristics.

The right not to use the Internet implies an obligation binding on the legislature to adopt legislation that will ensure the possibility of not using the Internet. This requires legislative activity aimed at drafting appropriate guaranteeing and protective legislation. The content of such legislation should include a categorical formulation of legal norms establishing the principle that the choice of the form of action – offline or online – should be left to the discretion of each person. This aspect will be of particular importance in both horizontal and vertical relations. Colliding interests shall be balanced according to the principle of proportionality. In particular, one should consider the limitation of parties' contractual freedom to restrict the choice of offline and online form in a given contract.

The right in question implies that public authorities are not allowed to interfere through legal norms with the decision-making freedom of individuals when they do not want to use the Internet. Legislation should not make it mandatory to use the Internet. This dimension of the right in question is especially important in the context of individuals' relations with public authorities. In particular, public services and proceedings conducted by public authorities should be carried out in two ways: in the real world and in the virtual space using online applications. These forms must be equivalent and the choice of the offline form should not involve any additional procedural difficulties that could discourage individuals from making this choice.

6.2 The constitutional basis for the right not to use the Internet

It is generally accepted that the primary function of any constitution – as an act with the highest legal force within a given legal system – is to define the basic norms (principles or rules) that determine the shape of both the political system and the socio-economic system of a state (Bożyk, 2020, p. 27; Garlicki, 2022, p. 45). Therefore, the matter to be regulated in constitutions should include all manifestations of human activity that are crucial for proper self-fulfillment in political, social, professional, or private and family life. However, today there is no longer any doubt that the Internet has become a tool that is widely used in all spheres of human activity. It is a tool for day-to-day communication, political or social participation, searching for and disseminating information, gaining knowledge (learning), as well as pursuing a profession or providing work. Internet has allowed mankind to create a new space for itself – the digital (cyber) space, understood as a network of infinite Internet connections through which users exchange information, transfer and process data, provide various types of services, etc. (Marczyk, 2018). What is also important is that public authorities also use information technology on a massive scale to carry out public tasks. In view of such proliferation – the Internet is no longer a "neutral" phenomenon from a constitutional point of view.

However, there is no universal model for the response of the legislature to the emergence of digital space. In some European countries, the decision has been made to regulate at least some issues related to the functioning of people in the new realities in constitutional provisions. Examples of such countries include Portugal and Greece. Since 1997, the Portuguese Constitution has guaranteed everyone access to public information technology networks.[1] On the other hand, in 2001, the Greek legislature recognized everyone's right to participate in the information society, while pointing out that facilitating access to electronically transmitted information, as well as its production, exchange, and dissemination, are among the positive duties of public authorities.[2] In other countries, where the constitutional provisions do not regulate explicitly the rights and obligations associated with the use of the Internet, standards are set by constitutional courts, through so-called creative interpretation (Wiśniewski, 2021).[3] In 2009, in the *HADOPI* case, French Constitutional Council, ruling on the basis of the "classical" freedom of expression and opinion guaranteed by Article 11 of the 1789 Declaration of the Rights of Man and of the Citizen, stated that

> [i]n the current state of the means of communication and given the generalized development of public online communication services and the importance of the latter for the participation in democracy and the expression of ideas and opinions, this right implies freedom to access such services.
>
> (Constitutional Council, 2009)

Access to information technology and communication services was thus considered an element of general freedom of expression (Falque-Pierrotin, 2012).

The Constitution does not directly address the issue of rights and obligations in the digital space. There is no doubt, however, that the catalog of rights and freedoms contained therein includes not only those rights and duties that are expressed explicitly in its provisions, but also those that can be interpreted on the basis of those provisions. As a living instrument, the Constitution retains its regulatory capacity also in the changed realities of political, social, and economic life. The Polish Constitutional Tribunal has already had an opportunity to confirm that

> [a]lthough the Constitution does not explicitly refer to the functioning of the individual in virtual space, the protection of the constitutional freedoms and rights of individuals in connection with the use of the Internet and other electronic means of remote communication is no different from that concerning

> traditional forms of communication or other activities. (…) Due to the complexity of the Internet, the activity of individuals in this sphere corresponds to the relevant forms of constitutionally protected activity.
>
> (Constitutional Tribunal, 2014)[4]

According to the Constitutional Tribunal:

> [t]he Internet should thus be viewed as one of the tools that enable the exercise of substantive freedoms and rights, and not as a separate sphere or a sphere that is not covered by constitutional protection. In this state of affairs, an evaluation of provisions that allow interference with substantive freedoms and rights, and that relate to the use of, among other things, the Internet by individuals, should be carried out taking into account the normative content of the relevant provisions of the Constitution in a given case that guarantee the protection of fundamental rights.
>
> (Constitutional Tribunal, 2014)

Consequently, the "classical" constitutional guarantees should also be appropriately applied to activities that involve the use of the Internet, which entails positive obligations on the part of the state "to ensure at the statutory level the protection of the individual on the Internet in a manner analogous to the adequate guarantees for the functioning of the individual in non-virtual spaces" (Łakomiec, 2023, p. 69).

In Polish legal literature, there have been attempts to construct a specific right of access to the Internet on the basis of the provisions of Chapter II of the Constitution, which focuses on "Freedoms, rights, and duties of man and citizen". Two aspects of this right were singled out in particular, namely the right of access to an Internet connection and the right to access the resources of the World Wide Web (Rzuciło, 2010). Demands have been formulated to include a provision in the Constitution that would explicitly establish the freedom to use the Internet, with arguments that "the right of access to the Internet has already left the stage of conceptualization and entered the stage of normativization and even constitutionalization" (Zieliński, 2013). Of course, these considerations are part of the current debates being made around the world (De Hert & Kloza, 2012; Mehrotra, 2021). However, as already indicated, it is now necessary to consider the possibility of constructing, on the basis of the provisions of the Polish Constitution, the right not to use the Internet.

The fundamental argument in favor of the right not to use the Internet is the aforementioned right of access to the Internet. If it is assumed that the right to access the Internet is, in its nature, primarily that of a freedom, the content of which consists of, among other things, the ability to decide to connect to the Internet and the freedom to use its resources,[5] then the right not to use the Internet is a reflection of the former, a kind of other side of the same coin. An individual entitled to the right of access to the Internet thus has the freedom to be *online*, but at the same time also has the freedom to remain *offline*. This kind of reasoning is typical of the interpretation of constitutional guarantees of freedoms. For example, the freedom of conscience and religion established in Article 53 of the Constitution includes not only the freedom to adopt and practice a religion of one's choice, but also the freedom not to profess any religion (Constitutional Tribunal, 2015).[6] The freedom of association in trade unions and being their active members – protected under Article 59(1) of the Constitution – also includes the so-called negative freedom of association, which means the possibility to decide not to be a member of any trade union without suffering any negative consequences (Constitutional Tribunal, 2008).[7] Also, the freedom to choose and pursue an occupation arising from Article 65(1) of the Constitution inevitably includes the possibility to decide to change an occupation or not to have one (Garlicki & Jarosz-Żukowska, 2016a). One of the elements of the freedom in question is therefore the freedom to decide not to work (Garlicki & Jarosz-Żukowska, 2016b).[8]

At least some constitutional provisions relating to certain aspects of an individual's daily activities can also be used as the basis for constructing the right not to use the Internet. Typically, the very right of access to the Internet in vertical relations between citizens and the state is derived from Article 61 of the Constitution, which guarantees the right to obtain information about the activities of public authorities, including the right to access documents containing public information. The legislature intended an official information and communication technology publication, referred to as the Public Information Bulletin, to be the primary means for the exercise of this right. It takes the form of a uniform web page system on an ICT network (Act of 6 September 2001; Chomicka, 2012),[9] which is, in practice, precisely the Internet. In principle, this is where all public information, including official documents, should be posted. At the same time, if a piece of information has been posted – either due to a statutory obligation or at the discretion of a public authority – in the Public Information Bulletin, the public authority is no longer required to make it available by "analog" means (e.g., in writing or orally), even if such means is requested by a citizen (Wyporska-Frankiewicz, 2023).[10] Thus, the legislature restricts the eligible individual's freedom to decide how to access public information, which must be considered a form of restriction on the exercise of the constitutional right guaranteed under Article 61 of the Constitution. In extreme cases, it can even lead to a complete obstruction of access to public information. In this context, the right not to use the Internet becomes a guarantee of the constitutional right to access public information in the form desired by the individual enjoying this right.

Examples can also be identified of such areas of horizontal interaction between individuals, where the right not to use the Internet appears as a guarantee of the effectiveness of constitutional regulation. One such example is Article 49 of the Constitution, which protects the freedom and secrecy of communication. The legislator, aware of technological advances, no longer speaks only of the freedom and secrecy of "correspondence" and instead takes into account newer forms of communication than the epistolary form (including correspondence *via* electronic mail). However, there is no doubt that the personal freedom in question necessarily includes the freedom to choose the form of communication, and therefore the possibility to choose communication "outside" the Internet, such as through the exchange of traditional letter correspondence.[11]

The social rights listed by the Constitution include workers' right to safe and sanitary working conditions and to rest, which are provided for in Article 66. In today's economy, where the Internet is sometimes the primary tool for work (not only for communication with the employer, contractors, or customers), the right to be offline is becoming a condition for maintaining a work and life balance and resting. Article 76 of the Constitution, on the other hand, imposes an obligation on the state to protect the consumer as the "weaker" party – compared to the entrepreneur – in the process of providing goods or services. This obligation should necessarily include countering the negative effects of the phenomenon occurring in the trade and services sector, namely the fact that the increasing use of digital solutions is accompanied by a systematic reduction in access to "analog" solutions, including through a reduction in the number of physical customer service points and a lack of investment in offline customer contact tools. The right not to use the Internet must be seen in this case as a means of strengthening consumer protection against exclusion in access to goods or services. This measure becomes particularly relevant in the case of access to goods and services that can be considered basic necessities (e.g., access to medical care services).

6.3 The right not to use the Internet in vertical relations in proceedings before public authorities

The right not to use the Internet also applies to an individual's relations with public authorities. When using various services of the public administration or in court proceedings, any individual should be given the opportunity to choose the form in which the matter case is to be handled (offline or online) and the form in which the proceedings are to be conducted. According to Article 7 of the Constitution, public authorities act on the basis of the law and within its limits. This provision is applicable to both the legislative and executive branches of government, as well as to all entities performing public tasks (Winczorek, 2008, p. 28). On the basis of certain categories of social relations, legislation usually defines the form in which letters are to be filed and meetings of public authorities with parties are to be held. This issue is within the regulatory freedom of the ordinary legislature. However, it is important to implement all constitutional values, which include the protection of human rights. The freedom established in Article 31 of the Constitution means the freedom to make acts of will and choice (Bosek, 2016, p. 763). The Constitutional Tribunal, on the basis of the above-mentioned provision, assumed that everyone can decide how to act and behave (Constitutional Tribunal, 2007). This means that a person is free to involve in any behavior that is not expressly prohibited by law. The freedom of choice of the offline form should be provided for in legislation that governs proceedings before public authorities. The protection of specific values alone can justify a limitation of the principle of individual freedom in Article 31 of the Constitution. The point is not to provide complete freedom, but to create a legal framework of free choice for the individual within the limits of the law.

It seems particularly important to guarantee the possibility of choosing the form of activity in the proceedings relating to administrative proceedings or court cases, as well as the filing of letters on paper form with the possibility of ensuring direct contact. The practice of recommending that a person who does not use the Internet should seek the support of other family members in handling a matter is not acceptable, as it does not respect human dignity as required by Article 30 of the Constitution. The right not to use the Internet is founded on the principle of protection of human dignity, which requires each person to be treated with respect.

A reduction of the options for handling a matter to the online option only is not the right solution. Merely guaranteeing an alternative at the level of legislation by ensuring the possibility of choosing either the offline or the online form seems to be insufficient, as the totality of factual and technical circumstances that may determine the choice of the form due to possible factual barriers should also be taken into account. In other words, the offline form of handling a case should be treated as equivalent to the online form, and no additional restrictions should be imposed on its selection that are not justified and necessary. Examples of such unacceptable action that has a discouraging effect include establishing a higher fee charged for filing documents in paper form, longer processing times for cases initiated in this manner, etc. It is equally unacceptable to limit the possibility of filing an application or an appeal only to electronic communication channels, as this forces people to use the Internet.

Indeed, the possibility to communicate remotely using modern technology can be used in administrative and court proceedings, but it is particularly important that this does not come at the expense of other values of procedural justice. The Constitution does not restrict in any way how administrative and judicial matters should be handled or how meetings should be held, and only adopts the principle of openness of the actions of public authorities. According to Article 61(2) of the Constitution, "the right to obtain information includes access to documents and admission to meetings of collective bodies of public authorities elected by universal suffrage, with the possibility of audio or video recording". Such access, of course, applies to both online and offline meetings.

With the development of new technologies and the COVID-19 pandemic, it is possible to note a dynamic increase in the scope of application of remote communication in administrative and judicial proceedings, which should generally be viewed positively, but involves the need to respect the rights of those who do not wish to use the Internet. It is worth briefly presenting selected pieces of legislation on this matter and evaluating them from the point of view of respect of the right not to use the Internet.

Pursuant to the Act of 7 July 2023, amending the Code of Civil Procedure, the Act on the system of common courts of law, the Code of Criminal Procedure, and certain other acts (Act of 7 July 2023), Article 151(2) of the Code of Civil Procedure of 17 November 1964, as amended (hereinafter referred to as CCP) (Code of Civil Procedure, 2023), provides for the possibility of ordering "the holding of a public hearing using technical devices that allow it to be held remotely (remote hearing)". It is also important that a court, when informing participants that a remote hearing has been ordered, must inform them of the possibility of appearing in the courtroom or the obligation to declare their willingness to participate in the remote hearing. This makes it possible to respect the rights of those who do not want to use the Internet.

The legislation allows for a request to examine a witness remotely pursuant to Article 235(1) CCP. What is particularly important in the case of people who do not choose the offline form of the proceedings, such a request may be rejected with by a party, who has 7 days from the date of obtaining information about the intention to take evidence to file an objection. The above-mentioned legal provision may be of particular interest to people who prefer face-to-face contacts in the real world. It is also necessary to clarify the legal solutions and counteract the possible risk of abuse of this provision for the purpose of procedural obstruction. This requires a careful balancing of values between the parties' freedom of choice and the principle of speed of proceedings.

Whenever the remote form of a court session is used, everyone should be provided with adequate technical support, for example, by making computer equipment available to the person concerned at the seat of the court or the office of the public administration body. This is because some people may not have the skills or equipment required to use information technology tools, or simply prefer face-to-face human contact. It is particularly important for a remote meeting before a public authority should be held with the consent of all parties and participants in the proceedings.

In criminal cases, in accordance with Article 374(4) of the Code of Criminal Procedure of 6 June 1997, the presiding judge may exempt the accused, an auxiliary prosecutor, or a private prosecutor from the obligation to appear at the trial, if they are detained, if the participation of these parties in the trial by means of technical devices that allow remote participation in the trial with simultaneous direct video and audio transmission is ensured. In such cases, a court registrar or a judge's assistant, as well as a defense attorney (unless he or she appears in the court), must be present at the place where these persons are staying. At the same time, it should be noted that a remote session is not allowed, among others, in cases involving felonies, since in such situations the presence of the accused in the courtroom is mandatory. In criminal proceedings, the participation of a party in offline proceedings should be particularly safeguarded due to the need to guarantee the defendant's right to defense. Its exercise, it seems, requires personal participation. The use of remote hearings in criminal proceedings requires special caution due to the unique nature of the taking of evidence, which relies heavily on the explanations of the accused and the testimony of witnesses.

6.4 The right not to use the Internet in horizontal relations on the basis of civil and labor contracts

The hallmark of horizontal relations is the equality of the contracting parties. According to Article 353(1) of the Civil Code of 23 April 1964, as amended (Civil Code, 2023), "parties entering into a contract may arrange the legal relationship at their own discretion, as long as its content or purpose do not oppose the properties (nature) of the relationship, a statute, or the principles of social interaction". In general, Polish civil law recognizes as equal the handwritten form and the electronic form of signature for declarations of intent. From the point of view of the above-mentioned legal provision, it is necessary to consider whether it would be permissible in a contractual relationship to restrict the freedom of the parties to choose the form of submission of declarations of intent in writing in favor of the exclusively adopted electronic form.

The adoption of the permissibility of concluding contracts exclusively using electronic signature, and thus assuming the need to use the Internet, appears to be too far-reaching and may lead to the actual exclusion of a certain group of people from the possibility of concluding such contracts. Also, at least the financial argument should be added. It costs approximately €50 to produce an electronic signature in Poland. These are the costs associated with acquiring the necessary tools to perform the act of signing documents, including a cryptographic card, card reader, and software. Expenses are not limited to the decision to obtain an electronic signature. It is also necessary to pay for the renewal of the certificate, which fluctuates around €25. Paying these fees may be too difficult or impossible for some people. This is because the possibility of placing the so-called "trusted signature", which is provided for in Polish law, does not exist in the case of obligation contracts with financial consequences. A trusted signature is only a proof of identity. Of course, its use also presupposes the need for Internet access, although the mere submission of a trusted signature does not involve any additional costs than those associated with access to an Internet connection. Therefore, it should be concluded that the exclusion in a contract of the possibility of making declarations of intent in writing would constitute an illegal clause in view of the applicable laws and principles of social interactions.

The right not to use the Internet can refer not only to the clear-cut issue of using the Internet or opting not to do it, but also to the online availability in time. An example is labor relations in the private sector. An employee has the right not to use the Internet and the offered applications with notifications installed on phones and smartwatches. The literature expresses the demand for the right of an employee to be offline beyond working hours (Moras-Olaś, 2021). It should be noted that it is closely linked to the right not to use the Internet and can be considered a specific right. The right not to use the Internet after the working hours should be especially protected for the sake of labor rights and the protection against harassment. For example, it should be considered unacceptable to use provisions in employment contracts regarding the obligation to check email on an ongoing basis after working hours. It should be emphasized that any expectation of using notification systems for incoming messages using Internet access is incompatible with the right to rest. It also seems necessary for legislation to specify in detail the right not to use the Internet.

6.5 Conclusions

It should be advocated that a separate category be added to the catalog of human rights in Poland: the right not to use the Internet. To ensure a proper balance of the protection against coercion to use or not to use the Internet, it is worth considering adding a right to the Internet with two aspects – positive and negative – in a separate article in Chapter II of the Polish Constitution. Furthermore, appropriate legal regulations in this regard should be also included in acts of international law for the protection of human rights, including the European Convention for the Protection of Human Rights and Fundamental Freedoms. Dealing with the issue would require an adequate political debate in order to reach a compromise on the normative content.

The constitutional provisions presented herein, from which the right not to use the Internet can be reconstructed, concern particular spheres of social life, but they are too general and insufficient to adequately protect an individual. First, the right not to use the Internet is the result of the process of interpretation of the normative content of the existing legislation, and there is a risk that with technological advances, the interpretation of these laws will change in favor of the protection of the right to the Internet in the positive sense to the exclusion of guarantees for those who prefer to operate in the real world rather than the virtual world. Constitutional provisions explicitly stating protection against coercive use of the Internet will radiate throughout the legal system, so that legal protection can be systemic, and this can help ensure the axiological consistency of the Polish legal system. The alternative is to introduce appropriate legal changes at the legislative level, but this seems inexpedient from the point of view of the principles of legislative technique, since, first, this right may be overseen in a particular sphere of social relations, and second, it is an excessive proliferation of legal provisions. It seems that the only reasonable solution is to include such normative regulations in the general provisions on administrative proceedings, administrative court proceedings, tax proceedings, criminal proceedings, criminal fiscal proceedings, penal executive proceedings, and civil and criminal proceedings.

It should also be emphasized that the exercise of the right not to use the Internet requires not only appropriate legal action, but also factual action. Simply guaranteeing this right does not mean making it a reality. Public authorities should take several measures to ensure that people can operate offline without discrimination. Examples include the operation and development of analogue service points for customers in government offices, and support in the submission of applications and other letters in paper form. It is necessary to strive to maintain the traditional form of meetings before public authorities, as it allows persons who do not use the Internet to make decisions freely and can contribute to establishing the material truth. At the same time, it should be emphasized that such measures are also necessary from the point of view of the need to ensure the security of legal transactions.

Notes

1 Article 35(6) of the 1976 Constitution of Portugal:

> Everyone is guaranteed free access to public-use information technology networks. The law shall define the regime governing cross-border data flows, and the appropriate means for protecting both personal data and other data whose safeguarding is justified in the national interest.

2 Article 5A(2) of the 1975 Constitution of Greece:

> All persons have the right to participate in the Information Society. Facilitation of access to electronically transmitted information, as well as of the production, exchange and diffusion thereof, constitutes an obligation of the State, always in observance of the guarantees of articles 9, 9A and 19.

3 A similar approach is taken by international courts, including the European Court of Human Rights.

4 The Constitutional Tribunal further specified:

> The transmission of correspondence by electronic means (e.g., e-mail) is subject to the same constitutional protection as the transmission of a letter in traditional paper form (Art. 47, Art. 49, Art. 51). Transmission of information to a defense counsel *via* the Internet or other means of electronic communication – to the same guarantees as its transmission in a personal conversation (Art. 42). The protection of intimacy in dealing with persons working in professions of public trust is the same regardless of the form of communication (Art. 47). The expression of views, the acquisition and dissemination of information by electronic means are fully subject to the protections provided for in Art. 54 of the Constitution. Likewise, the protection of the freedom of the press and the means of social communication is the same, regardless of the form in which this freedom is exercised (Art. 14, Art. 54). The constitutional protection of the freedom of economic activity (Art. 20 and Art. 22) also extends to undertaking and carrying out such activity on the Internet or through other forms of electronic communication. The same is also true of the protection of the freedom to choose and pursue an occupation (Art. 65), the freedom of artistic creativity, scientific research, and the publication of its results, as well as the freedom of teaching and freedom to enjoy cultural assets (Art, 73) or the right to file petitions, requests, and complaints to public authorities (Art. 63).

5 Thus, this is not a substantive social right containing a demand that the state create a certain information and communication technology infrastructure and provide everyone with (free) access to it.

6 As the Constitutional Tribunal explained, it is indisputable that the freedom not to profess any religion is guaranteed at the same level as the freedom to cultivate any faith. In exercising the freedom of conscience, both the "freedom to religion" and "freedom from religion" can be exercised (see the judgment of October 7, 2015, ref. K 12/14, OTK ZU 9/A/2015, item 143).

7 In the opinion of the Constitutional Tribunal:

> [t]he negative freedom of assembly and association is manifested in the freedom not to be a member of a trade union and the protection from the negative consequences thereof. (…) the negative freedom of association is established in the Constitution, even though Article 59(1) of the Constitution explicitly guarantees only the freedom of association in trade unions. However, it is reasonable to assume that the essence of the freedom of association consists of two aspects: a positive and a negative one. Thus, since the freedom of association in trade unions is guaranteed, so is the freedom not to join a trade union.
>
> (judgment of July 1, 2008, ref. K 23/07, OTK ZU 6/A/2008, item 100)

8 Article 65(2) of the Constitution clearly implies the constitutional prohibition of forced labor, exceptions to which may be provided by law.

> The negative aspect of the freedom to work is the prohibition to introduce an obligation (compulsion) to work, non-compliance with which would give rise to criminal or administrative sanctions. In other words, public authorities cannot require taking a job of those who, for whatever reason, do not intend to work. (…) This is because the guarantee of the freedom to work includes the freedom to remain unemployed.

9 As specified in Article 8(1) of the Act of September 6, 2001 on access to public information. In addition to the Public Information Bulletin, some public authorities maintain separate data portals, access to which also requires an Internet connection. For example, the case law of the Constitutional Tribunal is published in the collection "Orzecznictwo Trybunału Konstytucyjnego – Zbiór Urzędowy" [Jurisprudence of the Constitutional Tribunal – Official Collection] which is in electronic form only (see Article 115 of the Act of November 30, 2016 on the organization and procedure before the Constitutional Tribunal, Journal of Laws of 2019, item 2393). One should also not forget that since 2012, normative and other legal acts have been promulgated in the relevant official journals only in the form of an official document; official journals are issued in electronic form, with the issuing authority maintaining a separate website for each such journal (see Article 2a of the Act of July 20, 2000 on the promulgation of normative acts and certain other legal acts, Journal of Laws of 2019, item 1461).

10 This is because it is assumed that

> the primary way of acquaintance with public information is the Public Information Bulletin [PIB], and the publication of information in the PIB excludes the obligation to make it available again at the request of an interested party, or in other forms provided for in the act, for example, by displaying or posting. Therefore, if the public information requested by an applicant has been made public, then the entity to which the access request is submitted should only refer the interested party to the relevant publication.

11 This, in turn, implies a positive obligation on the part of the state to create an infrastructure to enable individuals to gain access to a certain minimum range of universal postal services. In Poland, the function of an operator designated to provide universal postal services is performed by Poczta Polska Spółka Akcyjna (the Polish Post), whose sole shareholder is the State Treasury.

Bibliography

Act of July 7, 2023, Amending the Code of Civil Procedure, the Act on the system of common courts of law, the Code of Criminal Procedure, and certain other acts. *Journal of Laws of 2023, item 1860.*

Act of September 6, 2001, On access to public information. *Journal of Laws of 2022, item 902.*

Batorski, D. (2009). Wykluczenie cyfrowe w Polsce [Digital exclusion in Poland]. In Grodzka, D. (Ed.), Społeczeństwo informacyjne, vol. 3(19). *Studia BAS.*

Bosek, L. (2016). A commentary to Art. 31. In Bosek, L. & Safjan, M. (Eds.), *Konstytucja RP. Komentarz. Tom I. Art. 1 – 86* [Constitution of the Republic of Poland. A commentary. Volume I. Art. 1 – 86]. Wydawnictwo C.H. Beck.

Bożyk, S. (2020). Rozdział II. Konstytucja jako podstawowe źródło prawa konstytucyjnego [Chapter II. Constitution as the basis source of constitutional law]. In Bożyk, S. (Ed.). *Prawo konstytucyjne* [Constitutional law] (pp. 27–53). Temida 2.

Chomicka, D. (2012). Problematyka udostępniania aktów prawnych i orzeczeń w Internecie [The problem of posting of legal acts and judgments on the Internet]. *Kwartalnik Prawa Publicznego*, *2*, 127–140.

Civil Code of April 23, 1964. *Journal of Laws of 2023, item 1610.*

Code of Civil Procedure of November 17, 1964. *Journal of Laws of 2023, items 1550, 1429, 1606, 1615, and 1667.*

Code of Criminal Procedure of June 6, 1997. *Journal of Laws of 2024, item 37.*

De Hert, P., & Kloza, D. (2012). Internet (access) as a new fundamental right. Inflating the current rights framework? *European Journal of Law and Technology*, *3*(3). https://ejlt.org/index.php/ejlt/article/view/123 (accessed: April 30, 2024).

Falque-Pierrotin, I. (2012). La Constitution et l'Internet. *Nouveaux cahiers du Conseil constitutionnel*, *36*, 31–44.

Garlicki, L. (2022). *Polskie prawo konstytucyjne. Zarys wykładu* [Polish constitutional law. A lecture outline]. Wolters Kluwer.

Garlicki, L., & Jarosz-Żukowska, S. (2016a). Note 14 to Article 65. In Garlicki, L. & Zubik, M. (Eds.). *Konstytucja Rzeczypospolitej Polskiej. Komentarz. Tom II* [Constitution of the Republic of Poland. A commentary. Volume II]. Wydawnictwo Sejmowe.

Garlicki, L., & Jarosz-Żukowska, S. (2016b). Note 29 to Article 65. In Garlicki, L. & Zubik, M. (Eds.). *Konstytucja Rzeczypospolitej Polskiej. Komentarz. Tom II* [Constitution of the Republic of Poland. A commentary. Volume II]. Wydawnictwo Sejmowe.

Constitutional Council of the French Republic, 2009-580 DC, HADOPI, 10 June 2009.

Constitutional Tribunal of the Republic of Poland, Judgment K 12/14, 7 October 2015. OTK ZU 9/A/2015, item 143.

Constitutional Tribunal of the Republic of Poland, Jugdment K 23/07, 1 July 2008. OTK ZU 6/A/2008, item 100.

Constitutional Tribunal of the Republic of Poland, Judgment K 23/11, 30 July 2014. OTK ZU 7/A/2014, item 80.

Constitutional Tribunal of the Republic of Poland, Judgment K 28/05, 7 March 2007. OTK-A 2007, no. 3, item 24.

Kowalik, W. (2009). Wykluczenie cyfrowe jako nowa płaszczyzna podziałów w społeczeństwie informacyjnym [Digital exclusion as a new area of divisions in an information society]. *Studia Humanistyczne AGH*, *7*, 73–84.

Łakomiec, K. (2023). Prawa i wolności jednostki w społeczeństwie informacyjnym a regulacja funkcjonowania platform internetowych [The rights and freedoms of individuals in an information society and the regulation of the functioning of online platforms]. *Państwo i Prawo*, *12*, 64–84.

Marczyk, M. (2018), Cyberprzestrzeń jako nowy wymiar aktywności człowieka – analiza pojęciowa obszaru [Cyberspace as a new dimension of human activity – conceptual analysis of the area]. *Przegląd Teleinformatyczny*, *1–2*, 59–72.

Mehrotra, A. (2021). Access to Internet as a human right – Justification and comparative study. *Comparative Law Review*, *27*, 313–327.

Moras-Olaś, K. (2021). Prawo do bycia offline jako podstawowe prawo pracownika [The right to being offline as a fundamental employee right]. *Studia z zakresu Prawa Praca i Polityki Społecznej*, *4*, 305–323.

Rzucidło J. (2010). Prawo dostępu do Internetu jako podstawowe prawo człowieka (część I) [The right of access to the Internet as a fundamental human right (part I)]. *Prawo Mediów Elektronicznych*, *2*, 38–46.

Winczorek, P. (2008). *Komentarz do Konstytucji Rzeczypospolitej Polskiej z dnia 2 kwietnia 1997 r.* [A commentary to the Constitution of the Republic of Poland of 2 April 1997]. Liber.

Wiśniewski, A. (2021). The European Court of human rights and internet-related cases. *Bialystok Legal Studies*, *23*(3), 109–133.

Wyporska-Frankiewicz, J. (2023). Note 1 do Article 14. In Piskorz-Ryń, A. & Sakowska-Baryła, M. (Eds.). *Ustawa o dostępie do informacji publicznej. Komentarz* [Act on access to public information. A commentary]. Wolters Kluwer.

Zieliński, M. (2013). Dostęp do Internetu jako prawo człowieka? W sprawie potrzeby nowej wolności w Konstytucji Rzeczypospolitej Polskiej [Access to the Internet as a human right? On the need for a new freedom in the Constitution of the Republic of Poland]. *Przegląd Sejmowy*, *4*, 9–22.

7 Non-use of the Internet as human rights enabler?

The curious cases of the right to privacy and the right to health

Władysław Jóźwicki and Łukasz Szoszkiewicz

7.1 Introduction

The diffusion of the Internet has revolutionised how we communicate, access information and receive public services. However, this technological innovation has also brought forth challenges that raise critical questions about its inherent features and their impact on the enjoyment of human rights. The excessive collection and commodification of personal data remain beyond the control of an individual. Paradoxically, countermeasures such as obligatory informed consent for personal data processing (i.e., cookies) have led to "privacy fatigue", a phenomenon when individuals "disclose personal information despite their privacy concerns" (Choi *et al.* 2018). Massive collection of personal data implies exposure of sensitive information to data breaches, for instance in healthcare (Seh *et al.* 2020). Network effects magnify these issues by enabling misinformation to spread rapidly and creating echo chambers where individuals are insulated from diverse perspectives. While the Internet serves as a powerful tool for social mobilisation, its network-based dynamics of information flow and content filtering algorithms can also facilitate polarisation (Peralta *et al.* 2021). Furthermore, algorithmic manipulation poses a distinct challenge to informational self-determination. By creating micro-profiles of individuals based on their online behaviour, these algorithms enable personalised targeting that can be harnessed for political campaigning (Martino *et al.* 2020).

For this reason, we will analyse whether non-access to the Internet can be seen as a human rights enabler and what consequences that brings to the realisation of particular human rights as well as to the proportionality analysis in a case of conflict of rights. We argue that the non-use of the Internet should be taken seriously when assessing all the requirements of proportionality in the large sense, as well as when applying the principle of progressive realisation of economic, social and cultural (ESC) rights. This is due to the fact that by choosing not to be online, individuals can protect themselves from the trade-offs inherent in the digital environment and exercise their rights in ways that are not achievable online. Also, the states and monitoring bodies should not forget about the threats to human rights, which are inherent in the nature of being online when Internet technologies are being used as a means to enable human rights. We will analyse these paradoxes through the lens

DOI: 10.4324/9781003528401-9

of two human rights – privacy and health – to demonstrate how informed choices regarding Internet non-use can influence their enjoyment and how that needs to be reflected in human rights policies and their review. In this analysis, we will primarily rely on the United Nations (UN) international human rights framework and, if necessary, integrate regional and national developments that relate to the non-use of the Internet.

7.2 Non-use of the Internet as an enabler of the right to privacy

The Internet is a technology based on the transmission of data over a network of computers and other devices, such as servers or mobile devices. Any data transmission is carried out through infrastructure maintained by intermediary entities (e.g., Internet service providers or operators of cloud-based services), which inevitably involves the possibility of third-party access. Even the most advanced data encryption methods (Stoykova 2023) and other privacy-enhancing tools (e.g., Virtual Private Networks, Tor network) do not provide complete protection against unauthorised access to data on online behaviour. The sense of privacy and anonymity relies on the assumption that the financial and organisational burden of identifying a given person will be too excessive for third parties. Nevertheless, any sharing of personal data means a potential loss of control over it. Even if reidentifying a person were not currently possible, advancements in technology could make it feasible in the (near) future. By not participating in the digital environment, individuals avoid the traps of data exploitation and maintain a degree of autonomy over their personal data that is increasingly difficult – or impossible – to achieve online.

However, non-use of the Internet is not about the complete rejection of technology but about making informed choices concerning when and how to engage with the digital environment to maintain control over one's personal data. It can be driven by the desire to protect one's private life, avoid personal data collection or minimise exposure to unwanted online digital tracking by corporations and public authorities for various purposes ranging from mass surveillance to targeted advertising.[1] An example of non-use in this context could be choosing not to use Internet-based health services to protect sensitive health data from digital collection and potential misuse or data breaches. It is estimated that between 2005 and 2019 the total number of individuals affected by data breaches in healthcare systems was nearly 250 million worldwide, with most of them affected in the last five years.[2] In the future, we will likely observe leakages of neural data, which is increasingly collected by business actors, and which can be decoded to reveal one's most intimate features (Yuste & De La Quadra-Salcedo 2023).

In this sense, the decision not to use the Internet can be seen as a form of exercising the right to informational self-determination, which was coined in the 1980s and, since then, penetrated regional and national human rights frameworks.[3] It has been invoked *expressis verbis* in the jurisprudence of the European Court of Human Rights (ECtHR 2023), Inter-American Court of Human Rights (IACtHR 2024), and selected Asian countries[4] as one of the fundamental components of the right to privacy. Invoked, for the first time, by the German Constitutional Court in the *Census* case of 1983, the right to informational self-determination "confers upon the individual the authority to, in principle, decide themselves on the disclosure and use of their personal data" (BVerfG 1983). The Court has also emphasised that the lack of "sufficient certainty" over the kind and scope of personal data known to third parties "impede[s] freedom to make self-determined plans or decisions" (BVerfG 1983, para. 146).

As with other human rights, the right to informational self-determination is not absolute and can be restricted. It can, therefore, be subjected to a proportionality analysis, which requires all the proportionality tests to be conducted and passed in order to allow a limitation of a particular right or freedom. In this text, we adhere to a broad understanding of the proportionality analysis. Limitations in the enjoyment of rights and freedoms, in order to be legitimate and proportionate *sensu largo*, must cumulatively meet six requirements. First, they need to be determined/prescribed by law, which also contains legislative quality requirements. Second, they need to realise a legitimate aim, which in the context we are analysing is predominantly the rights and freedoms of others (the ones provided with the use of online methods). Third, they need to be suitable/appropriate to achieve the above aim. Hence, they must lead to genuine progress in the realisation of the right in question. Fourth, they need to be necessary to do that, meaning that there is no other less restrictive to the limited right method to achieve progress in the concurring right. Fifth, the limitation needs to be proportionate *sensu stricto*, meaning "[t]he harm (cost, burden, sacrifice) caused by the limitation must be 'proportional in a strict sense' to the benefit (gains, good) it contributes to produce" (Tremblay 2014, 865). Lastly, sixth, while introducing limitations in the enjoyment of rights and freedoms, we have to bear in mind that the essence of the limited right or freedom must always remain intact so the right may not become annihilated or drained out of its content.

Given the nature of the Internet, any transition to the digital environment will inherently involve limitations in the enjoyment of the right to informational self-determination. In other words, every digital solution perceived as an enabler of individual rights (e.g., personalised medicine as an enabler of the right to health) will require an assessment of proportionality that involves the right to informational self-determination. As we will show, the non-use of the Internet (and implications for the right to informational self-determination) is frequently overlooked in that context. However, if we take rights and freedoms seriously, we need to apply all the above-mentioned proportionality analysis elements.

First, the limitations need to be determined/prescribed by law. This means that the courts must determine whether the collection, retention, processing and authorisation of access to personal data are "in accordance with the law". Therefore, the legal basis must meet certain qualitative requirements (i.e., the "quality of the law"), which implies accessibility for the individual and predictability of its application (ECtHR 2015, para. 236). The law must also provide adequate and effective safeguards against arbitrariness and the risk of abuse (ECtHR 2015, para. 302). The German Federal Constitutional Court, in assessing a case on predictive policing, ruled that "the severity of interference with the right to informational self-determination primarily depends on the type, scope and possible uses of the data, as well as the risks of abuse" (BVerfG 2023). For this reason, an individual should have sufficient certainty over the further use of one's personal data, in particular requirements under which data can be used for purposes other than initially collected. For example, under what requirements data taken as part of healthcare can be made available to law enforcement authorities for the purpose of crime prevention. In recent years, international and national legal instruments and case law has provided cases that involved "repurposing" of personal data processing, which implies the possibility of changing the legitimate aim for which the data was originally collected. For instance, the EU's proposal for establishing the European Health Data Space aims to introduce the secondary use of electronic health data for, *inter alia*, healthcare, scientific research, education and training of AI-based systems.[5] Hence, the technical and legal possibility of changing the purpose of processing should already be clearly determined by the law allowing the collection of data.

Second, limitations need to realise a legitimate aim. Sometimes, a collection of digital data is justified with the protection of national security or public order, particularly in countries where law enforcement agencies have extensive powers to search computer systems. Other commonly invoked legitimate aims include the protection of the rights and freedoms of others (in particular, an increasing accessibility and quality of a given social right) or public health (e.g., preventing the spread of COVID-19). The invocation of these values can lead to various actions in the digital environment. An analysis of the recommendations formulated under the Universal Periodic Review shows that in some countries, the Internet is primarily a tool to strengthen the protection of the right to freedom of expression or the right to assembly. Therefore, such countries are recommended to refrain from restricting and shutting down the Internet (UPR – Uganda 2022; Gabon 2023; Morocco 2023). At the same time, another group of states is recommended to ensure the right to privacy and freedom from censorship on the Internet, which suggests that they leverage digital connectivity for surveillance (UPR – the Netherlands 2022; Nauru 2021).

Although the Internet – like any technology – is described in terms of both risks and opportunities for human rights, some authors suggest that "preventive repression [will] increase as technology continues to develop in the future" (Dragu & Lupu 2021). In some states, digitalisation has become a tool that facilitates governmental control, such as in China or Egypt.[6] The preventive repression includes primarily non-violent forms of repression leading to chilling effect. In this context, the non-use of the Internet becomes not only an enabler of the right to privacy but the last stronghold of individual autonomy.

The broad powers of law enforcement agencies are also used in countries with strong protection of individual rights. This is demonstrated by the EncroChat case, in which the Dutch and French services, Europol as well as Eurojust successfully infiltrated the EncroChat network, which was facilitating communication (mainly) between organised crime groups. A series of cases before courts across Europe has revealed the lack of binding digital forensics standards in criminal proceedings which would be compliant with the right to a fair trial (Stoykova 2023).

Third, limitations need to be suitable/appropriate to achieve the legitimate aim. Interventions involving the collection of personal data (and consequently limiting the right to informational self-determination) are usually motivated either by the protection of national security or the progressive realisation of other rights, in particular social rights such as the right to health or the right to education. However, to be considered appropriate, digital services should genuinely facilitate legitimate aims. For instance, despite their limitations, tracing apps have proven beneficial in preventing the spread of COVID-19. The deployment of smartphone applications enabled near real-time data collection and analysis, whereas traditional surveillance methods are typically delayed by one to three weeks (as seen in the United States) (Pandit *et al.* 2022). Timing is crucial in preventing the spread of the virus, whose incubation period is typically less than 14 days (O'Connell *et al.* 2021). While the collection of personal data interferes with privacy, it serves dual purposes: forecasting the transmission of the virus (thus protecting public health) and assessing an individual's likelihood of exposure when moving through various spaces or interacting with others (thus facilitating the right to health).

Fourth, limitations need to be necessary, which indicates that any limitation of an individual right should be the least restrictive means to achieve a legitimate aim. In the context of digital public services, the legitimate aim often hinges on their increasing quality (e.g., due to the better allocation of financial and organisational resources) and enhanced accessibility, which leads to the progressive realisation of ESC rights, such as the right to health. However, this rise in quality and accessibility cannot be justified by a proportional – or even exponential – enabling of the realisation of a given right if it leads to a restriction of another right. According to the requirement of necessity, any restriction of rights should be made only when there is no other way to achieve the legitimate aim, and to the narrowest possible extent for the realisation of a specific legitimate aim. This means that if it is possible to strengthen the realisation of a given right by allowing it to be exercised online while at the same time maintaining the possibility of offline exercise, public authorities should ensure both forms of realisation of the right. Both the Human Rights Committee (HRC 2014, para. 37) and the Committee on Economic, Social and Cultural Rights (CESCR 2000, para. 47) highlighted in various contexts that rights include "core obligations" which cannot be conditioned on the availability of resources and the same should apply to the right to informational self-determination.

Fifth, the limitation needs to be proportionate *sensu stricto*. Due to the "indivisibility, interdependence and interrelatedness"[7] of human rights, strengthening the realisation of one right often impacts the realisation of another. Assessment of proportionality *sensu stricto* then requires consideration of the proportion of an interference. The transfer of public services to the digital environment, in many cases, will involve strengthening the realisation of various rights, such as the right to participation in public life (e.g., voting online) or the right to health (e.g., telemedicine). At the same time – due to the specific features of the Internet described in the introduction – it will always interfere with the right to privacy, particularly informational self-determination. As long as the infringing upon privacy remains proportional to strengthening the realisation of another right, it could be justified. Proportionality will become increasingly difficult to justify as privacy protection becomes more burdensome, e.g., when a significant reduction in the grid of polling places accompanies the introduction of an optional form of online voting. When the difference between the possibility of exercising a given right online and offline reaches such great differences that exercising it in the latter form will be extremely burdensome, such an action should be considered disproportionate. One can claim that it was possible for public authorities to act in such a way as to make it possible to organise online voting without unduly restricting the right to informational self-determination.

Estonia's Internet voting system exemplifies a careful balance between protecting privacy and promoting the right to public participation. Introduced in 2005, this system enhances participation by making voting more accessible to those who cannot or do not like to visit polling stations in person. However, despite its convenience, Internet voting poses privacy concerns, such as potential cyberattacks that could compromise ballot secrecy. The Supreme Court upheld that the individual, once properly informed of the risks related to Internet voting, should decide whether or not to cast his or her vote online (Madise & Vinkel 2011, 8). Therefore, Estonia maintains traditional paper ballots as an alternative, allowing individuals who prioritise privacy over digital convenience to vote in a traditional way.

Last but not least, limitations cannot infringe upon the essence of the right to informational self-determination. In this context of digital-only public services, it will be necessary to analyse the nature and scope of the data acquired, the retention period (which should be as short as possible), the authority processing the data, as well as the permissibility of changing the purposes of the processing. The degree of datafication of the society may also play a role in the assessment – the higher it is, the more likely it is that public authorities can create an accurate digital profile of an individual, which, in our opinion, could lead to the infringement of the essence of the right to informational self-determination.[8] It seems reasonable to claim that selected data, e.g., on the content of the vote cast in an election, should never be processed for different purposes than initially collected. However, most of the data protection regulations allow for further processing of personal data (even so called sensitive data) if certain conditions are met (e.g., for research and statistical purposes, when data is properly anonymised,[9] for the protection of equally important public interest).

7.3 Non-use of the Internet as an enabler of the right to health

One of the rights often associated with the benefits the Internet can provide to its realisation is the right to health. The Internet may enhance especially the accessibility and availability of the right to health. Regarding physical accessibility, the Internet opens the possibility of providing medical services, in cases not requiring in-person contact, *via* long-distance care (Pawelczyk 2018, 620). Regarding economic accessibility (affordability), online medical care does not require costly and time-consuming travel to specialists unavailable in the neighbourhood. Also, the costs of consultations may be reduced. Internet access may alleviate health inequality (Yu & Meng 2022), thus serving non-discrimination in the enjoyment of the right to health. That applies especially when it comes to underprivileged groups, which are particularly economically vulnerable, as Internet access mitigates the negative impact of income inequality on healthcare access (Yu & Meng 2022). Internet access may also improve healthcare quality due to increased access to scientific knowledge for medical personnel, for instance, through databases of medical literature or Large Language Models, which are increasingly trained on medical papers (Clusmann *et al.* 2023). Finally, being online can significantly increase information accessibility. The latter should not, however, be considered as a possible replacement for professional medical care but as a supplement to it.

Recently, the COVID-19 pandemic revealed some health-beneficial force of the Internet and access to information. Regardless of community type, mortality rates were generally higher during the pandemic in places with limited Internet access (Lin *et al.* 2022). Moreover, being online may lead to increased demand for medical services. Searching for health information significantly affects an individual's demand for healthcare (Suziedelyte 2012). All in all, Internet access generally improves the average health condition (Yu & Meng 2022). As the UN Committee on the Rights of the Child (CRC) underlined regarding the relatively better digitally included group, which are young people:

> the Internet provides opportunities for gaining access to online health information, protective support and sources of advice and counselling and can be utilised by States as a means of communicating and engaging with adolescents. The ability to access relevant information can have a significant positive impact on equality.
>
> (CRC 2016, para. 47)

Being online in different ways serves as, and potentially increasingly so, an enabler of the right to health. This needs to be considered while undertaking the proportionality analysis with other rights and freedoms endangered by being online, such as the right to privacy, which was analysed in more detail in the previous section, but also other rights which can be negatively affected through (algorithmic) bias and discrimination or function creep, which often accompanies Internet-based healthcare services (Sun *et al.* 2020, 23). In all such cases, a method to be applied is the proportionality analysis of whether the advance in the realisation of one right is proportional to the detriment of another.

The situation when it comes to the right to health is, however, more complex than that. While being online provides certain benefits for the right to health, it also poses certain threats to this right. This is the case regarding both the very same aspects of the right that it may enhance but also regarding other ones. Digital health technologies can contribute to health inequity by deepening the consequences stemming from the "digital divide" between those who can and cannot access such interventions, some of which may be mitigated with different means like review and accountability mechanisms (Sun *et al.* 2020, 23, 25, 29). Some, however, may not. Some threats to the right to health may not be prevented by legal mechanisms or technological solutions but are inherent to the nature of being online. All the benefits from the online right to health enablers may be enjoyed only by those who also enjoy Internet access (ca. two-third of the population worldwide). The issue is that some vulnerable groups are overrepresented in offline groups (e.g., indigenous peoples). That may be eliminated by the increase in Internet access availability and digital literacy promotion. Before that becomes universal, the divide and the most basic stemming from it right-to-health-related consequences remain, however, inevitable.

When it comes to equality, the health-related information gathered and available for the development of diagnosing, results analysis and research on the sources of and treatment methods of different diseases represents only those who actually are connected, which reflects the imbalance of the spread of connectivity, and privileges particular regions or particular groups. The so-called "health data poverty" disables individuals, certain groups or even whole populations from benefiting from discovery or innovation due to a scarcity of representative data. That may prevent some (groups of) people from the benefits of data-driven digital health technologies or even lead to them being harmed by such technologies (Ibrahim *et al.* 2021, 260–261). That, again, may, to some extent, be mitigated by different means, which, however, cannot be immediate. Also, an extended history of data availability may create something of a kind of "connectivity capital", resulting in more accurate and effective data-driven digital health technologies applications for certain groups. In 2021, 86.3% of genomics studies including genome-wide association studies have been conducted in individuals of European descent. This proportion has increased from 81% in 2016 at the cost of the underrepresented populations (Fatumo *et al.* 2022), which shows that both the current situation and tendency are counter-egalitarian.

Another significant issue is the access to health-related information. Generally, the Internet threatens with disinformation or information overload as well as shallowness or superficiality of the information offered (Kloza 2024). These threats become particularly hazardous when it comes to health-related information. The information may quickly turn out to be incomplete, imprecise or even represent misinformation, and thus be useless or even harmful in the hands of a recipient. An unprecedented and increasing majority of parents and guardians are using the Internet for information concerning their children's health. They are, however, not necessarily using reliable and safe sources of information (Pehora *et al.* 2015). Reliance on non-traditional health sources, amplified by network effects and algorithmically designed echo chambers, led, already before the COVID-19 pandemic, to increasing vaccine hesitancy (Getman *et al.* 2018). The COVID-19 pandemic may, however, serve as a particularly telling example of the potential scale of health misinformation, which arose to an extreme example of an "Infodemic" (Borges do Nascimento *et al.* 2022).

There are methods to minimise that kind of threats. It is undoubtedly advisable that "health care providers should begin to focus on improving access to safe, accurate, and reliable information through various modalities including education, designing for multiplatform, and better search engine optimization" (Pehora *et al.* 2015). This and other means can also be implemented on policy-making and legal grounds. None of them may, however, be fully implemented together with connectivity. Access to the Internet or health-related information may not be made in any way conditional upon meeting certain requirements by the receivers. Also, a full or limited selection of available Internet information does not rest in any single state or international organisation's capacities. Therefore, it is imminent that misinformation, misinterpretation or misapplication of information on the web might lead to health-threatening choices by the receivers. A new challenge has been created by the development of the Large Language Models, which, admittedly, may have some potential to democratise medical knowledge and facilitate access to healthcare but – due to their design – are also prone to "distribute misinformation and exacerbate scientific misconduct due to a lack of accountability and transparency" (Clusmann *et al.* 2023). The balance between benefits and damages stemming from an almost unlimited flow of information on the Internet and access to it by anybody is, in many aspects, extremely shaky.

The CRC already in 2013 expressed concern

> by the increase in mental ill-health among adolescents, including developmental and behavioural disorders; depression; eating disorders; anxiety; psychological trauma resulting from abuse, neglect, violence or exploitation; alcohol, tobacco and drug use; obsessive behaviour, such as excessive use of and addiction to the Internet and other technologies; and self-harm and suicide.
>
> (CRC 2013a, para. 38, see as well: CRC, 2013b, para. 46)

Being online is one of the factors increasingly endangering mental health. Children represent a particularly vulnerable group in that regard, but not the only one. The most apparent threats seem to be addictions and the so-called FOMO ("fear of missing out") (Kloza 2024), but the constant connectivity can impair people's well-being in many ways and is related to the most severe clinical phenomena like depression but also anxiety, loneliness and other mental health outcomes related to subjective well-being (Cai *et al.* 2023). "Digital detox" or simply a choice of limiting connectivity may be one of the means to challenge this threat (Radtke *et al.* 2022).

However, that has become more and more difficult also due to the increased supply of online services. For those who do not have Internet access, "especially on a 'smart' device, life has become unduly burdensome and, at times, even impossible" (Kloza 2024). That applies also to the digital services provided in order to facilitate certain human rights availability. Therefore, the related to being online mental health threats become accompanied also by the accumulated enablement of other rights *via* online means, which increases the scale of the problem and thus of the risks that excessive use of the Internet brings to people's health. That calls for an in-depth proportionality analysis of the increased demand for connectivity required by enabling other human rights by the online services and resulting from that adverse effects on the right to health, which have to be considered as limitations of the latter and allowing the increase in the services available online only if all the proportionality requirements in limiting the right to health are met. Their offline availability becomes thus yet another parameter to be considered under the proportionality test while introducing their online equivalents at the cost of other rights, like the right to health. That is yet another example of the first of the general conclusions that stem from our analysis.

However, while being a threat, online solutions may also be effectively used to solve at least some of the mental health issues. The earlier arguments regarding healthcare improvement through the possibilities the Internet provides also apply to mental health issues (Reglitz & Rudnick 2020). That is yet another example of the second of the general conclusions that stem from our analysis. Enabling the right to health *via* the Internet requires an in-depth analysis of the being online effects on the health of people under the framework of progressive realisation of the right to health in both the mental and physical dimensions and increasing the services available online only if the overall result is positive, especially in the light of "strong presumption that retrogressive measures taken in relation to the right to health are not permissible" (CESCR 2000, para. 32). Enabling the right to health *via* the Internet also requires the guarantee that the right will be exercised without discrimination of any kind, which is an immediate obligation of the states (CESCR 2000, para. 30), not a progressive one (Saul *et al.* 2014, 133–213). In light of what has been shown, the latter seems especially challenging in the context of the "digital divide" and other threats to equality connected to online enablers of the right to health.

7.4 Concluding remarks

Being online indisputably enhances the enjoyment of different human rights. At the same time, it brings some trade-offs to some of them, like the right to privacy or, to some extent, the right to health. Some of the challenges may be avoided or mitigated by adjusting policies or legal solutions to be implemented on the state or international level. Nevertheless, certain trade-offs remain inherent in the very nature of being online, and it is not possible to eliminate them.

Inevitably, an increasing number of services, be they public or private, become available *via* the Internet (Kloza 2024). When it comes to enabling human rights and endangering other human rights by those services, it becomes an issue of proportionality analysis. It must become increasingly applied at policy-making, judicial review or other monitoring levels. That applies equally, irrespective of whether we recognise online services as enablers of human rights or as a self-standing right of access to the Internet, which, not being absolute, also is a subject of proportionality (Dror-Shpoliansky & Shany 2021, 1274). Similarly, it applies irrespective of whether we consider non-access to the Internet as a choice driven by the realisation of human rights and hence their enabler (as we do in this text) or whether we opt for the recognition of a new, standalone human right not to use the Internet, which neither is absolute and is thus subject of proportionality (Kloza 2024).

The competent bodies should carefully take all the stemming from being online consequences for the enjoyment of human rights under consideration. That means that they should consider the benefits to human rights available through online means, but also the threats stemming therein. They should remember that progress in one right achieved *via* online means may adversely affect other human rights, but also that online realisation of a particular right may, in one aspect, enhance its enjoyment while, in another, deteriorate it. The proportionality methodology should be applied with all the tests it requires and with particular sensitivity to the being-online-related consequences for both rights at stake – the one that benefits and the one enjoyment of which is being limited. That concerns the proportionality analysis and the tests it requires. As a result, the enthusiasm for connectivity should not lead to disregarding the offline availability of rights and freedoms. Another issue is the cost-benefit analysis within the scope of one particular right that its online realisation might bring about. That applies especially to ESC rights like the right to health. In the ESC rights realm, the critical issue becomes the principle of progressive realisation of those rights so that the progress achieved by online services outweighs the detriments caused by it and is not discriminatory.

Perhaps the concept that "[t]he same rights that people have offline must also be protected online", which has dominated the recent international discourse about human rights in cyberspace (Dror-Shpoliansky & Shany 2021, 1253–1256), should become supplemented with two caveats. As the first caveat, we propose: While enabling human rights online, we may not resign from providing them offline if the protection of other rights requires that. That may seem somewhat self-evident. However, not necessarily so, as the recent pandemic crisis revealed, for example, when travellers' obligation to complete the passenger location form upon arrival in Belgium could be fulfilled only through the Internet (Kloza 2024). As the second caveat we propose: While enabling human rights online, we may do that only as far as it leads to genuine and non-discriminatory progress in the realisation of the particular right. However, this kind of in-depth analysis seems so far to be absent in the policy-making process or in the activity of human rights monitoring bodies.

Notes

1 It should be noted, however, that companies are able to create profiles of offline people they know exist and supplement the information with information coming in from various sources, such as friends who are online. See: Dunbar *et al.* (2015).

2 The number of data breaches in healthcare has been on the rise since 2005. See: Seh *et al.* (2020).

3 Nevertheless, it has not been recognised *expressis verbis* in the universal human rights framework. The General Comment no 16 on the right to privacy does not mention the concept, nor the individual communications of the Human Rights Committee (for more: Vaitkunaite 2023). The Universal Human Rights Index, the most comprehensive database of human rights recommendations adopted by the UN Treaty Bodies, Human Rights Council special procedures and within the Universal Periodic Review, discloses only one mention of this concept made by the Independent Expert on the enjoyment of all human rights by older persons. See: IE Older persons (2020, para. 115).

4 For instance, in India. See: Writ Petition (Civil) No 494 of 2012. Although Indian Supreme Court uses the phrasing "informational privacy", it draws parallels with the German Census case of 1983 and the concept of "informational self-determination" (see paras. 207, 241).

5 European Union, Proposal for a Regulation of the European Parliament and of the Council on the European Health Data Space, COM/2022/197 final, Article 34.

6 In the Arab Spring countries, social media initially empowered activists but quickly became a tool for repression. Government and military forces transformed platforms like Facebook and Twitter into arenas of harassment and danger for dissidents, leading to arrests and forced exiles. See: Tufekci (2019).

7 World Conference on Human Rights in Vienna, Vienna Declaration and Programme of Action, 25 June 1993.

8 Federal Constitutional Court of Germany, when adjudicating on the permissibility of AI-based software for law enforcement agencies noted that their use

> can also come close to developing a full profile. This is because the software can open up new possibilities of filling in the available information on a person by factoring in data and algorithmic assumptions about relationships and connections surrounding the person concerned.
>
> See: BVerfG (2023)

9 Although anonymised data is no longer considered "personal data", it could potentially be reidentified and linked back to an individual in the future. This likelihood increases with ongoing advancements in datafication of society and increasing computational power.

Bibliography

Books and articles

Borges do Nascimento, I. J., A. B. Pizarro, J. M. Almeida, N. Azzopardi-Muscat, M. A. Gonçalves, M. Björklund, & D. Novillo-Ortiz (2022), Infodemics and Health Misinformation: A Systematic Review of Reviews, *Bulletin of the World Health Organization*, 100(9), 544–561.

Cai, Z., P. Mao, Z. Wang, D. Wang, J. He, & X. Fan (2023), Associations Between Problematic Internet Use and Mental Health Outcomes of Students: A Meta-analytic Review, *Adolescent Research Review*, 8, 45–62.

Choi, H., J. Park, & Y. Jung (2018), The Role of Privacy Fatigue in Online Privacy Behavior, *Computers in Human Behavior*, 81, 42–51.

Clusmann, J., F. R. Kolbinger, H. S. Muti, Z. I. Carrero, J-N. Eckardt, N. Ghaffari Laleh, C. M. L. Löffler, S-C. Schwarzkopf, M. Unger, G. P. Veldhuizen, S. J. Wagner, & J. N. Kather (2023), The Future Landscape of Large Language Models in Medicine, *Communications Medicine*, 3. www.nature.com/articles/s43856-023-00370-1

Dragu, T., & Y. Lupu (2021), Digital Authoritarianism and the Future of Human Rights, *International Organization*, 75(4), 991–1017.

Dror-Shpoliansky, D., & Y. Shany (2021), It's the End of the (Offline) World as We Know It: From Human Rights to Digital Human Rights – A Proposed Typology, *The European Journal of International Law*, 32(4), 1249–1282.

Dunbar, R., V. Arnaboldi, M. Conti, & A. Passarella (2015), The Structure of Online Social Networks Mirrors Those in the Offline World, *Social Networks*, 43, 39–47.

Fatumo, S., T. Chikowore, A. Choudhury, M. Ayub, A. R. Martin, & K. Kuchenbäcker (2022), Diversity in Genomic Studies: A Roadmap to Address the Imbalance. Available at: www.ncbi.nlm.nih.gov/pmc/articles/PMC7614889/, Accessed on 16 May 2024 (published in final edited form as: A roadmap to increase diversity in genomic studies, *Nature Medicine,* 2022; 28(2)).

Getman, R., M. Helmi, H. Roberts, A. Yansane, D. Cutler, & B. Seymour (2018), Vaccine Hesitancy and Online Information: The Influence of Digital Networks, *Health Education & Behavior*, 45(4), 599–606.

Ibrahim, H., X. Liu, N. Zariffa, A. D. Morris, & A. K. Denniston (2021), Health Data Poverty: An Assailable Barrier to Equitable Digital Health Care, *The Lancet. Digital Health*, 3(4), 260–265.

Kloza, D. (2024), The Right Not to Use the Internet, *Computer Law & Security Review: The International Journal of Technology Law and Practice*, 52. https://doi.org/10.1016/j.clsr.2023.105907

Lin, Q., S. Paykin, D. Halpern, A. Martinez-Cardoso, & M. Kolak (2022), Assessment of Structural Barriers and Racial Group Disparities of COVID-19 Mortality With Spatial Analysis, *JAMA Network Open*, 5(3). https://jamanetwork.com/journals/jamanetworkopen/fullarticle/2789619

Madise, Ü., & P. Vinkel (2011), Constitutionality of Remote Internet Voting: The Estonian Perspective, *Juridica International Law Review*, VIII, 8.

Martino, G. D. S., S. Cresci, A. Barrón-Cedeño, S. Yu, R. Di Pietro, & P. Nakov (2020), A Survey on Computational Propaganda Detection, *arXiv preprint arXiv:2007.08024.*

O'Connell, J., M. Abbas, S. Beecham, J. Buckley, M. Chochlov, B. Fitzgerald, L. Glynn, K. Johnson, J. Laffey, B. McNicholas, B. Nuseibeh, M. O'Callaghan, I. O'Keeffe, A. Razzaq, K. Rekanar, I. Richardson, A. Simpkin, C. Storni, D. Tsvyatkova, J. Walsh, T. Welsh, D. O'Keeffe (2021), Best Practice Guidance for Digital Contact Tracing Apps: A Cross-disciplinary Review of the Literature, *JMIR Mhealth Uhealth*, 9(6), e27753. https://doi.org/10.2196/27753. PMID: 34003764; PMCID: PMC8189288.

Pandit, J. A., J. M. Radin, G. Quer, et al. (2022), Smartphone Apps in the COVID-19 Pandemic, *Nature Biotechnology*, 40, 1013–1022.

Pawelczyk, B. (2018), Art. 12. Prawo do ochrony zdrowia, in: Z. Kędzia & A. Hernandez-Połczyńska (eds), *Międzynarodowy Pakt Praw Gospodarczych, Socjalnych i Kulturalnych*. Komentarz, C.H. Beck, Warszawa.

Pehora, C., N. Gajaria, M. Stoute, S. Fracassa, R. Serebale-O'Sullivan, C. T. Matava (2015), Are Parents Getting it Right? A Survey of Parents' Internet Use for Children's Health Care Information, *Interactive Journal of Medical Research*, 4(2). https://pubmed.ncbi.nlm.nih.gov/26099207/

Peralta, A. F., M. Neri, J. Kertész, & G. Iñiguez (2021), Effect of Algorithmic Bias and Network Structure on Coexistence, Consensus, and Polarization of Opinions, *Physical Review E*, 104(4), 044312.

Radtke, T., T. Apel, K. Schenkel, J. Keller, & E. von Lindern (2022), Digital Detox: An Effective Solution in the Smartphone Era? A Systematic Literature Review, *Mobile Media & Communication*, 10(2), 190–215 (Special Issue: Digital Wellbeing in an Age of Mobile Connectivity).

Reglitz, M., & A. Rudnick (2020), Internet Access as a Right for Realizing the Human Right to Adequate Mental (and other) Health Care, *International Journal of Mental Health*, 49(1), 97–103.

Saul, B., D. Kinley, & J. Mowbray (2014), *The International Covenant on Economic, Social and Cultural Rights: Commentary, Cases, Materials*. Oxford University Press, Oxford.

Seh, A. H., M. Zarour, M. Alenezi, A. K. Sarkar, A. Agrawal, R. Kumar, & R. A. Khan (2020), Healthcare Data Breaches: Insights and Implications. *Healthcare (Basel, Switzerland)*, 8(2), 133.

Stoykova, R. (2023), Encrochat: The Hacker with a Warrant and Fair Trials? *Forensic Science International: Digital Investigation*, 46, 301602.

Sun, N., K. Esom, M. Dhaliwal, & J. J. Amon (2020), Human Rights and Digital Health Technologies, *Health and Human Rights Journal*, 22(2), 21–32.

Suziedelyte, A. (2012), How Does Searching for Health Information on the Internet Affect Individuals' Demand for Health Care Services?, *Social Science & Medicine*, 75(10), 1828–1835.

Tremblay, L. B. (2014), An Egalitarian Defense of Proportionality-based Balancing, *International Journal of Constitutional Law*, 12(4), 864–890.

Tufekci, Z. A. (2019), Response to Johanne Kübler's A Review of Zeynep Tufekci – Twitter and Tear Gas: The Power and Fragility of Networked Protest (2017, New Haven: Yale University Press). *International Journal of Politics, Culture, and Society*, 32, 365–369.

Vaitkunaite, I. (2023), *Reinventing the Right to Privacy Towards Full-Fledged Informational Self-Determination A doctrinal study of the evolutive interpretation of Article 17 of ICCPR*, MA Thesis, Lund University.

Yu, J., & S. Meng (2022), Impacts of the Internet on Health Inequality and Healthcare Access: A Cross-Country Study, *Frontiers in Public Health*, 10. www.frontiersin.org/journals/public-health/articles/10.3389/fpubh.2022.935608/full

Yuste, R., & T. De La Quadra-Salcedo (2023), Neuro-Rights and New Charts of Digital Rights: A Dialogue Beyond the Limits of the Law, *Indiana Journal of Global Legal Studies*, *30*(1), 15–37. https://doi.org/10.2979/gls.2023.a886161

Documents

BVerfG, Judgment of the First Senate of 16 February 2023 – 1 BvR 1547/19.

BVerfG, Order of 15 December 1983 – 1 BvR 209/83.

CESCR, General Comment No 14 (2000), The right to the highest attainable standard of health (article 12 of the International Covenant on Economic, Social and Cultural Rights), E/C.12/2000/4, from 11 August 2000.

CRC, General Comment No 15 (2013a) on the right of the child to the enjoyment of the highest attainable standard of health (art. 24), CRC/C/GC/15, from 17 April 2013.

CRC, General Comment No 17 (2013b) on the right of the child to rest, leisure, play, recreational activities, cultural life and the arts (art. 31), CRC/C/GC/17, from 17 April 2013.

CRC, General Comment No 20 (2016) on the implementation of the rights of the child during adolescence, CRC/C/GC/20, from 6 December 2016.

ECtHR (2015), *Zakharov v. Russia*, 47143/06, 4 December 2015.

ECtHR (2023), *L.B. v. Hungary*, 36345/16, 9 March 2023.

European Union, Proposal for a Regulation of the European Parliament and of the Council on the European Health Data Space, COM/2022/197 final.

HRC, General Comment No 35 (2014) on ICCPR article 9 on liberty and security of person.

IE Older persons, Report of the Independent Expert on the enjoyment of all human rights by older persons: Visit to New Zealand, A/HRC/45/14/ADD.2, 13 July 2020.

Inter-American Court of Human Rights, Members of the Corporation Lawyers Collective "José Alvear Restrepo" (CAJAR) Vs. Colombia, 18 March 2024.

UPR (Universal Periodic Review), 2021-2023. Recommendations toward Uganda (from Canada). A/HRC/50/11, 2022, para. 123.132; Recommendation toward Gabon (from Estonia), A/HRC/53/6, 2023, para. 136.83. Recommendation toward Morocco (from Greece), A/HRC/52/7, 2023, para. 57.109; Recommendations toward the Netherlands (from Cuba), A/HRC/52/16, 2022, para. 147.121. Recommendation toward Nauru (from France), A/HRC/47/17, 2021, para. 99.94.

World Conference on Human Rights in Vienna, Vienna Declaration and Programme of Action, 25 June 1993.

8 Digital disconnection as a plight or right?

A manifesto to re-imagine digital disconnection as a reasonable accommodation

Mariek M. P. Vanden Abeele, Marijn Martens, Sarah Anrijs, Sara Van Bruyssel and David de Segovia Vicente

8.1 Introduction

Digital disconnection as a concept refers to the voluntary actions that individuals undertake to set limits to their digital connectivity (Nassen et al., 2023; Syvertsen, 2020). Examples of such actions are temporarily abstaining from using a device or platform (i.e., digitally detoxing; Radtke et al., 2022), adjusting device settings to minimise distractions – for instance by disabling notifications or grey scaling (Dekker & Baumgartner, 2023; Liao & Sundar, 2022) and talking oneself down from the use of digital media when a craving occurs (Brevers & Turel, 2019). Digital disconnection as a phenomenon is growing: in Flanders (Belgium) alone, the number of adult citizens that sets limits to their digital connectivity through smartphones has grown from 58% in 2017 to 88% in 2022 (De Marez et al., 2022; Vanhaelewyn & De Marez, 2017).

From a conceptual point of view, digital disconnection is often considered an agentic response, allowing individuals to 'reclaim control' over their digital media use and screen time (Karsay & Vandenbosch, 2021). Underlying this idea of an agentic response is the assumption that digital well-being is enhanced when individuals can optimally balance their connectivity and disconnectivity, so that they maximise the benefits of digital media use while minimising drawbacks (Vanden Abeele, 2020). The phenomenon of digital disconnection responds to this idea: it comes with the hope and aspiration that – even in a culture of ubiquitous connectivity – it is still possible to focus and be productive, feel present in the moment and enjoy a sense of privacy (Syvertsen, 2020).

The assumption that digital disconnection as an agentic response can improve digital well-being is corroborated by empirical research findings suggesting that the use of digital disconnection products, such as the use of apps for monitoring and limiting screen time, mitigates against problematic or excessive screen use and in doing so, safeguards against the negative effects of problematic screen use

DOI: 10.4324/9781003528401-10

on well-being (e.g., Schmuck, 2020). The rationale, then, is that individuals can resort to digital disconnection products and services to better succeed in regulating their screen behaviour, especially in those contexts where rational decision-making over this behaviour is important, yet challenged by the digital environment (Lyngs et al., 2019).

The former conceptual approach to digital disconnection is fruitful in that it acknowledges the ambivalent experiences of individuals in relation to 24/7 connectivity (Ytre-Arne et al., 2020) and recognises the human capacity and right to intervene in one's own digital reality, among others by developing, adopting and implementing instruments that help modify it in line with one's goals and values (Karsay & Vandenbosch, 2021; Syvertsen, 2023). Yet, at the same time, the phenomenon of digital disconnection – and with it the commodification of disconnection through a wide range of products and services – is also fiercely criticised: scholars warn that approaching digital disconnection as an agentic response can reinforce processes of individual responsibilisation, leading to digital disconnection being framed foremost as a rational act of self-care towards digital well-being, even a luxury, that individuals should strive for – and thus choose to spend their money and energy on (Kuntsman & Miyake, 2022; Van Bruyssel et al., 2023).

For some individuals, however, digital disconnection is not a luxury or choice, but rather becomes a moral obligation – a necessary instrument of (self-)governance to feel digitally well (Fast, 2021). We argue in this chapter that in an 'always-on' and 'digital first' society, this obligation falls disproportionately on the shoulders of individuals with an underdeveloped or impaired capacity for self-regulation, who are more likely to be the young and/or the neurodiverse. After all, in this society it has become near impossible to opt out of the use of digital devices and platforms and many are intentionally designed to prey on vulnerabilities in executive functioning (Flayelle et al., 2023). Hence, for persons with impaired self-regulation – and by extension those who care for them – digital disconnection has become a plight they are condemned to if they wish to fully participate in contemporary digital society.

We therefore plead to understand digital disconnection as a necessity for some, and therefore a reasonable accommodation our society should provide. As we will argue, this re-imagination of digital disconnection has implications for how we conceive of digital disconnection and its potential to be recognised as a human right (see also Hesselberth, 2018; Kloza, 2024): it critically interrogates the individualisation of the responsibility for digital disconnection, as it forces already disadvantaged persons to take on the burden of 'disconnective work' (Fast, 2021) and therefore invites to think of ways in which we can collectively resist an attention economy (Odell, 2019).

In what follows, we will further elaborate on why digital disconnection is a necessity for persons with impaired self-regulation. We start by explaining what impaired self-regulation is, and reason how it can be considered a disability when surrounded by a technological environment that is designed to capitalise on attention.

8.2 Impaired self-regulation: a biopsychosocial perspective

Self-regulation, as an umbrella concept, is defined and used in different ways in different fields of research. Nonetheless, there is scholarly consensus that self-regulation refers to an individual's capacity for systematically 'setting personal goals and steering behaviour toward the achievement of established goals' (Zeidner et al., 2000, p. 751). *Impaired* self-regulation, then, occurs when individuals face difficulty in controlling and regulating their behaviour, which shows among other things, in failures of executive functions required to monitor, evaluate and instruct oneself (Wagner & Heatherton, 2015).

Impaired self-regulation is in itself not considered a disability *per se*, but it is identified as a core feature (and thus also a diagnostic criterion) of several developmental and learning disabilities, including attention deficit hyperactivity disorder (ADHD) and autism spectrum disorder (American Psychiatric Association, 2013). The World Health Organization (WHO) implicitly recognises impaired self-regulation as a disabling impairment, listing several executive functions that provide the capacity for self-regulation in its International Classification of Functioning, Disability and Health (ICF), including impulse control, attention and the capacity for organisation and planning (WHO, 2002).

Following a biopsychosocial model, however, the ICF makes explicit that what makes a disability is *more* than just the impairment in one's bodily or mental functions (WHO, 2002): disability occurs especially when a society is neither designed for, nor provides sufficient accommodations to compensate for the impairment, thus setting limits to the activities one can perform and disadvantaging those who are not 'able' without aid or intervention.

If we apply this lens to the case of impaired self-regulation, we can conclude that an impairment in executive functions becomes especially disabling when surrounded by a context in which this vulnerability is being deliberately exploited. We argue that the current digital environment represents such a context (Flayelle et al., 2023) that is omnipresent. Yet, it is difficult to opt out from this context, given that our contemporary society has developed a culture of ubiquitous connectivity, in which the use of digitised services and anytime, anyplace availability have become the norm. As we explain in the following, this catches individuals with impaired self-regulation in a double bind.

8.3 The triple trap of the digital society: addictive design, digital first and always on society

We observe three major developments in contemporary western(ised) societies that present a 'triple trap' to individuals with impaired self-regulation, making it difficult for them to live *with* digital media, but also *without*. These developments are situated in the digital, the service and the broader cultural environment that surrounds people.

8.3.1 Addictive design: the deliberate commodification of human attention

A first development concerns the digital environment itself: people today are surrounded by digital platforms designed for the commodification of their attention. This is because the (tech) industry has increasingly turned human attention into a quantifiable commodity (Marazzi, 2008): driven by a logic of surveillance capitalism (Zuboff, 2019), this industry develops and maintains evermore parts of our everyday digital surroundings (devices and platforms) to make a profit from the large-scale and real-time commodification of human behaviour through processes of dataveillance and datafication (Dijck, 2014; Haggart, 2019; Lai, 2023; Sadowski, 2019).

To serve the attention economy, digital platforms are tailored to maximise the amount of human attention – in the form of user engagement – they can capture. After all, as tech companies compete with each other for user engagement, those devoting substantial resources to 'hacking' human attention gain a competitive advantage. In doing so, however, this industry capitalises on design features, often labelled as addictive, that exploit the psychological mechanisms of attention in a way that challenges users' self-control, often leading to problematic usage patterns (Flayelle et al., 2023).

These addictive design features are embedded in a variety of different types of digital platforms. Social media platforms, for instance, use likes and reposts to target users' behaviour through random-ratio schedule reinforcement, and online shopping and gaming platforms often offer special deals at limited times to attract more attention from their users (Flayelle et al., 2023). Recognising the value of data, these design logics also increasingly pervade in the (public) service industry, where users are nudged to provide data in exchange for better service; think for instance of health insurance companies that nudge clients to share passively monitored health data (e.g., step count) in exchange for a discount, a point to which we will return in the following.

For now, it is clear that in this capitalist context, the goals of companies to gain more datapoints and the goals of individuals to limit their digital connectivity are inherently opposing. Due to the addictive design implemented by the tech industry, however, this quickly becomes an unfair fight, especially for those with impairment in self-regulation. Indeed, research shows that those with underdeveloped or impaired self-control capabilities see themselves disproportionately affected (Hofmann et al., 2016; Reinecke et al., 2022) and more easily fall into patterns of problematic use (Kim et al., 2016; West et al., 2021). Recent empirical work, for instance, shows how especially individuals with lower self-control experience mindless scrolling as a behaviour that impedes them from reaching their goals, resulting in feelings of guilt and decreased well-being (de Segovia Vicente et al., 2024).

One might argue that individuals suffering from impaired self-regulation can easily solve this by simply not using such tech products. As we explain in the following, however, this decision is complicated by the increasing expectation of connectivity in a digital first and always-on society.

8.3.2 The digital first society: the marginalisation of offline life

A second 'trap' results from society noticeably developing into a *digital first society*. This term refers to how the service industry, including the semi-public and public service industry, is increasingly adopting digital-first or digital-only strategies and nudging individuals to use digital services (Anrijs et al., 2023; Schou & Pors, 2019). Indeed, in order to realise daily or basic needs like arranging taxes, housing, healthcare and other administration, individuals are increasingly expected to go online and connect digitally with service providers. For some of these needs, the digital service has become the only service option. In Western countries, including Belgium, for instance, tremendous investments are being made in transforming (public) services into online or digital (public) services (Heponiemi et. al., 2020; Reutter, 2022).

The rationale behind this digital transformation of services is the belief that both service providers and receivers benefit from this evolution (Bovens & Zouridis, 2002). Compared to how they were organised in the past, digital services are considered cost-effective and time-saving and are believed to be easier and simpler to use. Moreover, digital services promise to be more transparent and responsive towards citizens compared to former analogue services (Mergel et al., 2019). Furthermore, service providers can also be motivated to go all-in on a digital strategy because it allows them to access and collect more data about their clients (Jayasree, 2013); data that they can subsequently use for business intelligence purposes (Arner et al., 2022; Hormozi & Giles, 2004).[1]

Recent studies question, however, whether these beliefs and hopes of increased efficiency, ease of use, transparency and business intelligence are actually fulfilled. Several studies have demonstrated how the digitisation and automation of service delivery, might have complicated the service delivery processes (Redden et al., 2020; Reutter, 2022). For service providers, new challenges arise from the digitisation and automation of services that require ample investment to be mitigated. For example, they need to invest to mitigate privacy or security issues, but also more complex issues related to transparency, bias and quality control (Redden et al., 2020; Reutter, 2022; Schiff et al., 2022). For service receivers, the move towards digital services is criticised for shifting the work and thus the responsibility from service providers to service receivers (Goedhart et al., 2022; Madsen et al., 2022; Schou & Pors, 2019). Examples of this are how bank transactions used to be performed by a bank clerk but are now in the hands of the user, or how citizens now need to request, download and print official documents through online portals instead of public administrations delivering these documents *via* physical mail or public counters.[2]

Although public service providers might still provide non-digital alternatives, these non-digital or physical service alternatives are often inferior: providing access at a slower pace, in a more restrictive manner and/or at a higher cost. As such, individuals are *de facto* nudged to go online to use digital services (Schou & Hjelholt, 2018). This is further complicated when service providers themselves start embedding addictive and commercial design features (e.g., gamification elements and marketing cookies) into their digital service platforms in order to increase the user engagement for their digital products.

Based on the above, we argue that (public) service providers have knowingly and unknowingly become complicit in re-organising our society into a digital first society. In this digital first society, citizens depend increasingly on digital environments for basic needs such as finances, administration, mobility, housing, etcetera. This is especially challenging for individuals with impaired self-regulation, who thus need to constantly access and use digital devices and platforms to make use of digitised services. The embedding of design logics following industry standards into these services (e.g., the use of cookies), as well as their convergence on the same device where people use a variety of other 'addictively designed' apps (e.g., social media, shopping, gaming), contribute to a context in which individuals with impaired self-regulation are set up for failure. The pervasiveness of digital services in everyday life, however, implies that it is difficult, if not impossible, to opt out.

8.3.3 The always-on society: the cultural normativity of 24/7 connectivity

Finally, our society is not only a digital first society, but also an *always-on society*: social norms surrounding availability and reciprocity have been altered as a result of ubiquitous connectivity, resulting in a permanently online, permanently connected lifestyle as the default mode of living (Vorderer et al., 2017). Currently, in an increasing number of professions, but also in non-professional social roles, individuals face pressures for continuous connectivity (Freytag et al., 2021; Nguyen, 2021). Effective parenting, competent management and employment are now perceived, at least in part, as functions that require online presence and a constant vigilance for what is happening online (Büchler et al., 2020; Nurmi & Hinds, 2020). For example, children (and their parents) are assumed to regularly be online to receive notifications from educational applications utilised by their schools. Similarly, managers and employees are expected to maintain availability for their colleagues through digital channels.

Once again, design logics play a role: normative expectations to be constantly online and respond immediately to any incoming communication are enforced through a variety of design cues embedded in communication applications (such as messaging apps, mailing apps, social media platforms, etc.), ranging from presence awareness cues to read receipts (Ling & Lai, 2016). These design features promote 'perpetual contact' (Katz & Aakhus, 2002), thereby creating a sense of obligation to respond promptly and remain continuously available, thus demanding a relentless connectivity to not miss out and stay on top of one's responsibilities (Van Bruyssel et. al., 2024).

These shifted norms to be available or present for others are in conflict with the ideal of digital disconnection, as disconnection inherently renders individuals unavailable or absent. Disconnection behaviour can, therefore, be perceived as breaking with social norms or expectations and can be perceived as less acceptable or appropriate, making it less likely, or harder, for individuals to engage in it (Fast, 2021; Geber et al., 2024). Those who disconnect need (implicit) approval or acceptance from those they disconnect from to be unavailable or absent for a while. This approval or acceptance might however be easier to realise for some than for others. While some people have the privilege to decide to spontaneously cut all social ties for a while (Beattie, 2020), others do not have, or want this possibility as disconnecting from social ties could be contested and would disrupt the lives of those they care for and about (Portwood-Stacer, 2013; Fast, 2021; Van Bruyssel et al., 2024).

In sum, the social complexity arising between the contradictory norms of disconnecting in an always-on society shows that initiating and certainly maintaining disconnection is going against the stream. Although practiced by an individual, digitally disconnecting involves everyone as part of a connected network. In this logic, if people with impaired self-regulation want to disconnect, it quickly becomes counterproductive and ineffective. They can be left with the choice to either ease their sensory load, being absent and falling short of the increasing amount of social expectations and responsibilities embedded in connectivity; or, suppress regulatory disfunctions and try to keep up and be focused. In short, trying to tend to one's well-being becomes increasingly incompatible with societal expectations.

8.4 Breaking free from the triple trap: facilitating effective digital disconnection as a reasonable accommodation

Based on our above argumentation, one might think we plead *against* digitisation. This is, however, not what we argue for. Rather, we want to question whether our digitising society deprives individuals with impaired self-regulation of equal opportunities; opportunities to focus, to achieve goals and to overall feel well and guilt-free, whether related to their private, social or professional life. Especially when evermore aspects of our daily lives are being digitised through platforms that prey on attention, we can ask if persons with impaired self-regulation are not disproportionately burdened to deal with this 'unfair' reality.

In what follows, we therefore make explicit what we do plead for, namely to shift the mindset surrounding digital disconnection, considering it not as a luxury but as an often necessary aid and therefore deserving of being recognised as a reasonable accommodation and an act of care work. We argue that by re-imagining digital disconnection this way, we can also re-imagine the actions and interventions that can assure the realisation of digital disconnection without jeopardising one's personal or professional life. We argue that this re-imagination of digital disconnection is required to truly approach digital disconnection as a *right* and not just a plight among those who suffer from impaired self-regulation.

8.4.1 Step one: recognising digital disconnection as a reasonable accommodation

Above we have argued that the addictive design of digital devices and platforms sets people with impaired self-regulation up for experiencing self-control failure. We believe that, in these circumstances, digital disconnection should first of all be recognised as a necessity and not a luxury or magical solution to impaired self-regulation.

There is increasing evidence that supports this view. This evidence shows that although people with impaired self-regulation more often turn towards digital disconnection, they still report a lack of self-control over their screen time – i.e., in spite of practicing disconnection more, they *still* suffer. Vanden Abeele and Nguyen (2023), for instance, found that the persons who practiced disconnection more, were those who reported *less* control over their screen time. Similarly, Schmuck (2020) found that persons who used digital detox apps were (still) more likely to be problematic smartphone users. These observations can explain why empirical evidence on the effectiveness of digital disconnection for improving well-being currently remains mixed (Nassen et al., 2023; Radtke et al., 2022; Vanden Abeele et al., 2024) and can help understand the heterogeneity in the effects of disconnection on well-being (Nguyen & Hargittai, 2024): digital disconnection might not simply be a *helpful means for all* to protect against the burdens of relentless connectivity, but rather completely unnecessary for those with good self-regulation capacity, while a *necessary accommodation* to those who struggle with impaired self-regulation. This assumption is supported by recent psychological research, which suggests that people high in trait self-control exert less self-control at the state level by simply 'avoiding the need to exert it in the first place' (Inzlicht & Roberts, 2024).

A parallel could be drawn with people who have a learning disability, for instance, dyslexia: dyslectic persons have persistent issues with reading and decoding text, even after high-quality intervention (Elliott, 2020). Reading aids are accommodations that help them navigate our written world and that somewhat level the playing field for them (Barden, 2014), but they will not magically 'absolve' them from their reading difficulties. Similarly, people with impaired self-regulation might resort to the use of digital disconnection as an aid to somewhat level the playing field for them in navigating our contemporary digital first and always-on society, to somewhat stay afloat when surrounded by an inescapable digital environment that is designed to provoke self-regulation failure. Digital disconnection can in other words help to (somewhat) re-adjust digital environments so that there is a lesser need for regulating media behaviour through directly applying will-power and self-control.

Essential here, is the recognition that, if true, digital disconnection does not give persons with impaired self-regulation an advantage over others – on the contrary, it rather aims to remove a disadvantage that they face. In a society that values equality and non-discrimination, disconnecting therefore deserves to be recognised as a *reasonable* accommodation, meaning that it reasonably compensates for an unfair disadvantage.

The former understanding has profound implications for how we approach disconnection products, services and strategies. Rather than seeing screen time reducing apps, disconnection gadgets and digital well-being trainings as part of the self-improvement industry, we can approach them as support tools and instruments that are potentially helpful for making reasonable accommodations to individuals with impaired self-regulation. For instance, in several countries, reading software is offered for free to students with dyslexia. Disconnection tools could by default be similarly offered to students – an evolution that we already see taking effect in schools that enforce localised digital disconnection, e.g., by asking students to put phones in a magnetically sealed pouch during school hours.

This shift in how we understand digital disconnection also broadens our perspective on already existing accommodations. For instance, in recent years there has been ample debate over the overdiagnosis of disorders characterised by impaired self-regulation, including ADHD. In this literature, scholars explain the currently observed overdiagnosis by pointing towards the 'cult of performance' (Gascon et al., 2022, p. 2374), leading individuals to rather seek diagnosis and treatment than to accept their human limitations; while this is likely a reason for the rise in diagnoses, we may however also explore alternative reasons. For instance, we could ask if the digitisation of society has not led to an amplification of the disadvantages that come with impaired executive functioning, thus largening the group who experiences a clinically diagnosable functional impairment. As Sophie McBain wrote in the Magazine The New Statesmen (McBain, n.d.):

> It is not pure coincidence that ADHD diagnoses have risen alongside the internet's attention economy. Nor is it a coincidence that they have increased during this era of cut-throat capitalism, in which ever more people are consigned to desk-bound jobs that place huge demands on their time. We are also still contending with the aftermath of the pandemic: is it any surprise that so many of us feel rudderless and unable to concentrate?

If we can indeed link the increase in ADHD diagnoses to the rise of the attention economy, then a provocative question is whether treatments for ADHD, among others through the use of medication, are not just a far reaching way to help people digitally disconnect so they can focus and concentrate.

8.4.2 Step two: recognising digital disconnection as an act of care work

Simply recognising digital disconnection as a reasonable accommodation is not enough, however. Current disconnection strategies are responsibilising the individual, while *collective* action is needed, as connection and disconnection in their essence are collective practices (Van Bruyssel et al., 2024). We should, therefore, be vigilant to how we allow and organise dis/connection in our private and professional lives, as well as which responsibilities we assign to whom in that process.

An ethics of care approach here is useful (Tronto, 2013). First, it allows to understand disconnection as a form of care work that is *essential* work – existing equally and not subordinately, with being connected. Second, an ethics of care, rather than starting on an individual level, departs from the collective: it seeks to understand how people and things are dependent on one another to function sustainably. It questions who – in this web of interdependent relationships – is more burdened with the work of care.

From this perspective, then, we can understand how individually practiced digital disconnection to protect oneself against the disabling nature of this environment is a potentially ill-fitted (and maybe even perverse) solution to this problem. After all, at its core, an ethics of care and subsequently a politics of care, implies pinpointing where caring responsibilities need to be more equally distributed and revealing where a lack of caregiving is damaging the necessary resources to adequately participate in society. To that end, we must look at the distribution of responsibilities, both between individuals versus institutions (e.g., schools, caregivers) and between social groups (e.g., the 'post-digital housewife') who are (or are not) burdened to care for dis/connection.

A politics of care perspective subsequently also holds political life, including governmental institutions, responsible to provide caring systems. In the case of the struggles of impaired self-regulation in a digital first and always-on society, this means providing adequate time and space for disconnection without jeopardising societal participation. To that end, being online cannot be the default for interactions with people and institutions, as it translates disconnecting – as 'not doing' something – to systematically falling short of basic needs and expectations. Disconnection – just like connection – is a collective behaviour and responsibility. As such disconnection as a right must go hand in hand with ensuring the stakes of disconnecting are not disproportionately high, by making sure there are valued, equal alternatives to catch the ties that are being (temporarily) disconnected from. For example, digital communication between schools, pupils and parents *via* dedicated online school platforms has facilitated many time-consuming tasks, but it has also brought along new and demanding online availability patterns that come with 'real' life expectations. For pupils, teachers or parents with impaired self-regulation offline communication alternatives could make a meaningful difference, both to provide and accept time to disconnect.

8.4.3 Step three: re-designing digital dis/connection environments

Up until here, we consider digital disconnection no longer as a luxury but as an intervention that is reasonable, albeit requires care work and caring circumstances to be a sustainable, attainable and inclusive practice. However, it seems logical to explore if the playing field could also be levelled more collectively and preventively through a universal re-design of the environment, referring both to the re-design of the digital environment as well as to the re-design of our society's institutions and our culture's normative expectations. We argue that this latter approach of re-designing the technological, institutional and social environment is currently not being sufficiently explored – on the contrary. In this final section we therefore explore options for the re-design of digital (dis)connection environment through regulation and education. Regulation and education can be seen as *preventive* interventions, attempting to prevent inequalities rather than to remedy inequalities afterwards.

Regulation for industry and society could, for instance, be realised by means of standards for non-addictive design that must be met (cf. Web Content Accessibility

Guidelines (WCAG) and data protection guidelines (General Data Protection Regulation)) and/or by imposing taxes or fines on those who do not meet or ignore standards. In addition, regulation or legislation could also be made for public services and essential sectors (e.g., governments, schools, banks, health insurance companies), in that these must always offer equivalent non-online alternatives. In doing so, individuals must be able to choose an alternative that delivers a similar service at a similar time or cost investment (e.g., a school that chooses to work with digital handbooks must ensure that this handbook is also available as a pdf and not just online/if connected to the Internet). Only when there are worthy alternatives, there is some guarantee that for these interactions individuals can choose not to connect.

To date, however, little regulation or legislation exists that obliges service providers to provide non-digital services with similar quality and efficiency. Non-digital services often become an after-thought, with (public) service providers adopting neoliberal tactics that prioritise cost reduction through digitising service delivery processes above equal non-digital services and as such inclusive access to services. This market-driven focus on cost-cutting instead of inclusivity could make legislation more difficult.

With respect to the always-on society, several European countries now have labour law legislation that specifies 'the right to disconnect'. In this legislation, however, the problem is often very narrowly interpreted as the 'right to be unavailable after working hours' (see de Leyn et al., 2024), thereby overlooking the struggle of employees to set boundaries around their connectivity *during* work hours to accommodate 'deep' and 'slow' work (Fast, 2021), for instance because they fear booking 'focus time' in their calendar will be disrespected or frowned upon.

In addition to regulation and legislation, disconnection could also be supported through education. We imagine this to include basic education that from a young age offers individuals knowledge and awareness of the use of addictive design and motives for digitising public and essential services in order to cultivate the necessary critical and caring thinking on digitising societies. Including this into higher education curricula for future digital product designers, policymakers and public servants can also be a solution on a structural level. By giving young citizens an understanding of the potential inequities that addictive design and/or digital-first services can create, they can make informed decisions, but most importantly interpret the struggles of dis/connecting in a critical societal framework rather than taking the blame. This could be realised through the integration of courses on media psychology, sociology and economy within IT, policy and economic science programmes in higher education.

8.5 Conclusion

To conclude, we argue that individuals with impaired self-regulation are disadvantaged in our contemporary Digital Society: they are confronted with a reality in which they are surrounded by addictively designed digital devices and platforms that prey on their vulnerability to lose self-control. Yet, these devices and platforms are often also useful and even necessary to access a wide variety of digitised (public) services. Ubiquitous connectivity has become necessary to meet expectations surrounding 24/7 availability and reciprocity that have become locked into our professional and personal social networks.

Given this conundrum, it should not be a surprise that digital disconnection is more common among individuals with impaired self-regulation, who likely seek to set limits to their digital connectivity to re-shape their digital environment so that it becomes less exploitative of their vulnerability. However, digital disconnection is too often approached as an individual responsibility and/or a luxury, rather than as a necessity for people with impaired self-regulation. What is then often forgotten, is that digital disconnection is not a magical solution but an act of care that requires work. Indeed, to participate equally in a digital first and always-on society, individuals with impaired self-regulation (and their caregivers) must invest ample effort into re-adjusting the environment so that it optimally protects against self-regulation failure. This work, however, all-too-often remains invisible, undervalued and ultimately remains an uphill battle.

For these reasons, we plead to give digital disconnection the status of a reasonable accommodation. This recognition, then, comes with an invitation to explore how society could shift the burden of responsibility for implementing this accommodation, as well as to consider how preventive measures could reduce the need for digital disconnection to begin with.

Acknowledgements

Funding support for this chapter was provided by the European Union's Horizon 2020 research and innovation programme under the European Research Council Starting Grant agreement 'DISCONNECT' No. 950635 and the Research Foundation Flanders (FWO-Vlaanderen) under Grant agreement 'Disconnect to Reconnect' No. S005923N.

Notes

1 Already two decades ago it was found that banks use data mining to analyse patterns that can predict how customers would react on interest rates, product offers and default payments (Hormozi & Giles, 2004). By analysing data, banks could increase their efficiency and improve customer targeting (Königstorfer & Thalmann, 2020). It should be noted that, for some services, such as banking, regulation has come into effect. The revised Payment Services Directive (PDS2), for example, forces banks to share their payment data to third party FinTech parties when requested by consumers, lessening their grip and ownership on this personal data.

2 Note how, in contrast with their expectations and hopes, this shift in responsibilities also have created *more* work for service providers, due to the many questions and complaints from individuals that they have to deal with. Some argue this has negated the proposed efficiency gains (see for example Løberg, 2021).

Bibliography

American Psychiatric Association. (2013). *Diagnostic and statistical manual of mental disorders: DSM-5* (5th ed.). American Psychiatric Association.

Anrijs, S., Mariën, I., De Marez, L., & Ponnet, K. (2023). Excluded from essential internet services: Examining associations between digital exclusion, socio-economic resources and internet resources. *Technology in Society*, *73*, 102211. https://doi.org/10.1016/j.techsoc.2023.102211

Arner, D. W., Castellano, G., & Selga, E. (2022). Financial data governance: The datafication of finance, the rise of open banking and the end of the data centralization paradigm. *SSRN Electronic Journal*. https://doi.org/10.2139/ssrn.4040604

Barden, O. (2014). Facebook levels the playing field: Dyslexic students learning through digital literacies. *Research in Learning Technology*, *22*. https://doi.org/10.3402/rlt.v22.18535

Beattie, A. (2020). *The manufacture of disconnection*. University of Wellington.

Bovens, M., & Zouridis, S. (2002). From street-level to system-level bureaucracies: How information and communication technology is transforming administrative discretion and constitutional control. *Public Administration Review*, *62*(2), 174–184. https://doi.org/10.1111/0033-3352.00168

Brevers, D., & Turel, O. (2019). Strategies for self-controlling social media use: Classification and role in preventing social media addiction symptoms. *Journal of Behavioral Addictions*, *8*(3), 554–563.

Büchler, N., Ter Hoeven, C. L., & Van Zoonen, W. (2020). Understanding constant connectivity to work: How and for whom is constant connectivity related to employee well-being? *Information and Organization*, *30*(3), 100302. https://doi.org/10.1016/j.infoandorg.2020.100302

Dekker, C. A., & Baumgartner, S. E. (2023). Is life brighter when your phone is not? The efficacy of a grayscale smartphone intervention addressing digital well-being. *Mobile Media & Communication*, 20501579231212062. https://doi.org/10.1177/20501579231212062

De Marez, L., Sevenhaut, R., Denecker, F., Georges, A., Wuyts, G., & Schuurman, D. (2022). *imec.digimeter 2022: Digitale trends in Vlaanderen* (p. 86). imec.

de Segovia Vicente, D., Van Gaeveren, K., Murphy, S. L., & Vanden Abeele, M. M. (2024). Does mindless scrolling hamper well-being? Combining ESM and log-data to examine the link between mindless scrolling, goal conflict, guilt, and daily well-being. *Journal of Computer-Mediated Communication*, *29*(1), zmad056.

Elliott, J. G. (2020). It's time to be scientific about dyslexia. *Reading Research Quarterly*, *55*(S1), S61–S75. https://doi.org/10.1002/rrq.333

Fast, K. (2021). The disconnection turn: Three facets of disconnective work in post-digital capitalism. *Convergence*, *27*(6), 1615–1630.

Flayelle, M., Brevers, D., King, D. L., Maurage, P., Perales, J. C., & Billieux, J. (2023). A taxonomy of technology design features that promote potentially addictive online behaviours. *Nature Reviews Psychology*, *2*(3), 136–150.

Freytag, A., Knop-Huelss, K., Meier, A., Reinecke, L., Hefner, D., Klimmt, C., & Vorderer, P. (2021). Permanently online—Always stressed out? The effects of permanent connectedness on stress experiences. *Human Communication Research*, *47*(2), 132–165. https://doi.org/10.1093/hcr/hqaa014

Gascon, A., Gamache, D., St-Laurent, D., & Stipanicic, A. (2022). Do we over-diagnose ADHD in North America? A critical review and clinical recommendations. *Journal of Clinical Psychology*, *78*(12), 2363–2380. https://doi.org/10.1002/jclp.23348

Geber, S., Nguyen, M. H., & Büchi, M. (2024). Conflicting norms—How norms of disconnection and availability correlate with digital media use across generations. *Social Science Computer Review*, *42*(3), 719–740. https://doi.org/10.1177/08944393231215457

Goedhart, N. S., Verdonk, P., & Dedding, C. (2022). "Never good enough." A situated understanding of the impact of digitalization on citizens living in a low socioeconomic position. *Policy & Internet*, *1*(21). https://doi.org/10.1002/poi3.315

Haggart, B. (2019). The age of surveillance capitalism: The fight for a human future at the new frontier of power. *Journal of Digital Media & Policy*, *10*(2), 229–243.

Heponiemi T., Jormanainen V., Leemann L., Manderbacka K., Aalto A., & Hyppönen H. (2020). Digital divide in perceived benefits of online health care and social welfare services: National cross-sectional survey study. *Journal of Medical Internet Research*, *22*(7). https://doi.org/10.2196/17616

Hesselberth, P. (2018). Discourses on disconnectivity and the right to disconnect. *New Media & Society*, *20*(5), 1994–2010. https://doi.org/10.1177/1461444817711449

Hofmann, W., Reinecke, L., & Meier, A. (2016). Of sweet temptations and bitter aftertaste: Self-control as a moderator of the effects of media use on well-being. In *The Routledge handbook of media use and well-being* (pp. 211–222). Routledge.

Hormozi, A. M., & Giles, S. (2004). Data mining: A competitive weapon for banking and retail industries. *Information Systems Management*, *21*(2), 62–71. https://doi.org/10.1201/1078/44118.21.2.20040301/80423.9

Inzlicht, M., & Roberts, B. W. (2024). The fable of state self-control. *Current Opinion in Psychology*, *58*, 101848. https://doi.org/10.1016/j.copsyc.2024.101848

Jayasree. (2013). A review on data mining in banking sector. *American Journal of Applied Sciences*, *10*(10), 1160–1165. https://doi.org/10.3844/ajassp.2013.1160.1165

Karsay, K., & Vandenbosch, L. (2021). Endlessly connected: Moving forward with agentic perspectives of mobile media (non-) use. In *Mass communication and society* (Vol. 24(6), pp. 779–794). Taylor & Francis.

Katz, J. E., & Aakhus, M. A. (2002). 19 Conclusion: Making meaning of mobiles – A theory of Apparatgeist. *Perpetual Contact*, 301–318. https://doi.org/10.1017/CBO9780511489471.023

Kim, Y., Jeong, J.-E., Cho, H., Jung, D.-J., Kwak, M., Rho, M. J., Yu, H., Kim, D.-J., & Choi, I. Y. (2016). Personality factors predicting smartphone addiction predisposition: Behavioral inhibition and activation systems, impulsivity, and self-control. *PLOS ONE*, *11*(8), e0159788. https://doi.org/10.1371/journal.pone.0159788

Kloza, D. (2024). The right not to use the internet. *Computer Law & Security Review*, *52*, 105907.

Königstorfer, F., & Thalmann, S. (2020). Applications of Artificial Intelligence in commercial banks – A research agenda for behavioral finance. *Journal of Behavioral and Experimental Finance*, *27*, 100352. https://doi.org/10.1016/j.jbef.2020.100352

Lai, S. S. (2023). "She's the communication expert": Digital labor and the implications of datafied relational communication. *Feminist Media Studies*, *23*(4), 1857–1871. https://doi.org/10.1080/14680777.2021.1998181

Leyn, T. D., Verlinden, A., Lemahieu, L., Geldof, L., Mennes, M., Cocchi, A., Martens, M., & Abeele, M. V. (2024). Unburdening the (sis)connected individual? A digital disconnection policy paradox in Flanders (Belgium). *Media and Communication*, *12*(0). https://doi.org/10.17645/mac.8588

Liao, M., & Sundar, S. S. (2022). Sound of silence: Does muting notifications reduce phone use? *Computers in Human Behavior*, *134*, 107338.

Ling, R., & Lai, C.-H. (2016). Microcoordination 2.0: Social coordination in the age of smartphones and messaging apps. *Journal of Communication*, *66*(5), 834–856.

Løberg, I. B. (2021). Efficiency through digitalization? How electronic communication between frontline workers and clients can spur a demand for services. *Government Information Quarterly*, *38*(2), 101551. https://doi.org/10.1016/j.giq.2020.101551

Lyngs, U., Lukoff, K., Slovak, P., Binns, R., Slack, A., Inzlicht, M., Van Kleek, M., & Shadbolt, N. (2019). Self-control in cyberspace: Applying dual systems theory to a review of digital self-control tools. *Proceedings of the 2019 CHI Conference on Human Factors in Computing Systems*, 1–18. https://doi.org/10.1145/3290605.3300361

Madsen, C. Ø., Lindgren, I., & Melin, U. (2022). The accidental caseworker – How digital self-service influences citizens' administrative burden. *Government Information Quarterly*, *39*(1), 101653. https://doi.org/10.1016/j.giq.2021.101653

Marazzi, C. (2008). Capital and language: From the new economy to the war economy. *No Title*. https://cir.nii.ac.jp/crid/1130282273072840832

McBain, S. (n.d.). Driven to distraction: Why are so many more adults being diagnosed with ADHD? *New Statesman, London*, *151*(5692), 32–37.

Mergel, I., Edelmann, N., & Haug, N. (2019). Defining digital transformation: Results from expert interviews. *Government Information Quarterly*, *36*(4), 101385. https://doi.org/10.1016/j.giq.2019.06.002

Nassen, L.-M., Vandebosch, H., Poels, K., & Karsay, K. (2023). Opt-out, abstain, unplug. A systematic review of the voluntary digital disconnection literature. *Telematics and Informatics*, *81*, 1–24.

Nguyen, M. H. (2021). Managing social media use in an "always-on" society: Exploring digital wellbeing strategies that people Use to disconnect. *Mass Communication and Society*, *24*(6), 795–817. https://doi.org/10.1080/15205436.2021.1979045

Nguyen, M. H., & Hargittai, E. (2024). Digital disconnection, digital inequality, and subjective well-being: A mobile experience sampling study. *Journal of Computer-Mediated Communication*, *29*(1), zmad044.

Nurmi, N., & Hinds, P. J. (2020). Work design for global professionals: Connectivity demands, connectivity behaviors, and their effects on psychological and behavioral outcomes. *Organization Studies*, *41*(12), 1697–1724. https://doi.org/10.1177/0170840620937885

Odell, J. (2019). *How to do nothing: Resisting the attention economy*. Melville House.

Portwood-Stacer, L. (2013). Media refusal and conspicuous non-consumption: The performative and political dimensions of Facebook abstention. *New Media & Society*, *15*(7), 1041–1057. https://doi.org/10.1177/1461444812465139

Radtke, T., Apel, T., Schenkel, K., Keller, J., & von Lindern, E. (2022). Digital detox: An effective solution in the smartphone era? A systematic literature review. *Mobile Media & Communication*, *10*(2), 190–215.

Redden, J., Dencik, L., & Warne, H. (2020). Datafied child welfare services: Unpacking politics, economics and power. *Policy Studies*, *41*(5), 507–526. https://doi.org/10.1080/01442872.2020.1724928

Reinecke, L., Gilbert, A., & Eden, A. (2022). Self-regulation as a key boundary condition in the relationship between social media use and well-being. *Current Opinion in Psychology*, *45*, 101296. https://doi.org/10.1016/j.copsyc.2021.12.008

Reutter, L. (2022). Constraining context: Situating datafication in public administration. *New Media & Society*, *24*(4), 903–921. https://doi.org/10.1177/14614448221079029

Sadowski, J. (2019). When data is capital: Datafication, accumulation, and extraction. *Big Data & Society*, *6*(1), 2053951718820549. https://doi.org/10.1177/2053951718820549

Schiff, D. S., Schiff, K. J., & Pierson, P. (2022). Assessing public value failure in government adoption of artificial intelligence. *Public Administration, 100*(3), 653–673. https://doi.org/10.1111/padm.12742

Schmuck, D. (2020). Does digital detox work? Exploring the role of digital detox applications for problematic smartphone use and well-being of young adults using multigroup analysis. *Cyberpsychology, Behavior, and Social Networking, 23*(8), 526–532.

Schou, J., & Hjelholt, M. (2018). Digital citizenship and neoliberalization: Governing digital citizens in Denmark. *Citizenship Studies, 22*(5), 507–522.

Schou, J., & Pors, A. S. (2019). Digital by default? A qualitative study of exclusion in digitalised welfare. *Social Policy & Administration, 53*(3), 464–477. https://doi.org/10.1111/spol.12470

Syvertsen, T. (2020). *Digital detox: The politics of disconnecting*. Emerald Group Publishing.

Syvertsen, T. (2023). Framing digital disconnection: Problem definitions, values, and actions among digital detox organisers. *Convergence, 29*(3), 658–674.

Tronto, J. C. (2013). *Caring democracy: Markets, equality, and justice*. New York University Press.

Van Bruyssel, S., De Wolf, R., & Vanden Abeele, M. (2023). Who cares about digital disconnection? Exploring commodified digital disconnection discourse through a relational lens. *Convergence*, 13548565231206504. https://doi.org/10.1177/13548565231206504

Van Bruyssel, S., De Wolf, R., & Vanden Abeele, M. (2024). From bliss to burden: An ethnographic inquiry into how social, material and individual obstacles to digital well-being shape everyday life. *New Media & Society*, 14614448241288159. https://doi.org/10.1177/14614448241288159

Vanden Abeele, M. M. P. (2020). Digital wellbeing as a dynamic construct. *Communication Theory, 31*(4), 932–955. https://doi.org/doi:10.1093/ct/qtaa024

Vanden Abeele, M. M. P., & Nguyen, M. H. (2023). Digital media as ambiguous goods: Examining the digital well-being experiences and disconnection practices of Belgian adults. *European Journal of Communication*, 02673231231201487. https://doi.org/10.1177/02673231231201487

Vanden Abeele, M., Vandebosch, H., Koster, E., De Leyn, T., Van Gaeveren, K., de Segovia Vicente, D., Van Bruyssel, S., van Timmeren, T., De Marez, L., Poels, K., DeSmet, A., De Wever, B., Verbruggen, M., & Baillien, E. (2024). Why, how, when, and for whom does digital disconnection work? A process-based framework of digital disconnection. *Communication theory, 34*(1), Article 1. https://doi.org/10.1093/ct/qtad016

van Dijck, J. (2014). Datafication, dataism and dataveillance: Big Data between scientific paradigm and ideology. *Surveillance & Society, 12*(2), 197–208. https://doi.org/10.24908/ss.v12i2.4776

Vanhaelewyn, B., & De Marez, L. (2017). *Imec.digimeter* 2017: *Measuring digital media trends in Flanders* (p.212). imec.

Vorderer, P., Hefner, D., Reinecke, L., & Klimmt, C. (2017). Permanently online and permanently connected: A new paradigm in communication research? In *Permanently Online, Permanently Connected*. Routledge.

Wagner, D. D., & Heatherton, T. F. (2015). Self-regulation and its failure: The seven deadly threats to self-regulation. In *APA handbook of personality and social psychology, Volume 1: Attitudes and social cognition* (pp. 805–842). American Psychological Association. https://doi.org/10.1037/14341-026

West, R., Ash, C., Dapore, A., Kirby, B., Malley, K., & Zhu, S. (2021). Problematic smartphone use: The role of reward processing, depressive symptoms and self-control. *Addictive Behaviors, 122*, 107015.

WHO. (2002). Towards a common language for functioning, disability, and health: ICF. In *The International Classification of Functioning, Disability and Health*. https://cir.nii.ac.jp/crid/1573668925447490176

Ytre-Arne, B., Syvertsen, T., Moe, H., & Karlsen, F. (2020). Temporal ambivalences in smartphone use: Conflicting flows, conflicting responsibilities. *New Media & Society*, *22*(9), 1715–1732. https://doi.org/10.1177/1461444820913561

Zeidner, M., Boekaerts, M., & Pintrich, P. R. (2000). Self-regulation: Directions and challenges for future research. In *Handbook of self-regulation* (pp. 749–768). Elsevier. www.sciencedirect.com/science/article/pii/B9780121098902500524

Zuboff, S. (2019). Surveillance capitalism and the challenge of collective action. *New Labor Forum*, *28*(1), 10–29.

Part II

Contexts

9 Right not to use the Internet

Lessons to be learned from the right not to be subject to automated decisions

Leonor Moral Soriano

9.1 Introduction

It is widely acknowledged that new rights emerge when the existing legal framework fails to adequately protect the political and moral values of a society. Several factors can contribute to this inadequacy (Serna 2024: 19). Among these is the belief that current rights are insufficient to address new challenges (such as the digital ones); additionally, technological and scientific advancements, such as the use of "black boxes" in decision-making processes, further require the establishment of new rights. However, sometimes the best answer to deal with these defies are not new rights but a reinforced interpretation of existing rights (Serna 2024: 21).[1] In this sense, the right not to use Internet can be conceptualized as an specific interpretation of the fundamental right of privacy (data protection); likewise, the right to be free from automated decisions may be considered a concretization of the right to judicial protection (and, ultimately, the Rule of Law).

In particular, automated decision-making (ADM) systems are artificial intelligence technologies designed to assist or even replace human judgments. Applied in the legal domain, this technology is used by legal operators. The idea of a robot judge or machine judge is unsettling, though it has ceased to be a science fiction image, and national legislations, such as in Spain, already regulate AI-assisted judicial decisions.[2] On the other hand, the use of ADM systems by the public authorities and governmental bodies is a well-established and widespread practice in all public services areas: health, education, contracting, transportation, etc. What is challenging is the use of ADM systems by public bodies to take decisions that have legal effects on citizens, so that it will be an algorithm that, *via* assistance or substitution, determines the sphere of rights and interests of those affected by the activity of governmental bodies.

ADM systems present formidable challenges for the legal framework: transparency, accessibility, accountability, fairness, biases, and the delegation of legal powers to machines, among others. To confront these challenges and safeguard the rationality of legal systems, some scholars advocate for establishing a human right to not be subject to automated decisions. I will explore the necessity of this new right from both a functional perspective (do we require a new right?) and a normative standpoint (why is the creation of a new right imperative?). These functional

DOI: 10.4324/9781003528401-12

and normative questions mirror those posed by other emerging rights, such as the right not to use the Internet, which is the main theme of this book. In addressing these inquiries, I will focus on the utilization of ADM by legal practitioners, particularly by public bodies whose decisions, whether partially or fully automated, directly impact individual rights. Do we truly need a new right not to be subjected to automated legal decisions? Are the "classic" rights providing us with sufficient protection?

9.2 Functional and normative concept of automated decision-making

In decision-making process, public administrations may employ ADM systems based on various technologies such as rules, regressions, predictive analytics, machine learning, deep learning, or neural networks; one or more of these technologies are selected or combined depending on the phase of the administrative procedure.[3] In this sense, their use is more prevalent in the initial stages of administrative actions, particularly in planning and in the early stages of file instruction (Hofman 2021: 4).

Ulrik Roehl (2022) has identified up to six types of ADM system usage in administrative actions depending on the level of autonomy attributed to AI, i.e., the extent to which the legal operator utilizes the technology.[4] This functional classification (non-normative) actually identifies different levels of interaction between humans and the ADM system used, that is, between the legal operator and the algorithm:

Type A: Minimal automation. The legal operator decides on all aspects of the administrative file and receives assistance from technologies like a word processor. They will use checklists, instructions, and other decision-making standards that are not embedded in algorithms.

Type B: Data retrieval and processing. The decision is shared between the legal operator and the technology. The technology collects, records, and presents relevant data to resolve the case. For example, awarding study grants requires a technology that examines applications and extracts relevant data from the public bodies' databases.

Type C: Procedural steps to follow. Similarly, a decision is shared between the operator and the technology. In this case, the technology not only retrieves and selects relevant data but also suggests the next steps in the procedure. For instance, the technology used in the United States to decide on aid for disabled children belongs to this category since the system evaluates applications: for simpler cases, an automatic recommended decision is made, whereas for more complex cases, the technology suggests direct evaluation by the legal operator.

Type D: Assisted decisions. The decision is shared between the legal operator and the technology. The technology collects, records, and presents some or all relevant data from a file and also suggests a limited number of solutions or even a specific decision. The previous example also applies here as the machine proposes or recommends possible decisions that the legal operator can adopt.

Type E: Automated decisions. The technology, not the legal operator, is the primary author of the decision. All aspects are entrusted to the technology, which operates automatically based on statistics and correlations, without the assistance of a public employee in the decision-making process. Following the grant example, after data retrieval and analysis, the algorithm decides the amount of the grant without the legal operator's intervention. Another example is the technology that identifies and notifies citizens of debt acquired from improper social benefits; if the citizen does not contest the notification within a certain period, the technology initiates debt recovery proceedings. Some aspects of these automated decisions may even be considered characteristic of the following type of technology.

Type F: Autonomous decisions. Again, the primary decision-maker here is technology. All aspects of the administrative decision are entrusted to technology based on dynamic unsupervised machine learning systems, where the legal operator does not intervene in the decision-making process.

All these ADM-assisted or fully automated decisions are adopted by a legal operator (Roehl 2022: 49), even in the realm of Types E and F decisions. Therefore, from a functional perspective, the necessary human intervention does not detract from the automation of the decision reached.

This functional definition of ADM appears, at first glance, to contradict the normative definition found in European legislation. Article 22 of the General Data Protection Regulation (GDPR) states that:

> The data subject shall have the right not to be subject to a decision based solely on automated processing, including profiling, which produces legal effects concerning him or her or similarly significantly affects him or her.

It appears that the inclusion of the term "solely" plays a pivotal role in determining when a decision is automated: if a decision is fully automated, we may assert a presumed right not to be subject to such judgment; conversely, if the decision relies partly on ADM systems, the level of legal protection changes, and we forfeit the right not to be subject to an automated decision. This concept of ADM under Article 22 GDPR, which centres on the element of "solely" (i.e., fully automated decisions), would enable the evasion of legal constraints on all partially automated decisions, thereby rendering the right not to be subject to automated decisions inapplicable.

The scope of Article 22 GDPR, and thus the concept of ADM, was addressed in a ruling by the Court of Justice of the European Union in case C-634/21 dated December 7, 2023. In this case, SCHUFA, an algorithm-based scoring company, assesses individuals based on their past behaviour to predict future conduct. The plaintiff, who applied for a loan, was denied credit by the lending institution due to SCHUFA's prediction. Upon exercising their right to access data protection against SCHUFA, the plaintiff received only generic information; moreover, SCHUFA refused access to their data and the weighting of that data used in the probability calculation. While SCHUFA did not directly deny credit, the decision of the lending institution was influenced by the information provided by SCHUFA.

According to the Court, the generation of a probability value by an entity like SCHUFA "constitutes an individual automated decision" because Article 22 GDPR refers not only to decisions that have legal effects on the data subject concerned but also to resolutions that significantly affect them (para. 44 C-634/21). In essence, the decision of the lending institution qualifies as an automated decision because it relied on a third-party ADM system that substantially influenced the final decision.

As Cotino indicates, the guarantees of Article 22 GDPR are thus linked to facts or acts that have an influence in the decision made (Cotino 2024). In other words, the individual decision is automated if it "draws strongly" on probabilistic calculations (para. 48 C-634/21) or is based on another ADM system. It is irrelevant whether the algorithm's result was provided by a third party and not the decision-making entity. The Court argues that there would be a risk of circumventing Article 22 GDPR if an interpretation were chosen according to which the generation of the probability value should be considered a mere preparatory act, and only the act adopted by the third party could, if applicable, be classified as a *decision* within the meaning of Article 22.1 of the GDPR.

The impact of this doctrine is extraordinary for determining the treatment of automated decisions in general and automated legal decisions in particular. The Court upheld a more protective rather than formalistic stance, since the veil of "entirely" automated decisions (Cotino 2024) is lifted, and automated decisions is a notion that includes also partially automated or semi-automated decisions based on ADM systems with greater or lesser human intervention. The scope of Article 22 GDPR extends to decisions that are determinatively based on ADM systems, and, therefore, human intervention should not automatically exclude the application of the guarantees for automated decisions conferred by Article 22 GDPR.[5]

The functional concept proposed by Roehl aligns with the legal interpretation of ADM by the Court. With the Court's ruling, the scope of the guarantees under Article 22 GDPR broadens, allowing the invocation of the right not to be subject to automated legal decisions when a decision (partially automated) is determinatively based on an ADM system. What constitutes this right? Is it a fundamental right?

9.3 The alleged right not to be subject to automated legal decisions

The purported right not to be subject to automated decisions should entail the prohibition of using ADM systems and the invalidity of automated decisions. However, the GDPR does not envisage that in this manner. In fact, Article 22 of the GDPR outlines significant exceptions to this alleged right. Automated decisions are permitted if:

a) is necessary for entering into, or performance of, a contract between the data subject and a data controller;

b) is authorized by Union or Member State law to which the controller is subject and which also lays down suitable measures to safeguard the data subject's rights and freedoms and legitimate interests; or
c) is based on the data subject's explicit consent.

Given the broad scope of these exceptions, the anticipated prohibition of ADM usage gives rise to a series of obligations for the data controller and a set of guarantees for the individual. On one hand, the GDPR mandates measures to safeguard the data subject's rights, freedoms, and legitimate interests.[6] On the other hand, the data subject is endowed with guarantees such as providing specific information to the interested party and with rights such as to obtain human intervention, express their viewpoint, receive an explanation of the decision taken after such evaluation, and challenge the decision (para. 66 C-634/21 and recital 71 of the GDPR).

The wording of Article 22 of the GDPR is peculiar if it is intended as a provision declaring a new human right. Let us imagine that the European legislator declares the right to education and then specifies that exceptions to it are allowed if expressly authorized by the Member States. Immediately, we would conclude that we are not facing the declaration of a human right because we know that rights are universal and, if they serve any purpose, it is to limit the power of public authorities (general exceptions are not admissible). Similarly, given the wide scope of exceptions in Article 22 of the GDPR, it does not declare a right not to be subject to automated decisions; rather, it assembles a set of guarantees that must be provided to protect citizens against decisions using ADM systems.[7]

There is no new right, although it recognizes a set of actions and guarantees. The question, then, is whether these guarantees should be grounded in a right not to be subject to automated legal decisions, and thus, whether such a right is necessary. Should a right not to be subject to automated decisions be established? Some authors (Dror-Shpoliansky and Shany 2021; Huq 2020) argue that new rights need to be created to shield us from the novel threats and challenges posed by the digital realm. Alongside offline rights, a second generation of online rights emerges with the aspiration to equalize the analog and the digital, at least in terms of the protection afforded in both realms.

Paradoxically, multiplying the number of fundamental rights diminishes their force, and if we do not wish to create a landscape inundated with hollow rights, we must recall García Figueroa's dictum (2022) *iura non sunt multiplicanda sine necessitate* that is inspired in Ockham's razor. It is worth remembering that a fundamental right is not merely any declaration prefaced by the words "right to ..."; rights are realms of freedom that exist even prior to the legal system and, for this reason, they constrain the legal framework (legal norms cannot contravene fundamental rights) and notably restrict the exercise of public powers. As Laporta states (1987: 27), rights precede actions, claims, demands, norms, normative freedoms, and status immunities.

Therefore, from the reading of Article 22 of the GDPR, it is erroneous to conclude that we are confronting a new fundamental right because there is a set of guarantees against automated decisions (obtaining human intervention, expressing their viewpoint, receiving an explanation of the decision taken after such evaluation, and challenging the decision). Instead, the argument would be that we have a set of actions and guarantees because we possess a right. However, I do not believe that this is a new right, nor is it necessary to be so. The rationale for the defence measures we are examining against automated legal decisions derives from the Rule of Law itself and the principle of due process.

9.4 Administrative law as the normative system for ADM-based decisions

Jennifer Raso (2021), in her contribution to the collective book "Artificial Intelligence and the Law in Canada", has proposed using Administrative Law as the normative framework (a system of rules and principles) for legal decisions made by public administration based on ADM. While she specifically discusses Canadian Administrative Law, it's important not to overstate the differences between Anglo-American and Roman-Germanic legal systems (Moral Soriano 2008). On both sides of the Atlantic, we share principles that shape our Public Law, notably, for our purposes, the principle of due process.

Indeed, administrative procedure is a structured series of actions aimed at ensuring that decisions are lawful, appropriate, and the most fitting. Moreover, administrative procedure primarily serves as a safeguard for stakeholders to defend their rights and legitimate interests. In this regard, it will be argued that the actions and guarantees considered in the GDPR related to the purported right not to be subject to automated decisions closely align with the actions and guarantees granted by the Rule of Law to all citizens, specifically, the rights outlined in Articles 41.2 and 47 of the EU Charter of Fundamental Rights (EU Charter), regarding the right to good administration, form the basis of the guarantees outlined in the GDPR.

9.4.1 Allegations. Hearing of the interested party

The first guarantee mentioned in Article 22 of the GDPR is the right to seek human intervention from the public agent and to express the viewpoint of the data subject. It represents a *reserve of humanity* (Ponce Solé 2022, 2019) that extends to ADM processes and the right to be heard at any stage of the administrative procedure, particularly before a decision is reached (Article 41.2.a) of the EU Charter).

When public administration makes a decision affecting our rights and interests, we have the right to participate in this decision-making process by making allegations at any stage of the proceeding, including during its instructional phase and prior to the decision's adoption. These forms of intervention presuppose human involvement since the allegations will be evaluated by the public agent, and if rejected, the reasons for rejection must be provided.

The human-in-the-loop model envisioned here is predominantly employed by ADM systems: human-in-the-loop-for-exceptions (HITLFE). It entails humans (legal operators) handling exceptions (allegations) to assess their relevance (Llano

2024: 141). This model assumes the fallibility of predictive models and also presupposes that the interested party is aware that the public body is resorting to ADM systems in the decision-making process. Thus, to exercise our right to be heard in administrative proceedings, we must be informed of the use and extent of ADM systems by public administration.

9.4.2 Notification and access to the file

This right to be informed (as a passive right) is closely linked to another inseparable guarantee of the administrative procedure: notifying the interested party that an administrative procedure has been initiated involving ADM systems. Additionally, it includes the right to access the administrative file as provided for in Article 41.2.b) of the EU Charter (based on the principles of contradiction and transparency). In cases of administrative decisions based on ADM systems, notification should include information on the interaction between the ADM system and the legal operator, the specific ADM system used, whether it proposes a specific decision, and its operation. Without this information, stakeholders will find it challenging to make relevant allegations or participate meaningfully in the hearing procedure.

Steps in this direction have been taken in French Administrative Law where the administration is obligated to notify when an administrative act has been adopted using an ADM system. Article L311-3-1 of the Code of Relations between the Public and the Administration (amended by the Digital Republic Act of 2016, known as the Lemaire Act) states that "*une décision individuelle prise sur le fondement d'un traitement algorithmique comporte une mention explicite en informant l'intéressé*".[8] However, accessing information about the use of ADM systems from the outset of the procedure is crucial for citizens involved in the decision-making process to defend their interests and rights. One must keep in mind that the purpose of notification is to gain a comprehensive understanding of the evidence used by the legal operator, so concealing relevant aspects impedes a robust challenge of automated administrative decisions.

Using an example provided by Raso (2021: 184), let's consider an individual imprisoned for a sexual assault offense. To determine their placement in low, medium, or high-security facilities, prison officials assess risks using technology that predicts inmate behaviour based on their history. The public body utilizes data provided by the individual and from other databases that feed the algorithm; the outcome of the ADM may be the indication that the inmate's future behaviour poses a medium risk to other prisoners. If the individual knew that the algorithm gave more weight to data correlations extracted from previous records than to their own responses, they could understand the decision criteria that have been followed. However, if they are unaware that aspects such as ethnic group weighting, postal code, criminal history, or the use of other databases overweight their own responses, they will have limited opportunities to challenge or make meaningful allegations (Raso 2021: 190).

9.4.3 Justification of the administrative decision

This brings us to the final guarantee of any legal decision, including automated administrative decisions: every legal decision must be justified. The obligation to provide legal justification for a decision lies at the core of our Rule of Law: only by understanding the reasons behind the decision can we exercise the right to challenge it through administrative review and judicial proceedings. The obligation to justify judicial decisions and the right to effective judicial protection are enshrined in Articles 41.2.c and 47 of the EU Charter, respectively. Automated legal acts adopted by public administration cannot evade this requirement for justification, nor can they evade scrutiny through administrative review or judicial recourse. The opposite scenario would be characteristic of an arbitrary state, where decisions made by its authorities evade legal scrutiny.[9]

Requiring administrative acts to be motivated is inherent to all legal activities, just as we demand that judicial decisions must be justified.[10] Public officials, like judges, are operators of a normative system, namely, the Law, and must base their decisions within this normative framework, providing not only relevant facts but also appropriate reasons (laws, regulations, precedents, legal principles, values, etc.).

Considering that the public official making an administrative decision is a legal operator and argues in legal terms, it is essential to distinguish between the principle of explainability (also covered in the GDPR) and the requirement of legal justification. In this regard, the technology of the ADM system must be explained to understand how more weight or relevance is attributed to the profile developed from previous cases; however, why ADM systems are used in a specific administrative act is a matter that should be justified, i.e., legally argued.

9.5 Explaining is not justifying

Explanation and justification cannot be confused because they belong to categorical domains with very different adjustment directions.[11] The notion of adjustment directions was developed by John Searle (1983: 7), who distinguishes between (i) adjusting our mind to the world and (ii) adjusting the world to our mind.[12] The adjustment direction of the mind (or language) to the world is present in technoscience and especially in computing: it describes reality. It tells us what is *normal*; it explains how the algorithm works or what correlations exist between the analysed data. On the other hand, the adjustment direction of the world to the mind (or language) pertains to normative systems such as law: it tells us what should be. It tells us *how the world should be*, not *how it is*; it informs us of the normative, and we must not confuse *normality* with *normativity*,[13] or *Sein* with *Sollen* (Kelsen 1991 [1960]).

These two adjustment perspectives are conceptually separate (García Figueroa 2017: 113). However, this separation does not imply that there is no place for artificial intelligence in the legal sphere. Rather, it suggests that the role of artificial intelligence in law in general, and ADM systems in legal decisions in particular, must be analysed considering that they are descriptive tools within a prescriptive context. These tools are essentially products of another world (the empirical) that also serve the normative (Moral Soriano 2023).

In this sense, behavioural patterns and predictions generated by technologies such as machine learning provide us with descriptive premises. This sets an important limit on the role they can play in legal argumentation, as we can explain if we consider Hume's Law:[14] it is impossible to derive normative claims solely from descriptive ones; therefore, deriving a legal decision (a judgment of duty) from a purely descriptive premise (the outcome of an algorithm) is unfeasible. Indeed, ADM systems are conceptually incapable of justifying or founding legal decisions (such as administrative acts or judicial decisions) on their own.[15]

The danger of this confusion between explanation and justification is evidenced by the use of ADM systems based on machine learning, and especially deep learning. In these cases, the machine makes connections between the vast amount of data it is fed and processes them in hidden intermediate layers until reaching the output layer: the decision, understood as an empirical statement (not prescriptive). Caution must be exercised regarding the application of this technology in the legal domain, particularly in the justification of legal decisions, because it lacks transparency: we do not know how it works, so we are unaware of what leads an ADM system to reach a specific outcome. Taken to the extreme, Eduardo Gamero (2021) argues that the obligation to justify administrative decisions (automated or not) prohibits the use of black box predictive algorithms in decision-making processes since it is impossible to know why the system makes the proposed decision.[16]

To address the transparency issue of black boxes used by the public administration in its legal activity, proposed solutions range from full access to the base code, partial access, to the most novel, and still in development, Explainable AI (XAI). Michèle Finck (2019: 14) argues that full access to the data and the artificial intelligence model used must overcome two significant hurdles: first, only a minority of citizens could understand the data and algorithm commands; second, intellectual property and data protection could be another obstacle to revealing the ADM system used. Therefore, explainability is the chosen route for technological developments to address the transparency issue. In projects like DARPA XAI,[17] machines understand the context and environment in which they operate and, over time, build explanatory models that allow them to characterize real-world phenomena. These may be based on technical factors, counterfactual explanations (Wachter *et al.*, 2018), or compliance systems (Hildebrandt 2011). For example, in medicine, LIME, Salency Maps, or Grad-CAM are some of the XAI systems in cancer detection that explain the diagnosis reached by highlighting the image of those areas that have been decisive for the machine to make the decision.

Explainability brings us back to the empirical world: we explain how the law of gravity works in the same way that we explain how an AI system works and how a specific outcome has been reached. However, once again, we must not confuse the world of *how an invention works* (empirical, composed of descriptive premises) with the world of *why we reach a decision* (normative, composed of prescriptive premises). In other words, for explanation, we need descriptive premises, while for justification / foundation / argumentation, we need, in addition, prescriptive premises. Clarifying this distinction prevents the reduction of legal discourse to empirical discourse (Alexy 1989: 225).

9.6 Predictive justice and the rule of law

Article 22 GDPR refers to safeguards that are deeply connected to fundamental rights entrenched in the Rule of Law, as articulated in Articles 41.2 and 47 of the EU Charter of Fundamental Rights. These rights include the right to be heard at any stage of the administrative process, access to administrative files, the obligation to justify legal decisions, and the right to effective judicial protection. Their application in European administrative procedures typically involves procedures such as allegations, hearings, notifications, access to files, justifications of administrative acts, and challenges in administrative or jurisdictional proceedings.

It has been emphasized that in order to exercise our right to effective judicial protection and to challenge automated legal decisions, we need something more than an explanation of the decision referred to in Recital 71 of the GDPR.[18] The reason is that we cannot legally challenge explanations that belong to the empirical world, in the same way that we cannot challenge the statement that gravity attracts every mass. The technology behind the ADM system used must be *explained* to understand how more weight or relevance is attributed to the profile developed from previous cases, or the relevance attributed to certain aspects of the specific case, or the weight of a fundamental right in conflict with other rights invoked in the case. All of this can be explained, and it is the purpose of XAI or another technology. However, it must be *justified* why ADM systems are used in a specific administrative decision, why certain elements of the case are given relevance while others are excluded, or why the weight of fundamental rights varies according to the elements of the case. From the obligation to justify a legal decision follows the obligation to notify and allow access to the administrative file in order to know all the judgment elements that the legal operator will use; only then can we make allegations both during the decision-making process and before reaching a decision (otherwise, we would be blindly stumbling and hoping to hit upon some grounds for challenge). These obligations will be refined with compliance systems and impact assessment on fundamental rights envisaged by the European Artificial Intelligence Act.

Meanwhile, let us not surrender to the language of technoscience. Machines can give us predictions of criminal recidivism, tax fraud commission, vulnerability status to qualify for social benefits, etc. There are even intelligent systems that predict the outcome of judicial procedures. All of this is characteristic of a model of legal realism "that does not strictly respond to an *ex iuris scientia* interpretation, but to a practical and forensic view of positive law" (Llano 2024). This vision is highly attractive in the case of public administration: who would not want to have an administration whose legal operators resolve matters quickly, economically, and (predictably) accurately thanks to ADM systems? However, in this transition to prediction (or predictive justice as Llano 2024, calls it), we cannot relinquish rights that are inherent to the Rule of Law. In short, I believe that in the case of automated decisions, as in the case of Internet, it is not advisable to erect new rights but to rely on those we already enjoy.

9.7 Conclusions

Two lessons can be learned from the right not to be subject to automated decisions that we can apply to the right not to use Internet. Firstly, automated legal decisions, including partially automated ones, present significant ethical and legal challenges related to human agency, privacy, transparency, non-discrimination, and accountability. One approach to tackling these challenges is to acknowledge new rights, often termed third or fourth-generation rights, such as the right not to use Internet, the right to navigate the digital landscape and to achieve a level of protection comparable to that in the analogue world. However, this strategy has drawbacks: multiplying new rights may dilute their effectiveness, potentially leading to a system of hollow rights.

And secondly, upon analysing Article 22 of the GDPR, it becomes evident that rather than introducing a new right, the focus should be on specific guarantees and actions that individuals can take against automated decisions or against the intrusion of Internet in our private sphere. These include seeking human intervention, expressing their viewpoints, receiving explanations for decisions, challenging them, and guarantees to protect our privacy and dignity.

Acknowledgements

This contribution is part of the Research Project I+D+i PID2021-126869OB-I00, Gobernanza de la Educación (GO-Educación), funded by MCIN/AEI/10.13039/501100011033/FEDER Una manera de hacer Europa.

Notes

1 The creation and evolution of rights have been the subject of extensive scholarly inquiry. Rights are generally categorized into several generations. The first generation consists of civil and political rights; the second generation encompasses economic, social, and cultural rights; the third generation includes rights related to social progress and well-being; and the fourth generation pertains to rights associated with new technological advancements.

2 Article 57 of Spanish Royal Decree-Law 6/2023, of December 19, approving urgent measures for the implementation of the Recovery, Transformation, and Regulating the Use of Information Technologies in the Administration of Justice Plan, regulates AI-assisted judicial decisions. These involve the generation of total or partial drafts of a document generated by algorithms, which may serve as the basis or support for a judicial resolution or a decision regarding the judicial procedure.

3 In an administrative procedure, legal practitioners may employ a combination of ADM systems. If gradually more phases of the procedure become subject to ADM, we will encounter what is known as cyberdelegation—essentially a form of delegating the exercise of administrative authority to an automated system. Cyberdelegation has been

studied by Coglianese and Lehr (2017) and Cuéllar (2016), among others. Cuéllar warns that reliance on computer programs, especially those that adapt autonomously (black boxes), may further complicate public deliberation on administrative decisions, as few observers, if any, will fully grasp how a specific decision was reached.

4 See Roehl (2022) for a comprehensive overview of the classifications and typologies of automation developed by scholarly doctrine.

5 The case law of the Court will require interpreting Article 41 of the Spanish Law 40/2015 on the Legal Regime of the Public Sector (LRJSP) to unveil the nature of automated decisions. This provision defines "administrative automated action" as "any act or action carried out entirely through electronic means by a Public Administration within an administrative procedure and without direct involvement of a public employee". According to European law, the key to assert whether a decision is automated is the decisive effect of ADM on the final decision, rather than the degree of intervention by legal operators.

6 Such measures must include the obligation for the controller to use appropriate mathematical or statistical procedures, implement technical and organizational measures appropriate to ensure that the risk of errors is minimized and inaccuracies are corrected, and secure personal data in a manner that takes account of the potential risks involved for the interests and rights of the data subject and prevent, *inter alia*, discriminatory effects on that person.

7 The European legislator is reluctant to recognize new rights. It does not seem to have done so in the specific case of Article 22 of the GDPR, but neither has it embraced this rhetoric in the Artificial Intelligence Act, although it has placed fundamental rights at the centre of the governance model for artificial intelligence developments.

8 Article L300-2 classifies the source code used in administrative proceedings as an administrative document, and the doctrine of the Commission d'Accès aux Documents Administratifs (CADA) has done the same with the algorithms used by the public administration, as well as technical documentation such as the software requirements specification document.

9 In Spanish administrative law, as in European legal systems, the failure to justify the administrative act invalidates it (Article 47 of Act 39/2015 on Common Administrative Procedure).

10 The distinction between reasons (for action) and motives has been accepted by all philosophers studying the topic (as María Álvarez indicates, 2016): Josef Raz in 1975, Derek Parfit in 1997, and Jonathan Dancy in 2000 are the most prominent authors in this field. A normative reason is a reason for action, while a motive is a reason why someone does something. In fact, etymologically, motives refer to what moves us to do something, and in this sense, they are intimately related to a purely psychological dimension. The example proposed by García Figueroa (2014), also mentioned by Álvarez (2016), clarifies this perfectly: when Othello kills Desdemona convinced that she has been unfaithful, "it can be said that Othello killed Desdemona motivated (that is, moved) by jealousy, but it would be strange to say that the Moor of Venice took Desdemona's life justified by jealousy" (García Figueroa 2014, 142).

11 The precursor of this notion, of adjustment direction, is Thomas Aquinas, who affirmed that truth is the correspondence between things (*res*) and the mind (*intellectus*). Thomas Aquinas, *Summa Theologica*, Part I, question 21, Article 2. When describing something, our mind fits the world; when regulating something, the world is meant to fit to our minds.

12 Searle refers to the example posed by Elizabeth Anscombe. Let's suppose a man goes to the supermarket with the shopping list his wife gave him, on which are written the words "beer, butter, and bacon". Let's suppose that as he goes around with his shopping cart selecting these items, he is followed by a detective who notes down everything he picks up. When they leave the store, both the buyer and the detective will have identical lists. But the function of the two lists will be quite different. In the case of the buyer's list, the purpose of it is, so to speak, to make the world match the words on the list: the buyer must make his actions fit the list. In the case of the detective, the purpose of the list is to make the words match the world: the detective must make the list describe the buyer's actions. The differences between both adjustment directions, Anscombe continues, can be further demonstrated by observing the role of an "error" in both cases. If the detective gets home and suddenly realizes that the man bought pork chops instead of bacon, he can simply erase the word "bacon" and write "pork chops". But if the buyer gets home and his wife tells him he bought pork chops when he should have bought bacon, he cannot correct the error by erasing "bacon" from the list and writing "pork chops" (Searle 1979: 347; 1999: 101). The adjustment direction of the husband is from the world to the list (to the word, to the mind) because it doesn't describe reality but rather changes it to match the list; on the other hand, the detective's adjustment direction is from the list to the world.

13 Finding patterns reveals what is normal, not necessarily normative. On the normal/normative dichotomy (normality/normativity), see García-Pelayo (1968: 68).

14 One of the best studies regarding Hume's Law has been elaborated by Bruno Celano (1994).

15 Moreover, when the ADM system is based on outcome prediction systems, they present data in terms of probability in a way that appears to be more neutral, more objective, and even more precise than it actually is (Tashea 2017). For example, a prison official may receive an automated report indicating that the defendant has an 80.2% chance of reoffending according to the legal analysis model (Surden 2019: 1336). However, according to the model, two out of every ten defendants will not reoffend. Therefore, it is not appropriate to base a legal decision on descriptive and deceptively precise premises (Surden 2019: 1337) without considering the model's limitations in terms of bias, discrimination, and lack of transparency.

16 Gutiérrez David applies the concept of the black box in the context of administrative activity assisted by ADM systems

> not only for machine learning or deep learning algorithms, but to any fully or partially automated decision-making model, regardless of the type of algorithm implemented, when it is not possible to verify the correctness and legality of the decisions taken by the model.
>
> (Gutiérrez David 2021: 166)

17 DARPA XAI: Explainable Artificial Intelligence, www.darpa.mil/program/explainable-artificial-intelligence

18 Article 86 of the Artificial Intelligence Act establishes "the right to obtain from the deployer clear and meaningful explanations of the role of the AI system in the decision-making process and the main elements of the decision taken" in cases where high-risk AI systems, as listed in Annex III, have an adverse impact on fundamental rights. The scope of this article is narrower than the implications of Article 22 of the GDPR. However, the coexistence of these provisions warrants further investigation.

Bibliography

Alexy, R. (1989). *Teoría de la argumentación jurídica (trad.)*. Centro de Estudios Constitucionales.

Álvarez, M. (2016). Reasons for Action: Justification, Motivation, Explanation. In Edward N. Zalta (ed.). *The Stanford Encyclopedia of Philosophy* (Winter 2017 Edition). https://plato.stanford.edu/archives/win2017/entries/reasons-just-vs-expl/

Celano, B. (1994). *Dialettica della giustificazione pratica: saggio sulla Legge di Humne*. Giappichelli.

Coglianese, G., and Lehr, D. (2017). Regulating by Robot: Administrative Decision Making in the Machine-Learning Era. *The Georgetown Law Journal*, 105, 1147–1223.

Cotino, L. (2024). La primera sentencia del Tribunal de Justicia de la Unión Europea sobre decisiones automatizadas y sus implicaciones para la protección de datos y el Reglamento de inteligencia artificial. *Diario La Ley*, 17th January 2024.

Cuéllar, M.-F. (2016). *Cyberdelegation and the Administrative State*. Stanford Public Law Working Paper No. 2754385. http://ssrn.com/abstract=2754385

Dancy, J. (2000). *Practical Reality*. Clarendon Press.

Dror-Shpoliansky, D., and Shany, Y. (2021). It's the End of the (Offline) World as We Know It: From Human Rights to Digital Human Rights – A Proposed Typology. *The European Journal of International Law*, 32(4), 1249–1282.

Finck, M. (2019). Automated Decision-Making and Administrative Law. Max Planck Institute for Innovation and Competition Research Paper, No. 19-10.

Gamero Casado, E. (2021). Necesidad de motivación e invalidez de los actos administrativos sustentados en inteligencia artificial o en algoritmos. *Almacén de Derecho*, 4th February 2021. https://almacendederecho.org/necesidad-de-motivacion-e-invalidez-de-los-actos-administrativos-sustentados-en-inteligencia-artificial-o-en-algoritmos (last consulted in 16th April 2024).

García Figueroa, A. (2014). *Teoría de la argumentación. Funciones, fines y expectativas*. In Gascón Abellán. M. (ed.), *Argumentación Jurídica*. Tirant lo Blanch.

García Figueroa, A. (2017). *Praxis*. Una introducción a la moral, la política y el Derecho. Atelier, Barcelona.

García Figueroa, A. (2022). *Algunos reparos a la doctrina del Mar menor*. Almacén de Derecho, 27th September 2022. https://almacendederecho.org/algunos-reparos-a-la-doctrina-del-mar-menor

García-Pelayo y Alonso, M. (1968). *Del mito y de la razón en la historia del pensamiento político*. Revista de Occidente.

Gutiérrez David, M. E. (2021). Administraciones inteligentes y acceso al código fuente y los algoritmos públicos. Conjurando riesgos de cajas negras decisionales. *Derecom*, 30, 143–228. www.derecom.com/secciones/articulos-de-fondo/item/download/411_6141b7998e1471e9b179a2b00c9f527a

Hildebrandt, M. (2011). Legal Protection by Design: Objections and Refutations. *Legisprudence*, 5, 223–248.

Hofman, H. (2021). *An Introduction to Automated Decision-Making and Cyber-Delegation in the Scope of EU Public Law*. University of Luxemburg Law Working Paper Series, n. 8.

Huq, A. (2020). A Right to a Human Decision. *Virginia Law Review*, 106, 611–688.

Kelsen, H. (1991) [1960]. *Teoría pura del derecho*. Roberto Vernengo (trad). Porrúa, México.

Laporta San Miguel, F. J. (1987). Sobre el concepto de derechos humanos. *Doxa: Cuadernos de Filosofía del Derecho*, 4, 23–46.

Llano Alonso, F. (2024). *Homo ex machina. Ética de la inteligencia artificial y Derecho digitial ante el horizonte de la singularidad tecnológica*. Tirant lo blanch.

Moral Soriano, L. (2008). Precedents: Reasoning by Rules and Reasoning by Principles. *Northern Ireland Legal Quarterly*, 59, 33–42.

Moral Soriano, L. (2023). Criaturas empíricas en un mundo normativo. La inteligencia artificial y el derecho. *Revista de Derecho Público: Teoría y Método*, 7, 151–174.

Parfit, D. (1997). Reasons and Motivation. *Proceedings of the Aristotelian Society*, (Supplementary Volume), 71, 99–129.

Ponce Solé, J. (2019). Inteligencia artificial, Derecho administrativo y Reserva de Humanidad: Algoritmos y Procedimiento Administrativo Debido Tecnológico. *Revista General de Derecho Administrativo*, 50.

Ponce Solé, J. (2022). Reserva de humanidad y supervisión humana de la inteligencia artificial. *El Cronista del Estado Social y Democrático de Derecho*, 100, 58–67.

Raso, J. (2021). *AI and Administrative Law*. In Martin-Bariteau, F., y Scassa, T., (eds.), *Artificial Intelligence and the Law in Canada*. LexisNexis.

Raz, J. (1975). *Practical Reasoning and Norms*. London: Hutchinson & Co., reprinted, Oxford University Press, 1990 and 1999.

Roehl, U. (2022). Understanding Automated Decision-Making in the Public Sector: A Classification of Automated, Administrative Decision-Making. In Juell-Skielse, G., Lindgren, I., Åkesson, M. (eds.), *Service Automation in the Public Sector*. Progress in IS. Springer, 35–63. https://doi.org/10.1007/978-3-030-92644-1_3

Searle, J. (1979). *A Taxonomy of Illocutionary Acts*. Cambridge University Press.

Searle, J. (1983). *Intentionality: An Essay in the Philosophy of Mind*. Cambridge University Press.

Searle, J. (1999). *Mind, Language and Society. Philosophy in the Real World*. Phoenix.

Serna, P. (2024). *El discurso de los nuevos derechos humanos. Perspectiva genético-crítica*. In Crespo, J. and Pereira Sáez, C. (eds.), *Los nuevos derechos humanos*. Comares, 17–50.

Surden, H. (2019). Artificial Intelligence and Law: An Overview. *Georgia State University Law Review*, 35, 1306–1337.

Tashea, J. (2017). *Courts are Using AI to Sentence Criminals. That Must Stop Now*. www.wired.com/2017/04/courts-using-ai-sentence-criminals-must-stop-now/

Wachter, S., *et al.* (2018). Counterfactual Explanations without Opening the Black Box: Automated Decisions and the GDPR. *Harvard Journal of Law & Technology*, 2018. https://arxiv.org/abs/1711.00399

10 The meaning of the limitation of the use of the Internet for criminal punishment from the perspective of extended mind thesis

Kamil Mamak

10.1 Introduction

Since the broad deployment of the Internet, there has been discussion of how it has changed our lives (see, e.g., Sparrow, Liu, and Wegner 2011; Floridi 2015). One of the many ideas discussed about the role of technologies in general, and the Internet, in particular, is that they become a literal part of us. This chapter explores such an idea by referring to the extended mind thesis (Clark and Chalmers 1998). It is a view according to which external artifacts could be counted as part of the extended mind. If we treat this thesis seriously, then there are ethical and legal consequences, including the discussion of the right to access the Internet and the right not to use the Internet. This chapter gives special attention to the consequences of adopting this view in relation to criminal punishment, showing that manipulating access to the Internet is a relevant issue from that perspective.

This chapter is structured as follows. After the introduction, there is a brief explanation of the extended mind thesis. Then, the focus shifts to the role of the Internet from an extended mind perspective. The following section is concerned with the ethical consequences resulting from the acceptance of the discussed philosophical thesis. Then, there is a section that focuses on the relevance of this thesis for the discussion on the right to access the Internet and the right not to use the Internet. The following section discusses the extended mind thesis in the context of punishment, specifically on imprisonment. This chapter ends with conclusions.

10.2 The extended mind thesis

The extended mind thesis is an idea that proposes a non-intuitive explanation for the interaction of humans with external, non-biological artifacts. In short, according to the extended mind thesis, cognitive processes are not locked up in the physical boundaries of the body but extend into the external environment. Andy Clark and David Chalmers formulated the most recognized version of this way of thinking about the mind. They start their seminal paper with the sentence, "Where does the mind stop and the rest of the world begin?" (Clark and Chalmers 1998, 7). They

DOI: 10.4324/9781003528401-13

express skepticism as to whether the boundaries of the body are the boundaries of the mind.

In their paper, the authors use examples that allow them to illustrate the problems; the most famous example from that paper is the one about Otto and Inga. Otto and Inga want to go to an exhibition at the Museum of Modern Arts in New York City. Inga, in order to get to the museum, recalls its location from her biological memory. Otto has Alzheimer's disease, and in order to get to the museum, he consults the location of the museum with his personal paper notebook, in which he wrote various pieces of information, including the location of the concerned institution. Authors claim that Otto's notebook serves the same role for him as biological memory for Inga. Thus, Otto's mind is extended to this external artifact (the notebook).

According to Clark and Chalmers, not every artifact could be considered an extension of the mind, but only one that could become coupled with the mind and be part of the cognitive loop. To be considered as part of the mind, the artifact needs to fulfill some criteria; they show those criteria in the example of Otto's notebook, formulating four of them. First, the notebook is an element of Otto's mind because it is a constant element in Otto's life, and Otto treats the notebook as a relevant element of taking action. Second, there is easy and direct access to the notebook. Third, when Otto finds information there, he automatically endorses (approves) it. Fourth, the information in the notebook was at some point endorsed by him in the past (Clark and Chalmers 1998, 17). Those criteria are sometimes referred to as "trust and glue" criteria (see, e.g., Record and Miller 2018, 106). Clark and Chalmers acknowledge the differences between the biological memory and the external artifacts, but they think that those differences are shallow, and more or less, the mind and the notebook play the same roles.

The paper referred to was published in 1998, about a decade before the smartphone revolution. The thesis advanced in the paper has gained more attention in recent times. Clowes et al. point out two main reasons for its recent popularity (Clowes, Smart, and Heersmink, 2024). First, it has explanatory power regarding the relations between humans and the technologies they use (see, e.g., Carter et al. 2018). Many people never give up their smartphones, smartwatches, personal computers, and so on. And what is important in the context of this chapter, as Clowes et al. point out, is that many of these smart devices have networking capabilities that enable them to be connected to the Internet. The second reason they point out is that in contemporary cognitive science, there is a strong ani-Cartesian direction (rejection of dualism that separates mind and body, treating them as distinct matters), and the extended mind thesis follows this trend. In that context, it is usually presented as part of 4E cognition, which stands for four words – embodied, embedded, enacted, and extended (see, e.g., Newen, Bruin, and Gallagher 2018). In short, the popular take on cartesian dualism suggests that mind and body are distinct and separable matters. The 4E framework points out that our cognitive processes are shaped by our bodies (embodiment) and the environment in which humans are living (embedment). Enactivism refers to the dynamic relations between organisms and their environment. The cognition arises through the interactions. Finally, the extended part, which is the focus of this chapter, allows for extending the cognitive process on the external artifacts. Together, those concepts are an alternative to dualist thinking (Rowlands 2013, 51; but see, e.g., Adams and Aizawa 2010).

10.3 The extended mind thesis and the Internet

Since the publication of the extended mind thesis more than 25 years ago, the concept has developed, and various aspects have been discussed (for overview, see, e.g., Gallagher 2018; Telakivi 2023). One of the specific subjects of interest is the Internet and its relationship with the mind. Could the Internet be part of the extended mind? Clark, one of the co-authors of the original paper that formulated the extended mind thesis, raised skepticism over treating the Internet as a part of extended cognition (Clark 2008).

However, not the whole Internet must be considered as a part of the extension, but it could be "some small piece of the Internet", as long as the conditions for extension, which are accessibility, relevancy, and trust, are met (Dempsey, Coin, and Dubljević 2024, 158). Later in this chapter, when I refer to the Internet as an extension of the mind, I mean that some parts of the Internet might constitute the mind, not that the whole Internet should be treated as part of someone's mind.

As mentioned, contemporary devices could be considered to constitute the self, and those devices are often connected to the Internet. I use the terms extended mind and extended self interchangeably. If the mind is part of myself, my mind is extended, and I am a whole extended. In some cases, access to some parts of devices is dependent on use to the Internet. For example, pictures that allow us to remember past events could be stored in the cloud. The typical way to access them is through a smartphone, but sometimes, this requires having access to the Internet. From that perspective, the smartphone, without access to the Internet, could not be seen as complete extension of the mind. In other words, the term "smartphone" is used here not as a sum of material components that are exclusively inside of the device but as something more significant that, together with the services and infrastructure, can be fully functional. For example, we could have access to some of the memories through our device, but to use that information, the device needs to be charged, and there must be access to the Internet, which allows us to connect to the service that is in the cloud.

For example, Heersmink discusses this idea in the context of autobiographical memory. He noticed that to access some of our past memories, we are dependent on access to the services that contain information about our past, and in that context, he claims that our autobiographical memory could be extended and distributed (Heersmink 2022). To use Facebook *via* smartphone and check the photos from vacations posted there a couple of years earlier, we need to have a device that is connected to the Internet. In his other work, he claims that personal identity cannot be reduced to psychology or biology, but it needs to be seen as an environmentally distributed and relational construct; he talks about "distributed selves" (Heersmink 2017a). He points out the ethical consequences. We should have a broader concept of self by including the social and external structures, focus on the external memory systems in studies of personal identity, and add that we should not interfere with one's distributed minds and selves. In other work, he notices that the more we depend on external information in cognitive functioning on an everyday basis, the more those artifacts are integrated into our cognitive system (Heersmink 2017b). We could read the above notions as the endorsement of the role of technology in constituting what the human self is. It shows the entanglement of humans with technology. The refusal of the role of technology for contemporary humans could not give a full description of who we are in a technologically textured world.

Another scholar who analyses the role of the Internet in the context of the extended mind thesis is Smart. He initially introduced the Web-Extended Mind hypothesis, which is the idea "that technological and informational elements of the web can (at least sometimes) serve as part of the mechanistic substrate that realizes human mental states" (Smart 2013, 447). In his later work, Smart proposes a slightly different definition of the "Web-extended Mind," which is "an extended cognitive system whose processes supervene on a set of constituent material elements that include one or more Web resources" (Smart 2017, 362). Smart considers whether the Web (current or future) can be part of the extended cognitive system and uses criteria ("trust and glue") that Chalmers and Clark used in their paper on the extended mind to answer the question of whether some artifact could be considered as an element of the extended mind. He concludes that the nature of our interaction with today's Internet allows for a variety of forms of Internet-extended cognition (Smart 2017, 369). Smart points out that the general trajectory of technology development reinforces the possibility of including the web in the cognitive system. He uses an example of Otto++. The most important aspect of this example for this chapter is that instead of a notebook, Otto uses a smartphone with an app that contains information in the cloud, and to have access to this information, there is a need to have access to the Internet (Smart 2018, 280). Smart believes that notebooks and apps connect to the Internet and fulfill the same function, and we could treat them as functionally equivalent to those realized by biological models (like biological memory).

Heersmink and Sutton believe that the "parts" of the Internet might be relevant for an extended mind thesis. They analyze the impact of the Web on cognition from various perspectives, including the extended one. They focus on the relations between the Web and users and conclude that while most current Web apps are not deeply integrated with the mind, they argue that some highly personalized Web applications accessed on wearable digital devices might have the capacity for deep integration (Heersmink and Sutton 2020, 139).

For clarification, accepting the extended mind thesis does not mean that every human is extended into technological devices in the same way, but rather that there could be people for whom external artifacts are important to such an extent that they should be treated as an extension of their minds, and by that, an extension of themselves. This reservation also concerns use to the Internet. For some people, the Internet could be an essential element that enables them to be truly themselves, and for others, it might be a relevant aspect of their lives.

10.4 Ethical risk and extended mind thesis

If we accept that the extended mind is a plausible explanation of the relationship of humans with external artifacts, such a statement entails legal and moral consequences. Those consequences are discussed in this section. Clark and Chalmers note that sometimes "interfering with someone's environment will have the same moral significance as interfering with their person" (Clark and Chalmers 1998, 18). For example, Søraker points out that the information in Otto's notebook could have moral status and, as such, deserves to be protected (Søraker 2008). Clowes et al. consider ethical risks more systematically and point out three areas of ethical concern related to the extended mind: mental privacy, mental manipulation, and agency (Clowes, Smart, and Heersmink 2024). Now, I will briefly unpack them.

Mental privacy is concerned with access to information. In short, the content of our memories that are stored in biological minds is hidden from the external observer, while the memories that are stored in external artifacts are exposed to risks of access to it, like in the case of Otto's notebook, which others might get unauthorized access to (see also, e.g., Carter, Clark, and Palermos 2018). Vold illustrates this in relation to criminal procedures (Vold 2018). In many legal systems, one could remain silent when accused of a crime. In other words, there is no way to access the content of the mind of the person accused of committing a crime. If we accept the extended mind thesis, then there is a problem with accessing personal technologies, such as smartphones. Should we treat the content of the smartphone in the context of a criminal investigation in the same way as we treat the content of the biological memory, to which there is no access? Should the right to remain silent extend to smartphones?

Palermos, in his recent paper about mental privacy, calls for making it impossible, legally and practically, to obtain such data (Palermos 2023). Clowes et al. point that privacy concerns are especially prominent in case of devices or services that are online or connected online, where the content is accessible to various social actors, including individual hackers, corporations, and governmental bodies (Clowes, Smart, and Heersmink 2024).

Related to privacy issues are risks of manipulation. Those who might have access to the information could not only see this information against the will of the owner but also could manipulate it (Clowes, Smart, and Heersmink 2024). Carter identifies two categories of risks related to manipulation: acquisition manipulation and eradication manipulation. The first is concerned with the possibility of creating new beliefs, and the second is with deleting memories (Carter 2021).

The third ethical group of risks discussed by Clowes et al. is related to autonomy. Cited authors base this risk on the observation that cognitive extension might impact mental autonomy. They refer to these risks, in particular, in the work of Vold and Hernández-Orallo on AI Extenders (Vold and Hernández-Orallo 2022; Hernández-Orallo and Vold 2019). In short, AI extenders are tools that constitute an extension of cognitive states resulting from the deployment of AI systems. Human agents that are going to make decisions might be impacted by the AI tools they use. Vold and Hernández-Orallo provide a definition of AI extenders (Vold and Hernández-Orallo 2022):

> An AI extender is a cognitive extender that is "fueled" by AI. This means that some AI technology is directly responsible for the cognitive capability that the extender is able to deploy, in conjunction with its user.

The mentioned issues regarding autonomy and responsibility are, for example, related to risks related to the fact that the tools could impact the way in which people who use them act, or there is a problem with who could be responsible for malfunctions or keeping up with systems that become some extension (see also on that topic: Telakivi et al. forthcoming). The problem with autonomy and responsibility for the effects of the deployment of AI systems is one of the most discussed problems within AI ethics (on issues with responsibility with AI see, e.g., Matthias 2004; Sparrow 2007; Müller 2020; Gordon and Nyholm 2021). The extended mind thesis applied to this problem makes it even more problematic due to the intimate connection of tools (in this case, AI-based) with humans.

The above categories of risks do not exhaust the list of potential ethical issues related to adopting the extended mind thesis. The presented issue shows, at least, the multidimensionality of ethical consequences related to that thesis. Some of the ethical risks are relevant from the perspective of the law. The following two sections further clarify this. First, the relevance of the extended mind thesis is presented for the discussion on the right to use the Internet as well as related issues of the right not to use the Internet. Second, access to the Internet is discussed from the perspective of the philosophy of punishment.

10.5 Right to use/not to use the Internet and the extended mind thesis

It was already mentioned that the Internet might be an element of the infrastructure of the extended self. Even if the Internet does not, as a whole, constitute the extension of the person, it might be a necessary ingredient of the personal technologies that are integral parts of the person. Such observation makes it a natural candidate of interest for those who are interested in the right to use the Internet and the right not to use the Internet. At the outset, it might be said that the extended mind thesis is relevant to both of them.

Kloza points out that over the years, there has been a change in the way in which access to the Internet is presented, which was accelerated by the public health crisis. Instead of being an option, it becomes an obligation. He wonders to what extent people could be forced to use it and argues that citizens should not be obliged to use the Internet. He formulates it as the right not to use the Internet (Kloza 2024). He reviews the main groups of arguments that could support the right to non-use of the Internet. The main arguments are the lack of willingness to use the Internet, second, that people could not afford the necessary hardware that allows them to use the Internet, and third, that some people are unable to use it. The extended mind thesis is the most relevant to the first group of reasons, which I am now focusing on.

Kloza, while discussing the reasons why people might not want to use the Internet, points at different possibilities, including religious beliefs, civil disobedience, and concerns about the environment. He also mentions concerns about privacy.

The extended mind perspective is especially relevant to privacy concerns. People might not want to use the Internet in specific contexts. Those are not people who do not use the Internet at all; quite the contrary. We are speaking now about people whose access to technology and the Internet constitutes who they are. However, when some institutions enforce the use of the Internet in some contexts, they might be worried that someone could get access to their data. It was mentioned that there are ethical risks related to the possibility of reading and analyzing personal data, and there are related risks of manipulating those data by erasing or changing them. In other words, some people might prefer to use the Internet on their own terms, not to connect to it in a context where they do not feel fully comfortable. This could mean a lack of willingness to use the Internet when they might worry that their data would be vulnerable to access, manipulation, or eradication.

It seems that the more clear relevance of the extended mind thesis is to the right to Internet access (see, e.g., Pollicino 2020; Pollicino and Susi 2019; Tully 2014; Reglitz 2020). If the technologies constitute who citizens are, there might be a formulated expectation that the state provides the necessary infrastructure that allows for the undisrupted use of technologies that constitute an extension of selves. People develop relationships with technologies on their own, but the state could be an actor who has the power to maintain the safety and continuity of its use. There is also another aspect related to that. There is a context in which the state deprives people (almost entirely) of access to technologies, which is connected with criminal punishment of deprivation of liberty. In the next section, more focus is placed on that aspect of use of the Internet.

10.6 Use of the Internet, extended mind, and philosophy of punishment

In this section, I want to focus on the use of the Internet in the context of punishment. Issues regarding unauthorized access to personal data or the possibility of manipulating content that is part of the extended mind have been presented. Consequences could also be found on the grounds of criminal law. Carter and Palermos wonder how we should treat the physical attack on the devices that constitute an extended mind, like personal computers. The idea is that the default legal classification of such attacks, which is attached to the property, does not reflect the nature of the wrong. According to them, the right approach is to treat attacks on the devices that count as extensions of the minds as personal assaults that underline the connection of devices with the owners (Carter and Palermos 2016). In other words, the destruction of personal devices should be treated as an attack on the person, not a mere act that interferes with the property of the owner.

Inspired by that paper, I considered whether it is possible to apply this thinking to punishment (Mamak 2021, 2024). When someone steals money and causes financial loss, then it is a crime, but when the same amount of money is imposed by the criminal court as a fine, it is considered a punishment. When someone is holding another person in some place against their will, it is a crime, but when the same person is against their will in prison, then it is a punishment. Going back to the idea of Carter and Palermos, they believe that when a wrongdoer interferes with someone's elements of their extended mind, it should be considered a crime. I ask whether the interference with elements of the extended mind could be treated as punishment when imposed by a criminal court. I frame it as a limitation of access to personal technologies and propose to recognize it as pain/hardship that is an element of punishment. If accepted, then it has consequences in various aspects of punishment and allows the formulation of normative notions.

Now, it is time to go back to the use of the Internet. As it was mentioned, the Internet might be a necessary element of technologies that are integrated with human beings in a way that could be considered an extension. Then, influencing the use of the Internet might indirectly impact someone's extended "infrastructure." There are at least three ways in which, at the ground of punishment, access to the Internet could be relevant, taking into account the perspective of the extended mind thesis.

First, when imposing the punishment of imprisonment, the court should take into account the fact that the person in most contemporary prisons will be deprived of access to personal technologies, which entails access to the Internet. If access to personal technologies and the Internet is not an option, the calculated punishment of imprisonment should include the hardship of limitation of access to technology. Bagaric et al. propose to calculate the punishment for the lack of the use of the Internet (Bagaric, Fischer, and Hunter 2018). One of the basic rules of imposing punishment is that it should be proportional; the gravity of the crime should be proportional to the severity of punishment (see, e.g., Bagaric 2014; Hirsch and Ashworth 2005). The court imposing punishment is obliged to reflect on the severity of negative consequences, which is derived from the principle of proportionality. If the court decided that the punishment that is adopted is imprisonment, the court should take into consideration the fact that some people would be deprived of access to their personal technologies as a consequence of imprisonment. The fact of deprivation of access to technologies, including access to the Internet, should be calculated by the court at the stage of imposing the length of the punishment.

Second, and it also concerns the punishment of imprisonment, access to the Internet in prisons should be provided. In contemporary practice, the norm is the lack of or limited access to the digital technologies (see, e.g., Järveläinen and Rantanen 2021; Reisdorf and DeCook 2022; Reisdorf and Jewkes 2016). There are different reasons for providing (some) access to the Internet in prisons, including rehabilitation, teaching to live in society, providing skills for the job market, education, connecting with families, and reducing misbehavior in prisons (for overview, see e.g., Järveläinen and Rantanen 2021; Bagaric, Fischer, and Hunter 2018; Reisdorf 2023). The extended mind gives additional justification for providing use of the Internet.

The subject of the punishment from an extended mind perspective is the "whole" person, which consists of the biological parts as well as non-biological artifacts that are not fully physically connected with the body of the person. The current dominant view on that matter is marked by dualism and allows no notice of the extended nature of the person. As mentioned, the extended mind thesis's popularity could not only be reduced to its explanatory power for humans' relationship with technology but also because it constitutes the replacement for cartesian dualism.

Dualism (of mind and body) is present in the law as an underlying theory of some institutions, not in an apparent way as a philosophical declaration of the lawgivers but more as a hidden assumption that needs to be revealed. Benforado points out that the distinction of the body and the mind is the language of the law and it is in the core of our culture (Benforado 2010, 3; see also on dualism and law Fox and Stein 2015; Shen 2013). The process of abandoning the dualist thinking force to find a better view on the subject of punishment and the extended mind thesis provides such an alternative view. To put it simply, the second point, out of the three presented in this section, is about imprisonment and argues for incarcerating the "whole" person, which includes their technologies, also connected to the Internet.

Third, the manipulation of access to technologies, including the Internet, might be considered punishment (Mamak 2024). Based on that, new forms of punishment might be formulated, or it gives additional support for formulated ideas. For example, Bagaric et al. propose deprivation of the Internet (Bagaric, Fischer, and Hunter 2018). I elsewhere formulated cyber banishment (Mamak 2023; see also 2021), which does not cover, as deprivation of the Internet, the whole access but is limited to specific areas of the online environment.

10.7 Conclusion

In this chapter, the main focus was on using the Internet as the necessary condition for being fully oneself and the meaning of such a view for criminal punishment. For some, the Internet might be an integral element of their existence, and such a position is relevant to criminal punishment. In order to consider the constitutive meaning of technologies for human beings, there is a need to look at humans from a non-intuitive philosophical perspective. The extended mind thesis is the view that allows a look at the relationships between humans and technologies in a more unified way. According to this thesis, external artifacts could be counted as elements of the mind. As an example, the smartphone might be considered our extension. This chapter considers especially the relevance of access to the Internet. If we accept that Internet access allows the artifacts to function as human extensions, then the manipulation of access to technologies has relevance to ethics and law. There is a discussion on the impact of the extended mind perspective on the discussion on the right to use the Internet and the right not to use the Internet. Finally, the relevance of criminal punishment is shown. First, the lack of access to technologies, including the Internet, should be counted as a hardship for the convicted while imposing proportional punishment. The second issue is a call for allowing the use of the Internet in prisons as a condition to be fully self while serving punishment.

Third, the limitations of the use of technologies, as well as the Internet, might be the basis or support for alternative punishments.

This chapter aimed to show how a change in the underlying philosophical assumption about the subject of punishment might impact the thinking about the current justice system practices. The extended mind thesis is interesting not only due to the coherence with intuitions of many about the transformative role of technology for humans but also because it allows us to show immediately, after its application, how institutions of criminal law could change. Alternatives to the dominant philosophical perspective also shed new light on the discussion on the right to use/not to use the Internet.

Bibliography

Adams, Frederick, and Kenneth Aizawa. 2010. "Defending the Bounds of Cognition." In *The Extended Mind*, edited by Richard Menary. Cambridge, MA: MIT Press.

Bagaric, Mirko. 2014. "Proportionality in Sentencing: The Need to Factor in Community Experience, Not Public Opinion." In *Popular Punishment*. New York: Oxford University Press. https://doi.org/10.1093/acprof:oso/9780199941377.003.0005.

Bagaric, Mirko, Nick Fischer, and Dan Hunter. 2018. "The Hardship That Is Internet Deprivation and What It Means for Sentencing: Development of the Internet Sanction and Connectivity for Prisoners." *Akron Law Review* 51 (2). https://ideaexchange.uakron.edu/akronlawreview/vol51/iss2/2.

Benforado, Adam. 2010. "The Body of the Mind: Embodied Cognition, Law, and Justice." *St. Louis University Law Journal* 54. https://papers.ssrn.com/abstract=1546674.

Carter, J. Adam. 2021. "Varieties of (Extended) Thought Manipulation." In *The Law and Ethics of Freedom of Thought, Volume 1: Neuroscience, Autonomy, and Individual Rights*, edited by Marc Jonathan Blitz and Jan Christoph Bublitz, 291–309. Cham: Springer International Publishing. https://doi.org/10.1007/978-3-030-84494-3_10.

Carter, J. Adam, Andy Clark, Jesper Kallestrup, S. Orestis Palermos, and Duncan Pritchard, eds. 2018. *Extended Epistemology*. Oxford, New York: Oxford University Press.

Carter, J. Adam, Andy Clark, and S. Orestis Palermos. 2018. "New Humans?: Ethics, Trust, and the Extended Mind." In *Extended Epistemology*, edited by J. Adam Carter, Andy Clark, S. Orestis Palermos, Jesper Kallestrup, and Duncan Pritchard. Oxford: Oxford University Press. https://www.oxfordscholarship.com/view/10.1093/oso/9780198769811.001.0001/oso-9780198769811-chapter-17.

Carter, J. Adam, and S. Orestis Palermos. 2016. "Is Having Your Computer Compromised a Personal Assault? The Ethics of Extended Cognition." *Journal of the American Philosophical Association* 2 (4): 542–60. https://doi.org/10.1017/apa.2016.28.

Clark, Andy. 2008. *Supersizing the Mind: Embodiment, Action, and Cognitive Extension*. 1st edition. Oxford: Oxford University Press.

Clark, Andy, and David Chalmers. 1998. "The Extended Mind." *Analysis* 58 (1): 7–19.

Clowes, Robert William, Paul R. Smart, and Richard Heersmink. 2024. "The Ethics of the Extended Mind: Mental Privacy, Manipulation and Agency." In *Neuroprosthetics: Ethics of Applied Situated Cognition*, edited by Jan-Hendrik Heinrichs, Birgit Beck, and Orsolya Friedrich, 13–35. Berlin, Germany: J. B. Metzler.

Dempsey, Ronald P., Allen Coin, and Veljko Dubljević. 2024. "Is the Internet a Cognitive Enhancement?" *Journal of Cognitive Enhancement* 8 (1): 155–69. https://doi.org/10.1007/s41465-024-00289-y.

Floridi, Luciano. 2015. *The Onlife Manifesto: Being Human in a Hyperconnected Era*. Cham: Springer Nature. https://doi.org/10.1007/978-3-319-04093-6.

Fox, Dov, and Alex Stein. 2015. "Dualism and Doctrine." *Indiana Law Journal* 90: 975–1010.

Gallagher, Shaun. 2018. "The Extended Mind: State of the Question." *The Southern Journal of Philosophy* 56 (4): 421–47. https://doi.org/10.1111/sjp.12308.

Gordon, John-Stewart, and Sven Nyholm. 2021. "Ethics of Artificial Intelligence." *Internet Encyclopedia of Philosophy* 2021. https://iep.utm.edu/ethic-ai/.

Heersmink, Richard. 2017a. "Distributed Selves: Personal Identity and Extended Memory Systems." *Synthese* 194 (8): 3135–51. https://doi.org/10.1007/s11229-016-1102-4.

Heersmink, Richard. 2017b. "Extended Mind and Cognitive Enhancement: Moral Aspects of Cognitive Artifacts." *Phenomenology and the Cognitive Sciences* 16 (1): 17–32. https://doi.org/10.1007/s11097-015-9448-5.

Heersmink, Richard. 2022. "Extended Mind and Artifactual Autobiographical Memory." *Mind & Language* 37 (4): 659–73. https://doi.org/10.1111/mila.12353.

Heersmink, Richard, and John Sutton. 2020. "Cognition and the Web: Extended, Transactive, or Scaffolded?" *Erkenntnis* 85 (1): 139–64. https://doi.org/10.1007/s10670-018-0022-8.

Hernández-Orallo, José, and Karina Vold. 2019. "AI Extenders: The Ethical and Societal Implications of Humans Cognitively Extended by AI." In *Proceedings of the 2019 AAAI/ACM Conference on AI, Ethics, and Society*, 507–13. AIES'19. New York, NY: Association for Computing Machinery. https://doi.org/10.1145/3306618.3314238.

Hirsch, Andrew von, and Andrew Ashworth. 2005. *Proportionate Sentencing: Exploring the Principles*. Oxford: Oxford University Press. https://www.oxfordscholarship.com/view/10.1093/acprof:oso/9780199272600.001.0001/acprof-9780199272600-chapter-7.

Järveläinen, Eeva, and Teemu Rantanen. 2021. "Incarcerated People's Challenges for Digital Inclusion in Finnish Prisons." *Nordic Journal of Criminology* 22 (2): 240–59. https://doi.org/10.1080/2578983X.2020.1819092.

Kloza, Dariusz. 2024. "The Right Not to Use the Internet." *Computer Law & Security Review* 52 (April): 105907. https://doi.org/10.1016/j.clsr.2023.105907.

Mamak, Kamil. 2021. *Filozofia Karania Na Nowo*. Kraków: Krakowski Instytut Prawa Karnego Fundacja.

Mamak, Kamil. 2023. "Cyber Banishment: An Old Sanction for Virtual Spaces." *Criminal Justice Studies* 36 (2): 133–145. https://doi.org/10.1080/1478601X.2023.2188449.

Mamak, Kamil. 2024. "A New Opening for the Alternative Punishments Debate: Applying the Extended Mind Thesis." *Ratio Juris* 37 (3): 248–68. https://doi.org/10.1111/raju.12414.

Matthias, Andreas. 2004. "The Responsibility Gap: Ascribing Responsibility for the Actions of Learning Automata." *Ethics and Information Technology* 6 (3): 175–83. https://doi.org/10.1007/s10676-004-3422-1.

Müller, Vincent C. 2020. "Ethics of Artificial Intelligence and Robotics." In *The Stanford Encyclopedia of Philosophy*, edited by Edward N. Zalta, Summer 2020. Stanford: Metaphysics Research Lab, Stanford University. https://plato.stanford.edu/archives/sum2020/entries/ethics-ai/.

Palermos, Spyridon Orestis. 2023. "Data, Metadata, Mental Data? Privacy and the Extended Mind." *AJOB Neuroscience* 14 (2): 84–96. https://doi.org/10.1080/21507740.2022.2148772.

Pollicino, Oreste. 2020. "The Right to Internet Access: Quid Iuris?" In *The Cambridge Handbook of New Human Rights: Recognition, Novelty, Rhetoric*, edited by Andreas von Arnauld, Kerstin von der Decken, and Mart Susi, 263–75. Cambridge: Cambridge University Press. https://doi.org/10.1017/9781108676106.021.

Pollicino, Oreste, and Mart Susi. 2019. "Internet and Human Rights Law: Introduction." *European Law Journal* 25 (2): 120–21. https://doi.org/10.1111/eulj.12309.

Record, Isaac, and Boaz Miller. 2018. "Taking iPhone Seriously: Epistemic Technologies and the Extended Mind." In *Extended Epistemology*, edited by J. Adam Carter, Andy Clark, Jesper Kallestrup, S. Orestis Palermos, and Duncan Pritchard. Oxford: Oxford University Press. https://doi.org/10.1093/oso/9780198769811.003.0007.

Reglitz, Merten. 2020. "The Human Right to Free Internet Access." *Journal of Applied Philosophy* 37 (2): 314–31. https://doi.org/10.1111/japp.12395.

Reisdorf, Bianca C. 2023. "Locked In and Locked Out: How COVID-19 Is Making the Case for Digital Inclusion of Incarcerated Populations." *The American Behavioral Scientist*, February, 00027642231155369. https://doi.org/10.1177/00027642231155369.

Reisdorf, Bianca C., and Julia R. DeCook. 2022. "Locked up and Left out: Formerly Incarcerated People in the Context of Digital Inclusion." *New Media & Society* 24 (2): 478–95. https://doi.org/10.1177/14614448211063178.

Reisdorf, Bianca C., and Yvonne Jewkes. 2016. "(B)Locked Sites: Cases of Internet Use in Three British Prisons." *Information, Communication & Society* 19 (6): 771–86. https://doi.org/10.1080/1369118X.2016.1153124.

Rowlands, Mark. 2013. *The New Science of the Mind: From Extended Mind to Embodied Phenomenology*. Reprint edition. Cambridge, MA: A Bradford Book.

Shen, Francis. 2013. "Mind, Body, and the Criminal Law." *Minnesota Law Review*, January. https://scholarship.law.umn.edu/mlr/375.

Smart, Paul. 2013. "The Web-Extended Mind." In *Philosophical Engineering*, 116–33. Chichester, West Sussex, UK: John Wiley & Sons, Ltd. https://doi.org/10.1002/9781118700143.ch8.

Smart, Paul. 2017. "Extended Cognition and the Internet." *Philosophy & Technology* 30 (3): 357–90. https://doi.org/10.1007/s13347-016-0250-2.

Smart, Paul. 2018. "Emerging Digital Technologies: Implications for Extended Conceptions of Cognition and Knowledge." In *Extended Epistemology*, edited by J. Adam Carter, Andy Clark, Jesper Kallestrup, S. Orestis Palermos, and Duncan Pritchard. Oxford: Oxford University Press. https://doi.org/10.1093/oso/9780198769811.003.0015.

Søraker, Johnny Hartz. 2008. "The Moral Status of Information and Information Technologies: A Relational Theory of Moral Status." In *Information Security and Ethics: Concepts, Methodologies, Tools, and Applications*, 3829–47. Hershey, PA: IGI Global. https://doi.org/10.4018/978-1-59904-937-3.ch261.

Sparrow, Betsy, Jenny Liu, and Daniel M. Wegner. 2011. "Google Effects on Memory: Cognitive Consequences of Having Information at Our Fingertips." *Science* 333 (6043): 776–78. https://doi.org/10.1126/science.1207745.

Sparrow, Robert. 2007. "Killer Robots." *Journal of Applied Philosophy* 24 (1): 62–77. https://doi.org/10.1111/j.1468-5930.2007.00346.x.

Telakivi, Pii. 2023. *Extending the Extended Mind: From Cognition to Consciousness*. London: Palgrave Macmillan.

Telakivi, Pii, Tomi Kokkonen, Raul Hakli, and Pekka Mäkelä. forthcoming. "AI-Extended Moral Agency?" *Social Epistemology*.

Tully, Stephen. 2014. "A Human Right to Access the Internet? Problems and Prospects." *Human Rights Law Review* 14 (2): 175–95. https://doi.org/10.1093/hrlr/ngu011.

Vold, Karina. 2018. "Are 'You' Just inside Your Skin or Is Your Smartphone Part of You?" *Aeon Ideas*. http://lcfi.ac.uk/media/uploads/files/Vold_Are_you_just_inside_your_skin_or_is_your_smartphone_part_of_you__Aeon_Ideas.pdf.

Vold, Karina, and José Hernández-Orallo. 2022. "AI Extenders and the Ethics of Mental Health." In *Ethics of Artificial Intelligence in Brain and Mental Health: Philosophical, Ethical & Policy Issues*, edited by M. Ienca and F Jotterand, 177–202. Cham: Springer.

11 Digitalisation of public services in Belgium

Enshrining the right not to use the Internet in the Constitution[1]

Elise Degrave

11.1 Introduction

Human rights were designed to be exercised in a human context. They are now threatened by the widespread digitalisation of society and, in particular, of public services. In this chapter, we argue for the right to choose how we exercise our human rights, whether online or offline, and for the importance of enshrining a new fundamental right in the Belgian Constitution: the right not to use the Internet (Degrave 2023, 2024).

First, the paper examines the benefits and risks of digitising public services. It then sets out the reasons why it is important to enshrine the right not to use the Internet. Finally, we explain why it is important to enshrine this right in the constitution rather than in legislation.

11.2 The benefits and risks of digitising public services

In the relationship between citizens and public services, digital technology is both a solution and a problem.

Digital technology is a *solution*, because behind the scenes of the public sector, the so-called "back office", administrations can work together with just a few clicks. It was this observation that led Belgium, as early as the 1990s, to become more efficient by developing the re-use of citizens' data between institutions, making the country a pioneer in the development of e-government.[2]

Administrative procedures are simplified[3] thanks to the "only once" principle, also known as the "single data collection" or "tell us once" principle.[4] This principle is binding on many administrations, whether federal, community-level or regional.[5] It means that citizens can only be asked once for the information that concerns them, unlike in the past, when individuals had to communicate their data to each administration with which they came into contact. In other words, once a citizen has provided information to one authority, other authorities can no longer ask for identical data. For example, if citizens move house, they no longer need to provide their new address multiple times. Instead, the information will automatically circulate between the administrations that need it. In legal terms, this principle

DOI: 10.4324/9781003528401-14

translates into an obligation for public authorities to "collect data indirectly", as set out in several pieces of legislation.[6] They are obliged, under certain conditions, to request the data from the institution that already has them. This system does not require citizens to provide their data to the authorities in digital form. They can provide it in paper form, with the onus on the administration concerned to encode the information in the IT system. For example, the birth of a child is reported verbally by the parents to the local authority or hospital. The local authority or hospital then enters the information into a computer system.[7]

The exchange of information between administrations also makes it possible to automate certain forms of assistance, which is granted to people without them having to apply for it. This is the case for the "gas and electricity" social tariff:[8] thanks to the exchange of data between administrations, some people automatically receive a reduction on their bill (Degrave 2014; Service de lutte contre la pauvreté 2020). This is the most automated right to date.

In practice, energy suppliers send the list of their customers to the Ministry of Economy, which compares this data with the data in the National Register in order to identify the identification numbers in the National Register for each person. The list of these numbers is then sent to the Crossroads Bank for Social Security, which finds the individuals entitled to the social tariff in the databases of the social security sector. The list of beneficiaries is then sent to the energy suppliers, who apply the discount immediately.

Beyond these benefits, digital technology can also be a *problem*, particularly in the relationship between the citizen and the administration, known as the "front office" (Degrave 2014; 2023).[9] This is linked to the fact that the state is the only entity against whom citizens can exercise their rights. The state has a monopoly on financial aid and legitimate coercion (through the police and the courts). As a result, we have no choice but to go through a public authority to obtain an identity card, claim an unemployment benefit or file a tax return. So when all or most of these steps take place online, citizens have no other option than to get used to it. Digital literacy becomes a new prerequisite for accessing rights and fulfilling obligations (Mazet 2021).

But the law is not designed to be applied by rigid machines. On the Internet, users could be blocked by "bugs" such as "404 errors", be surprised to have to tick a standardised box that does not correspond to the users' particular case, or be stressed by having to carry out procedures that were previously carried out by a human agent whose job it was to do so. On top of this, websites are not always easy to use.

These difficulties are not limited to older people or people with disabilities. The Digital Inclusion Barometer (2024) shows that 46% of Belgians aged between 16 and 74 (i.e., almost one in two Belgians) are in a situation of digital vulnerability because they do not use digital technology or have poor digital skills. It is therefore not just a question of age. Young people aged between 16 and 24, even though they are "digital natives", mainly use social networks from a smartphone. A third of them have poor general digital skills and struggle to fill in forms online (King Baudouin Foundation 2024).

But it gets worse. Among all the citizens who will one day be faced with a digital problem, there are some for whom a "bug" can be "fatal".[10] These people rely on the State for the exercise of basic rights such as access to social housing, unemployment benefits, social integration income, public transport passes, etc. They are in regular contact with the State, which has a responsibility to ensure that their rights are respected. They are also in regular contact with the administration, much more so than "privileged" citizens for whom interaction with public services is generally limited to identity cards, tax returns or passport applications for travel purposes. People who are vulnerable because of disability, job loss or illness depend on public services, sometimes for their very survival. Shifting the procedures for accessing these rights to the online environment has a paradoxical consequence. Because these people are in contact with public services more often than others, they will be required to take steps online more often than others. And yet it is precisely these people who have the most difficulty with digital tools because they do not have the right tools and/or do not know how to use them. Further, they rarely have contacts, especially professional contacts, who can help them overcome the technical barriers, in the same way that employees can turn to IT specialists at their workplace.

As a result, digital technology appears to be one of the causes of "non-take-up of rights", i.e., the fact that some people are legally entitled to a right but do not actually benefit from it. Discouraged by the increasing complexity of online administrative procedures, some people do not follow through to the end of the process to obtain their rights, even though these are rights that should enable them to feed, house and care for themselves and so on. In addition, digital technology creates a distance in the relationship between agents and beneficiaries, which is detrimental to informing people about their rights and further reinforces the phenomenon of "non-take-up" (Dumont 2020; Noël 2021).

11.3 Why should the right not to use the Internet be enshrined?

At the initiative of the European Commission and its "digital compass" (European Commission 2021), the European Parliament and the Council decided on 14 December 2022 that "100% of essential public services should be available online by 2030".[11]

In Belgium, this objective took a concrete form through the adoption of the Brussels Ordinance[12] of 25 January 2024,[13] known as "Digital Brussels". This ordinance is the first legal text in Belgium to organise the digitalisation of all administrative procedures, without a clear guarantee of a human alternative. This text has sparked an unprecedented public outcry and has attracted a great deal of legal criticism, which we will discuss in the following.

Concerns about "all-digital" do not mean that we should deny the benefits of digital technology. They point to the need to assess objectively how digital technology is a solution in some cases and a problem in others. In particular, the threats to fundamental rights need to be taken seriously, as does the importance of giving everyone the right to choose the non-digital route to exercising their rights.

The following sections explore the relationship between citizens and public services ('front office') in a context where digital technology is the primary gateway to government services.[14]

11.3.1 Fundamental rights threatened by "all-digital" public services

While the digitisation of public services offers advantages, it also undermines a number of fundamental rights enshrined in the European Convention on Human Rights ("ECHR") and in the Belgian Constitution.[15] These include the right to equality and non-discrimination, the right to privacy and protection of personal data, the right to integration of people with disabilities, the right to a life in dignity and the right to freedom of expression.

11.3.1.1 The right to equality and non-discrimination

Regulations requiring people to use digital means of communication with the authorities might violate *the fundamental right to equality and non-discrimination* (Article 14 ECHR, Articles 10 and 11 of the Constitution) and could therefore be invalidated by the Constitutional Court or the Council of State.

Requiring administrative procedures to be carried out online, without organising the maintenance of physical counters, would create an unjustified difference in treatment to the detriment of a section of the population, in this case people who, because of their lack of digital autonomy, would thus be excluded from access to certain rights and services (Langlois & Van Drooghenbroeck 2023). This situation should therefore be classified as indirect discrimination.

The Belgian Constitutional Court has already ruled about the online accessibility of official standards that must be published in the *Moniteur belge*. It annulled a law which stipulated that, apart from three paper copies, one of which was available for consultation at the *Moniteur belge*, all other public access was provided *via* the *Moniteur belge* website (Degrave & Verdussen 2021; Passaglia 2016).[16] Since this ruling, any member of the public is able to phone a human agent, *via* a freephone number, for help in finding any act or document published in the *Moniteur belge*, and to request a copy at cost price.[17]

Since then, the Legislation Section of the Belgian Council of State ("SLCE") has ruled along the same lines on several occasions. In its opinion of 17 August 2023 on the above-mentioned draft Digital Brussels decree, the SLCE argued that "the computerisation of online administrative procedures and communications with public authorities is likely to give rise to indirect discrimination on the grounds of disability, age, wealth, social origin or gender. Access to such administrative procedures or communications presupposes access to computer equipment and an Internet connection, as well as the digital skills needed to understand how they work. Numerous studies have shown the difficulties encountered by a number of people in accessing these technologies, in particular because of one or more of the differentiation criteria mentioned above".[18] It concluded that

> it would not be acceptable, in the light of Articles 10 and 11 of the Constitution, for a significant number of people to be deprived of effective access to the services provided by the public authorities as a result of the obligation (...) to ensure the digitisation of administrative procedures and communications with the public authorities.[19]

In the same vein, a few years ago the SLCE also had to note the risk of discrimination in relation to online education[20] on the one hand, and the obligation to use digital means to obtain a car license plate[21] on the other. Regarding distance education, the SLCE observes that transitioning from paper course modules sent by mail to online-only formats diminishes equal access for "learners". Such a shift requires access to a computer equipment and an Internet connection, which could disadvantage certain groups, including individuals deprived of their freedom.[22] Similarly, the SLCE states that the obligation to exclusively use digital means for obtaining a car license plate, without a non-digital option, could be viewed as discriminatory in violation of Articles 10 and 11 of the Constitution. This requirement could effectively exclude individuals who lack the necessary digital equipment or capabilities from submitting a registration request.[23]

On the judicial front, the Brussels Court of First Instance heard a case brought by the UNIA[24] against the Brussels Regional Parking Authority concerning the "scancars", which are increasingly replacing pedestrian checks in parking enforcement. Despite their high-tech appearance, these cars are unable to recognise a disabled person's card. As a result, many disabled people have been charged unfairly. In its ruling of 22 May 2022,[25] the Court found indirect discrimination on the grounds of disability, which is prohibited by "anti-discrimination" legislation (in this case, the Brussels Regulation of 5 October 2017). Although apparently neutral, the control by the scancar creates a difference in treatment between two categories of people in the parking order, on the one hand motorists who pay the fee and on the other hand disabled people who present their card. In the judge's view, it was unjustified to impose additional formalities on disabled people since, under the law, all they had to do to benefit from free parking was to display a parking card. The agency was therefore ordered to put an end to this illegal practice (UNIA 2022).

In the same vein, on 23 June 2023 the Parliamentary Assembly of the Council of Europe adopted a resolution[26] in which it emphasised that "the authorities have a particular responsibility in the digital field when they themselves dematerialise public services". The Assembly notes that "objectives such as rationalising administrative costs, simplifying case management or improving the efficiency or speed of processing cases may be legitimate", but reaffirms that

> the pursuit of these objectives must in no way leave people who do not have easy access to digital technologies behind, as this would deprive them of access to their rights and would constitute a breach of the obligation to ensure the continuity of public services.[27]

The Assembly therefore calls on the Member States to

> move away from an approach of entirely paperless public services towards an approach of *entirely accessible* public services,[28] including by maintaining non-digital access to public services in all cases where this is necessary [to] guarantee equal access to public services, their continuity and their adaptation to users.[29]

This resolution therefore embodies a political priority of the "wider Europe", which Belgium, as a member of it, cannot ignore.[30]

At European Union level, in their "European Declaration on Digital Rights and Principles for the Digital Decade",[31] the European Parliament, the Council and the European Commission recall that "technology should be used to unite, and not divide, people". They emphasise that the digital shift must contribute to "a fair and inclusive society and economy in the EU", while committing to "a digital transformation that leaves nobody behind". This shift should benefit everyone, by for instance achieving gender balance, and including elderly people, people living in rural areas, persons with disabilities, and marginalised, or vulnerable people and those who act on their behalf. Importantly, the digital transformation should also promote cultural and linguistic diversity.[32] This text is described as "a reference framework for citizens" that guides the EU and Member States in their journey to digitalisation.[33] It embodies the EU and Member States' commitment "to promote a digital transformation where people are at the centre".[34] The implementation of this text is monitored by the Commission, which publishes an annual report on progress and gaps in the Member States.

On 2 July 2024, the European Commission published the second annual report on the State of the Digital Decade. This study reviews how Member States have so far acted upon the European Declaration on Digital Rights and Principles.[35] The report on Belgium highlights that "Belgium's regions and its national level, the federal government, have all made it a priority to tackle the digital divide and promote an inclusive, green digital transformation".[36] Regarding the accessibility to public services, the report emphasises that "measures to promote the digitalisation of key public services are balanced, with a significant focus on skills".[37] However, the report does not address the provision of non-digital alternatives for public services. Notably, the term "human contact" is absent from the report.

11.3.1.2 The right to privacy and the protection of personal data

The imposition of digital access to public services also affects the right to privacy (Article 8 ECHR, Article 22 of the Constitution) and the protection of personal data (organised in particular by the General Data Protection Regulation, "GDPR"). Such a measure is not prohibited, but care must be taken to ensure that certain safeguards are respected.

First, whether online or offline, public authorities can only collect the personal data they need to do their job. This is the principle of data minimisation enshrined in Article 5 GDPR. In the same vein, the above-mentioned "European Declaration on Digital Rights and Principles for the Digital Decade" recalls that "however, we can see that there is a tendency to collect more data online than is necessary, resulting in a greater intrusion into people's private lives online than offline". For example, asking for information at a government counter does not necessarily mean you have to identify yourself. In digital form, many websites require you to provide your surname, first name and email address for simple information. The ONEM[38] website even asks for your national registration number on its "contact form".[39]

However, the right to privacy is understood as a *right to informational self-determination*, i.e., the right to control one's own data by deciding what may be communicated, to whom, and what may be done with it (Degrave 2014). This interpretation first came from the German Constitutional Court, which drew it from Articles 1 and 2 of its Basic Law, which are devoted to the rights to dignity and freedom. Since then, this interpretation has been applied in particular by the European Court of Human Rights, which recently recalled, in a case concerning the online publication of the identity and contact details of a tax debtor, that

> Article 8 thus enshrines a right to a form of informational self-determination which entitles individuals to invoke their right to privacy with respect to data which, although neutral, are collected, processed and disseminated to the public in such a way that their rights under Article 8 may be implicated.[40]

Put another way, it is the idea that, unless a law requires data to be processed for legitimate reasons and in a relevant and necessary manner, everyone can legitimately refuse to disclose information about themselves without trying to hide anything objectionable, just as they have the right to put curtains on their windows without revealing any suspicious behaviour. Informational self-determination and the principle of data minimisation underline the importance of maintaining a non-digital channel in relations with the authorities.

11.3.1.3 The right to inclusion for people with disabilities

Digital technology is also ambivalent for people with disabilities.

On the one hand, it can be a great help. For example, every smartphone has some very interesting features that make everyday life easier for people with disabilities, such as the ability to browse the Internet using only voice.[41]

However, when it comes to relations with public services, the digitisation of administrative procedures (despite the existence of appropriate tools) can jeopardise the fundamental right to inclusion of people with disabilities (Article 19 of the United Nations Convention on the Rights of Persons with Disabilities – Article 26 of the Charter of Fundamental Rights of the European Union – Article 22ter of the Constitution). This is due in particular to the fact that, despite a European Directive on the subject[42] in force since 2016, many government websites are only accessible with a mouse or a touch screen. They are unusable for 15% of people with visual, hearing, cognitive or physical disabilities.

11.3.1.4 The right to human dignity

According to Article 23 of the Belgian Constitution, which protects economic, social and cultural rights, "everyone has the right to lead a life in accordance with human dignity" and "this right includes in particular (...) 2° the right to social security, health protection and social, medical and legal assistance; 3° the right to decent housing; (...) 5° the right to cultural and social fulfilment (...)".

However, only offering administrative procedures online can hinder the exercise of these rights if, faced with the "humiliating bugs" mentioned above, people are prevented from applying for a social right – such as housing or social assistance – or an economic right – such as a subsidy or bonus – or are denied access to cultural life – such as access to museums *via* a QR code or prior online booking. Yet these rights are essential for upholding the dignity of citizens, i.e., the respect that is due to every individual. The right to dignity is broad, and "protects everyone against degrading or inhuman acts that could reduce them to the status of a thing" (Vie publique 2023). When digital technology obstructs access to these rights, it becomes a factory of human indignities (Fleury 2023). Furthermore, it is interesting to include the right not to use the Internet in Article 23, as it already imposes various positive obligations on the State, requiring it to "provide" the services indicated therein (Hachez 2000). Given the pervasive use of digital technology today, it is important to subject the State to a new positive obligation in favour of human dignity, the obligation to put in place the means to enable citizens not to use the Internet, so that they can benefit from the rights that are absolutely essential to the preservation of their human dignity.

11.3.1.5 The right to freedom of expression

Imposing the use of the Internet may also threaten the right to freedom of expression (Article 10 ECHR – Article 19 of the Constitution), as argued by Kloza (2021, 2024). The ECHR considers that everyone must be able to exercise his freedom of expression and access information through various channels, including the Internet. It therefore derives from Article 10 a right of access to the Internet as an additional means of exercising freedom of expression and of accessing information, even if that information is accessible by other means.[43] However, the right of access to the Internet does not mean that everyone is obliged to use the Internet to exercise their rights or fulfil their obligations. Consequently, although the Court has not yet ruled on the right not to use the Internet, we can reason by analogy with the right of access to the Internet. Imposing an obligation to use the Internet, without any alternative, in order to exercise freedom of expression and access to information would be tantamount to imposing on citizens a single means of exercising these rights.

11.3.2 The freedom to choose human interaction

In the context of "all-digital" services, even people who are generally comfortable with digital technology can experience annoying difficulties. Therefore, over and above the issue of fundamental rights, it is important to allow everyone to choose whether or not to use the Internet to exercise their rights.

Indeed, online procedures are often complex because they are not sufficiently adapted to the events in people's lives (a birth, buying a house, etc.). They are the implementation of the logic (or lack of it) of administrations. For these procedures, we therefore need a human agent whose job it is and who is trained to do so. Digital technology, on the other hand, shifts the burden of this work to the user, as if he were being asked to sit in the place of the civil servant and deal with his computer, even though he has no training in this area and is not paid for it.

In addition, there are technical problems that citizens cannot solve themselves (website down, multiple updates, etc.).

In Belgium, the right not to use the Internet is already enshrined in a number of legal provisions. At federal level, the Code of Economic Law,[44] which applies to relations between citizens and public services, states that "in the absence of legal provisions to the contrary, no one may be compelled to perform a legal act by electronic means". The legislatures of the French Community[45] and the Walloon Region[46,47] have also each adopted a similar provision, aimed at "citizens who are unable or *unwilling*[48] to use technology (…), particularly in their dealings with the administration".[49] This right should now be enshrined in the Constitution, for the reasons explained in the following.

Moreover, it is interesting to note that the Belgian legislator has recognised a "right to disconnect" to workers.[50] This measure aims to mitigate the "culture of 'permanent connection' which has a negative impact on respect for rest periods".[51] By acknowledging the need to limit digital technology's presence in citizens' lives, this legislation highlights the importance of balancing "online" and "offline" life, which is essential for mental well-being (Kloza 2024). Hence, it is crucial to avoid requiring individuals to connect at the end of the day to carry out essential and sometimes complex administrative tasks alone in front of a screen.

In addition, a law adopted on 9 February 2024[52] enshrines the consumer's right to choose between electronic payment and payment in cash, in particular because some people are uncomfortable with electronic payments or do not have access to them, such as "the elderly, immigrants, disabled people, socially vulnerable citizens and marginalised people".[53] This legislation underscores the importance of providing a non-digital alternative to ensure that all citizens, regardless of their social or economic situation, have access to essential services.

11.4 Why should the right not to use the Internet be enshrined in the Constitution?

In view of these observations, which are likely to become even more pronounced in the future in the light of the political projects like the Digital Brussels Ordinance and the European aim that "100% of essential public services should be available online by 2030",[54] it is crucial to enshrine in the Constitution the "right not to use the Internet", which could also be framed as the "right to human interaction" with public administrations. This is an important consideration, especially as the Belgian

Constitution currently does not address digital issues. In particular, it enshrines neither the right to access the Internet nor the right to abstain from using it (Verdussen 2019; Degrave & Verdussen 2021).[55]

Itis interesting to note that Switzerland has already begun the process of constitutionalising the right not to use the Internet. This is a world first. The canton of Geneva has enshrined the "right to digital integrity" in its constitution,[56] which "includes in particular the right to be protected against the abusive processing of data linked to one's digital life, the right to security in digital space, the right to an offline life and the right to be forgotten".[57] Other Swiss cantons are following suit. In Neuchâtel, for example, a draft decree to this effect was approved at first reading in April 2024.[58]

The inclusion of this new right in the Constitution is justified by the strength of the constitutional norm and the enrichment it represents for other fundamental rights.

11.4.1 The strength of the Constitution

Establishing the right not to use the Internet would have strong *symbolic value*, underlining the importance, stressed by the Constituent, of organising a digitally balanced society by keeping digital technology in its rightful place, as a tool serving the general interest and complementing human interaction (Verdussen, 2019).

Moreover, the Constitution is at the *top of the hierarchy of norms*. In Belgium, like above-mentioned, the right not to use the Internet is already enshrined in a number of legal provisions. However, these standards only have the force of law. Another standard of the same value could deviate from them. Therefore, in order to guarantee the reality of the right not to use the Internet regardless of future legislative reforms, and to enforce it at all levels of power in Belgium, it is important to give this right a constitutional basis and to enshrine it in the Constitution, which has the highest value and must be respected by all other norms in Belgium.

11.4.1.1 Enrichment of other fundamental rights

When digitalisation obstructs an individual's access to their rights, the constitutional rights to equality and non-discrimination, to inclusion of people with disabilities, and to a life in dignity can be invoked to compel the legislature to provide solutions for the benefit of those affected. However, it remains uncertain that measures taken in the name of these rights will guarantee human interaction. For example, in order to put an end to discrimination caused by digital technology, measures have been taken to support people in the digital age, such as digital public facilities. However, they do not solve the problems of digital rigidity and standardisation. What's more, existing fundamental rights do not protect those who choose (rather than are forced) to engage in human interaction.

The question is where to place this new fundamental right in our Constitution.

Article 23 of the Constitution, which enshrines the right to human dignity, is attracting attention because in recent years there have been several proposals in

Belgium to insert a "right to access the Internet" in Article 23 (Degrave 2023). This right to access the Internet could be complemented by a right not to use the Internet, to emphasise that the right to access the Internet does not imply an obligation to use it. Article 23 of the Constitution could therefore read as follows:

> Everyone has the right to lead a life worthy of human dignity. (…) These rights include in particular: (…) 7° the right of use the Internet and the right not to use the Internet for the exercise of one's rights and the fulfilment of one's obligations.

This would emphasise the concept of the Internet as a means of access to rights, alongside human interaction.

Another possibility would be to consider the right not to use the Internet as an aspect of freedom of expression, enshrined in Article 19 of the Constitution, based on the reasoning set out above in the European Court of Human Rights' interpretation of Article 10 ECHR.[59] It is considered that imposing the exclusive use of the Internet to express oneself constitutes a violation of freedom of expression since it restricts the means available for transmitting and receiving information by preventing this freedom from being expressed in human interaction, offline. In order to guarantee the right to this human interaction, "the freedom to express one's opinion on any subject" guaranteed by Article 19 of the Constitution could now be formulated as "the freedom to express one's opinions on any subject and in any form whatsoever". However, we feel that this solution is less appropriate than the previous one. Symbolically, linking the right not to use the Internet to freedom of expression reduces it to a question of communication and does not make us sufficiently aware of the damage that "all-digital" technology can cause to human dignity by being an obstacle to the rights necessary for the survival of each individual.

11.5 Conclusion

Digitisation of public services has a number of benefits in terms of reducing the administrative burden on citizens. Digitisation facilitates the exchange of information between administrations and makes it possible to automate the provision of certain forms of assistance. However, the generalisation of this digitisation also creates difficulties for a large number of people, including those who are generally comfortable with digital technology, who are unable to solve the technical "bugs" or complex procedures that used to be carried out by an agent. These difficulties can also exclude whole categories of people from accessing their rights. We are thinking in particular of people living in poverty or with disabilities, who are particularly dependent on the state and therefore increasingly subject to this forced digitisation.

With the increasing digitisation of public services, encouraged by the European target of "100% online by 2023", a new right should be enshrined in our Constitution: the right not to use the Internet.

The rationale for this right lies in the protection of a number of fundamental rights that are currently being undermined by digital technology, namely the right to equality and non-discrimination, the right to privacy and protection of personal data, the right to inclusion of people with disabilities and the right to lead a life in accordance with human dignity. This new right is also justified by the importance of being able to choose human interaction, in particular to ensure a balance between life "online" and life "offline".

This new fundamental right should be given a constitutional basis, as the Constitution is the common foundation of the nation, dominating all other norms. The right not to use the Internet could usefully enrich the right to lead a life worthy of human dignity or the right to freedom of expression, reflecting the work of the Council of Europe and the jurisprudence of the European Court of Human Rights.

These initial avenues for reflection and action are driven by the conviction that digital technology is not an end in itself. That it serves society and not the other way round. In this sense, the "European Declaration on Digital Rights and Principles for the Digital Decade" reiterates this by stating that "Artificial intelligence should serve as a tool for people, with the ultimate aim of increasing human well-being".[60]

We hope that they will stimulate constructive discussions within the states and enrich our constitutions with a breath of fresh air, ensuring that digital technology is put in its rightful place as a controlled and chosen tool.

Notes

1 ChatGPT4 was used for the editing of this chapter.

2 For more details see. Degrave, E. (2014).

3 In practice, see www.kafka.be/fr.

4 According to the French expression. See www.numerique.gouv.fr/services/guichet-dites-le-nous-une-fois/.

5 See e.g., a Law of 8 August 1983, Organizing a National Register of Natural Persons (1983); Law of 15 August 2012, Relating to the Creation and Organization of a Federal Service Integrator (2012); Ordinance of 17 July 2020, Guaranteeing the Principle of Single Data Collection in the Operation of Services and Bodies Under or Performing Certain Tasks for the Authority, and Simplifying and Harmonizing Electronic and Paper Forms (2020); Flemish Decree of 18 July 2008 on the Electronic Exchange of Administrative Data (2008).

6 The obligation to collect data indirectly is laid down in various pieces of legislation. See e.g., an Article 6 of the Law of 8 August 1983, Organizing a National Register of Natural Persons (1983); article 8, §3 of the Law of 15 August 2012, Relating to the Creation and Organization of a Federal Service Integrator (2012); article 6 of the Ordinance of 17 July 2020, Guaranteeing the Principle of Single Data Collection in the Operation of Services and Bodies Under or Performing Certain Tasks for the Authority, and Simplifying and Harmonizing Electronic and Paper Forms (2020).

7 For more information, go to www.belgium.be/fr/famille/enfants/naissance/declaration_de_naissance.

8 This automation is governed by the law of 29 April 1999 on the organisation of the electricity market.

9 There are also a number of problems in the back office, particularly as regards data errors and the use of biased algorithms.

10 In the words of a welfare recipient at the PUNCH (Pour Un Numérique Critique et Humain) conference on "Automatisation des droits et du contrôle" (by V. Englebert and E. Degrave) held in Brussels on 3 February 2023.

11 European Parliament and Council. (2022). *Decision (EU) 2022/2481 of 14 December 2022 establishing the action programme for the digital decade to 2030.* OJ, L 323/4, 19.12.2022, Art. 4(1)(4). The following day, the European Parliament, the Council and the Commission solemnly proclaimed the "European Declaration on Digital Rights and Principles for the Digital Decade", stating in particular that "everyone should have online access to essential public services in the EU", and pledging to "ensure that people living in the EU are given the opportunity (…) to access a wide range of digital services" while ensuring "the re-use of public sector information" (European Commission, European Parliament, & Council of the European Union. (2022). *European Declaration on Digital Rights and Principles for the Digital Decade* (Art. 7). OJ, C 23/1, 15.12.2022.).

12 An ordinance is a legal rule adopted by the Brussels Region. It has the same legal force as a law or decree.

13 More specifically, this concerns the Joint Decree and Order of the French Community Commission, the Brussels-Capital Region and the Joint Community Commission relating to the digital transition of public authorities (2024, January 25). *Moniteur Belge*, 21 February 2024, p. 25726.

14 For example, it should be remembered that the draft "Digital Brussels" ordinance provides for administrations to go online without guaranteeing that human interaction will be maintained.

15 The following sections will focus on these two legal texts.

16 C.C., judgment no. 106/2004, 16 June 2004.

17 Programme Law of 24 December 2002, Art. 475 bis (inserted by Law of 20 July 2005 containing various provisions, Art. 6).

18 SLCE. (2023, 17 août). *Opinion 74.001/2/V on a preliminary draft joint decree and ordinance of the Brussels-Capital Region, the Joint Community Commission and the French Community Commission 'relating to the digital transition of Public Authorities'*. p. 9.

19 SLCE. (2023, 17 août). *Opinion 74.001/2/V on a preliminary draft joint decree and ordinance of the Brussels-Capital Region, the Joint Community Commission and the French Community Commission 'relating to the digital transition of Public Authorities'*. p. 9.

20 SLCE. (2016, 12 avril). *Opinion No. 59121/2 on a preliminary draft decree of the French Community 'organising French Community distance education in e-learning'*. pp. 3–4.

21 SLCE. (2013, 11 février). *Opinion No. 52753/4 on a draft Royal Decree 'amending the Royal Decree of 20 July 2001 on the registration of vehicles'*. p. 4.

22 SLCE. (2016, 12 avril). *Opinion No. 59121/2 on a preliminary draft decree of the French Community 'organising French Community distance education in e-learning'*. p. 3.

23 *Tribunal de première instance de Bruxelles (francophone), 2 mai 2022*, www.unia.be/files/ 2022_05_02_Trib._Bruxelles.pdf.

24 Unia in an independent public institution in Belgium that advocates for equality and combats most forms of discrimination (such as racism, age, etc.). www.unia.be/fr.

25 UNIA, Samen voor gelijkheid, www.unia.be/files/Documenten/2022_05_02_Trib._Br uxelles.pdf

26 Council of Europe, Parliamentary Assembly. (2023). *Bridging the digital divide: Promoting equal access to digital technologies* (Resolution 2510).

27 Council of Europe, Parliamentary Assembly. (2023). *Bridging the digital divide: Promoting equal access to digital technologies* (Resolution 2510, para. 7).
28 Emphasis added.
29 Council of Europe, Parliamentary Assembly. (2023). *Bridging the digital divide: Promoting equal access to digital technologies* (Resolution 2510, para. 12.1).
30 For other cases in France, see. Kloza, D., & Rossi, J. (2023–2024). Du droit d'accéder à internet à la liberté de – ne pas – l'utiliser? *Revue européenne des médias et du numérique, 68*, 17 et seq.
31 OJ, C. 23, 23.01.23.
32 Chapter II, 2, C 23/3.
33 European Commission, European Declaration on Digital Rights and Principles, https://digital-strategy.ec.europa.eu/en/library/european-declaration-digital-rights-and-principles
34 European Commission, Monitoring of Digital Rights and Principles - Support Study 2024, https://digital-strategy.ec.europa.eu/en/library/monitoring-digital-rights-and-principles-support-study-2024
35 European Commission, Monitoring of Digital Rights and Principles - Support Study 2024, https://digital-strategy.ec.europa.eu/en/library/monitoring-digital-rights-and-principles-support-study-2024
36 European Commission, Report on the state of the Digital Decade 2024, https://digital-strategy.ec.europa.eu/en/library/report-state-digital-decade-2024, p. 5.
37 European Commission, Report on the state of the Digital Decade 2024, https://digital-strategy.ec.europa.eu/en/library/report-state-digital-decade-2024, p. 5.
38 The ONEM (National Employment Office) is a public institution that manages unemployment insurance for citizens and certain employment-related measures, such as career breaks.
39 National Employment Office, Formulaire de contact, www.onem.be/contact/formulaire-de-contact.
40 See recently ECHR, *L.B. v. Hungary,* 36345/16, 9 March 2023, §103. This was a case of "shaming" involving a Hungarian citizen with tax debts whose name was posted online on the Tax Authority's website, under Hungarian law.
41 ASBL Creth's "Les Tactiles" project aims to highlight the functionalities of consumer tactile technologies (particularly smartphones and tablets) to meet the needs of people with disabilities. Find out more here: http://creth.be/les-tactiles/.
42 Directive 2016/2102 of 26 October 2016 on the accessibility of websites and mobile applications of public sector bodies, OJ, L327/1, 2.12.2016.
43 See also ECHR, *Ramazan Demir v. Turkey*, 9 February 2021, 68550/17, §47.
44 Art. XII.25, §1er.
45 Decree of 3 April 2014 on communications by electronic means between users and the public authorities of the French Community, Art. 4.
46 Walloon Decree of 27 March 2014 on communications by electronic means between users and the Walloon public authorities, Art. 4.
47 We have not found any equivalent provision in Flemish legislation.
48 Emphasis added.
49 Projet de décret relatif aux communications par voie électronique entre les usagers et les autorités publiques de la Communauté française (2013–2014). *Documents du Parlement de la Communauté française*, n° 616, n° 1, p. 5.; Projet de décret relatif aux communications par voie électronique entre les usagers et les autorités

publiques wallonnes (2013–2014). *Documents du Parlement de la Wallonie*, n° 1000, n° 1, p. 7.

50 Article 29 of the Act of 3 October 2022 containing various provisions relating to employment.

51 Bill containing various provisions relating to labour, *Doc. Parl.* ch. repr. Sess. 2021-2022, Doc 55 2810/001, p. 18.

52 Law of 9 February 2024 containing various provisions relating to the economy, Art. 17.

53 Proposal for a law amending the Code of Economic Law in order to ensure that businesses are obliged to accept payment in cash from consumers, Ch. Repr., *Doc.* 2022-2023, Doc 55 3162/001, p. 5.

54 European Parliament and Council. (2022). *Decision (EU) 2022/2481 of 14 December 2022 establishing the action programme for the digital decade to 2030.* OJ, L 323/4, 19.12.2022, Art. 4(1)(4).The following day, the European Parliament, the Council and the Commission solemnly proclaimed the "European Declaration on Digital Rights and Principles for the Digital Decade", stating in particular that "everyone should have online access to essential public services in the EU", and pledging to "ensure that people living in the EU are given the opportunity (…) to access a wide range of digital services" while ensuring "the re-use of public sector information" (European Commission, European Parliament, & Council of the European Union. (2022). *European Declaration on Digital Rights and Principles for the Digital Decade* (Art. 7). OJ, C 23/1, 15.12.2022.).

55 While the Belgian Constitution does not currently enshrine a fundamental right to access the Internet, several proposals have nevertheless been submitted to the House of Representatives and the Senate. These proposals aim to amend Article 23 of the Constitution, which deals with economic, social and cultural rights, by adding a "right to access the internet", a "right to access the internet tool", a "right to access a public electronic communications network that is neutral", a "right to sufficient and neutral access to the internet", or a "right to access a neutral and open internet". However, none of these proposals have been examined.

56 Constitution of the Canton of Geneva, Art. 21A.

57 Constitutional Act amending the Constitution of the Republic and Canton of Geneva (Cst-GE) (For a strong protection of the individual in the digital space.) https://ge.ch/grandconseil/data/loisvotee/L12945.pdf.

58 Cf. Les députés en faveur d'un droit à l'intégrité numérique, RTN, 23 April 2024, https://www.rtn.ch/rtn/Actualite/Region/20240423-Les-deputes-en-faveur-d-un-droit-a-l-integrite-numerique.html and Projet de décret du groupe socialiste modifiant la Constitution de la République et Canton de Neuchâtel (Cst.NE) (Pour un droit à l'intégrité numérique et la protection d'un droit à une vie hors ligne), 12 janvier 2023, www.ne.ch/autorites/GC/objets/Documents/Rapports/2023/23108_com.pdf

59 See also ECHR, *Ramazan Demir v. Turkey*, 9 February 2021, 68550/17, §47.

60 Chapter III, 8.

Bibiliography

Degrave, E. (2014). *L'e-gouvernement et la protection de la vie privée. Légalité, transparence et contrôle* (Coll. Crids, No 33). Larcier. https://researchportal.unamur.be/fr/studentTheses/le-gouvernement-et-la-protection-de-la-vie-priv%C3%A9e

Degrave, E. (2023). Justice sociale et services publics numériques: pour le droit fondamental d'utiliser – ou non – internet. *Revue belge de droit constitutionnel*, *2023*(3), 211–244.

Degrave, E. (2024). *L'État numérique et les droits humains*. Académie Royale de Belgique (Collection Académie en poche).

Degrave, E., & Verdussen, M. (2021). Constitution, libertés et numérique. Belgique. In Annuaire International de Justice Constitutionnelle, *2020* (pp. 169–195). Economica, Presses Universitaires d'Aix-Marseille.

Dumont, D. (2020). Le phénomène du non-recours aux prestations, un défi pour l'effectivité (et la légitimité) du droit de la sécurité sociale. *TSR-RDS*, *2020*(3), 285–326.

European Commission. (2021). A digital compass for 2030: Europe points the way to the digital decade *(COM(2021) 118 final)*. Communication from the Commission to the European Parliament, the Council, the European Economic and Social Committee, and the Committee of the Regions. https://eur-lex.europa.eu/legal-content/EN/TXT/?uri=CELEX%3A52021DC0118

Fleury, C. (2023). *La clinique de la dignité*. Seuil.

Hachez, I. (2000). L'effet de standstill: Le pari des droits économiques, sociaux et culturels? *Administration publique*, 30–57.

King Baudouin Foundation. (2024). *Digital inclusion barometer 2024* (pp. 22–25). https://kbs-frb.be/nl/barometer-digitale-inclusie-2024

Kloza, D. (2021). *Its all about choice. The Right not to use the Internet*. https://voelkerrechtsblog.org/its-all-about-choice/.

Kloza, D. (2024). The right not to use the internet. *Computer Law & Security Review, 52*, 105907. http://hdl.handle.net/1854/LU-01HFBGZ9ZHQ8Z2TCC178J7S3RZ

Kloza, D., & Rossi, J. (2024). Du droit d'accéder à internet à la liberté de – ne pas – l'utiliser? *Revue européenne des médias et du numérique*, *68*, 17–20.

Langlois, C., & Van Drooghenbroeck, S. (2023). Digitalisation et discrimination: Enjeux d'une rencontre, agenda d'une réforme / Discriminatie en digitalisering: Inzet van een kruisbestuiving, stappenplan voor een hervorming. In J. Ringelheim et al. (Eds.), *Een hernieuwde impuls voor de strijd tegen discriminatie / Redynamiser la lutte contre la discrimination* (1st ed., pp. 35–73). Intersentia.

Mazet, P. (2021). *Les conditionnalités implicites de l'accès aux droits à l'ère numérique*. HAL. https://shs.hal.science/halshs-03218656/document

Noël, L. (2021). Non-recours aux droits et précarisation en Région bruxelloise. *Brussels Studies*, *2021*, 1–18. https://doi.org/10.4000/brussels.5569

Passaglia, P. (2016). Le droit d'accès à internet dans les jurisprudences constitutionnelles: Vers un droit commun jurisprudentiel? In A. Le Quinio (Ed.), *Les réactions constitutionnelles à la globalisation* (pp. 93–123). Bruylant.

Service de lutte contre la pauvreté. (2020). Automatisation des droits. www.luttepauvrete.be/wp-content/uploads/sites/2/2020/01/AUTOMATISATION.pdf

UNIA. (2022, 13 mai). *Les scancars jugées discriminatoires pour les personnes en situation de handicap*. www.unia.be/fr/articles/les-scan-cars-jugees-discriminatoires-pour-les-personnes-en-situation-de-ha.

Verdussen, M. (2019). *Réenchanter la Constitution*. Académie Royale (Collection Académie en poche).

Vie publique – au coeur du débat public. (2023). *Qu'est-ce que le principe de sauvegarde de la dignité humaine?* www.vie-publique.fr/fiches/290005-quest-ce-que-le-principe-de-sauvegarde-de-la-dignite-humaine

12 Is the dematerialisation of public services an elective progress?

A sociological analysis of the (non)uses by older people in France[1]

Sabrina Aouici

12.1 Introduction

Announced as necessary and aimed at better meeting the needs of users, the introduction of Information and Communication Technologies (ICTs) within French administrations appears as the main vector for the modernisation of service relations. The e-administration development policy, which aimed to improve the quality of public service as well as a simplification of relations with users, was launched in France in the late 1990s with the circular of 16 September 1996 and the launch of the governmental action programme for the information society in 1998 (Roux, 2010; Cour des comptes, 2019). By establishing a national digital council since 2011, the state indicated its determination to accelerate the digital transition; in September 2020, by recommending the allocation of one billion euros to 'fight against illectronism and for digital inclusion', the Senate confirmed this trend. Over the past decade, the dematerialisation of services has rapidly spread within French administrations. Today, almost all administrations provide a more or less profound redesign of their service offerings, relying on the communication means offered by digital technology.

These technological developments impose new practices and uses on individuals to interact with institutions and assert their social rights. Data from the Digital barometer (Credoc, 2015; Credoc, 2019) show that the number of individuals conducting administrative or tax procedures online has increased over the entire period: one in five French people considers that digital technology simplifies relations with the public administration; 68% of French people now consider that having Internet access is important to 'feel integrated into society'; this represents fourteen points more than in 2009. Although the introduction of ICTs within French administrations under the principle of adaptability (or mutability) of public services seems to be accepted without major difficulty by most of the population, even praising the facilitating aspects and the time saving (those equipped, educated and familiar with new technologies), numerous studies highlight the 'double penalty for vulnerable populations facing the all-digital' and emphasise that the process of dematerialisation of services can exacerbate pre-existing inequalities (language difficulties, influence of age, level of education, place of residence …) and increase

DOI: 10.4324/9781003528401-15

the difficulty for the most vulnerable populations to access their rights (Granjon, 2009; Alberola et al., 2016; Koubi, 2013) and raise the risk of excluding a population that remains distant from ICTs.

Nearly thirteen million people in France declare themselves uncomfortable with digital technology, representing between a quarter and a third of the French population aged eighteen and over (Les Petits Frères des Pauvres, 2018). More than one in three believe that the Internet makes these relations more complex; for a quarter of them, administrative procedures are too complex and 20% admit to lacking proficiency with digital tools (Credoc, 2019). Many studies have highlighted a number of concerns about the temptation of 'all-digital' and the question of access to social rights. The main alert was to raise awareness of the risks associated with the 'digital divide' (Hargittai, 2002; Vendramin & Valenduc, 2003; Ben Youssef, 2004; Granjon, 2009; Attour & Longhi, 2009). By distinguishing economic and social inequalities related to available equipment and infrastructure, those related to uses or even to learning methods, the same studies show that having a computer and Internet connection is not enough to ensure an equal regime of uses and recall that the digital divide is not limited to the phenomenon of e-exclusion. A new form of inequality emerges, 'the latest variation of pre-existing social inequalities' (Granjon, 2009: 23). Beyond equipment and usage appropriation, questions arise about illectronism[2] (digital illiteracy), digital literacy and usage appropriation: 17% of French people are in a situation of illectronism; 15% did not use the Internet in 2019 (64% of those aged seventy-five and over) and 38% lack basic digital skills[3] (Cousteaux, 2019). Indeed, the use of online services requires not only equipment and 'digital autonomy' (Revil & Warin, 2019) but also a good knowledge of French, understanding of the terms used, ability to understand administrative services and the system (Koubi, 2013).

The population that is uncomfortable with digital tools is very heterogeneous, but retirees, the less educated and low-income groups are the least equipped: while the Internet connection rate is 85% for the entire population, it is 57% among those over seventy, 54% among those with no diploma (compared to 94% of higher education graduates) and 40% among those with low incomes. The age criterion concerns the entire digital support sector, which notes that the older people are, the more difficulties they have with digital technology.[4] According to data from the Digital barometer (Credoc, 2019), 75% of respondents feel little or not at all comfortable with digital technology and just as many feel little or not at all capable of using the Internet to carry out procedures. With the intensification of the dematerialisation of public services, retirees are therefore among the most vulnerable populations (Donnat, 2007; Le Douarin & Caradec, 2009; Alberola et al., 2016).

The intensification of the dematerialisation of public services leads to a reflection on the transformation of relations with public services, especially for working-class, since relations with public services are more frequent within working-class category than in other social category, due to economic needs and precarious living conditions (unemployment, housing difficulties, foreign status …) which are overrepresented there (Siblot, 2005; Spire, 2005). This questions the role of the municipality, a local public service often identified by working-class people as a place of confidence. This feeling is particularly reinforced in small municipalities. All these questions are reinforced by the decline in multimodal access to public services and the reduction (or disappearance) of spontaneous physical receptions. The question of the role of the social environment (family, social network, affective proximities) and professional caregivers also arises.

Indeed, the introduction of digital technology leads individuals without tools or without knowledge of them to seek external support, especially towards the family sphere, to try to overcome the difficulties of accessing dematerialised services. Strong expectations also weigh on associative structures (National digital council, 2015; Revil & Warin, 2019). Whether from the social environment or the social sphere, these digital caregivers must deal with questions of trust, availability and confidentiality generated by e-administration. Professionals in the associative sector are poorly prepared for the digital transition and under-equipped and they also encounter difficulties in conducting these new missions. The use of social workers and associative relays as resources and facilitators also raises a number of questions. If associative structures can serve as local relays and provide support to public services, under what conditions can they ensure the management and implementation of this new mission?

12.2 Data and methods

This chapter aims to re-examine these questions by offering a reflection on the difficulties posed by the introduction of digital technology in accessing social rights, for both users and the caregivers surrounding them, whether they come from the family or the social sphere. Our analysis is based on data from a qualitative survey conducted by National Old-Age Pension Fund (CNAV) in 2018 and 2019 before COVID-19 among sixty-four individuals from two distinct populations: thirty-one interviews were conducted with users of public services (retirees or individuals approaching retirement age); around thirty professionals were also interviewed (twenty-one associative leaders or social workers, twelve institutional actors of public services). Our survey area is located in the Île-de-France region: most interviews were conducted in Paris or in the inner suburbs and a third were conducted in more rural areas of the Paris region. The interview guides addressed the personal trajectory of the respondents and, for insured individuals, their family situation; relationships and knowledge of public services (definition, roles and missions of public services, experiences and opinions on public services); the evolution of missions/service offerings following digitalisation and necessary assistance (for professionals); accessible procedures and resources mobilisable in case of difficulties (for users as well as professionals); the question of access to rights and non-use. Interviews with users, with an average duration of fifty-five minutes, generally took place at retirees' homes; those with professionals (average of seventy-five minutes) were conducted at their workplaces. All interviews were recorded after the researcher had previously ensured pseudonymisation (all names used in this chapter are fictitious) and obtained informed consent from the respondents, then fully transcribed.[5]

The main objective of this study was to analyse the perception that the various surveyed publics have of the dematerialisation of public services and the impact of e-administration on their respective practices (Aouici et al., 2021). We propose to focus this chapter around four questions: (1) Does the introduction of digital tools in administrative procedures transform the relationship of elderly users with public services? (2) Does the introduction of digital tools in administrative procedures place new populations in situations of vulnerability? (3) Does the generalisation of tele-services[6] generate new forms of non-use among elderly users? and (4) What are the consequences for social actors and professional caregivers?

12.2.1 Consequences of digitalisation on the relationships of elderly users with public services

We applied textual statistical methods to exploratively analyse the responses provided during interviews to the following question: 'When you think of public services, what comes to mind?' The analysis of the vocabulary used contrasts a positive vision of public services (synonymous with proximity and service missions they offer to users) with a more negative vision (discourses emphasising inaccessibility, loss of human contact and risks associated with digitalisation).

The cross-analysis of discourses from users, institutional actors and associative leaders/social workers identifies three main dimensions: the first refers to the founding values of public services and support and service missions; it mainly comes from institutional actors and users in urban areas. The second focuses more on the organisational aspects of public services with the mention of administrations offering public services. The third associates the notion of 'public service' with the question of (in)accessibility and thus mentions the obstacles and difficulties encountered (including digitalisation); this is mainly the discourse of users and associative leaders/social workers in peri-urban and rural areas. Users then mobilise their subjective experiences to highlight the obstacles they face; they also mention the intermediaries (municipality, prefecture, associations) with which they have regular contacts, as well as procedures and contact modalities (phone, website, reception, access, …). Associative leaders and social workers, on the other hand, mention the limitations caused by digitalisation perceived, in these discourses, as generating difficulties. Among the most specific words of this dimension are indeed the terms: 'digitalisation', 'difficulty', 'problem', 'delay', 'long', 'understand', 'explain', 'directly', 'fear', 'generation' and 'competence'.

The dematerialisation of services has been accompanied by a change in the operational mode of reception in agencies, limiting physical reception and proximity services. This transformation has generated increased distance from public services, which arouses fear and incomprehension. Beyond the proximity of services, the most pressing concerns relate to the gradual disappearance of human contact and the reduced diversity of access modes to services. In its 2019 Report, the French Defender of Rights emphasised the need to maintain multimodal access to public services. This precaution would be especially valuable for the most vulnerable, ensuring them various solutions for contacting and accessing information from administrations.

Online procedures require, at a minimum, access to computer equipment and a good-quality Internet connection. These two conditions are not met across the entire territory and in all households in France, creating inequalities in accessing online public services: difficulties in accessing digital technology, inequalities in digital use, difficulties related to electronic exchanges (use of email), difficulties related to the design or deployment of websites and finally cognitive or physical difficulties highlighted by digital technology.

12.2.2 Administrative autonomy challenged by digitalisation

> Everyone has at least one child or neighbour to help.
>
> (Mrs. Bouchez, administrative manager – Social Security, urban area)

Discussing the use of digital technology and tele-services by elderly individuals in the context of increasing dematerialisation and 'digital inclusion' as said in French administrations, leads to a broader questioning of 'digital autonomy': is digital autonomy an indispensable prerequisite for digital inclusion?

Four typical situations emerge based on individuals' degree of digital autonomy and their degree of administrative autonomy (Aouici & Gallou, 2023). The first category (the 'agile') concerns individuals in a situation of administrative autonomy who easily mobilise digital tools, meaning people who are autonomous in their administrative procedures before and after the dematerialisation of public services. In contrast to the 'agile', the 'dependent' individuals are distinguished by the combination of 'administrative dependence' and 'digital dependence': these are individuals who were assisted for paper-based administrative procedures and continue to be assisted in their use of tele-services. The group of 'hesitant' refers to people who are autonomous with digital tools but require assistance for their administrative procedures. Finally, the category of 'fragilised' refers to individuals who were previously autonomous in their administrative procedures but are now weakened in their use of public services due to the shift to digital. This is the case, for example, of Mrs. Walter, an ex-bank employee, who plays online games and knows how to send or read emails but now relies on her daughters for administrative procedures, especially her tax declaration (which she used to complete alone during the paper-based procedures).

> For my taxes, I ask my daughters to do it online. I let them do it. I give them all the information. If there are amounts to declare that I have noted, I give them and then they are the ones who do it, because I don't know. I don't dare because I'm afraid of making a mistake. I'm afraid of answering wrongly. When you write, when you fill a form by hand, it's different.
>
> (Mrs. Walter, eighty-four years old, retired, rural area)

This typology of user situations regarding the use of tele-services shows how the dematerialisation of public services can encourage administrative autonomy but also hinder it and bring about a new category of potentially vulnerable population.

Thus, there is a need for assistance and support for digital autonomy that has not been seen before: users newly struggling with e-administration (the 'fragilised'), especially difficult to characterise and approach because they have never experienced economic or social difficulties and are therefore unaware of traditional aid systems. Crossing all social categories and age groups, this population escapes traditional social service identification circuits. Prevention actions rarely reach them, either because they occasionally manage to get help from relatives or because they do not go to places where they could be assisted, as highlighted by this professional.

> We have to think of the well-endowed public who read, write, have not or never encountered much difficulty in accessing their rights. And because of the information technology brake and the communication brake – I don't know if that's the word … Is the information sufficiently clear? It seems it also makes vulnerable populations who until then had not encountered difficulties?
>
> (Mrs. Zerda, digital deployment manager at Social Security, urban area)

For retirees comfortable with digital tools and with sufficient resources (social, economic, intellectual and administrative autonomy), the intensification of e-administration may have no impact on their access to rights (or even facilitate it). Similarly, but for entirely several reasons, the dematerialisation of public services seems to have no consequences for the situation of the 'dependent' (who rely on a helper for their procedures, whether they are performed with or without teleservices) or the 'hesitant' (who remain dependent on someone despite their digital proficiency). However, for others (specifically the 'fragilised'), e-administration leads to a 'loss of autonomy' and, in a way, an entry into 'administrative dependence' since to obtain information or assert a right, these individuals rely on someone (a relative or a social worker).

The associative leaders and social workers met are particularly concerned about this transformation. While they can ensure a minimum level of autonomy for some users by training them and ensuring they 'work with' rather than 'instead of' them, the quest for autonomy remains futile for users furthest from digital technology and the most precarious, who are forced to entrust their procedures to others. This is notably the opinion of Mrs. Lebord, an association manager, who believes that by limiting physical contact and encounters between users and public service, digitalisation has severed the ties between administration and citizens. Those who used to visit counters and were thus fully involved in their procedures for accessing retirement status, rights or benefits, are now deprived of the act and lose part of their administrative autonomy. The following verbatim precisely questions the consequences, both social and symbolic of the ongoing evolution:

> I think there is a large portion that will never be autonomous with digital tools. We type for them, instead of them … By doing that, public administrations have taken away the little autonomy they had, when they used to go to the CNAV to get their retirement file and come back here for the appointment, they were proud of having conducted the procedure. Because they took part in their

> retirement process. Whereas today, we print it, we do it on the computer and it is done without them. They are completely excluded from their own procedure.
>
> (Mrs. Lebord, associative leader, urban area)

Beyond this loss of autonomy, some associative leaders and social workers fear that digital technology and the transformation of contact methods with administrations that accompanies it may engender or reinforce the risk of isolation among the elderly. They mention the phenomenon of desocialisation that can result from digitalisation: not only loss of social ties but also loss of connection with the administration (since individuals no longer visit counters or search for information), loss of meaning (integration into the world). The emergence of new forms of non-use to rights related to digital technology must also be analysed.

12.2.3 The different forms of non-use related to digitalisation

> The dematerialisation of public services improves access to rights for those who know how to do by themselves, making tasks easier. But for those who do not know, it's a real problem. So, if they are not accompanied or assisted, it has the opposite effect!
>
> (Mrs. Assour, associative leader, urban area)

Digitalisation can exacerbate existing difficulties (Koubi, 2013; Alberola et al., 2016; Revil & Warin, 2019). Online services can penalise users in accessing their rights by slowing down access through particularly lengthy processing of applications, for example (Chabert et al., 2018) and lead certain populations to no longer seek their rights. In the 'Access to rights survey' devoted to the relationship with public services carried out by the Defender of Rights in 2017, one of the most common difficulty in their relationships with public services is 'the difficulty contacting someone (38%)'; the various obstacles to completing administrative procedures then lead 12% of users to abandon their procedures (Défenseur des droits, 2017). Indeed, studies point out that

> the internet is sometimes accused of 'dehumanizing' the relationship with public services because, most often, there is neither voice nor physical presence in the relationship. In terms of service accessibility and equal treatment, some consider that electronic administration would accentuate social inequalities.
>
> (Roux, 2010: 25)

The professionals we met agree that full digitisation in administration, at the expense of proximity and humanised service, accentuates existing difficult situations. This section aims to examine situations of non-use related to the redesign of public services and the intensification of tele-services; we will not address forms of non-use due to ignorance of one's rights.

The first situation of non-use identified in our study is non-use due to abandonment or renunciation of a right due to digital skills (Koubi, 2013; Warin, 2016;

Chabert et al., 2018). This consists of a multitude of situations that lead users to discouragement: the complexity of skills required (digital, administrative, linguistic), the difficulty and/or slowness of administrative procedures (possibly errors by the administration such as loss of documents or difficulty in understanding administrative processes and language), lack of French language proficiency and/or illiteracy or lack of digital skills. In the following excerpt, for example, Mrs. Lombard (associative leader) describes the difficulties related to lack of linguistic and administrative skills that the populations she works with face and the consequences of these difficulties on the risk of non-use:

> The first difficulty is the lack of knowledge of the French language. When I say 'lack of knowledge,' it's not necessarily people who are not French or who do not speak French, it's people who are put off by reading or too much written content and who will not go all the way, so they will not grasp the subtleties or things like that.
>
> (Mrs. Lombard, associative leader, urban area)

The case of Mr. and Mrs. Clement (sixty-eight and sixty-five years old, retirees) illustrates how digitalisation can generate new difficulties in accessing rights and lead to abandonment. While Mr. Clément is quite comfortable with computers, his wife regularly postpones healthcare procedures due to her difficulties in reaching certain services with the new tools provided. In the following verbatim, the couple expresses the difficulties caused by automated telephone:

Mr. Clement: In the choices that the automated telephone answering systems offer you, sometimes, you … you can't place your request. (…) So we give up. We don't try again.

Mrs. Clement: Oh, I give up! It's been five or six months since I needed to go to the hospital for a cardio check. I call and I get these automated systems, but it annoys me. It annoys me so I give up. When I don't feel well sometimes that I said to myself: 'Oh no, I have to do it, I have to do it'. Then I don't do it because I struggle and because it annoys me!

(Mr. and Mrs. Clement, sixty-eight and sixty-five years old, retirees, former workshop manager and former cleaning employee, peri-urban area)

Like other users we met, Mr. Dos Santos (a seventy-years-old retiree) tries to carry out his online procedures alone: he does not want to burden others or bother his family. Not very comfortable with computers but curious to learn, he enrolled in a digital workshop. During the interview, he was quite satisfied: he said he had managed to file his tax return form online without any external help. However, the interviewer noted after the interview that Mr. Dos Santos had indeed managed to access the website only but had not logged into his personal account (and thus had not been able to complete his online declaration). This mishap clearly illustrates how approximate computer knowledge can lead to non-use of rights. Some users who think they know how to use tele-services try to carry out their online procedures alone to maintain their autonomy but in fact find themselves in difficulty or even in a situation of non-use due to lack of awareness of their digital condition (Alexopoulou, 2020). These situations of non-use due to lack of digital skills have an impact on users' relationship not only with the administration but also with themselves. In his analysis of the use of connected computers by working-class people, Granjon notes that 'the idleness felt when faced with the tool is thus transforms into a lack of consideration' for oneself (Granjon, 2009: 32). According to the author, this negative experience can be perceived as a form of inability to participate in common life, generating a 'feeling of diminishing their supposed social value'.

Non-use due to political rejection, on the other hand, concerns people who reject the public offer because it does not align with their values and principles. We did not encounter users in this category, but it was mentioned by institutional actors. Resistant to ICT or in disagreement with the public offer (ideological non-use due to distrust or rejection of digital), they want human contact, a face-to-face response. This is more of a political stance, as individuals express their disagreement either directly related to the offer or with the administration as a whole (the e-administration implemented in recent years, with the reduction of direct contact, has contributed to degrading, in the eyes of some users, the image they may have had of public services as a whole or of a particular administration). However, experiences of non-use due to political rejection lead to distinguishing between 'voluntary refractory non-use' mentioned previously (which is not always directly related to digitalisation) and 'fear of stigmatisation' non-use. Indeed, non-use due to political rejection can also reflect a rejection because of the stigmas associated with the proposed service (negative and demeaning image that the service projects onto the user), leading to 'social disqualification' (Warin, 2016).[7] Mr. Pasquier (associative leader) discusses a logic more related to this 'fear of stigmatisation' associated with the service to which the individual may be entitled:

> People fear a sense of social disqualification. I think there are people who defend themselves against the degradation of their social situation by somewhat denying this situation and notably by not taking that first step to get information. Which is indeed probably very hurtful, very degrading.
>
> (Mr. Pasquier, associative leaders, urban area)

Lastly, there is another form of non-use related to the reorganisation of public services and digitalisation: non-use due to the distance from services. This form of non-use refers to the difficulty of access to rights due to the geographical distance of services (Attour & Longhi, 2009). People living in rural areas are more likely to face this, both due to poor network coverage and the distance/disappearance of local services. The statements collected during the interview with Mrs. Maillard (seventy-three years old, retired) illustrate this situation: she repeatedly explains that it is constraining, even discouraging, for her to cross several cities to carry out her procedures:

> I don't know if the retirement counselor in charge of my file works there. They are relocated several kilometers away. I was supposed to go see her again, I had some information to ask her. But it's too far. And so, it discouraged me and I didn't go. And maybe that is why I could have had a slightly higher pension if I had completed the file. But I didn't want to go there.
>
> (Mrs. Maillard, 73 years old, retired, secretary, peri-urban area)

This form of non-use can also occur when the situation involves specific or unusual administrative cases or situations not considered in the architecture of websites (Koubi, 2013).

The introduction of digital technology leads individuals who lack tools or do not know how to use them to seek external support, especially from social workers and associative relays who are considered resource persons and facilitators.

12.2.4 When caregivers themselves are helpless

> We create this tool to speed up the processing of files. But it puts us in a completely illegal situation. We hold confidential information that the individuals themselves are not supposed to transmit.
>
> (Mr. Asram, associative leader, urban area)

The digital support sector is heterogeneous and remains mainly derived from the social, public or private sphere and mostly non-profit associative. These professionals working to support populations in difficulty encounter numerous obstacles in conducting their mission. Providing indispensable assistance while respecting privacy is a delicate balance to uphold. In the following examples, Mrs. Berger (association manager) and Mrs. Brochet (director of a home care association) report on the risks associated with the confidentiality of their users' personal data. Those being assisted often entrust their contact details, allowing access to their personal information, to those who aid during these tasks, placing caregivers (whether familial or professional) on the edge of legality. The creation of an email account or the using of usernames and passwords then forces these digital helpers to juggle not only with the question of data confidentiality but also with the freedom to manage administrative procedures and to decide for oneself, a freedom questioned when depending on someone else to assert their rights.

> We have to provide individual digital assistance. And here, real questions arise too. We talk about data protection with the GDPR. It questions professional practices: not all professionals have been trained themselves, nor are they always equipped regarding information technology and this new type of support. What

> do we do in terms of data protection with so many identifiers, secret codes, secret questions, answers to the secret question?
>
> (Mrs. Berger, association manager, urban area)

> Ethically, I cannot ask an employee to create codes to access a user's account. I don't know how I, a home care provider, could support this type of service for a user. Having bank codes and … It makes me wonder: how will those people who are truly isolated cope: no family, etc.? Has that been thought of? It's a challenge we will have to face. When I say 'we,' I mean society. Preparation is important.
>
> (Mrs. Brochet, director of a home care association, rural area)

In the 'Access to rights survey', 27% of respondents said they did not have access to the Internet or had difficulty finding administrative information on the Internet (Défenseur des droits, 2017). Many testimonies from professionals have confirmed the difficulty, for certain populations, of obtaining information or advice, getting a form or even just an appointment *via* the Internet. As several institutional representatives emphasise, the intensification of e-administration as implemented in France has introduced a form of distancing or even exclusion of certain populations (the elderly, youth, homeless people, migrants), already fragile in their procedures or weakened by the introduction of digital tools. Users need direct contact with the administration. To prevent digital exclusion from exacerbating social exclusion, the need for support in Internet usage for specific populations has quickly become apparent. However, it emerged after the initial digitalisation measures. For most social workers, the government has only recently recognised these difficulties and has not anticipated them. They lament a late digital support strategy that relies on poorly equipped social workers. While social organisations have tried to implement various support strategies (development of 'digital agencies', self-service kiosks for delivering documents or accessing the organisation's procedures, etc.), professionals feel that public services are shifting the consequences of these changes, which ultimately fall on social workers, which fear having to replace the expertise of public service agents.

> I think we're only reacting now actually. We're talking a lot now about digital exclusion, digital precariousness. But in fact, we didn't react early enough. I'm sure there are many people who don't have access to their rights because of this or who have paid too many taxes when they didn't have to. Institutions are starting to realise that it's complicated for people. But it's a bit late. I wouldn't say it's hopeless, there's still a lot to do, but there have been damages.
>
> (Mrs. Aghien, director of a social center, urban area)

Individuals who lack the tools or do not know how to use them often seek support from caregivers who themselves struggle with digital issues. Relatives do not always know the administrative intricacies. As for professional caregivers, they must face new responsibilities and are not always equipped. They are first confronted with a technical difficulty since they must have a constant connection for their home interventions. Juggling between confidentiality duties and support for the autonomy of elderly people, professionals engage in complex support. Among these new constraints to manage, we will mention the manipulation of identifiers or passwords, which forces these digital helpers to juggle with the question of the confidentiality of personal data. Finally, digitalisation raises two moral challenges. The first concerns a shift in their missions: digitalisation often forces them to move from a task to 'do with' the user to a task of 'doing instead of'. Caregivers are then torn between conflicting requirements. The second challenge concerns the autonomy of users: with the necessary intervention of helpers, the 'individual autonomy' of the retiree shifts towards an 'autonomy extended to the collective' or a 'distributed autonomy' (Hennion et al., 2012; Humbert, 2022). These transformations affect the freedom to manage administrative procedures and to decide for oneself, a freedom questioned when depending on someone to assert one's rights. However, this notion is central for elderly people (whether they are in functional or decision-making autonomy loss and therefore supported accordingly to accomplish daily life activities) as it contributes to their satisfaction, self-esteem and well-being (Ennuyer, 2013; Bailly & Pothier, 2022).

12.3 Conclusion

Digitalisation imposes new practices on individuals to face the changes brought about by the widespread use of online services. Digital autonomy is a crucial objective but out of reach for some. The 'agile' individuals with sufficient capital consider digitalisation as facilitating their access to rights and services. On the other hand, for those who are 'remote' from digital technology, it affects the process by transforming practices. Those in the greatest difficulty are forced to find external support.

Family members or associative workers are often presented as solutions for elderly users to access their rights: children, in particular, are seen as 'natural caregivers', while associations are seen as supports for vulnerable populations. However, being dependent on someone (professional or not) raises numerous questions, including those regarding the confidentiality of personal data (for relatives and professionals alike), data security and the freedom to manage administrative procedures and make decisions independently – a freedom limited when depending on someone else to assert one's rights.

New forms of vulnerability are indeed emerging due to dematerialisation of public services, including the emergence of a 'digitally vulnerable' public. Our study also highlights the consequences of digitalisation on the question of loss of autonomy / the risk of administrative dependence for a population not identified by social workers (as they have no or few contact with social services), on the forms of non-use directly linked to digitalisation and on the distancing from public services and the risk of isolation for certain users. This societal change creates difficulties for new groups by depriving them of their administrative autonomy and exposing them to an unprecedented risk of non-use, thereby questioning one of the three founding principles of French public services: equality of access to public services.

Furthermore, digital inequalities reflect pre-existing social inequalities (language inequality, education level, income, location, etc.). There is a risk that the digital revolution may favour certain better-equipped citizens thus generating ageism. The 'institutionalised ageism of indifference' (Caradec, 2023) stems from public policies that do not explicitly rely on age criteria but impose rules or produce effects that are not age-neutral and effectively discriminate against older individuals or at least part of the elderly population. Without ageist intent but by showing insensitivity to age, digitalisation has made certain administrative procedures impossible or very difficult to access other than *via* the Internet.

The COVID-19 pandemic has also given more visibility to these issues: confinement has undeniably accentuated the difficulties of the most precarious, who are used to rely on professionals or close relatives to assert their rights, thus reinforcing inequalities of access for the most vulnerable and potentially the furthest from public services. This context thus raises the question of the alternative to the use of the Internet for conducting procedures and more broadly the question to freedom of access to services and rights.

Finally, the introduction of digital technology in dealings with public administrations forces individuals to modify their practices and adapt to the constraints imposed by tele-services. But who should adapt: should it be users adapting to changes in public services or public services adapting to user practices to continue to uphold its founding values of equality, fairness and accessibility?

Notes

1 This chapter is based on a study by the French National Pension Fund (*Caisse nationale d'assurance vieillesse* – CNAV); the work Report (in French) is available online (Aouici et al., 2021). Some analyses presented in Part II have partly already been published in French (Aouici & Gallou, 2023).

This publication reflects the views only of the author. CNAV is not responsible for any use that may be made of the information contained therein. All responsibility for the content of this publication is assumed by the author.

2 This term refers to not having basic digital skills (sending emails, consulting online accounts, using software, etc.) or not using the Internet (material incapacity or impossibility).

3 Basic digital skills are divided into four areas: information search, communication, software use and problem solving.

4 However, elderly people constitute a heterogeneous population: seniors can be perfectly socialised but disinclined to use digital technology or, on the contrary, socially or geographically isolated, but very active on digital networks.

5 These interviews have all been transcribed and completely pseudonymised. All extracts cited in this chapter will be associated with a pseudonym (first and last name).

6 The national commission for information technology and liberties defines tele-services as 'any information system allowing users to carry out administrative procedures or

formalities electronically' (Article 1(2005-1516) relating to electronic exchanges between users and administrative authorities and between administrative authorities).

7 This fear of disqualification is regularly mentioned regarding the French Active Solidarity Income, a service sometimes reflecting this disqualifying image for individuals, including potential beneficiaries.

Bibliography

Alberola, É., Croutte, P., & Hoibian, S. (2016). La 'double peine' pour des publics fragilisés face au tout-numérique. *Annales des Mines – Réalités industrielles*, *3*, 32–36. https://shs.cairn.info/revue-realites-industrielles-2016-3-page-32?lang=fr

Alexopoulou, S. (2020). The portrait of older people as (non) users of digital technologies: A scoping literature review and a typology of digital older (non) users. *Gerontechnology*, *19*(3), 1–15. https://doi.org/10.4017/gt.2020.19.003.11

Aouici S. & Gallou, G. (2023). L'autonomie administrative à l'épreuve de la dématérialisation. *Revue des sciences sociales*, *70*, 42–53. https://doi.org/10.4000/revss.10501

Aouici, S., Gallou, G., Peyrache, M., & Rochut, J. (eds.) (2021). La dématérialisation des services publics. Enquête sur l'impact des difficultés d'accès aux services numériques. *Les cahiers de la Cnav*, *16*. www.statistiques-recherche.lassuranceretraite.fr/app/uploads/2021/07/Cahiers-Cnav-16_cahier-cnav.pdf

Attour, A., & Longhi, C. (2009). Fracture numérique, le chaînon manquant. Les services d'e-administration locale dans les communes françaises. *Les cahiers du numérique*, *5*, 119–146. www.cairn.info/revue-les-cahiers-du-numerique-2009-1-page-119.htm

Bailly, N., & Pothier, K. (2022). *Vieillir? Et Alors!*. Editions Mardaga.

Ben Youssef, A. (2004). Les quatre dimensions de la fracture numérique. *Réseaux*, *127–128*, 181–209. https://shs.cairn.info/revue-reseaux1-2004-5-page-181?lang=fr

Caradec, V. (2023). L'âgisme anti-vieux en pratiques. Petit essai de typologie. *Traits-d'Union, la revue des jeunes chercheurs de Paris 3*, *12*, 82–92. https://shs.hal.science/hal shs-04342363v1/file/Typologie%20%C3%A2gisme%20Caradec.pdf

Chabert, L., Valatchy, M., Davenne, A., Grellié, H., & Le Matt, Q. (2018). La transition numérique, menace ou opportunité pour le recours aux droits sociaux? Etude des usages de personnes âgées et de personnes en précarité en région Hauts-de-France. University of Lille, Master's Report.

Cour des comptes. (2019). La relation de service des caisses de sécurité sociale avec les assurés à l'ère numérique: des transformations à amplifier. Rapport, Chapitre X, 379–413. www.ccomptes.fr/sites/default/files/2023-10/RALFSS-2019-10-relation-service-entre-CSS-assures.pdf

Cousteaux, A.-S. (eds.) (2019). *L'économie et la société à l'ère du numérique*. Insee Références.

Credoc – Centre de recherche pour l'étude et l'observation des conditions de vie/ Research center for the study and observation of living conditions. (2015). Baromètre du numérique 2015. Rapport. www.credoc.fr/publications/barometre-du-numerique-edition-2015

Credoc – Centre de recherche pour l'étude et l'observation des conditions de vie / Research center for the study and observation of living conditions. (2019). Baromètre du numérique 2019. Rapport. www.credoc.fr/publications/barometre-du-numerique-2019

Défenseur des droits. (2017). Enquête sur l'accès aux droits – vol. 2: Relation des usagers avec l'administration. Rapport. www.defenseurdesdroits.fr/sites/default/files/2023-10/ddd_etude_Enquete-acces-aux-droits-volume2_relations-usagers-services-publics_20170329.pdf

Donnat, O. (2007). Pratiques culturelles et usages d'internet. *Culture Etudes*, *3*, 1–12. https://shs.cairn.info/revue-culture-etudes-2007-3-page-1?lang=fr

Ennuyer, B. (2013). Les malentendus de l'« autonomie » et de la « dépendance » dans le champ de la vieillesse. *Le Sociographe*, *5 (Hors-série 6)*, 139–157. https://shs.cairn.info/revue-le-sociographe-2013-5-page-139?lang=fr

Granjon, F. (2009). Inégalités numériques et reconnaissance sociale. Des usages populaires de l'informatique connectée. *Les cahiers du numérique*, *5*, 19–44. https://shs.cairn.info/revue-les-cahiers-du-numerique-2009-1-page-19?lang=fr

Hargittai, E. (2002). Second-Level Digital Divide: Differences in People's Online Skills. *First Monday*, *7*(4). https://doi.org/10.5210/fm.v7i4.942

Hennion, A., Vidal-Naquet, P., Guichet, Fr., & Hénaut, L. (2012). Une ethnographie de la relation d'aide: de la ruse à la fiction, comment concilier protection et autonomie. Rapport de recherche pour la MiRe (DREES). https://sciencespo.hal.science/hal-02556487/file/2012-hennion-vidal-naquet-guichet-une-ethnographie-de-la-relation-d-aide.pdf

Humbert, C. (2022). Vieillir chez soi en situation de dépendance: attachement au domicile et (dis)continuité identitaire au grand âge. *Enfances Familles Générations*, *39*. http://journals.openedition.org/efg/12569

Koubi, G. (2013). Services en ligne et droits sociaux. *Informations sociales*, *178*, 44–51. https://shs.cairn.info/revue-informations-sociales-2013-4-page-44?lang=fr&ref=doi

Le Douarin, L., & Caradec, V. (2009). Les grands-parents, leurs petits-enfants et les « nouvelles » technologies de communication. *Dialogue. Familles & couples*, *186*, 25–35. https://doi.org/10.3917/dia.186.0025

Les Petits Frères des Pauvres. (2018). L'exclusion numérique des personnes âgées. Rapport. www.petitsfreresdespauvres.fr/wp-content/uploads/2024/06/2018_10_01_Rapport_exclusion_numerique_personnes_agees_pfP.pdf

National digital council/Conseil national du numérique. (2015). Avis n°2015-3 relatif au projet de loi pour une République numérique. https://cnnumerique.fr/files/2017-10/Avis-du-CNNum-sur-le-projet-de-loi-numerique.pdf

Revil, H., & Warin, P. (2019). Le numérique, le risque de ne plus prévenir le non-recours. *Vie sociale, 28*, 121–133. https://shs.cairn.info/revue-vie-sociale-2019-4-page-121?lang=fr

Roux, L. (2010). L'administration électronique: un vecteur de qualité de service pour les usagers? *Informations sociales*, *158*, 20–29. https://shs.cairn.info/revue-informations-sociales-2010-2-page-20?lang=fr

Siblot, Y. (2005). Les rapports quotidiens des classes populaires aux administrations. Analyse d'un sens pratique du service public. *Sociétés contemporaines*, *58*, 85–103. https://shs.cairn.info/revue-societes-contemporaines-2005-2-page-85?lang=fr

Spire, A. (2005). L'application du droit des étrangers en préfecture. *Politix*, *69*, 11–37. https://shs.cairn.info/revue-politix-2005-1-page-11?lang=fr

Vendramin, P., & Valenduc, G. (2003). *Internet et inégalités. Une radiographie de la « fracture numérique »*. Éditions Labor.

Warin, P. (2016). *Le non-recours aux politiques sociales*. Presses universitaires de Grenoble.

13 The ethics of choosing not to use the Internet

A comparative case study of the education and healthcare sectors in Slovakia and Sweden

Oskar MacGregor and Barbora Badurova

13.1 Introduction

Novel technological developments are often met with an initial mixture of optimistic (sometimes idealised) musings about promises and benefits, along with pessimistic (sometimes dystopian) worries about the risks or harms that the developments might come to entail. However, this initial speculation is typically a poor guide to the actual real-world impacts of a technology as it matures and spreads and is progressively woven into the fabric of society.

For instance, early predictions about the promises of the Internet hailed it as an avenue for setting human thought and expression free, ushering in a truly global open society (e.g., Frederick, 1993; Jones, 1997; Mayer-Kress & Barczys, 1995). Meanwhile, sceptics voiced concerns about end-of-days Y2K scenarios and similar cataclysmic impacts (e.g., Kass, 1996; Kraut et al., 1998; Webster, 1998). In practice, however, both of these initial, naively optimistic and pessimistic views have been gradually replaced by our actual current digital landscape: a mix of pocket super-computers with unprecedented access to the world's social, cultural and scientific outputs on the one hand, and the cynically walled-garden, filter-bubble realities of social media and manipulative data exhaust-sniffing excesses of big tech on the other. In this sense, the Internet of today has not reached either of the extreme positive or negative poles predicted in the initial speculation around its impact, but has instead given rise to various other unforeseen benefits and harms. Prediction is, in a word, difficult.

However, wherever we might stand in our personal views on the overall utility of the Internet today, one thing is certain. As societies have moved towards increasingly digital offerings of basic services, so too has the impetus to use the Internet transformed, from an initially rare luxury into a ubiquitous near-necessity. And, until recently, the general assumption accompanying this development seems to have been that it implies two corresponding *de facto* obligations. One on nation states, to guarantee access and provide any necessary training to individuals to facilitate their active participation in the digital domain (cf. target 9.c of the Sustainable Development Goals, or SDGs; United Nations, 2015; Vuorikari et al., 2022). And the other on individuals themselves, to both work towards a baseline

DOI: 10.4324/9781003528401-16

digital competence (also sometimes referred to as *digital literacy*) and furthermore to willingly submit to the ongoing digitalisation. While the lattermost point has occasionally triggered protest (e.g., in relation to scientifically unfounded fears about 5G networks; Ahmed et al., 2020), close scholarly scrutiny of the issue—which turns out to give rise to a host of legal and ethical concerns—is a more recent development (cf. Hesselberth, 2018; Kloza, 2024).

Digitalisation (and its attendant increased reliance on the Internet, which we take as inherent to a contemporary gloss of the term) is a pervasive phenomenon and so there are any number of sectors within which we could choose to focus our inquiries here. To try to keep the ensuing discussion somewhat manageable, we have in this chapter limited it to an ethical analysis of the digitalisation of two specific sectors that are both crucial to the functioning of society:

- *Education*: The shift towards online learning platforms and digital classrooms has created various Internet requirements for students across all levels of education. This digital dependency is set to further increase with the proposed integration of artificial intelligence (AI) and virtual reality (VR) in educational settings (Chen et al., 2020; Cruz-Jesus et al., 2016; Schmidt & Tang, 2020).
- *Healthcare*: Telemedicine and electronic health (eHealth) records often require patients to navigate digital platforms for accessing medical services and information. This creates a level of Internet dependency that is particularly worrying when considering that it occurs within a sector that focuses particularly on the disabled and elderly, two groups that are vastly over-represented in facing digital competence challenges (Beaulieu & Bentahar, 2021; Blažič & Blažič, 2020; Johansson et al., 2021).

Although many research articles have been written on the legal and ethical dimensions of these two domains of digitalisation, they are essentially all focused on the issues from the perspective of *limited access*—due to either inadequate digital infrastructures and/or insufficient digital competence, e.g., among the aforementioned disabled or elderly—what is often termed the *digital divide* (Van Dijk, 2020). This is an important area of inquiry, but distinct from our focus here. In fact, to our knowledge, there have been no substantive, previous investigations into the ethical concerns that can arise from individuals *choosing* not to use the Internet despite having both the necessary digital infrastructure access and the required level of digital competence to do so.

In this chapter, we discuss this topic through a comparative case study of the current situations in Slovakia and Sweden, two European Union (EU) countries that inhabit opposite ends on a European spectrum of societal digitalisation. We begin by grounding our discussion in the weight that the Universal Declaration of Human Rights (UDHR) and the SDGs ascribe to education and healthcare, as a means of establishing the inherent ethical value of universal access to these two sectors. Next, we elucidate three ethical arguments that all support the general choice to *not* use the Internet. Then, we provide a brief overview of the state of digitalisation in Slovak and Swedish education and healthcare, respectively, before applying the three arguments to these specific, real-world cases. We end by concluding with some general ethical reflections on the various sorts of everyday situations that increasingly require individuals to use the Internet, regardless whether they prefer not to.

13.2 Ethical preliminaries

In this chapter, as just noted, we base our argument on the UDHR and SDGs. Our interest in these frameworks here lies not in their legal status or implications, but in their status as globally accepted expressions of the sorts of ethical values that a society *ought* to uphold. Although it should be acknowledged that there are several important criticisms of the frameworks (cf. Adelman, 2018; Kopnina, 2016; Tasioulas, 2007), by taking their edicts for granted here—if only for the sake of argument—we circumvent the need to take an extensive detour into justificatory ethical theory. (The corollary of this is, of course, that our argument is rendered relative to the two frameworks, but we accept this as a cost of being able to get into more practical ethical concerns.)

Now, in general, the UDHR and SDGs can be seen as broadly supportive of the overall thrust of digitalisation and pervasive reliance on the Internet. For instance, Article 19 of the UDHR states that "Everyone has the right to … seek, receive and impart information and ideas through any media and regardless of frontiers" (United Nations, 1948), while the "means-of-implementation" target 9.c of the SDGs aims specifically to "Significantly increase access to information and communications technology and strive to provide universal and affordable access to the Internet in least developed countries …" (United Nations, 2015).

At the same time, regarding specifically *education*, Article 26.1 of the UDHR states that "Everyone has the right to education. … Technical and professional education shall be made generally available and higher education shall be equally accessible to all on the basis of merit" (United Nations, 1948). Likewise, goal target 4.1 of the SDGs aims to, by 2030, "ensure that all girls and boys complete free, equitable and quality primary and secondary education leading to relevant and effective learning outcomes", while goal target 4.6 aims to, also by 2030, "ensure equal access for all women and men to affordable and quality technical, vocational and tertiary education, including university" (United Nations, 2015).

As regards *healthcare*, Article 25.1 of the UDHR states that "Everyone has the right to a standard of living adequate for the health and well-being of himself and of his family, including … medical care and necessary social services" (United Nations, 1948). Goal target 3.8 of the SDGs, meanwhile, aims to "Achieve universal health coverage, including … access to quality essential health-care services and access to safe, effective, quality and affordable essential medicines and vaccines for all" (United Nations, 2015).

What conclusions might be drawn about the ethical values inherent in these formulations? In this chapter, we will focus on three main points.

First, the fact that both the UDHR and the SDGs explicitly target both education and healthcare as individual rights, or goals to secure, demonstrates that these two sectors have an inherent ethical value for any society. It is, in other words, of great ethical importance for a nation state to ensure that both sectors are sufficiently well-developed to offer relevant variants of their respective services. Second, and following from the first point, the formulations in both frameworks have clearly universalist ambitions. It would therefore be ethically unacceptable to provide education and healthcare to only some subset of a population—instead, their services must be made generally available to *everybody* within the nation state.

Third, and most important for our current purposes, the universalism of the second point is left unspecified. So, for instance, in stating that education must be "generally available … to all", the UDHR leaves open different possible interpretations of what "availability" ought to mean in practice. On a very strong interpretation—where the term is taken to mean something like "offered in accordance with every individual's personal preferences"—any requirement on individuals to use the Internet against their will is in *prima facie* conflict with the frameworks and digitalisation might therefore *in and of itself* be considered an ethical problem. On a weaker (and arguably much more sensible) interpretation—where "availability" is just taken to mean something like "offered within reasonable practical constraints"—ethical issues are more likely to relate to digital-divide concerns and less, or perhaps even not at all, to an individual's personal choice not to use the Internet.

Relatedly, albeit on a more practical note, any service, such as those provided within education and healthcare, must necessarily be offered within some sort of deployment architecture, of which digital access is just one possible alternative among many. But any feasible deployment architecture will likely benefit some individuals while disadvantaging others. To put it concretely, by way of a higher-education example: traditional, analogue, campus-based university programmes have often suffered from accessibility issues for those with different disabilities. For instance, there might be restricted physical access to different buildings and floors (Church & Marston, 2003), or a lack of relevant, technological in-classroom aids for the visually or hearing-impaired (Bishop & Rhind, 2011; Brown & Foster, 1991). In fact, in this sense, increased digitalisation might provide net benefits for many groups' access, which would count as a point in general favour of increased digitalisation (cf. Bhutani & Paliwal, 2015). In other words: in terms of the practical implementation of the ethical values inherent in the UDHR and SDGs, digitalisation might turn out to provide an overall *net access gain* for various groups in society, even if it happens to simultaneously directly disadvantage any individuals who choose not to use the Internet.

In other words, it would be unreasonable to think of the espoused universalism of the UDHR and SDGs as *absolute* and *unqualified*. Instead, any right to education or healthcare must reasonably be considered a defeasible, *pro-tanto* right, whose ethical strength in any given context will be contingent on there not being sufficiently weighty countervailing considerations (cf. Kloza, 2024, where analogous legal issues are discussed under the heading of *proportionality*). This will—as for *pro-tanto* rights generally—vary from one context to the next, and therefore require case-by-case deliberation, as we undertake in this chapter.

13.3 Choosing not to use the Internet

Before proceeding to the details of our comparative case study, it is important to first establish some general ethical reasons why an individual with both the requisite access and the necessary competence might nevertheless choose not to use the Internet. One way of answering this question is to return to the initial point with which we began this chapter: prediction is difficult, and there will always be some uncertainties and other growing pains with any new technology, but we should not let that discourage us. This sort of response might opt for the oft-deployed comparison of the Internet with the printing press (cf. Dewar, 1998)—two revolutionary developments that have had a lasting and substantial impact on, among other things, information dissemination, in providing novel means for significantly enhancing the spread of various, e.g., scientific and political ideas (Füssel, 2020; Uhlendorf, 1932). According to this sort of argument, critique of digitalisation is taken, at least implicitly, to be just as misguided as critique of the printing press: a naive and irrelevant nostalgia for a time that no longer exists, and which almost certainly was not generally preferable anyway.

We believe, however, that this sort of argument grossly misrepresents the realities of digitalisation, glossing over significant ethical issues with its real-world implementation. Specifically, we see digitalisation not as being *inherently* problematic, but as being infused *in practice*—in its actual, historically contingent manifestation in the real world today—with a number of particularly malicious problems, of which we will raise just three: *environmental impacts*, *system-wide vulnerabilities* and *surveillance capitalism*. By looking closer at these three issues, we can begin to appreciate the ethical costs of the expectation that everybody must willingly submit to the ongoing digitalisation of society.

First, the Internet, as a technological development, is incredibly complex. For one, the physical architecture upon which it is implemented—the various cables and towers and modems, the servers and computers, the smartphones and devices—is almost incomprehensibly complicated (cf. Bischof et al., 2018). Furthermore, the various software implementations on which it depends—the operating systems and programs, the protocols and security certificates, the interfaces and apps—together constitute a vast digital ecosystem that is not only dizzyingly sophisticated in its technical implementation, but also in its explicit and implicit governance structures and rules, as distributed across numerous nation states, international and national organisations and large and small companies (DeNardis, 2014; DeNardis, 2020; Greengard, 2015).

Not surprisingly, this organic, dynamic, constantly-evolving system brings with it various problems and risks. One of these is the massive amounts of energy required to keep the Internet humming away, with some research-based estimates suggesting that soon 20% of global electricity consumption will go to power the IT industry (Jones, 2018; cf. also Lange et al., 2020). Similar concerns hold for the materials and resources—such as rare-earth elements—that are required to produce contemporary electronics, as well as the various economic and political impacts of this reality (Levy et al., 2017; Van Veen & Melton, 2020). In other words: digitalisation, of the variety and at the scale it is deployed today, already poses significant environmental threats. Therefore, continued digitalisation entails a further strain on energy and materials, as has been recently illustrated particularly notably by the enormous energy demands of generative AI systems (Chien et al., 2023). These environmental (and attendant political) costs constitute an important—but often neglected—ethically relevant side effect of digitalisation as a general phenomenon.

Second, there is a growing understanding that increasing reliance on real-world digital solutions brings with it an escalation of various system-wide risks. There is seemingly no end to the number of security breaches and hacks of different organisations and companies that have resulted not only in the widespread dissemination among cybercriminals of various forms of sensitive personal information but even outright attacks on different cyber-physical systems within, e.g., critical infrastructure, such as sewage treatment centres, railroad traffic, power plants and hospitals (Argaw et al., 2019; Ashibani & Mahmoud, 2017; Solove & Hartzog, 2022; Ten et al., 2010; Yaacoub et al., 2020). These risks are effectively summed up by Microsoft President Brad Smith, in an address to the United Nations in Geneva, Switzerland (Microsoft, 2017):

> We are entering a world where every thermostat, every electrical heater, every air conditioner, every power plant, every medical device, every hospital, every traffic light, every automobile will be connected to the internet. Think about what it will mean for the world when those devices are the subject of attack.

Most important to our current focus is the fact that these sorts of attacks—which, again, are already increasing in frequency and severity over time, in pace with continued digitalisation—are a significant risk only for specifically digital services. There is, simply put, no equivalent analogue capacity for would-be attackers to effectively disable entire sectors or networks within a society, short of full-scale warfare. In other words, the interconnectedness of the Internet brings with it an astounding array of near-instantaneous, global information exchanges but also entails system-wide security vulnerabilities that are far easier to remotely exploit than any of their conceivable analogue counterparts.

A further corollary of this is the manner in which authoritarian governments can (and do) utilise Internet shutdowns and restrictions as a means of exerting population control (De Gregorio & Stremlau, 2020; Ensafi et al., 2015). It follows logically that increasing reliance on digital solutions will render those solutions more immediately vulnerable to whosoever holds control of the digital infrastructure. In other words, digitalisation of basic services has, in the real world, allowed a centralisation of control that is unlike most known analogue equivalents. In this sense too, then, increased digitalisation incurs significant societal risks, which must be factored into any subsequent ethical deliberation.

Third and final, an additional, crucial limitation with obligatory use of the Internet is its *de facto* inextricability from what Zuboff (2018) calls *surveillance capitalism*, i.e., the "new economic order that claims human experience as free raw material for hidden commercial practices of extraction, prediction and sales" (p. 8; cf. also the discussions on technological "rentiership" in Birch, 2020; Birch & Cochrane, 2022). Although it is in principle possible to imagine certain individuals making use of the Internet in a manner that does not become subject to the forms of surveillance capitalism elucidated by Zuboff and others, it is almost inconceivable in practice.

For one, the vast majority of devices that we use are directly produced by, or come preloaded with software produced by, one of the major multinational big-tech giants (Alphabet, Apple, Microsoft, etc.). And even where this is not the case—e.g., where a tech-savvy individual builds their own computer from various separate, carefully chosen components in order to minimise or eliminate the insight any one company has into their personal use of the Internet—accessing digitalised services, such as education or healthcare, will still largely rely on various big-tech platforms. For instance, a vast proportion of well-known cloud services on the Internet are hosted by Amazon Web Services (AWS; Wittig & Wittig, 2023). Similarly, most smartphone-based solutions today only work on devices running Android (Google/Alphabet) or iOS (Apple) systems. In other words, in practice, even the most privacy-minded individual will not be able to access typical digital services without being required, in some manner, to contribute to the continued support of surveillance-capitalist big-tech giants.

Each of these three examples—environmental impacts, system-wide vulnerabilities and surveillance capitalism—must be kept in mind when considering the progressive digitalisation of society. That is, they each provide some support for the ethical view that people should be able to choose not to use the Internet.

13.4 The digitalisation of education and healthcare in Slovakia and Sweden

In this section, we provide a brief overview of the relative states of digitalisation in the education and healthcare sectors in Slovakia and Sweden. The two countries provide an interesting contrast, as they are generally considered to inhabit opposite ends of the range of digital development within the EU. Specifically, Slovakia tends to rank below the EU average across most of the Digital Economy and Society Index (DESI) measures (European Commission, 2023a), while Sweden tends—like its Nordic neighbours—to rank quite far above (European Commission, 2023b). In other words, where Slovakia has made some progress in its digitalisation efforts over the past few years, it currently lags quite far behind Sweden, where earlier adoption of the relevant technologies has led to more extensive connectivity and a highly digitalised public and private sector. Similar differences in the levels of digitalisation in the two countries can be found across various sources and methodologies (e.g., Bocean & Vărzaru, 2023; United Nations, 2022).

In concrete terms, this means that life in Slovakia today is characterised by a mix of digital and analogue service offerings, sometimes occurring concurrently within the same sector, while Sweden can be considered to have dived headfirst into a more thoroughly and exclusively digital future. As just one example,

Slovakia recently passed a constitutional amendment to protect the use of cash for payment (European Central Bank, 2024) while Swedish commerce is today instead characterised by a virtual absence of cash (Arvidsson, 2019). Likewise, where Slovakia has only recently begun relying on electronic identification (eID) solutions in relation to specific services (Gregušová et al., 2022), the Swedish national, smartphone-based eID system Mobile BankID is today used by 92% of the country's population (Internetstiftelsen, 2023), a development that has also seen an attendant increase in Sweden of phone and Internet fraud, online identity theft and related forms of cybercrime (Digg, 2024).

13.4.1 Education

The digitalisation of education in Slovakia and Sweden, respectively, has taken quite different paths. Sweden was early to embrace digital solutions for many aspects of education, a process driven largely by various national and international (primarily EU) strategies, as well as through the adoption of global technological developments (Gu & Lindberg, 2021). The COVID-19 pandemic also required the country to make some adjustments, although these were—given Sweden's pre-existing digital infrastructure and general openness throughout the pandemic—relatively limited in scope (Bergdahl & Nouri, 2021). Slovakia, meanwhile, faced significant, concrete pressures to provide online education to its students for the very first time as a direct result of the forced lockdowns implemented in the country during the same period. Given the state of education in the country prior to this—with very few digital solutions on offer—it proved to be an immense challenge.

Specifically, schools in Slovakia struggled to provide online education as they often lacked the necessary equipment, such as relevant hardware and software for their teachers or even suitable Internet connections (Ministry of Education, 2021). In addition, many students did not themselves have the necessary hardware and software or appropriate conditions: some were required to share a single computer with multiple other members of the household, while others did not have any computer or Internet access in the first place (Ministry of Investment, 2022). In this manner, the lockdown restrictions exacerbated existing problems related to the digital divide (Nevická & Mesarčík, 2022). As just one example, the District Court in Prešov found that the Ministry of Education had failed to "provide [a Roma girl] with equal access to online distance education during the Covid-19 pandemic" (Center for Civil and Human Rights, 2023). Some Slovak schools tried to offer solutions to these sorts of problems, including letting students travel to school to use computers available there, but the overall experience was one of significant restrictions.

What was the lasting impact of all these challenges? First, the lockdown restrictions seem to have directly caused a significant negative impact on student well-being in Slovakia (Rutkowska et al., 2021). This result is not surprising, given that fully online education is not considered ideal for children and adolescents, since the opportunity for social interactions is severely limited compared to traditional classroom-based teaching (Chaturvedi et al., 2021).

Second, as regards the level of digitalisation within Slovak education, a 2023 World Bank survey found that, even after the pandemic, only 44% of high-school teachers in the country regularly used digital tools in education, only 40% used digital tools to connect theory with practice and only 15% offered their students digital tools for self-study (TASR, 2023). This is in stark contrast to Sweden, where digital solutions are today pervasive within the education sector, covering all the following areas (Skolverket, 2018):

- *Digital learning environments*, which are used for managing courses, distributing materials, submitting assignments and facilitating communication between students and educators, as well as between educators and parents. In addition, Swedish educators spend a significant amount of time in the classroom familiarising children, from the age of six, with various digital tools, including dedicated time exploring tablets and computers (Skolverket, 2023).
- *Digital assessment tools*, which are typically deployed online and allow for immediate feedback and analysis. For instance, Skolverket (the Swedish National Agency for Education) has recently begun transitioning to running all of its national tests—taken by students across the entire country in the third, sixth and ninth grades, as well as in upper secondary school—in digital form (Skolverket, 2024).
- *Online-only courses*, in particular at the secondary and tertiary (higher-education) levels. In fact, most Swedish universities offer various complete, online-only Bachelor and Master programs, corresponding to between one and three years of full-time study in an exclusively digital context (Swedish Council for Higher Education, 2021).
- *Online administrative systems*, used for various tasks such as enrolment, registration, attendance tracking and grade transcript generation.

To take the last point—online administrative systems—as an illustrative example, it is not currently conceivable for an adult in Sweden to participate in higher education without heavy reliance on the Internet. Even if the prospective student were to choose to study a course that is run entirely on a physical campus, utilising physical books and a paper-based final exam, they would still need to (i) apply *via* the national higher-education admissions system (universityadmissions.se), (ii) register and enrol in the university's online student portal, (iii) visit the online course schedule to verify timing and location of all classes, (iv) visit the course website—typically located within some cloud-based learning management system (LMS) such as Canvas, Blackboard or Moodle—to access any additional course materials, including lecture slides, (v) regularly check their student email to stay up-to-date with any information sent out by the lecturers or course coordinator, (vi) register for examinations, (vii) check their course results and grades in the university's student portal and (viii) request a grade transcript *via* the national grade administration website (ladok.se) upon completion of the course. In comparison, while Slovak higher education—which has embraced digitalisation to a greater extent than primary or secondary education within the country—also tends to require some use of the Internet, this is usually restricted to a limited subset of only a few of the points listed previously.

13.4.2 Healthcare

Much like in the case of education, there are significant differences in the extent to which the healthcare sectors of Slovakia and Sweden have been digitalised (Ardielli, 2020). And, as in the case of education, this discrepancy holds despite both countries being subject to a two-decade EU push for increased adoption of eHealth initiatives (Currie & Seddon, 2014; European Commission, 2024; World Health Organization, 2022).

More specifically, the Slovak system for eHealth is the responsibility of the National Health Information Centre, which provides various services such as eHealth records (including vaccination records), digital prescriptions, digital bookings and similar (n.d.; 2024). The Centre released its first applications in 2015 and they have been more widely implemented since 2018, although uptake within the healthcare sector has been slow (Štempeľová et al., 2023). For instance, digital certificates for work incapacity ("temporary disability") were launched—in collaboration with the Slovakian Social Insurance Institution—only in June 2022, with all doctors obliged to work with the system only since June 2023 (Ministry of Health, 2023). Nevertheless, this push towards increasing digitalisation has seen a growing reliance on national identification cards, which these days include an electronic chip, to, e.g., enable digital access to the eHealth system (Štempeľová et al., 2023). In summary, although digitalisation of the Slovak healthcare sector has been slow, it seems to have picked up pace in the last few years, not least as a result of recent legal requirements that doctors and other healthcare-sector employees utilise the systems (cf. Bird & Bird, 2017).

In contrast to this, the Swedish healthcare sector has seen significant digitalisation over several decades, predating many of the EU initiatives and culminating in the country's current "vision" that it should, by 2025, be the

> best in the world at using the opportunities offered by digitisation and eHealth to make it easier for people to achieve good and equal health and welfare, and to develop and strengthen their own resources for increased independence and participation in the life of society.
>
> (e-hälsa 2025, n.d.)

In practice, this means not only that most healthcare appointment bookings, prescriptions, medical (e.g., incapacity or vaccination) certificates, personal health records and similar are all available through a centralised, national eHealth portal (1177.se) but also that Swedes are increasingly adopting digital doctor's visits *via* various private and public smartphone apps—a practice that took off during the COVID-19 pandemic and seems to have largely continued since then (Internetstiftelsen, 2023). Practically all of these services are facilitated by the aforementioned eID solution Mobile BankID.

13.5 Ethical analysis

As we have already established, the UDHR and SDGs provide a strong ethical mandate for the importance of making education and healthcare available to all, but how strongly to interpret this availability requirement must be determined on a case-by-case basis. To do so in the current context, we will now look closer at the Slovak and Swedish cases presented previously, through the prism of our three ethical arguments for choosing not to use the Internet.

First, as regards environmental impacts, the thorough digitalisation in Sweden—compared to Slovakia—entails a significant environmental, and hence also ethical, burden for the country. It is difficult to find estimates of the respective share of the two countries' energy use that goes to power the various electronics that facilitate Internet use within them, or indeed the environmental costs of specifically digital education or healthcare services in either, but there are various proxy measures that can be investigated in their place. For instance, official EU statistics on electronic waste (e-waste) show that Slovakia collects 9.57 kg of e-waste per person and year, whereas Sweden collects 12.98 kg (Eurostat, 2023). Given Slovakia's population of around 5.5 million inhabitants, to Sweden's 10.5 million, this leads to a noteworthy difference in the total amount of e-waste generated annually in each country: around 53,000 tons in Slovakia to around 135,000 tons in Sweden. These numbers are even more concerning when one considers that Slovakia manages to collect, as e-waste, 65% of the electrical and electronic equipment put on the market within the three preceding years, whereas Sweden only manages to collect a comparatively paltry 47% (Eurostat, 2023). In other words, the significantly larger amount of e-waste in Sweden is not due to more diligent e-waste recycling by its inhabitants; if anything, the numbers suggest the opposite.

Essentially then, the realities of general digitalisation in each country suggest that the ethical weight of environmental damage, as one reason for choosing not to use the Internet, weighs heavier in Sweden. That is: a more thorough general digitalisation in Sweden raises significantly greater ethical concerns about environmental impacts, which in turn entail stronger ethical support for anybody choosing not to use the Internet there.

Second, as regards system-wide vulnerabilities, the ongoing digitalisation of both the Slovak and Swedish education and healthcare sectors—although having reached quite different stages—has nevertheless resulted in a significantly increased prevalence of cyberattacks. For instance, in the summer of 2023, Matej Bel University in Slovakia was hacked by a group that installed ransomware on its computers, resulting in the university website, as well as its email and administrative systems, becoming unavailable, so that staff and students could not upload assignments, access the results of exams or grades and so on (RTVS, 2023). Although the university was able to restore its website and systems without paying the requested ransom of 500,000 USD, the risk of the breached personal data becoming publicly available in a leak seems to remain to this day (Denník N, 2023). Given the higher level of digitalisation in Sweden, it is perhaps not surprising to note that the country has suffered a spate of similar attacks on its higher-education institutions in recent years (SVT, 2023b). This seems to be part of a global increase in cybercriminals exploiting the sorts of vulnerabilities that follow from increased digitalisation of the higher-education sector more generally (Nature, 2024). In other words, as education in both countries has become increasingly digital, so too have the attendant cybersecurity risks grown.

As regards healthcare, the Slovak National Cybersecurity Centre documented 131 cyberattacks against Slovak healthcare organisations in 2021, resulting in substantial financial losses for hospitals forced to pay ransoms (SITA, 2022). In contrast, Sweden—with its more thoroughly digitalised healthcare system—saw on average 662 cyberattacks *per week* against Swedish healthcare organisations during the end of 2022 and beginning of 2023 (Cederberg, 2023). Similarly, a recent report warns that Swedish hospitals are now among the most frequent targets of cyberattacks in the country (Janzon, 2024). It is important to note that these attacks are not trivial: among other things, they have resulted in the Swedish national eHealth portal 1177.se being temporarily knocked offline and the sale of breached hospital data on the dark web (SVT, 2023a, 2024).

These cases clearly show a strong, positive, real-world correlation between increasing digitalisation and increased cybersecurity risks. And although a more thoroughly digitalised country, such as Sweden, might arguably also have more experience mitigating such risks, the reality seems to suggest the opposite: Sweden has suffered both more numerous and more serious threats to its education and healthcare sectors than its Slovak counterparts. Whether this is an effect of lax Swedish cybersecurity practices or a simple reflection of the sheer number of cyberattacks occurring in each country, the ethical conclusion is (currently) the same. For these two countries and sectors, the threat of system-wide vulnerabilities as an ethical argument for choosing not to use the Internet carries greater weight in the more thoroughly digitalised—and therefore more vulnerable—Swedish context.

Finally—and perhaps not surprisingly—surveillance-capitalism arguments in favour of choosing not to use the Internet also become more ethically pertinent in the Swedish context. The realities of digitalising education and healthcare tend to rely heavily on contracts with private big-tech corporations offering closed-source software and applications. So, for instance, the LMS favoured by almost all Swedish universities—Canvas—is hosted on AWS, while the most common default office suite—Microsoft365—is known to lead to various risks for different long-term lock-in effects (Lundell et al., 2021). Likewise, the Swedish eID system Mobile BankID is only available on Android and iOS devices (BankID, 2024). Similar nationwide trends towards overt reliance on big-tech giants are still largely lacking in Slovakia, most likely as a direct result of digitalisation in the country still being relatively underdeveloped.

In all then, across all three arguments—from environmental impacts, system-wide vulnerabilities and surveillance capitalism—it seems that Sweden's digitalisation of education and healthcare are, compared to Slovakia's, more ethically problematic. This, in turn, therefore supports the notion that individuals in (the more highly digitalised) Sweden have a stronger ethical claim to be free to *not* use the Internet. That the high level of digitalisation in the country entails that such options are often impractical or even impossible therefore constitutes a serious ethical failure. In contrast, the comparatively low level of digitalisation in Slovakia entails that the country largely lacks both the benefits that such digitalisation might provide but also its risks. Ironically, the need to protect an individual's ability to choose not to use the Internet is simply less relevant here, given that education and healthcare in the country are not as thoroughly digitalised.

It is worth noting, however, that this state of affairs does not demonstrate any *necessary* correlation between rate of digitalisation and ethical concerns—the two notions can be quite straightforwardly disentangled, at least conceptually if not practically. Even as the *more* digitalised country, it is not at all inconceivable that Sweden could have been better at repairing and recycling its e-waste, adopted stronger cybersecurity practices and fostered more reliance on open-source and other non-big-tech hardware and software solutions. That is, the ethical conclusions of this particular case study might look more deceptively straightforward ("more digitalisation = more ethical problems") than what might easily otherwise have been the case.

13.6 Conclusion

A choice not to use the Internet, despite access and competence, is not ethically obvious, and needs to be determined on a case-by-case basis. In this chapter, we have utilised a comparative case study—between Slovakia and Sweden—to demonstrate that the ethical support for such a choice is stronger in the latter country than in the former, at least as regards education and healthcare, relative to our three presented arguments: environmental impacts, system-wide vulnerabilities and surveillance capitalism. Nevertheless, other cases—even other sectors or arguments within the same countries—might have led to different conclusions. In this sense, at the very least, it should be obvious that the choice not to use the Internet is far more ethically complex than it might at first appear. As the ongoing digitalisation of our societies speeds ahead, it therefore behoves us to critically examine the various ethical ramifications of these developments with far greater scrutiny than has been undertaken so far.

Bibliography

Adelman, S. (2018). The Sustainable Development Goals, anthropocentrism and neoliberalism. In D. French and L. J. Kotzé (Eds.), *Sustainable Development Goals: Law, theory and implementation* (pp. 15–40). Edward Elgar Publishing. https://doi.org/10.4337/9781786438768.00008

Ahmed, W., Vidal-Alaball, J., Downing, J., & Seguí, F. L. (2020). COVID-19 and the 5G conspiracy theory: Social network analysis of Twitter data. *Journal of Medical Internet Research*, *22*(5), e19458. https://doi.org/10.2196/19458

Ardielli, E. (2020). eHealth in the European Union: Comparative study. *ACC Journal*, *26*(2), 7–18. https://doi.org/10.15240/tul/004/2020-2-001

Argaw, S. T., Bempong, N. E., Eshaya-Chauvin, B., & Flahault, A. (2019). The state of research on cyberattacks against hospitals and available best practice recommendations: A scoping review. *BMC Medical Informatics and Decision Making*, *19*, 10. https://doi.org/10.1186/s12911-018-0724-5

Arvidsson, N. (2019). *Building a cashless society: The Swedish route to the future of cash payments*. Springer. https://doi.org/10.1007/978-3-030-10689-8

Ashibani, Y., & Mahmoud, Q. H. (2017). Cyber physical systems security: Analysis, challenges and solutions. *Computers & Security*, *68*, 81–97. https://doi.org/10.1016/j.cose.2017.04.005

BankID. (2024). *Get Mobile BankID*. https://support.bankid.com/en/get-mobile-bankid/get-mobile-bankid

Beaulieu, M., & Bentahar, O. (2021). Digitalization of the healthcare supply chain: A roadmap to generate benefits and effectively support healthcare delivery. *Technological Forecasting and Social Change*, *167*, 120717. https://doi.org/10.1016/j.techfore.2021.120717

Bergdahl, N., & Nouri, J. (2021). COVID-19 and crisis-prompted distance education in Sweden. *Technology, Knowledge and Learning*, *26*(3), 443–459. https://doi.org/10.1007/s10758-020-09470-6

Bhutani, S., & Paliwal, Y. (2015). Digitalization: A step towards sustainable development. *OIDA International Journal of Sustainable Development*, *8*(12), 11–24.

Birch, K. (2020). Technoscience rent: Toward a theory of rentiership for technoscientific capitalism. *Science, Technology, & Human Values*, *45*(1), 3–33. https://doi.org/10.1177/0162243919829567

Birch, K., & Cochrane, D. T. (2022). Big tech: Four emerging forms of digital rentiership. *Science as Culture*, *31*(1), 44–58. https://doi.org/10.1080/09505431.2021.1932794

Bird & Bird. (2017, January 11). E-health in Slovakia: Background, current status, vision, and challenges. www.twobirds.com/en/insights/2017/uk/ils/e-health-in-slovakia-background-current-status-vision-and-challenges

Bischof, Z. S., Fontugne, R., & Bustamante, F. E. (2018). Untangling the world-wide mesh of undersea cables. In *Proceedings of the 17th ACM Workshop on Hot Topics in Networks*, 78–84. https://doi.org/10.1145/3286062.3286074

Bishop, D., & Rhind, D. J. (2011). Barriers and enablers for visually impaired students at a UK Higher Education Institution. *British Journal of Visual Impairment*, *29*(3), 177–195. https://doi.org/10.1177/0264619611415329

Blažič, B. J., & Blažič, A. J. (2020). Overcoming the digital divide with a modern approach to learning digital skills for the elderly adults. *Education and Information Technologies*, *25*, 259–279. https://doi.org/10.1007/s10639-019-09961-9

Bocean, C. G., & Vărzaru, A. A. (2023). EU countries' digital transformation, economic performance, and sustainability analysis. *Humanities and Social Sciences Communications*, *10*(1), 1–15. https://doi.org/10.1057/s41599-023-02415-1

Brown, P. M., & Foster, S. B. (1991). Integrating hearing and deaf students on a college campus: Successes and barriers as perceived by hearing students. *American Annals of the Deaf*, *136*(1), 21–27. https://doi.org/10.1353/aad.2012.0564

Cederberg, J. (2023, February 15). *Ökade IT-attacker mot sjukvård*. Läkartidningen. https://lakartidningen.se/aktuellt/nyheter/2023/02/okade-it-attacker-mot-sjukvard/

Center for Civil and Human Rights. (2023, November 28). *Judgment of the District Court in Prešov in the case of the digital divide and access to education*. https://poradna-prava.sk/en/strategic-litigation/judgment-of-the-district-court-in-presov-in-the-case-of-the-digital-divide-and-access-to-education/

Chaturvedi, K., Vishwakarma, D. K., & Singh, N. (2021). COVID-19 and its impact on education, social life and mental health of students: A survey. *Children and Youth Services Review*, *121*, 105866. https://doi.org/10.1016/j.childyouth.2020.105866

Chen, L., Chen, P., & Lin, Z. (2020). Artificial intelligence in education: A review. *IEEE Access*, *8*, 75264–75278. https://doi.org/10.1109/ACCESS.2020.2988510

Chien, A. A., Lin, L., Nguyen, H., Rao, V., Sharma, T., & Wijayawardana, R. (2023). Reducing the carbon impact of generative AI inference (today and in 2035). *HotCarbon '23: Proceedings of the 2nd Workshop on Sustainable Computer Systems* (pp. 1–7). https://doi.org/10.1145/3604930.3605705

Church, R. L., & Marston, J. R. (2003). Measuring accessibility for people with a disability. *Geographical Analysis*, *35*(1), 83–96. https://doi.org/10.1111/j.1538-4632.2003.tb01102.x

Cruz-Jesus, F., Vicente, M. R., Bacao, F., & Oliveira, T. (2016). The education-related digital divide: An analysis for the EU-28. *Computers in Human Behavior*, *56*, 72–82. https://doi.org/10.1016/j.chb.2015.11.027

Currie, W. L., & Seddon, J. J. (2014). A cross-national analysis of eHealth in the European Union: Some policy and research directions. *Information & Management*, *51*(6), 783–797. https://doi.org/10.1016/j.im.2014.04.004

De Gregorio, G., & Stremlau, N. (2020). Internet shutdowns and the limits of law. *International Journal of Communication*, *14*, 4224–4243.

DeNardis, L. (2014). *The global war for internet governance*. Yale University Press.

DeNardis, L. (2020). *The Internet in everything*. Yale University Press.

Denník, N. (2023, July 3). *Univerzite Mateja Bela vypršal čas na zaplatenie výkupného pre hekerov. Web jej zatiaľ funguje*. https://dennikn.sk/minuta/3456046/

Dewar, J. A. (1998). *The information age and the printing press: Looking backward to see ahead*. RAND Corporation. www.rand.org/content/dam/rand/pubs/papers/2005/P8014.pdf

Digg. (2024). *Strategiska prioriteringar för digitaliseringspolitiken 2025–2030: Mot ett digitalt Sverige 2030*. www.digg.se/download/18.6d003ad218d8fc9183012dd7/1709290044712/Mot%20ett%20digitalt%20Sverige%202030.pdf

e-hälsa 2025. (n.d.). *Vision for eHealth: In English*. https://ehalsa2025.se/english/

Ensafi, R., Fifield, D., Winter, P., Feamster, N., Weaver, N., & Paxson, V. (2015). Examining how the Great Firewall discovers hidden circumvention servers. *ICM '15: Proceedings of the 2015 Internet Measurement Conference* (pp. 445–458). https://doi.org/10.1145/2815675.2815690

European Central Bank. (2024). *Opinion of the European Central Bank of 11 January 2024 on a constitutional law on cash as legal tender and access to cash (CON/2024/1)*. https://eur-lex.europa.eu/legal-content/EN/TXT/PDF/?uri=CELEX:52024AB0001

European Commission. (2023a). *2030 digital decade – Annex Slovakia: Report on the state of the digital decade 2023*. https://ec.europa.eu/newsroom/dae/redirection/document/98664

European Commission. (2023b). *2030 digital decade – Annex Sweden: Report on the state of the digital decade 2023*. https://ec.europa.eu/newsroom/dae/redirection/document/98667

European Commission. (2024) *eHealth: Digital health and care overview*. https://health.ec.europa.eu/ehealth-digital-health-and-care/overview_en

Eurostat. (2023, October). *Waste statistics: Electrical and electronic equipment*. https://ec.europa.eu/eurostat/statistics-explained/index.php?title=Waste_statistics_-_electrical_and_electronic_equipment#Electrical_and_electronic_equipment_.28EEE.29_put_on_the_market_and_WEEE_processed_in_the_EU

Frederick, H. (1993). Computer networks and the emergence of global civil society. In L. M. Harasim (Ed.), *Global networks: Computers and international communication* (pp. 283–295). MIT Press. https://doi.org/10.7551/mitpress/3304.003.0021

Füssel, S. (2020). *Gutenberg and the impact of printing*. Routledge.

Greengard, S. (2015). *The internet of things*. MIT Press.

Gregušová, D., Halásová, Z., & Peráček, T. (2022). eIDAS regulation and its impact on national legislation: The case of the Slovak Republic. *Administrative Sciences*, *12*(4), 187. https://doi.org/10.3390/admsci12040187

Gu, L., & Lindberg, O. J. (2021). Understanding Swedish educational policy developments in the field of digital education. In J. B. Krejsler and L. Moos (Eds.), *What works in Nordic school policies? Mapping approaches to evidence, social technologies and transnational influences* (pp. 213–233). Springer. https://doi.org/10.1007/978-3-030-66629-3_11

Hesselberth, P. (2018). Discourses on disconnectivity and the right to disconnect. *New Media & Society*, *20*(5), 1994–2010. https://doi.org/10.1177/1461444817711449

Internetstiftelsen. (2023). *Svenskarna och internet 2023*. https://svenskarnaochinternet.se/app/uploads/2023/10/internetstiftelsen-svenskarna-och-internet-2023.pdf

Janzon, B. (2024, April 27). *Varningen: Sjukhus bland de främsta målen för cyberattacker*. Sveriges Radio. https://sverigesradio.se/artikel/varningen-sjukhus-bland-de-framsta-malen-for-cyberattacker

Johansson, S., Gulliksen, J., & Gustavsson, C. (2021). Disability digital divide: The use of the internet, smartphones, computers and tablets among people with disabilities in Sweden. *Universal Access in the Information Society*, *20*(1), 105–120. https://doi.org/10.1007/s10209-020-00714-x

Jones, N. (2018). How to stop data centres from gobbling up the world's electricity. *Nature*, *561*, 163–166. https://doi.org/10.1038/d41586-018-06610-y

Jones, S. (Ed.). (1997). *Virtual culture: Identity & communication in cybersociety*. SAGE.

Kass, I. A. (1996). Regulating bomb recipes on the internet: Does First Amendment law permit the government to react to the most egregious harms? *Southern California Interdisciplinary Law Journal*, *5*, 83.

Kloza, D. (2024). The right not to use the internet. *Computer Law & Security Review*, *52*, 105907. https://doi.org/10.1016/j.clsr.2023.105907

Kopnina, H. (2016). The victims of unsustainability: A challenge to sustainable development goals. *International Journal of Sustainable Development & World Ecology*, *23*(2), 113–121. https://doi.org/10.1080/13504509.2015.1111269

Kraut, R., Patterson, M., Lundmark, V., Kiesler, S., Mukophadhyay, T., & Scherlis, W. (1998). Internet paradox: A social technology that reduces social involvement and psychological well-being? *American Psychologist*, *53*(9), 1017–1031. https://doi.org/10.1037/0003-066X.53.9.1017

Lange, S., Pohl, J., & Santarius, T. (2020). Digitalization and energy consumption: Does ICT reduce energy demand? *Ecological Economics*, *176*, 106760. https://doi.org/10.1016/j.ecolecon.2020.106760

Levy, S., Rosen, C. M., & Iles, A. (2017). Mapping the product life cycle: Rare earth elements in electronics. *Case Studies in the Environment*, *1*(1), 1–9. https://doi.org/10.1525/cse.2017.000265

Lundell, B., Gamalielsson, J., Katz, A., & Lindroth, M. (2021). Perceived and actual lock-in effects amongst Swedish public sector organisations when using a Saas solution. In H. J. Scholl, J. R. Gil-Garcia, M. Janssen, E. Kalampokis, I. Lindgren, & M. P. Rodríguez Bolívar (Eds.), *Electronic Government: EGOV 2021. Lecture Notes in Computer Science* (vol. 12850, pp. 59–72). Springer. https://doi.org/10.1007/978-3-030-84789-0_5

Mayer-Kress, G., & Barczys, C. (1995). The Global Brain as an emergent structure from the Worldwide Computing Network, and its implications for modeling. *The Information Society*, *11*(1), 1–27. https://doi.org/10.1080/01972243.1995.9960177

Microsoft. (2017, November 10). *Microsoft president Brad Smith on cybersecurity and a digital Geneva Convention* [Video]. YouTube. https://youtu.be/EMG4ZukkClw?si=V8gpwfMx9DO1uW4M&t=870

Ministry of Education. (2021). *Program informatizácie školstva do roku 2030*. www.minedu.sk/data/att/6e3/23246.a80016.pdf

Ministry of Health. (2023, May 31). *Zdravie je na prvom mieste – s povinnými ePN už žiadne behanie po úradoch*. www.health.gov.sk/Clanok?mzsr-elektronicka-pn

Ministry of Investment. (2022, March 16). *Vicepremiérka Remišová: Desaťtisíce Slovákov ohrozuje digitálna chudoba, máme plán ako im pomôcť.* https://mirri.gov.sk/aktuality/digitalna-agenda/vicepremierka-remisova-desattisice-slovakov-ohrozuje-digitalna-chudoba-mame-plan-ako-im-pomoct/

National Health Information Centre. (n.d.). *eHealth programme*. ezdravie. https://old.ezdravotnictvo.sk/en/eHealth_Programme/Pages/default.aspx

National Health Information Centre. (2024). *eslužby*. ezdravie. www.ezdravotnictvo.sk/sk/esluzby

Nature. (2024). Cyberattacks on knowledge institutions are increasing: What can be done? *Nature*, *626*, 234. https://doi.org/10.1038/d41586-024-00323-1

Nevická, D., & Mesarčík, M. (2022). Why are you offline? The issue of digital consent and discrimination of Roma communities during pandemic in Slovakia. *International Journal of Discrimination and the Law*, *22*(2), 172–191. https://doi.org/10.1177/13582291221096615

RTVS. (2023, June 22). *Univerzita Mateja Bela zrejme čelí kyberútoku: Nefungujú webové stránky školy ani AIS*. rtv: Správy. https://spravy.rtvs.sk/2023/06/univerzita-mateja-bela-zrejme-celi-kyberutoku-nefunguju-webove-stranky-skoly-na-ais/

Rutkowska, A., Liska, D., Cieślik, B., Wrzeciono, A., Broďáni, J., Barcalová, M., Gurin, D., & Rutkowski, S. (2021). Stress levels and mental well-being among Slovak students during e-learning in the COVID-19 pandemic. In *Healthcare*, *9*(10), 1356. https://doi.org/10.3390/healthcare9101356

Schmidt, J. T., & Tang, M. (2020). Digitalization in education: Challenges, trends and transformative potential. In M. Harwardt, P. F.-J. Niermann, A. M. Schmutte, and Axel Steuernagel (Eds.), *Führen und Managen in der digitalen Transformation: Trends, Best Practices und Herausforderungen* (pp. 287–312). Springer Gabler. https://doi.org/10.1007/978-3-658-28670-5_16

SITA. (2022, December 11). Počet hackerských útokov na Slovensku v zdravotníctve rastie, na výkupnom môže stratiť milióny eur. https://sita.sk/vzdravotnictve/pocet-hackerskych-utokov-na-slovensku-v-zdravotnictve-rastie-na-vykupnom-moze-stratit-miliardy-eur/

Skolverket. (2018). *Digitaliseringen i skolan: Möjligheter och utmaningar*. www.skolverket.se/getFile?file=3971

Skolverket. (2023, October 11). *Digitalisering i förskolan och skolan: Vad och varför?* www.skolverket.se/om-oss/var-verksamhet/skolverkets-prioriterade-omraden/digitalisering/digitalisering-i-forskolan-och-skolan---vad-och-varfor

Skolverket. (2024, April 17). *Om digitala nationella prov*. www.skolverket.se/skolutveckling/digitala-nationella-prov/om-digitala-nationella-prov

Solove, D. J., & Hartzog, W. (2022). *Breached! Why data security law fails and how to improve it*. OUP.

Štempeľová, I., Hudáková, H., & Takáč O. (2023). Polish and Slovak electronic health care (eHealth). *International Journal of Advanced Natural Sciences and Engineering Researches, 7*(9), 261–266.

SVT. (2023a, February 11). *Cyberattack mot VGR: Störningar hos flera regioner och 1177.* www.svt.se/nyheter/inrikes/flera-stora-sjukhus-hemsidor-ligger-nere

SVT. (2023b, February 12). *Attacker mot svenska universitets hemsidor.* www.svt.se/nyheter/inrikes/storningar-pa-svenska-universitets-hemsidor

SVT. (2024, March 4). *Data från cyberattack mot Sophiahemmet till salu.* www.svt.se/nyheter/lokalt/stockholm/data-fran-cyberattack-mot-sjukhus-till-salu

Swedish Council for Higher Education. (2021, March 2). *Distance education.* www.studera.nu/startpage/road-to-studies/other-ways/distance-education/

Tasioulas, J. (2007). The moral reality of human rights. In T. Pogge (Ed.), *Freedom from poverty as a human right: Who owes what to the very poor?* (pp. 75–102). OUP.

TASR. (2023, September 29). *Prieskum Svetovej banky: Takto dopadlo digitálne vzdelávanie na školách.* Teraz.sk. www.teraz.sk/slovensko/prieskum-svetovej-banky-odhalil-medzery/744093-clanok.html

Ten, C. W., Manimaran, G., & Liu, C. C. (2010). Cybersecurity for critical infrastructures: Attack and defense modeling. *IEEE Transactions on Systems, Man, and Cybernetics – Part A: Systems and Humans, 40*(4), 853–865. https://doi.org/10.1109/TSMCA.2010.2048028

Uhlendorf, B. A. (1932). The invention of printing and its spread till 1470: With special reference to social and economic factors. *The Library Quarterly, 2*(3), 179–231.

United Nations. (1948). *Universal Declaration of Human Rights.* www.un.org/en/about-us/universal-declaration-of-human-rights

United Nations. (2015). *Sustainable Development Goals.* https://sdgs.un.org/goals

United Nations. (2022). *E-government survey 2022: The future of digital government.* https://desapublications.un.org/sites/default/files/publications/2022-09/Web%20version%20E-Government%202022.pdf

Van Dijk, J. (2020). *The digital divide.* John Wiley & Sons.

Van Veen, K., & Melton, A. (2020). *Rare earth elements supply chains, part 1: An update on global production and trade.* United States International Trade Commission. www.usitc.gov/publications/332/executive_briefings/ebot_rare_earths_part_1.pdf

Vuorikari, R., Kluzer, S., & Punie, Y. (2022). *DigComp 2.2: The Digital Competence Framework for Citizens – With new examples of knowledge, skills and attitudes* (No. JRC128415). Joint Research Centre (Seville site). https://doi.org/10.2760/490274

Webster, B. F. (1998). *The Y2K survival guide: Getting to, getting through, and getting past the year 2000 problem.* Prentice-Hall.

Wittig, A., & Wittig, M. (2023). *Amazon Web Services in action: An in-depth guide to AWS.* Simon and Schuster.

World Health Organization. (2022, September 13). Countries in the European Region adopt first-ever digital health action plan. www.who.int/europe/news/item/13-09-2022-countries-in-the-european-region-adopt-first-ever-digital-health-action-plan

Yaacoub, J. P. A., Salman, O., Noura, H. N., Kaaniche, N., Chehab, A., & Malli, M. (2020). Cyber-physical systems security: Limitations, issues and future trends. *Microprocessors and Microsystems, 77*, 103201. https://doi.org/10.1016/j.micpro.2020.103201

Zuboff, S. (2018). *The age of surveillance capitalism: The fight for a human future at the new frontier of power.* Profile Books.

14 The right not to use the Internet to play videogames

Jonathan Keller

14.1 Prolegomena

If the idea of single-player videogaming brings to most people the image of a console or PC game running of a disc as a discrete, self-contained experience, the advent of always-online gaming and commercial distribution makes for a different reality.

Systematically, outside of a diminutive offer of "indie" titles, games are effectively sold, delivered and experienced as a service, regardless of whether the actual features and gameplay require it.

This comes with a lot of ancillary effects: from the temptation to ship half-finished products (to-be-fixed-later), to the prevalence of optional ("premium") for-pay content and features without which a product value may be markedly impaired, and brings on a number of privacy concerns and issues, when the user-facing product becomes a not-always-explicit vehicle for marketing, advertising and, in some instances, surveillance of users.

From a societal and public health perspective, the insistence that "everything must be online, always", is not devoid of pitfalls: it makes more difficult to protect children and vulnerable users from unwanted influence by third parties when being connected to an ill-understood (and sometimes hidden to the user) plethora of online servers exposes the user's activities at all times, and opens the possibility of unrestricted interactions with strangers.

In addition, the various Digital Rights Management (DRM) schemes put in place by publishers and associated End User Licence Agreements (EULA) go against most consumers intuitive understanding as to who owns the products ostensibly and expensively sold to them. Rules and laws applicable to digital content means they are really only effectively renting access to a service, through sometimes onerous contractual bonds users may not be fully cognisant of.

While some of these concerns are arguably brought on by the very nature of online gaming and digital distribution, many of these issues can be addressed by legislative and practical means – at least when it comes to single-player gaming – despite the publishing industry longstanding efforts to take advantage of the public and lawmakers' confusion as to how the digital sausage is made, exactly.

DOI: 10.4324/9781003528401-17

14.2 Introduction

14.2.1 Purpose of single-player videogaming

Everyone wishes to be a hero. Everyone aspires to be admired or acclaimed "for great qualities and achievements".[1] Videogames provide stimulating environments for players to test one's ingenuity, courage or strength. People crave a sense of accomplishment and being Luke Skywalker, single handedly defeating legendary evil empires from the comfort of one's sofa, is enticing. Even though those videogames that are designed for solo play may share a general presentation not dissimilar to videogames of yore, they typically operate in the always-connected and always monitored ecosystem of Internet gaming. Whether this is to the advantage of the user, consumer, and citizen is debatable, and that is the main question this chapter aims to explore.

Solo games purport to offer escapism, discovery, challenges, skill building opportunity, and general fun at the users' leisure, and typically at their chosen pace. Compared to "true" online gaming, they intuitively offer a self-contained experience, insulated from outward interference and social pressures to compete or interact with others (even though those may be made available), which in the eye of their players can be a feature rather than a limitation.

Because of their discrete presentation, solo games also suggest completeness. Like a book, one picks up a solo game with the expectation everything required to enjoy the full experience is included between the covers. Where online games present themselves as ongoing services, with – hopefully stable – ever evolving playgrounds, solo games (in between major releases in the case of franchises) promise capsule universes to be enjoyed revisited at leisure, reliably constant.

Since many users can enjoy a dopamine discharge from hitting a goalpost or defeating a monster, uncorrelated to how challenging the task, and careful not to alienate the least "hardcore" shares of a game's potential audience, most contemporary single-playing games are not geared for high difficulty or complexity, instead focusing more on providing a curated, adaptive experience more akin to what one may go through on a theme park ride than an actual competitive event (Bazar du Grenier, 2024).

This preference for reduced-challenge experiences eases access to first-time players, and controls consumers tolerance for frustration when deciding to pick up a game, and allows purposeful leverage thereof to stimulate the opt-in purchase of in-game content and advantages when faced with less easily surmountable odds at any later point in the game.

How readily pleasurable the experience significantly impacts the appreciation of a videogame by its players, which is critical for the industry. Thus, the release of dopamine in the player's brain upon a victory is key (Carpita et al., 2021). It directly relates to the players' "libidinal" requirement (Hunyadi, 2023) to the point where studies highlight the efficacy of serious games as the learning tools (Girard, Ecalle & Magnan, 2012).

Using a slightly provocative perspective, videogaming, like pharmaceutics, can be used by people to access "artificial paradises" described as a source of addiction (Cleveland Clinic, 2022; WHO, 2024). This questionable perception is often used as a justification to increase control on children's access to the Internet (Commission Enfants et écrans, 2024). Both pharmaceutical and videogames sectors require huge investments at the development phase, but enjoy huge margins once the product is on the market.

14.2.2 Legal protection of the videogame

Again, video games and pharmaceuticals share some characteristics when it comes to their legal description. Both classes of products are slippery and ill-classified legal creatures, owing in part to the relative "opacity" of their inner workings and microscopic or electronic nature. Videogames are clumsily striding the two branches of traditional intellectual property (IP) framework. On the one hand, both the continental *propriété littéraire et artistique* (Gaudrat, 2010), and the Anglo-Saxon copyright (Coats & Radfer, 1993) protect the originality of creation, explicitly including software and all derivatives, such as videogames. On the other hand, patent law, harmonised at European and international levels, grants a legal protection to software through (somewhat disputed) interpretations of the law as reward for investment (Keller, 2017). Even though both protections cannot be invoked at simultaneously, such accumulation of legal avenues and the exclusivity they *de facto* grant to right holders provide same with ample resources to be used – even beyond protective needs – as means to squelch competition and engage in abusive commercial practices. These compounds with technical and contractual means to subordinate the enjoyment of a videogame to a persistent connection to the Internet.

14.2.3 Delimitation of the subject

In stark contrast with yesteryear's model of selling CD or DVD copies of playable games, sometimes augmented by online-only components and features, the always-online games publishers that have emerged and come to dominate the market since the advent of 3G cellular network and generalised domestic broadband access regard games as loss-leader products, aimed at luring in consumers for services and on-demand for pay content, and in some cases, are mere data-gathering devices designed to syphon as much user data as possible, to be sold to advertisers and other interested parties.

In this new economy of video games, new actors, such as smartphone manufacturers (e.g., Samsung, Apple, Huawei), operating system publishers (e.g., Google Android, Apple iOS), platform providers (e.g., Google Play, Apple Store), and mobile game publishers (e.g., Tencen, Activision blizzard, SuperCell) have come to dominate by fully embracing these doctrines of software as a service and customer as a product, with the traditional industry heavyweights quickly following suit (Electronic Arts ranking in 700+ million US dollar in 2023). Those traditional "videogame-as-a-product publishers" (e.g., Ubisoft, Take2, Warner

Bros Discovery) and console manufacturers (e.g., Microsoft, Nintendo and Sony) have, thanks to this evolution, increasingly shifted towards the provision of such online services.

14.2.4 The right not to use the Internet to play videogames

Videogames, as a class of products, are eerily familiar and yet poorly understood by the general public. This owes in part to how diverse the offer has grown over the years, but mainly to how pervasive gaming and gamification have become in a society of always-online personal computing and mobile devices. Crucially, videogames of today do not exist in the same social, technical and economical space their antecessors debuted in. They are no longer self-contained, discrete objects, "living" on some hard drive, CD or proprietary storage medium, meant to come alive on demand and only within the confines of a personal computer or gaming console.

Almost all current games are designed, marketed and operated with the expectation of permanent broadband connectivity as a given, and the legal and contractual frameworks which rules the relations between manufacturers, publishers and consumers ranges from confusing to opaque for the latter. Other considerations, such as customer acquisition (for publishers) and cost of entry (for players), along with competition with online gaming experiences where freemium/premium sales models have come to dominate – initially in the mobile gaming markets, but then spreading into the PC and console ones – have a strong bearing on game design evolutions. Solo gaming in the 2020s needs to be – initially a least – cheap and easy to get into, incessantly enticing and rewarding to keep the player engaged and nagging, if need be, for the player to return often. The management, engineering and leveraging of player frustration, which used to be a staple of massively multiplayer online role-playing game (MMORPG). Skinner-box designs has become the *de facto* standard in mainstream game design, solo games not to be spared.

More and more, publishers use the Internet as an environment that could be considered as a "virtual kindergarten", where people – including children – are playing under the publisher's oversight acting as an unconcerned arbitrator within their social interactions. A last remark is necessary.

As this chapter will demonstrate, the right not to use the Internet shall be applied to play videogames to reverse the shift generated from solo to offline play transforming the videogame-as-a-product to online multiplayer games-as-a-service. The right not to use the Internet will free the players for the videogame providers' monitoring allowed by the constant Internet connection. The right not to use the Internet within this domain could be understood as the right to enjoy freely, i.e., without any kind of supervision, a finished product, i.e., stripped of any critical flaw or bugs. But the use of the Internet to play videogames is just an excuse used by publishers to "explain" their laziness, reflecting in many legal interactions with the players. Therefore, we will plead in favour of a right not to use the Internet to enjoy a finished product.

First, the IP on videogames offers to the publisher a way of escaping any kind of contractual liability and any warranty towards the end-user (Section 14.3.1). This latter faces an expensive flawed product allegedly on an ongoing maintenance allowed by the connection to Internet. Furthermore, the publisher dictates his own conditions through the End-User Licence Agreement (EULA). This contract allows the player to use the videogames within its terms creating an unilateral framework limiting the player's freedom to correct, maintain or enhance the flaws of the videogame (Section 14.3.2). Unfortunately, such contractual dodge is also present with a one-fits-all privacy policy, allegedly respecting users' personal data (Section 14.4). Publishers choose the stricter legal requirement among privacy laws before leaving the sole application of the adequate law to the player. This illusion of transparency only operates a "privacy-washing" justifying the constant monitoring of players (Section 14.4.1). Moreover, the constant connection to the Internet redesigns the videogames into a platform of commercials violating the gamers' right to be let alone. The ubiquitous proposing of sale creates addictions and moral harms to a vulnerable audience (Section 14.4.2).

14.3 The right not to use the Internet to play videogames as a circumvention strategy to evade the publisher's absolute control

In this section, it will be demonstrated that the right not to use the Internet to play videogames guarantees players to enjoy a stable product and not flawed betaware. However, EULAs emphasise the IP attributes of videogames. This empowers the publishers to control the distribution and the maintenance of their work (Section 14.3.1). Videogame as IP keeps the gamers subjected to the publishers' goodwill. As a copyrighted work, EULA are restricting the freedoms of the players to make a reasonable use of what they assume to be their property (Section 14.3.2).

14.3.1 The licence as means of control over videogames distribution and quality

Publishers' control over the distribution and the quality of videogames is being done through the use of the licence and technical means. Both are enforced through a compelled use of the Internet. Such control restrains the freedom of the player to use their copy of the videogame at their leisure.

14.3.1.1 The copyright as a legal control over the copy of the videogame

The right not to use the Internet to play a videogame constitutes a way for the player to claim her ownership over their copy of the videogame. Indeed, IP distinguishes the support (medium) from the work itself (Benabou, 2005). Thus, copies of the work *per se* are protected whoever possesses the support. This legal fiction allows to transfer to the player the right of possessing a reproduction of the work and, possibly, to assign the right to use the game. In other words, a legitimate user has the right to sell his hardcopy/digital copy but selling the right to use the game is much harder even if the Court of Justice of the EU (CJEU) case law grants this transfer under the reservation of a previous distribution within the European Union market.[2] As we will see in the following, Digital Right Management (DRM) tools, systematically implemented in the hard copy or/and the subsequent Internet registration, transform the standard contract into an *intuitu personae* contract. DRM establishes a link between a copy of the game and an individual device or user, strengthening the contractual connection with the first-buyer. Such technique hampers customers' ability to transfer ownership of their digital goods (Wong, 2012). Indeed, most licences prohibit the player from selling her account to third parties. Such behaviour could be considered as a breach of contract,[3] bringing termination and, ultimately, the annulment of the account.

Lack of account activity (i.e., connection to the game or service) can also be used as grounds by the publisher or by the device manufacturer to terminate an account, despite the legal provisions provided by Directive 2019/770 of 20 May 2019 on certain aspects concerning contracts for the supply of digital content and digital services.[4] Particularly, its Article 16 states the conditions of termination of a service supply contract applicable to digital content, curtailing the discretion of publishers and device manufacturers in deleting the game from the player's device past a certain inactivity period. Even if reality obviously contradicts the aforementioned directive, this is routine behaviour, justified by dubious operating costs reasoning (burden of permanent players' account storage).

Another way through which publishers often deprive consumers of the reasonably expected enjoyment of their goods is by voluntarily ending the post-sale maintenance and support of their products. As shown in the following, any videogame is "by default" originally flawed by bugs or incompatibilities, requiring publisher-provided patches. Issues of critical incompatibility often arise, preventing normal operation of a game on its intended platform, resulting in a denial of usage functionally indistinguishable from the removal of the game from the user's library. Halting maintenance is usually justified by the dissolution of the publisher company (Chalk, 2023) or the extinction of the franchise licence on which the game is based (Ricchiuto, 2017).

Of course, players may sue the publisher over the absence of conformity as stated by Article 8 of Directive 2019/770 electing the videogame as a "digital content".[5] The digital content or digital service shall

> be of the quantity and possess the qualities and performance features, including in relation to functionality, compatibility, accessibility, continuity and security, normal for digital content or digital services of the same type and which the consumer may reasonably expect, given the nature of the digital content or digital service and taking into account any public statement made by or on behalf of the trader.

Paragraph 3 of this very provision limits this right by allowing the publishers to shift the blame towards gamers failing to install the mandatory updates, even if only made available on the Internet.

Traditionally, courts' position tends to uphold the publishers'[6] view of videogames as works of art.[7] Such benefits could be extended to the device manufacturer for its hardware, as an inventor, or to the platform that is hosting a third party's game (e.g., Google Play), as an author. IP laws ease judicial fast-track through *prima facie* orders. As underlined previously, even if required, the author is not required to provide any rationale for their handling of products licensed to consumers (Reddit, 2022; Streamcommunity). Videogames as "digital content" do not offer such protection or rights to the player, seen as a licensee without the protections normally afforded to private consumers. Furthermore, the technicity of the digital domain requires experts, resulting in long and costly procedures. Directive 2019/770 applies solely to online sales, withholding protection from consumers who purchased their goods by brick'n'mortar retailers from the publishers' whim.

14.3.1.2 The technical control over the copy of the videogame

A central aim of IP laws in this context is to incentivise publishers investing in the creation of a work, which in this context is a videogame. Even if efficient, this protection is both punitive and, more and more, preemptive. Aside from raising public awareness of copyright issues (Captain Copyright, 2006), the entertainment industry established DRM early on as the default means of stemming piracy. Enshrined in law to the point of subjecting membership to the World Trade Organization (WTO)[8] to its recognition by individual states, DRM tools aim to enforce a single-beneficiary per licensed copy doctrine. Depending on convenience, these tools straddle criminal and copyright laws to assert their legal authority. The case for intrusive DRM implementation relies primarily on the notion that PCs provide easy access to the means of illicit duplication of proprietary software, by simply "burning" a DVD.

In fact, all types of gaming devices, from consoles to smartphones provide means of control over the installation and execution of protected software, typically through unique identifiers (Apple or Google's ID, Sony ID) for the hardware copy, the device, the user's account or IP address, or a combination thereof. Oftentimes, a superfluous registration on the publisher's website to create a mandatory player account is sometimes required despite other means of copy verification being already in play.

DRM tools' purpose evolved beyond mere copy protection to means of policing user behaviour and experience, such as preventing the use of cheating tools in online gaming. Under the rationalisation of protecting code integrity and ensuring quality of their products, publishers prevent users and third parties from fixing flaws in a product they wouldn't address themselves. The right to repair as projected by the EU falls before this goal through empowering consumers to repair by themself a material product (European Parliament, 2024). As we will demonstrate, Directive 2019/770 provides a framework constraining the publisher to provide a conform product as expected.

In some cases, DRM tools come as "RootKits" embedding themselves deep into a user's system files, usually unbeknownst to them, and provide fertile grounds for software and hardware incompatibilities and glitches. DRM becomes a way to check the players' legitimate accreditation, i.e., the right to use the game granted by the licence, through the automatic registration at every launch of the game (Korben, 2024). Offline activity makes technically impossible any upload of this information by DRM. In such a case, the player would probably not have access to all functionalities or, less probably, may be completely denied usage of the product, even in pure single-player mode. Besides copyright protection, DRM embodies publishers' claims of legitimate interest in gathering personal user data, under the rationale of protection of the publishers' interests, either of the cyber kind or to re-assert the publisher's property rights over their IP assets.

On paper the use of these means of control is conditional upon the player understanding and agreement to this oversight. But players generally do not read licence agreements, nor do they expect the extent to which the DRM entitles the publishers to invade their privacy. The symbiotic entanglement between DRM and EULAs morphs boilerplate contracts into an *intuitu personae* bind.

14.3.2 The right not to use the Internet as a way to evade the publisher's contractual grasp

The right not to use the Internet to play videogames could contribute to close two legal loopholes currently benefiting publishers through IP rights: contractual limitation of liability (Section 14.3.2.2) and the formalism of the contract *per se*, including the code of conduct (Section 14.3.2.1).[9]

14.3.2.1 The licence as a way to "defraud" the player

Through the EULA, publishers rely on the contractual framework established with a player. This framework requires an explicit licence recognised by the jurisprudence (Beurskens, Kamocki & Ketzan, 2013) as a guarantee of legal certainty avoiding copyright infringement (Keller, 2017, pp. 149–150) or hacking litigations (Sieber, 2006; Chopin, 2013). In other words, the agreement of licence is a mandatory commitment by the end user to not infringe any copyright law. But through this formal agreement to the "terms and conditions" electronically displayed, publishers can edict unfavourable obligations to the gamers. This very formalism may collide with consumer protection laws, as discussed in the following.

The formalism of the EULA needs to be reviewed. This contract restricts certain players' behaviour, justifying a constant oversight by publishers. To some, this is enough to make the case for a gamers' right not to use the Internet to play videogames when not strictly necessary to the gameplay. Outside the few people with commercial interests related to the game who would really read such documents,[10] general audience does not have a lawyer on retainer for everyday acts. Even if players are getting older, this audience is not familiar with the subtlety of the legalese. Clarity of purpose and legibility are only a concern for publishers insofar as they might deter players from agreeing to the terms of use and get in the way of players signing EULAs. *Per se,* such a contract is usually a 30-page document written in technical terms and never provided in a printed version as required by Article 19 of Directive 2019/770. Typical EULAs come in three forms: a long scrolling electronic text with a ticking box at the end, a "licence" text document located in the installation folder for PC games or, for hardcopy only, the famous "shrinkwrap licence" technique.[11] DRM completes this almost obsolete formalism by tacitly enforcing the agreed-upon rules by checking the legitimate access of the players, their behaviour and the use of prohibited third party software. Under any assumption, the players are not fully aware of what they agreed to, including the way their behaviour is framed by the code of conduct codifying "Do's and Don'ts" into the player's gameplay (Sheshounet, 2024).

A EULA appendix might also describe some kind of "gameplay ethics" defined unilaterally by the publisher. Any violation of this code is grounds to terminate the agreement, as the player is presupposed "to (having) read and accepted the full terms and conditions". Those ethic stipulations represent the very purpose of the licence as it stipulates the way the videogame, as an IP work, may be used by the gamer. EULAs contain legal dispositions to protect the IP *per se*, such as the prohibition to copy it or to intervene within the code, but also stipulations limiting gamers' behaviour during their gaming experience. Such stipulations rely indirectly on the "traditional" IP rights by limiting the purpose of the work to a specific purpose – i.e., the way the licensee uses it. Yet, the gamer are licensees allowing the publisher to limit the freedom of the players. Even if the game is completely scripted,[12] the interactions between all experiences *lived* by the players cannot be completely expected or regulated by the publishers. Some actions can be subject to serendipity effects due to the numbers of players or to development bugs (Sheshounet, 2023). Even as an IP work, the videogame could evolve independently, eluding the author's control, through the players' social interactions. Thus, publishers try to regulate those unexpected behaviour through the code of conduct. However, the publisher alone is able to appreciate what constitutes a behavioural misdemeanour,[13] which would lead to a breach justifying the termination of the agreement. Such termination would result in the player's account being deleted and, eventually, to the player himself being banned from all associated services, including those intended to provide appellate venues against this sanction. In other words, the right not to use the Internet to play videogames would protect the solo player's right to be free from any kind of oversight (see, infra, at 14.4). But this freedom is strictly limited to a one player campaign. In a multiplayer game the solution developed through case law for the social media platform's community guidelines could be applied to regulate interactions between players (IMCO, 2020). The latter's situation is handled mainly by the communication law; multiplayers' games could be perceived as an adapted social media support. Since social media is an "Internet-based platforms which allow for interactions between individuals or the broadcast of content to the wider world and which are far more interactive than traditional broadcast media" (LexisNexis, 2024) and that multiplayers' games fill to all those conditions.

14.3.2.2 The right not to use the Internet to play videogames allows to minimise the impact of publisher's deficiency

According to the established narrative associated with videogames as a copyright work, the publisher is free from any liability associated with IT developments errors. A copyright work enjoys the right of integrity, prohibiting any modification by unauthorised third party (corrective patches included). The EULA prohibits licensed players from attempting repairs on their own, regardless of functional bugs, security flaws or system errors. This integrity protection clause was grandfathered by the general software industry, where paid maintenance is a traditional ancillary service (Huet & Bouche, 2011; Le Tourneau, 2015). At the dawn of this industry, public authorities raised this issue, to which the publishers objected such a liability would place an unnecessary burden on their trade development. A few decades later, the threat of shouldering liability for such flaws came to be regarded as threatening enough to warrant further restriction of end-user recourses, due to the sheer costs stemming from a wider insurance cover (Keller, 2017; Weber, 2012). In other words, acknowledging responsibility for such flaws would trigger judicial reparations leading to increased insurance costs, leading to raising the price of software. Thus, several regimes were set up: a specific one for B2B allowing the mitigation of such stipulation through negotiation. Players, on the other hand, are end-consumers, and lack the opportunity to negotiate the standard contract provided by the publisher.[14] Thanks to the American kinship of the EULA, Article 2-719 of the Uniform Commercial Code requires publishers to emphasise the formalism of the stipulations related to limitation of liability by making it "conscionable", i.e., written in capital letters or in bold. Hence, publishers remain solely liable for "physical" damage, but not for bugs and errors. Videogames are allowed all the inherent flaws of software, i.e., programming mistakes. The protection granted by IP laws over publishing a flawed videogame is justified by the pretense of the will of the "artist" to publish his work "as is" (Bitan, 2010). Laws reserve the right to correct those flaws solely to the author, granted on his right of integrity on his work, even if, in reality, that monopoly is deemed to be a reward for investment (Geiger, 2004). For example, French IP laws offer the authorised user the right to correct errors (Gaudrat, 1988), but only if the author does not retain this right (L 122-6-1 CPI), i.e., through the licence/EULA, which prohibits it by default.

Regarding sectoral specificities, an unfinished videogame is deemed to materialise the original idea of the author and thus enjoys the copyright benefits. For many titles the winter holiday season and its associated gift giving is critical and justifies shipping first and fixing later. The assumption of always-online has enabled publishers to normalise post-sales fixes in the form of patches, update, etc., and to establish these practices as industry standards. The United States (US) Federal Trade Commission (FTC) has solved this issue by using consumer law.[15] EU law take on the matter comes in the aforementioned Directive 2019/770 and through the New Product Liability Directive. Nonetheless, the CJEU keeps repeating that

IP laws prevail on the contractual aspect, negating any hope of effective protection for players.[16] The "Game-as-a-Service" model advocates for an "infinite work in progress" interpretation, sheltering publishers from any kind of liability.

To conclude, from an IP perspective, commercially releasing a videogame is equivalent to publishing a finished work, which is protected by the "integrity" right from any third-party action. In such situation, the right not to use the Internet to play videogames could compel the publisher to supply a "conform", as demanded in Article 8 of Directive 2019/770, videogame which means a bug-free version of the game, i.e., not requiring any upgrade. The publisher would then be in a situation similar to what it was prior to the generalisation of the Internet, without the ability to upgrade an unfinished product or to oversee the player's activity. While Directive 2019/770 and contract law could provide an adequate answer, its application relies on costly procedures triggered and supported by players.

In the eyes of publishers, the player is not only suspected of being a fraudster, a cheater or unwilling to pay for the product, yet also regarded as a "cash cow" to tap for never ending streams of revenue. That perspective translates into the limitations stipulated by the EULA and the code of conduct, as that contractual framework justifies intruding into the player's gameplay. This argumentation underpins the progressive transformation of videogames from end-products to support for derivatives and secondary income. Same rationale justifies publishers processing personal user data to every extent possible. Thus, the right not to use the Internet can be supported by the right to privacy.

14.4 The privacy protection enhanced by the right not to use the Internet to play videogames

The right not to use the Internet to play videogames could be seen as integral to the protection of players privacy (Section 14.4.1), and simultaneously spare them unwanted solicitations (Section 14.4.2).

14.4.1 The right not to use the Internet: enhancing the right to privacy

The right not to use the Internet to play videogames is supported by the two different temporal periods of the right of privacy: the right to be let alone (ancient conception) and the protection of personal data (new conception) (Rossi, 2024). The first conception applies fully in our context as leaving the player to enjoy the gameplay without any third-party interference (see 14.4.1.2), whereas the modern conception is specifically aimed at the protection of personal data and the associated data processing during an offline experience (see 14.4.1.1).

14.4.1.1 The scrutiny of offline gameplay

Going through six different privacy policies edited by five different publishers (Ubisoft, Take 2, Warner Bros Discovery, Epic Games, Bandai Namco), all of them touch on matters of offline player's privacy. These documents inform the player on the nature of the personal data collected, how such data are collected and processed, and for how long.

A first issue rises from the determination of applicable law. Rather than picking a single doctrine, publishers choose to refer to both the dispositions of the EU General Data Protection Regulation (GDPR) and the California Consumer Privacy Act (CCPA) in their privacy policies. Yet, publishers willingly ignore some classes of gaming devices (PC and consoles) where the same rules of personal data protection shall apply, as they do to mobile devices. For example, Article 5(2) of the ePrivacy Directive[17] requires that any deposit of files on the players' device should receive their prior consent. Analysis of those different privacy policies shows this requirement is met only for the cookies stored on players mobile devices and publisher's servers.[18] No information is available for other devices where similar exchanges happen, such as consoles or computers.

Further inspection reveals the true flaws of such data gathering: its inaccessibility and its unreadability by the user whose information is harvested. The whole process is therefore impossible to be grasped by the player, and comforts two decades worth of legal design studies. Those show how a full grasp of privacy policies evade anyone without a PhD in law (McDonald & Cranor, 2008). The issue is worsened in a consumer space where people are unlikely to read the fine print. The phrasing of privacy policies drafted by publishers' privacy officers actively works against legibility and accessibility by the layman. See, for example, Warner Bros Discovery's privacy policies that use a unique form to describe all the processes related to the collection of personal data in (1) their videogames, (2) their theme parks, and (3) their websites.[19] To give another example, Bandai includes its job application process in its videogames' privacy policy.[20]

Such a situation highlights the challenges of the race to the best law, i.e., the opportunistic choice of a law by a publisher among several applicable laws, particularly problematic for a "sovereign" domain[21] such as personal data. For example, game console manufacturers' privacy policies mainly focus on the hardware maintenance, including cybersecurity and software compatibility issues.[22] For those purposes, they use the dubious notion of "legitimate interest", i.e., a data processing without the player's consent – even the knowledge – of the data subject, which is generally accepted in such a context. The question of uploading gameplay data after a certain disconnection time of the game console raises a similar issue. Even if explicit rights are granted to the player, with the provision not to be banned for contract breach, it is impossible to know which data are uploaded. To sum it up, the ability to play videogames on a console implies accepting the privacy policies. Due to all this legalese, intertwinement complicates the determination of which data are collected from offline activities.

The alleged "choice" takes the form of an "opt-in", which actually forces the player to endure an undetermined process of personal data collection, and, in particular, an analysis of the player's gameplay behavioural record. For example, some privacy policies stipulate things like "profile inference",[23] "usage data",[24] or "deriving aggregated data".[25] Such terms are synonyms for "personalised recommendation system" using such processes to promote some commercials within the game to entice the player into in-game purchases.

14.4.1.2 "The only way to get smarter is (not only) to play with a smarter opponent"

Playing does not automatically mean competing. Gaming is known to be a way to relieve stress, to develop cognitive skills and to combat loneliness (APA, 2023). Some players just want to have fun without any intervention from any third parties. Even if some videogames enable competition between players through small skirmishes,[26] those interactions have little or no impact on the narrative of a solo campaign. A videogame is an entertainment medium supposed to satisfy the players' specific needs according to the modalities of their choice. And this is where the right not to use the Internet to play videogames shall be understood as the right to be let alone to enjoy one's pleasure without any incursions from third parties.

In such a case, players shall enjoy a freedom similar to bookreading (Tricoire, 2002; Lochak, 1994) or to use a "stimulant for auto-eroticism".[27] Users consider the videogame as a manifestation of privacy much wider than what happens behind the closed doors of their home because of their actions with the work, players are not just a passive audience as in traditional IP work but real actors in their gameplay. In a solo campaign, players don't expect nor desire their behaviour and playstyle judged by a third party, and should be free to express their best or worst version of oneself. The reasonable expectation of privacy (Winn, 2016; Kerr, 2007) is at its highest level. As Justice Harlan explained it in US Supreme Court's *Katz*,[28] the reasonable expectation of privacy is a "twofold requirement, first that a person have exhibited an actual (subjective) expectation of privacy and, second, that the expectation be one that society is prepared to recognise as 'reasonable'". Both conditions should be easy to meet, as players do not expect to be oversighted during their gameplay.

In his dissenting opinion in *Chocholáč*, European Court of Human Rights (ECtHR) Judge Wojtyczek proposes to include within privacy protection "any domain an individual considers important for (oneself)". Such extension may include videogames as it already does for pornography. Both domains provide fantasies where victims or partners are either artificial or consented. Both cases are fictions without any other purpose but to satisfy the customer's enjoyment of a fantasy. There is no (direct) damage incurred from this consumption, even for the most violent acts.[29] However, in videogames, those abuses are strictly limited to violent content because explicit sexual behaviour displayed by a videogame are prohibited for public order reasons. Even if sex sales, videogames displaying sexual or suggestive content are kept from the common distribution networks since those products are subjected to a systematic censorship by American law.[30] Of course, suggestive contents are present in regular videogame, but those contents are rewards offered by developers to adventurous players as easter eggs (Houston Press, 2012) or as a marketing gossip to attract strollers (Gamefaqs, 2023; Tro-online, 2020). Videogames have more leeway in portraying acts of violence, as is customary in traditional plots of "*classic pieces of literature*".[31] Because videogame publishers and console manufacturers cannot certify efficiently the actual age of players (which is self-declared), videogames platforms can only offer some "adult" content but not "adult only games".[32] Even if such content can be displayed on any other medium[33] under the reservation to not "appeal to prurient interest"[34] be obscene (Silverstein, 2020).

As it was with comics and mangas in many countries, the case for children protection is raised to bear in restricting distribution of "harmful" contents (Silverstein, 2020). However, even as customs and laws stay the same players grow older and their entertainment needs in solo gameplay evolves. Modern videogames allow players to be, within their framework, either a saint or a demon. Such freedom could be linked to the protection of the right to personal development, and more precisely to personal autonomy,[35] away from any unwanted attention.[36] Such rights are directly linked to Article 8 of the European Convention of Human Rights (ECHR) and specifically for children by Article 6 of United Nations Convention on Rights of a Child (UNCRC). However, the disclosure of such private behaviour would not have any real impact on the public where all acts are … fictional.

The right to not use the Internet to play videogame could extend the same guarantees offered to preserve the privacy from any kind of unlawful interference at home as entitled by Article 8 ECHR and subsequent personal data texts (Convention 108+, GDPR, …). In a solo gameplay, the player has a reasonable expectation of privacy while being in a fantasy world. There is no expectation of personal data processing based on "usage information".[37]

14.4.2 The right not to use the Internet to play videogames offers a protection from distress and addiction

The right not to use the Internet would compel publishers to rethink their business models by easing off relentless sales pitches and commercials within the game (Section 14.4.2.1). But, more importantly, this right may allow children to fully enjoy the best of this industry by keeping them from toxic communities (Section 14.4.2.2).

14.4.2.1 Addictions as a business plan

Current online games sometimes bring "Ubik" to mind. In this Philip K. Dick's novel, the main character pays systematically for each single service provided by his own apartment's commodities. "Microtransactions"/"in game purchases" seem to use Ubik's fiction as a recipe for online games design, where purchases are pushed on players as a way to save themselves from the "fun pain", i.e., the toil of repetitive tasks and chores (like "farming" or "looting") required of them to advance through the game.

In-game sales are not *per se* detrimental to players. Some publishers provide decent freeware and only request players to pay for new features. But this benevolent business model is unfortunately limited. Microtransactions in videogames represent the best reason to enact a right not to use the Internet to play videogames. This business model directly impacts children's psyche by nurturing a blur between "virtual currency" and "real money" through the implementation of dark patterns schemes (EDPB, 2022) pushing children to "borrow" their parents' credit cards to get to desirable content. Unsurprisingly, publishers have shown little enthusiasm in providing consumers preventative or remedial mechanics to mitigate such "impulse buys" (Latham, 2023; Ouest France, 2023).

A few political initiatives are encouraged by lawmakers in Europe, but except for game console manufacturers implementing better controls, the mobile game publishers have been unresponsive to these calls, leading the European Parliament to draft a resolution aiming at providing a safer framework for microtransactions in videogames.[38] So far, no actual real case-law addresses has created precedent on that issue, resulting in the European Data Protection Board (EDPB) to provide some indirect clarity on the matter with the concept of "dark patterns" in its binding decision 2/2023 regarding TikTok. This authority takes note of their "negative impact for the protection of (…) their fundamental rights and freedoms". In that decision, dark patterns are qualified as leading "subconsciously" (children) "to decisions violating their privacy interests", and are amplified through "video Posting Pop-Up", reinforcing the nudging effect. But such reasoning based on "obfuscation techniques" is correlated to personal data, even if used in videogames to hide the amount spent by the player (Latham, 2023).

Some recent US decisions explain this lack of reaction from the industry, despite the EU's will to push for a sectoral regulation, in a twofold reasoning.[39] The first part lies on the immunity of the "interactive computer service" provided by both defendants. Even if they receive some fees from every microtransaction billed by a publisher, the distribution platforms are merely displaying content that was placed on that service by another party, and – on a legal standpoint – aren't acting as an official agent. The second and main part of the judges' reasoning is based on the absence of harm caused to the end-users from playing videogames.

14.4.2.2 The right not to use the Internet to play videogames as a safeguard against moral harm to children

Moral harms resulting from both videogames and the Internet are a complex "social issue" (Manrique, 2021). Apart from creating a chilling effect (De Marco & Aeris, 2022; Lequesne & Keller, 2023) around the censorship of the content, thus endangering freedom of speech, such recognition would open many litigations, jeopardising the videogame industry first, then possibly every brand of entertaining industry displaying violent content. Both the United States and Europe envision freedom of speech as the support of the right to "shock, offend or disturb the State or any sector of the population".[40] However, children are deemed vulnerable to outside influence to an extent beyond that of the adult population, warranting specific protections for them to thrive as stated by the UNCRC. Salesmen in game stores do not really care about the matching the purchaser' age and the labels edited by PEGI/ESRB.[41] Moreover, the lack of serious age control (Lausson, 2024) questions the efficiency of the mechanisms aiming to prevent the youngest ones from accessing "mature" videogames.

There is no doubt that a violent game may cause children to have nightmares, but an important reservation is made about opening the Pandora's box of awarding judicial damages on the basis of emotional distress. In other words, so far, no case-law recognises a direct harm from electronic content (mis)uses (Levallois-Barth & Keller, 2022). Furthermore, the two sides of the Atlantic have a different legal interpretation of such prejudice, even if, in both cases, judicial courts do not qualify it as a damage.

14.5 Conclusion

The right not to use the Internet to play videogames requires a claim in order to save the realm of dreams of the entertainment from a complete privatisation. The absolute risk being to ransom gamers from their artificial paradise with an annuity system demanded by a constant connection instead of granting them a positive right on their copy of the game. The multimedia nature of the videogame, i.e., the mix of photographic and video material based upon a software development, put this work under an unlimited protection against its users, even if the videogame maintenance is ended for decades, even if the operating system emulating it is obsolete, even if the publisher's company has been terminated. Thus, creating a right not to use Internet to play videogame allows the legitimate players to enjoy their possession as they should. Furthermore, the right not to use Internet to play videogames allows an informational privacy to the gamers to put third parties add-on or patches to enhance the gameplay and to go beyond a scripted adventure. This bubble also keeps vulnerable audience from facing a tailored commercial communication hidden within the videogames. Where traditional works allow fandoms, i.e., the rewriting or side quests of some popular novels/characters, modern works deny this right thanks to the constant connection.

Notes

1 Oxford Dictionary, Hero, https://en.wikipedia.org/wiki/Hero
2 CJEU, 3 July 2012, *Oracle v. Usedsoft*, C 127/11.
3 Paris Court of appeal, 19 march 2021, ref. n° 19/17493.
4 JOUE 22/05/2019, L 136/1.
5 Rec. 19 of Directive 2019/770:

> In order to cater for fast technological developments and to maintain the future-proof nature of the notion of digital content or digital service, this Directive should cover, *inter alia*, computer programmes, applications, video files, audio files, music files, digital games, e-books or other e-publications, and also digital services which allow the creation of, processing of, accessing or storage of data in digital form, including software-as-a-service, such as video and audio sharing and other file hosting, word processing or games offered in the cloud computing environment and social media.

6 CJEU, 18 December 2019, Development SAS c. Free Mobile SAS, C-666/18, IT, US District Court, D. Arizona, MDY Industries, LLC, *Plaintiff/Counterdefendant, v. Blizzard*, (D. Ariz. Jul. 14, 2008).
7 CJEU, 23 January 2014, Nintendo Co. Ltd et a. c./ PC Box Srl et 9Net Srl, n° C-355/12.

8 §1201 of US's Digital Millenium Copyright Act of October 28 1998; Art. 6 of Directive 2001/29/EC of the European Parliament and of the Council of 22 May 2001 on the harmonisation of certain aspects of copyright and related rights in the information society; Art. 11 of Loi n° 2006-961 du 1 août 2006 relative au droit d'auteur et aux droits voisins dans la société de l'information.

9 Ubisoft' Skull and bones requires the player to accept the code of conduct as a mandatory condition to play.

10 Streamers or third parties proposing independent microtransactions/services related to the game.

11 In such a case, the simple unwrapping of the plastic packaging of the game is deemed to express the player's agreement to the licence (Lemley, 1995).

12 I.e., the players are steered towards a predefined destination without true freedom.

13 Ubisoft, "Privacy policy", May 2020, https://legal.ubi.com/privacypolicy/fr-FR

> If you do not comply with these rules, you may be penalised, particularly in the event of anti-gambling, cheating or toxicity. We retain your data for as long as is necessary to apply these sanctions, for example your Account ID, your game data, your IP address, your terminal ID and your chat history.
>
> If you have been sanctioned on our Services, we will not be able to give you access to the Data related to your sanction in order to maintain our ability to detect or act against such behavior.

14 Art. 1110 of French Code Civil.

15 US Federal Trade Commission, In re Microsoft Corp 134 FTC 102 (2005) recognizing Microsoft's liability for not ensuring a high level of security.

16 CJEU, 6 October 2021, *Top System SA v. Belgian State*, C-13/20.

17 ePrivacy directive is a *lex speciali* framing the European personal data treatment from electronic telecommunication.

18 Take-Two Interactive, "Privacy policy", 2018, available at www.take2games.com/privacy/2018/index.html (last consultation 6th September 2024),

> You may choose to voluntarily provide us with various personal information and non-personal information through your use of the Online Services. We also may use "cookies" and other passive technologies including clear gifs to collect certain other information from you in connection with your use of the Online Services, such as the pages you visit and the features you use. Our cookies are linked to personal information.

19 Warner Bros. Discovery, "Consumer Privacy Policy", 2024, available at www.wbdprivacy.com/policycenter/b2c/en-emea/ (last consultation 6 September 2024).

20 Bandai Namco, "Privacy policy", available at https://en.bandainamcoent.eu/privacy-policy (last consultation 6 September 2024).

21 CJEU, 6 October 2015, *Maximillian Schrems v Data Protection Commissioner*, C-362/14.

22 Sony's Playstation, "Privacy policy", 2024, www.playstation.com/en-gb/legal/privacy-policy/

> Legitimate Interests – to fulfil our legitimate interests, or those of a third party in conducting and managing our business and our relationship with you as described in this Privacy Policy. For example, we rely on legitimate interest to (a) detect and prevent fraud, the unauthorised use of our Services, and other harmful or illegal activity, including by reviewing reports submitted by other PlayStation users, (b) improve our

products and services, including by performing analytics and business reporting in relation to how you use our Services and any issues you may encounter, and (c) share information with other Sony Group Corporation companies where necessary to support the security of our Services.

23 See Take 2, "Privacy policies", 26 April 2023, www.take2games.com/privacy/en-US, "inferences made from your information and web activity to help create a personalized profile so we can identify goods and services that may be of interest".
24 See Bandai Namco, "Privacy policy", ref supra, "Usage data which may collectively contain non-technical data. Certain usage data may be associated, linked or able to be cross-referenced with other information in your account, including personal data".
25 See Warner Bros Discovery, "Privacy Policy", ref supra.
26 Such as Ubisoft's Watchdogs 2 creating multiplayer game as a sidetrack in the solo campaign narrative but allowing the unsolicited player to escape easily from it.
27 ECtHR, 07 July 2022, – 81292/17, *Chocholáč v. Slovakia.*
28 U.S. Supreme Court, *Katz v. United States*, 389 U.S. 347 (1967).
29 GTA V constrains the player to torture a NPC in a scene.
30 US Supreme Court, *Roth v. United States*, 354 U.S. 476, (1957); *Miller v. California*, 413 U.S. 15 (1973).
31 US Supreme Court, concurring opinion, Justice Scalia, in *Brown v. Entm't Merchs. Ass'n*, 131 S. Ct. 2729, 2736–37 (2011), quoting Homere's Odyssey, Dante's Inferno and Golding's *Lord of the flies* as illustration.
32 Label provided by the Entertainment Software Rating Board (ESRB) which has for European equivalent the Pan European Game Information (PEGI). Videogames displaying sexual content are only available on PC devices.
33 *Brown v. Entm't Merchs. Ass'n*, ref supra.
34 *Roth v. United States*, ref. supra.
35 ECtHR, 16 December 1992, – 13710/88, *Niemietz v. Germany*; ECtHR 29 April 2002, – 2346/02, *Pretty v. UK.*
36 ECtHR, 10 January 2019, – 65286/13 and 57270/14, *Khadija Ismayilova v. Azerbaijan.*
37 As referenced by all the privacy policies quoted previously.
38 European Parliament, "Protecting gamers and encouraging growth in the video games sector", Press Release, 18 January 2023, www.europarl.europa.eu/news/en/press-room/20230113IPR66646/protecting-gamers-and-encouraging-growth-in-the-video-games-sector (last consultation 06 September 2024).
39 Northern District of California, 10 January 2022, *Taylor, et al., v. Apple, Inc.*, No. 20-CV-03906-RS; Northern District of California, 10 January 2022, *Coffee, et al., v. Google*, LLC, No. 20-CV-03901-BLF.
40 ECtHR, 13 September 2005, – 42571/98, *I.A. v. Turkey*, 2005.
41 We discard the hypothesis of a pedophile buying kids game to prey on them.

Bibliography

American Psychological Association (APA). (2023) "Video Games Play May Provide Learning, Health, Social Benefits, Review Finds", www.apa.org/news/press/releases/2013/11/video-games

Bazar du Grenier. (2024) « Mais pourquoi l'IA est pourrie? », Youtube, www.youtube.com/watch?v=VEeukZBgNFA

Benabou, M.-L. (2005) “Pourquoi une œuvre de l’esprit est immatérielle”, *Revue Lamy droit de l’immatériel (RLDI)*.

Beurskens, M., Kamocki, P., and Ketzan, E. (2013) “Les autorisations tacites – une révolution silence en droit d’auteur numérique, perspectives étasunienne, allemande et française”, *Revue internationale du droit d’auteur (RIDA)*.

Bitan, H. (2010) *Droit des créations immatérielles*, Lamy.

Captain Copyright (2006). Wikipedia. https://en.wikipedia.org/wiki/Captain_Copyright

Carpita, B., Muti, D., Nardi, B., Benedetti, F., Cappelli, A., Mirko Cremone, I., Carmassi, C., and Dell’Osso, L. (2021) “Biochemical Correlates of Video Game Use: From Physiology to Pathology. A Narrative Review”, *Life (Basel)*, https://doi.org/10.3390/life11080775

Chalk, A. (2023) “FTX collapse has done lethal damage to an up-and-coming card game”, *PCGamer*, www.pcgamer.com/ftx-collapse-has-done-lethal-damage-to-an-up-and-coming-card-game/

Chopin, F. (2013) “La cybercriminalité”, *Répertoire de droit pénal et de procédure pénale [Encyclopédie juridique Dalloz]*.

Cleveland Clinics. (2022) “Video Game Addiction”, https://my.clevelandclinic.org/health/diseases/23124-video-game-addiction

Coats, W. S., and Rafter, H. D. (1993) “The Games People Play: Sega v. Accolade and the Right to Reverse Engineer Software”, *15 Hastings Comm. & Ent. L.J.*

Commission d'experts sur l'impact de l'exposition des jeunes aux écrans, Enfants et écrans -À la recherche du temps perdu, 2024, available at www.elysee.fr/emmanuel-macron/2024/04/30/remise-du-rapport-de-la-commission-dexperts-sur-limpact-de-lexposition-des-jeunes-aux-ecrans (last consulted 10/01/2025).

De Marco, E., and Aeris. (2022) *Impacts of the use of biometrics and behavioural mass surveillance technologies on human right and the rule of law*, www.greens-efa.eu/en/article/study/impacts-of-the-use-of-biometric-and-behavioural-mass-surveillance-technologies-on-human-rights-and-the-rule-of-law

European Data Protection Board, Guidelines 03/2022 on deceptive design patterns in social media platform interfaces: how to recognise and avoid them, 2023, available at www.edpb.europa.eu/our-work-tools/our-documents/guidelines/guidelines-032022-deceptive-design-patterns-social-media_en (last consulted 10/01/2025).

European Parliament, Right to repair: Making repair easier and more appealing to consumers, Press Release, 23-04-2024, www.europarl.europa.eu/news/en/press-room/20240419IPR20590/right-to-repair-making-repair-easier-and-more-appealing-to-consumers (last consulted 10/01/2025).

Games FAQ. (2023) “Tomb Raider I-III Remastered Starring Lara Croft”, https://gamefaqs.gamespot.com/boards/426393-tomb-raider-i-iii-remastered-starring-lara-croft/80575591

Gaudrat, P. (1988) “La protection des logiciels par le droit d’auteur”, *RIDA,* n°1.

Gaudrat, P. (2010) Commentary of 1ere 25/06/2009, *RTD Com*, p. 319.

Geiger, C. (2004) “De la nature juridique des limites au droit d’auteur”, *PI*, n°13.

Girard, J. Ecalle, A. and Magnan, A. (2012) “Serious games as new educational tools: how effective are they? A meta-analysis of recent studies”, *Journal of Computer Assisted Learning, 29*(13), 207–219.

Huet, J., and Bouche, N. (2011) Les contrats informatiques, Dalloz, p. 128, EAN: 9782711014262.

Hunyadi, M. (2023) Faire confiance à la confiance, Erès.

Internal Market and Consumer Protection (IMCO) of the European Parliament, Online Platforms' Moderation of Illegal Content Online (2020) www.europarl.europa.eu/RegData/etudes/STUD/2020/652718/IPOL_STU(2020)652718_EN.pdf

Keller, J. (2017) *La notion d'auteur dans le monde des logiciels*, Université de Nanterre, PhD Thesis, François Pellegrini & Sylvia Preuss-Laussinotte (dir.).

Kerr, O. (2007) "Four models of Fourth Amendment protection", *Stan. L. Rev. 60*, https://papers.ssrn.com/sol3/papers.cfm?abstract_id=976296

Korben. (2024) "Le DRM Denuvo d'Hogwarts Legacy à nouveau cracké", https://korben.info/denuvo-drm-hogwarts-legacy-cracke-developpeur.html

Latham, K. (2023) "How computer games encourage kids to spend cash", *BBC*, www.bbc.com/news/business-65372710

Lausson, J. (2024) "Ce qui cloche avec le contrôle de l'âge par CB pour les sites pornos", *Numerama*, 15 avril 2024, www.numerama.com/politique/1724638-ce-qui-cloche-avec-le-controle-de-lage-par-cb-pour-les-sites-pornos.html

Lemley, M. A. (1995) "Intellectual Property and Shrinkwrap Licenses", *Southern California Law Review* 1239, https://ssrn.com/abstract=2126845

Lequesne, C., Keller, J. (2023) « Surveiller les foules », Observatoire de l'éthique publique, www.observatoireethiquepublique.com/nos-propositions/livres-blancs/surveiller-les-foules.html

Le Tourneau, P. Contrats informatiques et électroniques (édition 2014/2015), Dalloz, 2014.

Levallois-Barth, C., and Keller, J. (2022) *Analyse d'impact relative à la Protection des Données: le cas des voitures connectées*, Institut Mines-Télécom, Télécom ParisTech, CNRS LTCI. ⟨hal-03456922 ⟩ https://hal.science/hal-03456922

Lexis Nexis, Glossary, Social Media Definition, www.lexisnexis.co.uk/legal/glossary/social-media

Lochak. D. (1994) "Le droit à l'épreuve des bonnes moeurs. Puissance et impuissance de la norme juridique" in *Les bonnes moeurs*, PUF (hal-01670208).

Manrique, T. (2021) *Les questions sociétales et la jurisprudence des Cours européenne et interaméricaine des droits de l'homme*, Université de Toulouse, PhD Thesis, Joël Andriantsimbazovina (Dir.).

McDonald, A.M., and Cranor, L.F. (2008) "The Cost of Reading Privacy Policies", *I/S: A Journal of Law and Policy for the Information Society*, 4(3), 548–568.

Ouest France. (2023) "À 10 ans, elle dépense près de 3 000 € dans un jeu vidéo avec la carte bancaire de sa mère". www.ouest-france.fr/leditiondusoir/2023-05-24/a-10-ans-elle-depense-pres-de-3-000-euro-dans-un-jeu-video-avec-la-carte-bancaire-de-sa-mere-c909ce63-0bbf-4080-86c3-9882529c784f

Reddit. (2022) "Warning: Publishers can remove games from your library", www.reddit.com/r/Steam/comments/w9jpd5/warning_publishers_can_remove_games_from_your/?rdt=46170

Ricchiuto, M. (2017) "Activision is Removing Licensed Transformers and Legend of Korra Games from Online Retailers", 21 December 2017, *Bleeding cool*, https://bleedingcool.com/games/activision-removing-licensed-games/

Rossi, J. (2020) Protection des données personnelles et droit à la vie privée : enquête sur la notion controversée de « donnée à caractère personnel », Phd Thesis under the direction of Virginie Julliard, Jérôme Valluy, COSTECH, Université de technologie de Compiègne.

Rouner, J. (2012) "Top 10 Smuttiest Video Game Easter Eggs (NSFW)", Houston Press, www.houstonpress.com/arts/top-10-smuttiest-video-game-easter-eggs-nsfw-6394277

Sheshounet. (2023) "Texas Chain Saw Massacre – EXCESSIVEMENT NUL", www.youtube.com/watch?v=0cl85c3WOes

Sheshounet. (2024) « Skull & bones – Elu pire jeu 2024", www.youtube.com/watch?v=8TC-M2bVm_Q

Sieber, U. (2006) "International cooperation against terrorist use of the Internet", *Revue Internationale de droit pénal*, 3.

Silverstein, R. (2020) "The Law of Obscenity in Comic Books", *Touro Law Review*, https://digitalcommons.tourolaw.edu/lawreview/vol35/iss4/10

Thomson, L. (2014) "CIA infosec guru: US govt must buy all zero-days and set them free", *The register*, www.theregister.com/2014/08/07/geer_we_have_to_destroy_the_software_industry_in_order_to_save_it/

Tricoire, A. (2002) "L'art, la censure et les droits de l'homme", *Légipresse*, n°196.

Troonline. (2020) "Nude Raider". www.tro-online.com/jeu-nuderaider.html

Weber, L. (2012) "Bad bytes: the application of strict products liability to computer software", *St John L. Rev.* 66.

Winn, P. (2016) "*Katz and the Origins of the Reasonable Expectation of Privacy Test*", McGeorge L. Rev., 40 https://scholarlycommons.pacific.edu/mlr/vol40/iss1/1

Wong, C. (2012) "Can Bruce Willis Leave His iTunes Collection to His Children?: Inheritability of Digital Media in the Face of EULAs", *Santa Clara High Tech. L.J.*

World Health Organization. (2024) "6C51 Gaming disorder" in *ICD-11 for Mortality and Morbidity Statistics*, 2024, https://icd.who.int/dev11/l-m/en#/http%3a%2f%2fid.who.int%2ficd%2fentity%2f1448597234

15 An exploration of the child's right not to use the Internet

Disentangling from the digital web

Eva Lievens and Valerie Verdoodt

15.1 Introduction: children's increasingly digital lives

Recent policy documents at international (United Nations Committee on the Rights of the Child, 2021) and European level emphasise how essential Internet access is for the realisation of children's rights, and more specifically "for their inclusion, education, participation and for maintaining family and social relationships" (Council of Europe, 2018). In the different spheres of children's lives, and for educational, communication and leisure purposes in particular, the Internet has become indispensable. Schools impose the use of online learning platforms, friendships are maintained predominantly through mobile apps and online gaming platforms have taken over from playgrounds.

The shift towards a more intense and seemingly obvious use of technologies intensified during the COVID-19-crisis (Madigan et al., 2022; OECD, 2021). Amidst this digital transformation, the fundamental question regarding whether children have or should have a right not to use the Internet emerges as a pertinent concern. Childhood in a digital era is datafied and recorded to an unprecedented extent (Lupton and Williamson, 2017), leaving increasingly little room for experimentation in a phase of life where this is crucial (United Nations Committee on the Rights of the Child, 2016). Indeed, as the digital environment they are exploring, communicating and learning in is no longer free of supervision and tracking, concerns have been raised about its potential chilling effects (Center for Democracy & Technology, 2022). For example, children may become hesitant to search for certain information, engage in certain conversations or ask critical questions. Moreover, the lack of control over the management of their personal data can hinder their ability to develop, learn and explore their own identities (Milkaite, 2021).

In the broader debate on a right for children not to use the Internet, different strands of ideas are apparent, reflecting the "3Ps" that have been argued to be engrained in the United Nations Convention on the Rights of the Child ("UNCRC"; UN General Assembly, 1989): provision, protection and participation (United Nations Committee on the Rights of the Child, 2009). Many of the provisions of the UNCRC are rooted in a protectionist approach offering safeguards against specific dangers to which children are vulnerable, such as Article 34 on protection from sexual exploitation. However, the UNCRC also emphasises children's

DOI: 10.4324/9781003528401-18

capacities and strengths as active rightsholders. A key principle of the UNCRC is that children should not be viewed solely as vulnerable victims, but also as social actors who require support as they grow up. Thus, the UNCRC also includes a provision dimension, as children have the right to be provided with the resources, the skills and services needed for their development. Additionally, the participation dimension of the UNCRC requires that children be empowered to actively engage in society, such as by having a voice in the decision-making process on policy issues that impact their lives.

Whereas in recent policy and academic discourse on children's rights in the digital environment the focus has been on the importance of *providing* children with Internet access and opportunities to benefit from digital technologies more in general, there are also increasing concerns about the risks that children encounter online, and the time they spend on apps and mobile devices. This had led a number of policymakers in different countries and regions to consider restricting access to devices (predominantly smart phones) and online applications – either in general for children under a certain age or in specific contexts for certain periods of time (such as schools). Such proposals are inspired by the (perceived) need to *protect* children by means of prohibitions to use the Internet, and not necessarily by a right that children would have not to use the Internet. The question arises whether such a right would be in the best interest of the child (Article 3 UNCRC) or whether the rights that are contained in the UNCRC that aim to offer protection to children (e.g., the right to privacy, the right to protection from economic exploitation and the right to protection from violence) offer sufficient safeguards to remedy the risks in the digital environment. Whereas both the discussions on provision and protection measures affect children significantly, they are still only rarely actively asked to *participate* in those debates (Article 12 UNCRC).

In this chapter, we explore how the established debates on provision of Internet access to children and protection through restricting access and use are linked to the emerging discussions on the right not to use the Internet for children. We investigate recent policymakers' initiatives, academic literature and studies which include children's voices to identify arguments both in favour of and against the shaping of such a right, from a children's rights perspective. Our focus lies on children's rights instruments and debates at the level of the United Nations, the Council of Europe and the European Union. In addition, we use illustrations from a selection of countries where policies have been proposed or adopted which impact children's access to and use of digital technologies.

15.2 Provision: the importance of access to the digital environment

The Committee of Ministers of the Council of Europe adopted the first comprehensive recommendation on the rights of the child in the digital environment in 2018. It could be argued to be symbolic that "access to the digital environment" was put first in the order of the rights that are discussed in this document. The committee emphasises that having no or limited access to the digital environment (for instance, due to poor connectivity) may affect children's ability to fully exercise their human rights (para. 10), such as their freedom of expression and to receive information or their freedom of assembly and association. Moreover, states are encouraged to ensure that "all children have adequate, affordable and secure access to devices, connectivity, services and content which is specifically intended for children" (para. 11). Aside from this general statement, guaranteed access in specific settings, such as education or care settings, is also stressed.

The same approach was taken by the United Nations Committee on the Rights of the Child in their General Comment No. 25 on children's rights in relation to the digital environment, highlighting that "[m]eaningful access to digital technologies can support children to realize the full range of their civil, political, cultural, economic and social rights" (2021, para. 4). To ensure digital inclusion, states are encouraged to allocate public resources to "promote the equality of access to, and affordability of, services and connectivity" (para. 28). They should also guarantee that children have access to information in the digital environment and that the exercise of that right is limited only if the conditions included in Article 13 UNCRC are fulfilled (i.e., restrictions must be provided by law and be necessary for the respect of the rights or reputations of others; or for the protection of national security or of public order or of public health or morals). In specific areas, such as health (para. 93) and education (para. 99, 101 and 102), or for particular target groups, such as children with disabilities (para. 89) or children who live in remote areas (para. 102), access to the digital environment is put forward as particularly important. In relation to education, children themselves pointed to the importance of digital technologies to enhance their access to education and support their learning and participation in extracurricular activities (para. 99) during the consultations that were held in the run-up to the drafting of the General Comment. States should thus, according to the committee, invest in tech infrastructure in schools and for distance learning, where this is necessary (para. 101 and 102).

At the level of the European Union (EU), the European Declaration on Digital Rights and Principles for the Digital Decade (European Commission, 2023) commits to providing all EU citizens – hence, including children – with access to affordable and high-speed digital connectivity. The Better Internet for Kids + Strategy (European Commission, 2022) also emphasises that children need a reliable and affordable Internet connection, and suitable digital devices, in order to benefit from digital opportunities.

The red thread in and across these policy documents is that states should remove potential barriers to access to the digital environment for children – which may be infrastructural (lack of mobile coverage or connectivity), financial (low incomes), linguistical or political – because of the rich opportunities for the realisation of their rights that such access could provide them with. Yet, having actual access to the Internet does not automatically mean that children also want to use the Internet. Reasons why children may choose not to use the Internet could vary, from a desire to live their lives away from social media, for instance, to acts of civil disobedience (Kloza, 2024; e.g., online or virtual school strikes; Mattheis, 2022) or as a reaction to intimidation they have experienced online. In certain circumstances, children may not have a say in whether they want to use the Internet or not. Using the Internet might be contrary to religious beliefs, imposed by parents on their children. Moreover, as Kloza (2024) argues:

> the use of the internet has increasingly ceased to be a mere option, a choice, a (legal) entitlement or (some form of) a right, [...] people have become (de facto) obliged to or – at least – nudged towards the use of internet to exercise their rights or fulfil their duties, as a way of partaking in social or economic life.

Arguably, this is also the case for children. To what extent can a child or their parent(s) object to using a digital learning platform if the school mandates this, for instance?

From a children's rights perspective, these questions could be framed against the principle of the best interests of the child, laid down in Article 3 UNCRC. This principle entails that in all actions concerning children, their bests interest must be a primary consideration (United Nations Committee on the Rights of the Child, 2013). Whereas there is a strong consensus on the fact that having access to the Internet could be essential for the realisation of certain rights, there might perhaps also be circumstances in which it might be in the best interests of the child not to use it, to disconnect from it or to have offline alternatives for certain activities (e.g., in educational settings or in the context of play). The question then arises whether "a right not to use the internet" could be derived from the principle of the best interests of the child, and in which circumstances this might be relied upon and to what extent. The "best interests of the child" is a particularly useful principle where various children's rights conflict or are in tension (Livingstone et al., 2024), which could be argued to be the case when reflecting on whether access to the internet should be reconsidered where it for instance negatively impacts mental or physical health (see also, *infra*, under 15.3. Protection).

At the same time, in the context of the UNCRC, we could wonder whether a specific "right not to use the internet" is actually necessary in this context, or whether this is already engrained in the rights that are included in the UNCRC or – at least – could be read in them, when interpreted in a teleological manner. An example, for instance, relates to the right to play (Article 31 UNCRC). While the General Comment No. 25 acknowledges the importance of digital forms of play, the committee also points out that it is vital that this is balanced with offline alternatives, in physical locations where children live, and which allow for face-to-face interaction (para. 109). Whereas such alternatives should be provided by states, the industry can also play an important role, for instance by offering settings that allow to set time restrictions and introducing responsible videogame design, such as pop ups that show how much time a child spends in a game and nudge them to switch to offline forms of play after some time (Livingstone and Pothong, 2021). A similar observation relates to Article 13 UNCRC, which attributes the right to receive information and ideas of all kinds, through any media of the child's choice. While this includes online information, of course, it also still applies to offline forms of information.

It thus seems that (at least) certain rights should be understood by states as requiring them to offer or support "offline" alternatives to online experiences or content. Whether this also means that educational institutions, for instance, should provide students with the possibility to opt out of the use of digital platforms or devices for school activities or schoolwork might be less obvious and depend on the way in which school systems are organised at the national level. In certain countries, such as Belgium and the Netherlands, the constitutionally guaranteed freedom of education entails high levels of autonomy for educational institutions to organise the running of schools, including deciding on teaching methods and the pedagogical project, without interference from the government (Eurydice, 2023). Schools will be able to make decisions on the use of digital platforms and devices, and parents who want to register their child as a student, will often be required to agree to the school rules which detail which and how digital platforms will be used. Parents who do not agree to the school rules will need to enrol their child in another educational institution. Interference by the government with the institutions' autonomy could be justified in cases where other fundamental rights are under threat but requires a careful balancing exercise of the rights and interests at stake. This might become increasingly relevant considering the emerging and increasing evidence regarding the impact of the use of digital devices in school settings on the development, well-being and learning activities of children (Smale et al., 2021; UNESCO, 2023; *infra*). In certain countries, awareness about the pressure children experience because digital platforms allow teachers to send assignments at any given time or parents can continuously monitor grades is growing (De Standaard, 2024). Such concerns increasingly lead platforms to include "disconnection" features in their design. This could, for instance, entail that messages cannot be sent or delivered between 7 p.m. and 7 a.m.

Another context in which the right not to use the Internet is often explored for adults relates to the interaction with government or public bodies, for instance, regarding the availability of local government offices where citizens can engage in face-to-face interaction, or the possibility to submit tax returns through other than digital channels. It could be argued that specifically for children, questions regarding the right not to use the Internet are perhaps somewhat less relevant in this particular context, given the fact that it will often be the parent who will represent the child in interactions with the government.

Reflecting on whether there should be a right not to use the Internet for children, we might wonder whether we are asking the right question. Do we perhaps mean a right to *sometimes* not use the Internet or to have *offline alternatives* in certain contexts? Are we not searching for a balance between online and offline activities for children, benefiting optimally from the opportunities of technologies while being mindful of the advantages of offline alternatives? Arguably, the latter is engrained in certain articles related to provision in the UNCRC and should motivate states to pay sufficient attention to this when establishing policies and regulatory frameworks.

15.3 Protection: prohibiting or restricting children's use of digital devices or apps

Aside from policymakers' consensus on the importance of providing children with the possibility to access the Internet, in recent years, policy debates in different countries around the world increasingly focus on protective measures that, to varying degrees, directly or indirectly *limit* children's ability to use the Internet or enjoy screen time.

15.3.1 Overview of different types of restrictive measures proposed or introduced

The strictest measures being proposed are aimed at completely banning or significantly limiting children's access to screens or connected devices such as smartphones and game consoles, with notable examples in France or China.

In France, a multidisciplinary committee of experts in psychiatry, neurology, epidemiology, education and law was set up by the government in January 2024 to evaluate children's exposure to screens and develop recommendations for policy. The committee's final report, which included input from young people, recommends a range of measures tailored to different age groups (Bousquet-Bérard and Pascal, 2024). In particular, it calls for a complete ban on screen time for children under the age of three and suggests that screen use from the age of six should be allowed only under supervision.

Similarly, in 2023, the Chinese government issued draft guidelines for public consultation on children's screen time, consumption of online content and their autonomy in downloading apps and content (China Law Translate, 2023). These "Guidelines for the Establishment of Minors' Modes for the Mobile Internet"[1] propose, among other things, limiting smart device use to forty minutes per day for children under eight years old, focusing the content they consume on education, hobbies and interests, and having parents give permission for app downloads (Daum, 2023). In addition, app developers, app store providers and smartphone manufacturers would have to work together to create a comprehensive mode for minors (Yang, 2023). This would be a built-in setting in all mobile devices, apps and app stores that would limit time and select content based on the age group when using the mode, although parents can bypass the restrictions.

Other restrictive measures proposed or implemented target the use of specific devices or the use of such devices in specific contexts. In France, the committee report mentioned previously recommends that children under eleven should not use mobile phones at all (Bousquet-Bérard and Pascal, 2024). In several countries, a ban on the use of mobile phones in schools is recommended by the government and implemented in schools. In the United Kingdom, the Department of Education has issued non-statutory guidelines for schools on how to incorporate a ban on mobile phones during the school day into their school policies (UK Department of Education, 2024). Also in Belgium, for example, the 373 kindergartens, primary and secondary schools of the network *Wallonie-Bruxelles Enseignement* have implemented smartphone bans for school year starting in September 2024 (vrtnws, 2024), and the Flemish government recently announced that a complete ban on smartphone use will take effect in Flemish primary schools and the first four years of secondary schools from September 2025 onwards (De Tijd, 2024).

Some measures target specific types of services or applications, particularly social media or online games, or prescribe what content children can access. For example, the French committee report recommends smartphone use from the age of thirteen, but without social media applications, which should only be available from the age of fifteen (Bousquet-Bérard and Pascal, 2024).

Similarly, in Australia, the federal government has drafted legislation to impose a minimum age of sixteen to use social media platforms (Kaye and Jose, 2024; Campbell, 2025).

The Chinese government has been enacting restrictions on children's playtime since the early 2000s (Zendle et al., 2023). In 2019, the "Notice on the Prevention of Online Gaming Addiction in Juveniles"[2] introduced a gaming limit for children (individuals under the age of eighteen) for up to ninety minutes each day and three hours on public holidays. This Notice was updated in 2021 in an even stricter way, stipulating that online gaming companies may only offer services to minors for one hour between 20:00 and 21:00, and that they are only able to do so on Fridays, Saturdays, Sundays and statutory holidays (Xiao, 2021).

In the European Union and United States, discussions are also emerging around the banning of the addictive elements contained in certain digital services that are particularly popular with children (i.e., online games, social media, streaming). Such features include endless scrolling and default autoplay. The European Parliament has even stressed the need for a digital *right not to be disturbed*, as they consider that these addictive features are currently not (or insufficiently) addressed in the existing EU legislative framework (EP, 2023). In the United States, the New York bill known as the "Stop Addictive Feeds Exploitation (SAFE) For Kids Act"[3] aims to regulate how social media companies present posts to children. It would require posts to appear in the order they are issued by followed accounts, effectively eliminating the role of algorithms that currently curate and shape children's content streams on these platforms.

15.3.2 A children's rights perspective on proposed or introduced restrictions: is a right not to use the Internet necessary?

From a children's rights perspective, it can be questioned whether and what types of restrictions on children's Internet and screen time are in their best interests? The more restrictive these limitations are, the greater the risk of infringing on other rights, not only of children but also of their parents, who are also afforded autonomy in the decision-making about their children's upbringing in Article 5 UNCRC. According to the UN Committee on the Rights of the Child, states should implement safety and protective measures in accordance with children's *evolving capacities* (UN Committee on the Rights of the Child, 2021: para 82).

Children – who are defined in the UNCRC as every human being under the age of eighteen years – are not a homogenous group. As they progress throughout childhood, they develop, become more mature and their needs in terms of protection or agency change. This does not only mean that parents or caregivers must adapt their direction and guidance as children grow older, but also that policy measures that restrict children's behaviour or acts might need to be differentiated according to age (Varadan, 2019). Deciding on which measures are appropriate for which age is difficult as children develop at a different pace. Such decisions often fall short of individual children's needs but might be considered necessary to benefit children as a group (United Nations Committee on the Rights of the Child, 2013). Decisions – for instance, on age-based access or time restrictions or default settings – need to balance children's interests and should be evidence-based and grounded in research on child development and effects of technology use. In a next stage, to effectively implement age-specific measures, digital service providers would need to have reliable age assurance mechanisms in place. Such mechanisms are, however, controversial, and scholars, policymakers as well as data protection authorities have voiced concerns about both the effectiveness of current methods and the potentially invasive data collection practices they involve (Sas and Mühlberg, 2024).

Another consideration regarding restrictions is the potential negative impact on children who are vulnerable due to their socio-economic status or family situation. For example, in households where a smartphone is the only device through which children can access the Internet, smartphone bans could deny a significant group of children access to important opportunities for accessing information, play and socialisation.

The debates on prohibitions or restrictions on the use of devices, the Internet or specific services for children should be guided by the best interests of the child, which requires balancing their different rights and interests and that of others. In the context of this chapter, a pertinent question is whether a right not to use the Internet would be helpful in carrying out this balancing exercise? The rationale underlying the prohibitions and restrictions on the use of devices, the Internet or specific services for children clearly relates to protecting children from negative impacts on their rights to development and well-being, health and protection from harmful content or violence. Cyberbullying is often cited as a factor in driving these measures (Reed and Dunn, 2024), due to its harmful effects on children's mental health. Preventing or combating Internet (or specifically gaming) addiction or excessive spending online is another driver. Efforts to prevent obesity and the negative effects of excessive screen time and sedentary lifestyles have also contributed to the push to limiting screen time (e.g., Barnet et al., 2018). More specifically, research has shown that screen use can contribute to, among other things, sleep deprivation and eye disorders (Bousquet-Bérard and Pascal, 2024), further impacting children's overall health and development. In addition, there is an increased focus on the educational benefits of reducing screen use, as excessive screen use has been linked to poor academic performance (UNESCO, 2023).

At the same time, the scientific evidence of the harmful effects of screen use or specific applications on children's health and well-being is not (yet) robust, conclusive or generalisable (e.g., Orben et al., 2022; Valkenburg et al., 2022), and scholars have argued that the relationship between digital technology and children's (mental) health is more complex than often assumed (Johns Hopkins Bloomberg School of Public Health and United Nations Children's Fund, 2022). To illustrate, researchers exploring the link between adolescents' use of digital technology and their mental health in different countries found *inter alia* that time spent on the Internet did not appear to be strongly linked to children's life satisfaction and concluded that results from one country should not be assumed to transfer to another (Kardefelt-Winther et al., 2020). A meta-analysis has shown that the most robust studies suggest that moderate use of digital technology tends to be beneficial for children and young people's mental well-being (Kardefelt-Winther, 2017). A systematic review of existing evidence linking social media and adolescents' health also concluded that it "did not support the conclusion that social media causes changes in adolescent health at the population level" (National Academies of Sciences, Engineering, and Medicine, 2024).

Other scholars warn about the discourse of policymakers and media outlets who claim a national mental health crisis is to blame on smartphone use and social media (boyd, 2024). They refer to it as a new moral panic reappearing time and again whenever new technological developments take place. Phenomena which emerge in society, such as mental health issues, tend to be caused by a variety of socio-economic factors, rather than just by the technology which is at the centre of a moral panic (Livingstone, 2007). Simply banning access to technology will hence not provide a magic solution to such complex problems. On the contrary, it has been argued that bans could inadvertently increase children's vulnerability online. Restricting their ability to interact freely may limit valuable social opportunities, and when children bypass these restrictions, they may be less likely to seek help from adults when needed (Third, 2024). Importantly, conflicting or non-conclusive evidence on the effects of certain technologies, devices or applications does not necessarily mean that states should not act at all. In a children's rights context, the precautionary principle might require states to act if there are certain – not necessarily absolute – scientific indications of a potential danger and if not acting upon these indications could inflict harm (Livingstone, 2007; Lievens, 2021). Where the threshold lies is complex, and, in any case, all relevant rights and interests must be weighed against each other. Yet, even if states would act, given the rationale, it can be argued that the legal ground for states to do this can be found in the provisions of the UNCRC regarding the child's right to health (Article 24) and protection from violence (Article 19). Other provisions, relating to the right to privacy (Article 16) and protection from commercial exploitation (Article 32 UNCRC), might be relied on to address concerns about data-driven commercial practices which keep children engaged on platforms for long periods of time. This means that, arguably, a new right not to use the Internet is in this context not imperative to compel states to take actions that would benefit children.

15.4 Participation: giving children a voice

Over the past years, although still too sparsely, increasing attention has been devoted to listen to what children have to say regarding their experiences in and attitudes towards the digital environment (European Schoolnet, 2021), in line with Article 12 UNCRC and the child's right to be heard. Studies and consultations with children predominantly focus on their opinions on the importance of having access to digital devices, platforms and services, on the one hand, and the risks they encounter throughout the use thereof, on the other hand. To date, conversations with children on whether they think there should be a right not to use the Internet are not yet happening, or not yet reported on (to the best of our knowledge).

At the same time, children do express certain doubts or concerns that might be related to the issues discussed previously. In the Flemish *Apestaartjaren* study (Vanwynsberghe et al., 2024), for instance, 25% of child respondents express that they experience stress if they receive messages from teachers outside of schooltime or that they keep thinking about school because they might get messages through the digital learning platform. Additionally, 45% of respondents indicate that they spend too much time on screens. As another example, in the international consultation with children to inform the UNCRC General Comment No. 25, children articulated a nuanced perspective on the health aspects of (excessive) digital technology use. On the positive side, they noted its value in accessing information and support for various health issues. However, they also associated the overuse of digital technology with serious mental and physical health effects (Third and Moody, 2021). More specifically, children expressed concerns that spending long periods engaged with digital technologies could reduce time for physical activity and hinder the development of social skills. These results seem to indicate that a certain right to disconnect or as it could be put – not use the Internet *sometimes* – would benefit at least some children.

15.5 Conclusion

Children's lives today are entangled with digital technologies and online spaces, which is neither only beneficial nor only detrimental, but much more complex (Reed and Dunn, 2024). Our research shows that the debate regarding a potential right not to use the Internet for children is still in its infancy and that it can be approached from various angles. At this moment in time, and in the context of this debate, we believe that the UNCRC and the way it has been interpreted in General Comment No. 25 provides promising guarantees for reaching the multidimensional objectives engrained in the instrument.

From a provision perspective, although efforts are being undertaken to afford children optimal access to the Internet, they might not always want this, or at least not all of the time. The UNCRC does provide incentives for states to offer children offline alternatives in an increasingly digital world. Being disconnected at times might be in the best interests of (certain) children, and hence, states should take measures to achieve this.

From a protection perspective, states might want children not to use the Internet in order to mitigate a negative impact. At present, evidence is not conclusive about the actual harm that certain risks may cause, but the precautionary principle might justify state action. When action is taken, states will be able to rely on existing UNCRC obligations to shield children from harm and ensure their physical and mental health and do not necessarily need a right of the child not to use the Internet in order to compel them do so. Balancing different rights in that regard is key.

From a participation perspective, it is important to be aware the debate might suffer from generational bias (Reed and Dunn, 2024), where adults decide on whether children may or may not have a right not to use the Internet without consulting them. Moreover, the fact that we see potential in the UNCRC and its teleological interpretation does not mean that states, industry, educational institutions and parents should not engage in a more profound dialogue on the desirability or need for such a right in the future, what it entails and what it could achieve. Such dialogues imperatively need to occur with the involvement of children. Their views on whether a right not to use the Internet is meaningful, necessary or completely redundant, would provide valuable input for policymakers who are considering the adoption of measures in this area.

Acknowledgments

This chapter is linked to the research project G000325N, funded by the Fonds Wetenschappelijk Onderzoek Vlaanderen – Research Foundation Flanders, Belgium (FWO).

Notes

1 For an unofficial English translation of these draft guidelines see China Law Translate (2023). Guidelines for the Establishment of Minors' Modes for the Mobile Internet (Draft for solicitation of comments). www.chinalawtranslate.com/en/kid-mode-guidelines/.
2 For an unofficial English translation of this instrument see Xiao, L. Y. (2019). People's Republic of China Legal Update: The Notice on the Prevention of Online Gaming Addiction in Juveniles (published 25 October 2019, effective 1 November 2019). www.google.com/url?sa=t&source=web&rct=j&opi=89978449&url=https://osf.io/j2uz9/download&ved=2ahUKEwihjbmug8yIAxVBzwIHHb9ZPVsQFnoECBkQAQ&usg=AOvVaw0gA3tb4pSPqQuLMSiG34lW.
3 Senate Bill S7694A. www.nysenate.gov/legislation/bills/2023/S7694/amendment/A.

Bibliography

Bousquet-Bérard, C., & Pascal, A. (2024). Enfants et écrans: A la recherche du temps perdu. www.elysee.fr/admin/upload/default/0001/16/fbec6abe9d9cc1bff3043d87b9f7951e62779b09.pdf.

boyd, d. (2024, April 18). Struggling with a moral panic once again. www.linkedin.com/pulse/struggling-moral-panic-once-again-danah-boyd-1ozsc.

Campbell, M. (2025, January 15). Social-media bans won't work — there are better ways to keep kids safe. *Nature*. https://www.nature.com/articles/d41586-025-00051-0.

Center for Democracy & Technology. (2022). The chilling effect of student monitoring: Disproportionate impacts and mental health risks. https://cdt.org/wp-content/uploads/2022/05/2022-05-05-CDT-Civic-Tech-Chilling-Effect-and-Student-Monitoring-final.pdf.

China Law Translate. (2023, August 2). Guidelines for the establishment of minors' modes for the mobile internet (Draft for solicitation of comments). www.chinalawtranslate.com/en/kid-mode-guidelines/.

Council of Europe. (2018). Recommendation CM/Rec(2018)7 of the Committee of Ministers to Member States on guidelines to respect, protect and fulfil the rights of the child in the digital environment. https://search.coe.int/cm/Pages/result_details.aspx?ObjectId=09000016808b79f7.

Daum, J. (2023, August 4). Proposed guidelines for "Minors' Modes". *China Law Translate*. www.chinalawtranslate.com/proposed-guidelines-for-minors-modes/.

De Standaard. (2024, September 9). Kinderrechtencommissaris Caroline Vrijens: "Zoals we kinderen monitoren via Smartschool, geen enkele volwassene zou dat verdragen" [Children's rights commissioner Caroline Vrijens: 'The way we monitor children through Smartschool, no adult would put up with that']. www.standaard.be/cnt/dmf20240910_97442189.

De Tijd. (2024, December 20). Vlaamse regering bant smartphones in middelbare scholen. [Flemish government bans smartphones in secondary schools]. www.tijd.be/politiek-economie/belgie/vlaanderen/vlaamse-regering-bant-smartphones-in-middelbaar-onderwijs/10579917.html.

European Commission. (2022). A Digital Decade for children and youth: The new European strategy for a better internet for kids (BIK+). https://eur-lex.europa.eu/legal-content/EN/TXT/?uri=COM:2022:212:FIN/.

European Commission. (2023). *European declaration on digital rights and principles for the digital decade*. https://digital-strategy.ec.europa.eu/en/library/declaration-european-digital-rights-and-principles#Declaration.

European Parliament. (2023). European Parliament resolution of 12 December 2023 on addictive design of online services and consumer protection in the EU single market (2023/2043(INI)). www.europarl.europa.eu/doceo/document/TA-9-2023-0459_EN.html.

European Schoolnet. (2021). How to make Europe's digital decade fit for children and young people? https://data.europa.eu/doi/10.2759/096742.

Eurydice (European Commission). (2023). Belgium – Flemish Community. https://eurydice.eacea.ec.europa.eu/.

Johns Hopkins Bloomberg School of Public Health and United Nations Children's Fund. (2022). On my mind: How adolescents experience and perceive mental health around the world. www.unicef.be/sites/default/files/2022-05/UNICEF-%20ON%20MY%20MIND%20-%20FINAL%20REPORT%202022.pdf.

Kardefelt-Winther, D. (2017). How does the time children spend using digital technology impact their mental well-being, social relationships and physical activity? An evidence-focused literature review. Innocenti Discussion Paper 2017-02. www.unicef.org/innocenti/documents/how-does-time-children-spend-using-digital-technology-impact-their-mental-well-being.

Kardefelt-Winther, D., Rees, G., & Livingstone, S. (2020). Contextualising the link between adolescents' use of digital technology and their mental health: a multi-country study of time spent online and life satisfaction. *Journal of Child Psychology and Psychiatry*, *61*(8), 875–889. https://doi.org/10.1111/jcpp.13280.

Kaye, B., & Jose, R. (2024, September 10). Australia plans social media minimum age limit, angering youth digital advocates. *Reuters*. www.reuters.com/technology/australia-plans-social-media-ban-children-2024-09-09/.

Kloza, D. (2024). The right not to use the internet. *Computer Law & Security Review*, *52*, 105907. https://doi.org/10.1016/j.clsr.2023.105907.

Lievens, E. (2021). Growing up with digital technologies: How the precautionary principle might contribute to addressing potential serious harm to children's rights. *Nordic Journal of Human Rights*, *39*(2), 128–145. https://doi.org/10.1080/18918131.2021.199295.

Livingstone, S. (2007). Do the media harm children?: Reflections on new approaches to an old problem. *Journal of Children and Media*, *1*(1), 5–14. https://doi.org/10.1080/17482790601005009.

Livingstone, S., Cantwell, N., Özkul, D., Shekhawat, G., & Kidron, B. (2024). *The best interests of the child in the digital environment*. www.digital-futures-for-children.net/digitalfutures-assets/digitalfutures-documents/Best-Interests-of-the-Child-FINAL.pdf.

Livingstone, S., & Pothong, K. (2021). *Playful by design: A vision of free play in a digital world*. Digital Futures Commission. https://digitalfuturescommission.org.uk/wp-content/uploads/2021/11/A-Vision-of-Free-Play-in-a-Digital-World.pdf.

Lupton, D., & Williamson, B. (2017). The datafied child: The dataveillance of children and implications for their rights. *New Media & Society*, *19*(5), 780–794. https://doi.org/10.1177/1461444816686328.

Madigan, S., Eirich, R., Pador, P., McArthur, B., & Neville, R. (2022). Assessment of changes in child and adolescent screen time during the COVID-19 pandemic: A systematic review and meta-analysis. *JAMA Pediatrics*, *176*(12), 1188–1198. https://doi.org/10.1001/jamapediatrics.2022.4116.

Mattheis, N. (2022). Unruly kids? Conceptualizing and defending youth disobedience. *European Journal of Political Theory*, *21*(3), 466–490. https://doi.org/10.1177/1474885120918371.

Milkaite, I. (2021). *A children's rights perspective on privacy and data protection in the digital age: A critical and forward-looking analysis of the EU General Data Protection Regulation and its implementation with respect to children and youth* [Doctoral thesis, Ghent University].

National Academies of Sciences, Engineering, and Medicine. (2024). *Social media and adolescent health*. https://doi.org/10.17226/27396.

OECD. (2021). *Using digital technologies for early education during COVID-19*. www.oecd.org/en/publications/using-digital-technologies-for-early-education-during-covid-19_fe8d68ad-en.html.

Orben, A., Przybylski, A. K., Blakemore, S. J., & Kievit, R. A. (2022). Windows of developmental sensitivity to social media. *Nature Communications*, *13*, 1649. https://doi.org/10.1038/s41467-022-29296-3.

Reed, J., & Dunn, C. (2024). Postdigital young people's rights: A critical perspective on the UK government's guidance to ban phones in England's schools. *Postdigital Science and Education*. https://doi.org/10.1007/s42438-024-00464-6.

Sas, M., & Mühlberg, J. T. (2024). *Trustworthy Age Assurance? A study commissioned by the Greens/EFA Cluster on Green and Social Economy*. www.greens-efa.eu/en/article/study/trustworthy-age-assurance.

Smale, W. T., Hutcheson, R., & Russo, C. J. (2021). Cell phones, student rights, and school safety: Finding the right balance. *Canadian Journal of Educational Administration and Policy / Revue canadienne en administration et politique de l'éducation, 195*, 49–64. https://doi.org/10.7202/1075672ar.

Third, A. (2024, September 12). Instead of banning kids from online spaces, here's what we should offer them instead. *The Conversation.* https://theconversation.com/instead-of-banning-kids-from-online-spaces-heres-what-we-should-offer-them-instead-238798.

Third, A., & Moody, L. (2021). *Our rights in the digital world: A report on the children's consultation to inform UNCRC General Comment 25.* https://5rightsfoundation.com/uploads/OurRightsinaDigitalWorld-FullReport.pdf.

UK Department of Education. (2024). *Mobile phones in schools.* https://assets.publishing.service.gov.uk/media/65cf5f2a4239310011b7b916/Mobile_phones_in_schools_guidance.pdf.

UNESCO. (2023). *Global Education Monitoring Report 2023: Technology in education – A tool on whose terms?* Paris, UNESCO. https://unesdoc.unesco.org/ark:/48223/pf0000385723.

UN General Assembly. (1989). Convention on the Rights of the Child, 20 November 1989, United Nations, Treaty Series, vol. 1577.

United Nations Committee on the Rights of the Child. (2009). *General Comment No 12: The Right of the Child to be Heard.* CRC/C/GC/12.

United Nations Committee on the Rights of the Child. (2013). *General comment no. 14 on the right of the child to have his or her best interests taken as a primary consideration (art. 3, para. 1).* CRC/C/GC/14.

United Nations Committee on the Rights of the Child. (2016). *General comment No. 20 (2016) on the implementation of the rights of the child during adolescence.* CRC/C/GC/20.

United Nations Committee on the Rights of the Child. (2021). *General Comment No. 25 on children's rights in relation to the digital environment.* CRC/C/GC/25.

Valkenburg, P. M., Meier, A., & Beyens, I. (2022). Social media use and its impact on adolescent mental health: An umbrella review of the evidence. *Current Opinion in Psychology, 44*, 58–68. https://doi.org/10.1016/j.copsyc.2021.08.017.

Vanwynsberghe, H., Van Damme, K., Peeters H., D'haeseleer, S., Schokkenbroek, J. M., Martens, M., Sevenhant, R., Vanden Abeele, M., Ponnet, K., Callens, J., & Schreuer, C. (2024). Onderzoeksrapport Apenstaartjaren: de digitale leefwereld van kinderen en jongeren [Research report *Apestaartjaren:* the digital world of children and young people]. https://assets.mediawijs.be/2024-05/apenstaartjarenrapport_2024_lr_1_3.pdf.

Varadan, S. (2019). The principle of evolving capacities under the UN Convention on the Rights of the Child. *International Journal of Children's Rights, 27*(2), 306–338. https://doi.org/10.1163/15718182-02702006.

vrtnws. (2024, August 22). Ruim 370 Franstalige scholen verbieden smartphones komend schooljaar, voorlopig geen plannen in Nederlandstalig onderwijs [Over 370 French-speaking schools ban smartphones next school year, no plans in Dutch-speaking education for now]. *VRT Nieuws.* www.vrt.be/vrtnws/nl/2024/08/22/smartphone-waalse-scholen-verboden-brussel/.

Xiao, L. Y. (2019). People's Republic of China Legal Update: The Notice on the Prevention of Online Gaming Addiction in Juveniles (published 25 October 2019, effective 1 November 2019). www.google.com/url?sa=t&source=web&rct=j&opi=89978449&url=https://osf.io/j2uz9/download&ved=2ahUKEwihjbmug8yIAxVBzwIHHb9ZPVsQFnoECBkQAQ&usg=AOvVaw0gA3tb4pSPqQuLMSiG34lW.

Xiao, L. Y. (2021). People's Republic of China legal update: The notice on further strictly regulating and effectively preventing online video gaming addiction in minors. *Gaming Law Review*, *25*(9), 379–382. https://doi.org/10.1089/glr2.2021.0026.

Yang, Z. (2023, August 9). China is escalating its war on kids' screen time. What Beijing's new restrictions on child internet use mean for privacy protection. *MIT Technology Review*. www.technologyreview.com/2023/08/09/1077567/china-children-screen-time-regulation/.

Zendle, D., Flick, C., Gordon-Petrovskaya, E., Ballou, N., Xiao, L. Y., & Drachen, A. (2023). No evidence that Chinese playtime mandates reduced heavy gaming in one segment of the video games industry. *Nature Human Behaviour*, 7, 1753–1766. https://doi.org/10.1038/s41562-023-01669-8.

Index

Note: Endnotes are indicated by the page number followed by "n" and the note number e.g., 111n5 refers to note 5 on page 111.

MIX
Papier | Fördert gute Waldnutzung
FSC® C083411

Kolibri 360 GmbH
Ferdinand-Jühlke-Straße 7
99095 Erfurt, Deutschland
produktsicherheit@kolibri360.de